ADVENTURES
IN
FLYING

Jack Elliott (signature)

Jack Elliott

Foreword by Phil Boyer

ALEXANDER & RAY
BOOK PUBLISHERS

Gillette, New Jersey

Publisher's Cataloging-in-Publication Data

Library of Congress Control Number (LCCN) 2007902794

Elliott, Jack 1924-
 Adventures in Flying / Jack Elliott; Foreword by Phil Boyer

 p. cm.
 ISBN 978-0-615-13294-5 (cloth : alk. paper)
 1. Aeronautics. 2. African American air pilots. 3 Air pilots.
4. Airplanes. 5. Airships. 6. Balloons. 7. Flight. 8. Gliders.
9. Helicopters. 10. Parachutes. 11. Women air pilots. I. Title.
387.7
629.133

Manufactured in the United States of America

Dedication

To Esta-Ann,
Amy and Stephen,

the three most important people in my life.

Many of the communities and airports in these stories are located in New Jersey. In the interest of avoiding excessive repetition the state is not always mentioned. Where it does not appear, the state is New Jersey. In every case where the community is in another state, that state is always identified.

All photos in the book which do not have a specific credit line are Jack Elliott photos

Contents

Acknowledgments

The greatest advance in the art of writing, many writers would agree, was the coming of the computer. If a writer wants to make a change, and most writers make thousands of changes all the time, they no longer have to cross things out, they don't have to erase anything, they don't have to use correction tape. The computer does all that.

But all that good stuff adds up to a plus only if you are in command of the computer, which as it happens, I was not. Then you have problems. Computers are like animals or children. They have a mind of their own. You might want to do this, but the computer wants to do that. And you want to know who wins? It's not you.

So I am grateful to Mary Sullivan and Marty Balk for rescuing me on innumerable occasions from the idiosyncrasies of the computer. There were countless times in the writing of this book when I ran into trouble with my domineering computers (I started out on a PC and wound up on a Mac.). I had problems with both.

The computers were smarter than I was and they always insisted on having things their way. Mary and Marty came to my rescue time and again because they wouldn't take any nonsense from the computer. That has something to do, I believe, with understanding computers, which is not one of my strong points.

Mary also typed several chapters because she claimed to type faster than I do. She was probably right about that, although I'm not the slowest typist in the world. A bonus went with this service. I thoroughly enjoyed listening to her constant chuckles as she typed the chapter near the end of the book about bullfighting in Mexico.

Mary Ann Balk (Mrs. Marty Balk) spent many hours retyping the entire book and making corrections in spelling and grammar as she typed.

I am grateful to Tom Benenson, senior editor of *Flying* magazine, for editing the manuscript for me.

When the editing was done, Marty set the type, scanned the photos and incorporated them into the book.

I had many questions about publishing the book and people like Walter Boyne, the prolific aviation writer and former director of the Smithsonian National Air and Space Museum; George Larson, founding editor of *Air & Space Smithsonian*, and current senior editor of *Business & Commercial Aviation*; and Spencer Lane, author of the the prize-winning, *First World Flight; the Odyssey of Billy Mitchell*, were among those helpful with advice.

And the book, which had been in my head for several decades, would probably never have become a reality without the constant encouragement of my wife, Esta-Ann, daughter, Amy, and son, Stephen.

Their encouragement and help reinvigorated me on numerous occasions when I was running out of steam. All three have pretty good credentials. Esta-Ann worked in a school library for 20 years. She proofread my column for more than three decades. She did considerable research, proofread, and indexed the book. Amy wrote the first biography of Congresswoman Millicent Fenwick, published by Rutgers University Press, so she had the experience to provide me with some professional advice. Stephen, who holds a masters degree in Journalism and edited several online newsletters, has also been published in several trade magazines.

This book was actually born in 1963 when I was Sunday editor of the *Star-Ledger*, New Jersey's largest newspaper. Mort Pye was the editor at the time and I suggested to him that I thought we ought to have a flying column. I had a pilot's license and proposed that I write such a column. He listened and said, "Okay. Try it". The first column, titled, "Wings Over Jersey," ran on June 9, 1963. Since Pye never said, "Stop," I kept turning in copy every week. This book would never have come into this world if Pye hadn't given me his approval to try the column.

I never dreamed it would last more than 38 1/2 years, longer than any other newspaper aviation column ever written. Over the years I came across many highly unusual and sometimes incredible stories. Those years of weekly columns provided the core of this book.

I want to thank Jim Willse, current editor of the *Star-Ledger* for granting permission to publish these stories which are based on columns that originally appeared in the *Star-Ledger*.

I am indebted also to aviation artist Paul E. Rendel who did the beautiful painting which graces the dust jacket cover. The painting, titled, "Decision Time," was especially created for this book. It captures the feeling of space and freedom in the boundless skies and the beauty, color, and form of the cloud formations floating across the sky. A former president of The American Society of Aviation Artists, his work has been exhibited in several museums and has won many awards.

And a thank you to Barbara Noble, an enormously talented graphics artist, who designed the book's dust jacket cover, and contributed valuable advice on the book's design.

The book was published with the help of a grant from the Wolf Aviation Fund of Gavilan, New Mexico.

I must acknowledge also, the first man to suggest that I publish a collection of my columns. This occurred many years ago when the column was still in its youth. This man was Larry Burian who was then president of the NATA (National Air Transport Association).

I am grateful to Phil Boyer, President of the Aircraft Owners and Pilots Association for his insightful foreword.

I am greatly indebted to Pascal Landi for making last minute corrections under severe time constraints and for designing my web site www.adventuresinflying.net.

And finally, a big thank you to all those whose names I have inadvertently omitted.

Without the help of these people, each of whom made a contribution, this book would probably never have seen the light of day. Writing the book was an adventure in itself and I'm grateful to all those who helped see me through it.

Foreword

Like most pilots I flip through the pages of my old logbooks from time to time. Beyond fulfilling regulatory requirements, logbooks are a record of our flying experiences. The brief entries will mean little to a casual reader. But those same notes to me conjure up vivid memories of specific flights, planes and people. The first trip with their young grandchildren onboard to visit my parents that "flying" was really useful, that first encounter with bad weather, and so many other small notations that conjure up full stories.

In this volume, Jack Elliott has compiled a logbook of aviation experiences. But it is a logbook unlike any other. It is in many ways a gift to those of us who love general aviation and to those who want to know more about its joys, challenges and rewards.

For more than 38 years, Jack wrote the weekly "Wings Over Jersey" column for the *Newark Star-Ledger* newspaper. My first knowledge of Jack and his work was through this column, when I lived across the Hudson River from his home in New Jersey. He presented the multifaceted and fascinating world of general aviation to a general public, who even today continue to lack an understanding of GA. He captured the essence of flying in accessible, down-to-earth prose. And while the name of the column implies it was about airplanes in a single state, it was--and, especially as collected in this book, is -- about much, much more than that.

Jack's columns covered virtually all of GA from ultralights, to gliders to piston and turbine aircraft, to balloons, helicopters, seaplanes, and parachutes. He informed the public about aircraft from the Wright Flyer to the Concorde. He wrote about everything from short hops to round-the-world flights. He documented the joyful and tragic, the relatively mundane and the absolutely magnificent. It would be difficult to find a body of work about GA so comprehensive and utterly readable as *Adventures in Flying*.

Even more than the adventures, the places and the aircraft, Jack wrote about people. He encountered both ordinary and extraordinary individuals whose stories collectively describe the full breadth of GA experiences. Readers who are not pilots will enjoy the range of entertaining and informative tales. So will pilots like myself, who will recognize many of the characters who could just as easily be at their local airports today as when Jack met them.

While *Adventures in Flying* is by its nature a work of history, it is completely applicable to today's events. Many of the same challenges and battles we face--airport closures, public misunderstanding and media ignorance--have been around since airplanes have been flying. Jack's stories serve as a reservoir of wisdom, perspective and inspiration.

So this is a logbook of GA flying. But in larger sense, it is about life -- Jack's life in writing about general aviation, the lives of the people he chronicled, the lives all of those served by GA, and the life of GA in America. Like the logbooks kept by all pilots, *Adventures in Flying* will serve as an invaluable record and reminder of the value, challenge and the beauty of flying.

Phil Boyer
AOPA President
Frederick, MD

Preflight

All of us eventually find our own tiny niche in the vast scheme of things. Like water finding its own level or a river finding its twisting course to the sea. And like the river, there are many twists and turns along the way. But we get there.

For me, the journey toward that niche began when I was a small boy, although at the time I didn't know where I was heading. Whenever an airplane flew overhead, it was like an irresistible force, a magnet, pulling me out of the house. I'd run out to the backyard to stare up at the sky.

I've never outgrown that. I still gaze skyward every time an airplane passes overhead.

When I got a little older, the fascination with airplanes steered me to building balsa wood models, which many boys did in those days. Sometimes, as I recall, I paid as little as ten cents for a kit.

My mother gave me a board to work on which she had used to roll dough. I spread the plans that came with the kit on the board and, with straight pins from my mother's sewing kit to hold them in place, laid out balsa wood strips on the plans along with parts I cut out of a stamped sheet of balsa wood. I glued the pieces together to form fuselage sides and then connected the two sides, top and bottom, to complete the fuselage.

The wings and the tail were made in a similar fashion and then all the parts were covered with tissue that came with the kit. There was a tremendous fascination in seeing the model aircraft take shape.

I remember building a Gull Wing Stinson Reliant. I thought that airplane was a thing of beauty. I still do.

I modified the kit so that it had controls that worked by fashioning tiny hinges for the ailerons, elevators, and rudder from the aluminum bottle caps that came on the glass milk bottles of the time.

As I built those models, I dreamed of flying an airplane. But I knew that was far-fetched, even for a dream. Years later, however, as unlikely as it had seemed, that dream became a reality.

A couple of years after my discharge from the Army at the end of World War II, I went out to Westfield Airport in New Jersey and began taking flying lessons in a Piper Cub. It was an incredible experience to sit in a real airplane, inhale the smell of oil, manipulate the controls, and feel the magical response.

I was just about ready to solo when, after the last landing of the day on the turf strip, the instructor in back of me, who usually spoke with a roar, leaned over and said softly, "I'm not sure, but I think you caught the prop." We got out and looked at it. He was right. About an inch was missing from each end of the wooden propeller.

They had another prop on the airplane before I left. But I felt so bad about the incident that I never went back.

The dream of flying, however, didn't go away. It stuck with me and five years later I went out to a flight school at Morristown Airport run by the same people who ran the school at Westfield Airport, which by then had closed. And in 1954, I got my license.

Nine years later, when I was Sunday Editor of the *Star-Ledger* in Newark, N.J., I told Mort Pye, the editor, that I thought the paper should have an aviation column and I'd like to write it.

He thought about it for a moment and said, "Okay. Try it."

He never said stop, so I kept writing the column for the Sunday editions--for more than 38 years. It ran from June 9, 1963, until the last Sunday of 2001.

The column was written for the average reader, not just pilots. I tried to cover all aspects of aviation and to concentrate on adventure and human interest stories that would appeal to a broad spectrum of readers. I wanted to bring the excitement, the thrill, the beauty, and the rapturous sense of freedom associated with general aviation flying (all flying except airline and military) to the average reader.

There were columns about people nobody ever heard of whose aviation exploits were overflowing with drama, suspense, and excitement rivaling the exploits of aviation's greatest heroes. Those stories encompassed memorable experiences not only in powered aircraft, but in gliders, ultralights, balloons, seaplanes, helicopters, and blimps.

Some of the most inspiring stories I encountered were about people who overcame severe physical handicaps to become pilots.

There were columns about mercy flights in which volunteer pilots contribute their time, their aircraft and fuel, to fly patients to hospitals and treatment centers where, in many cases, their lives were saved. Most of these people had no other way of getting to these facilities. Sometimes they were not able to stand in long lines for extended periods of time. Many had exhausted their life savings battling their illnesses.

Aviation is full of colorful characters, including old-timers with fascinating stories about the early days of flying , often steeped in nostalgia. You will meet some of them in the pages which follow.

I always tried to present stories of a varied nature that would offer a well-rounded picture of the fascinating world of flying.

More than 25 years ago, readers started suggesting that I put some of those columns into a book.

Well, I finally did. And this is it.

Chapter 1

The Adventurers

There is a special breed of men and women infused with a driving impulse to push back horizons, to stretch the limits which restrain the majority of us. It is a yearning for the ultimate freedom, a desire to break the bonds which tie us to the earth and to soar aloft like a bird.

They yearn to go where no one has gone before, to go faster, farther, higher. Who are these people? They are aviators, men and women with unlimited horizons.

When we think of people of this breed, names like Charles Lindbergh and Amelia Earhart immediately spring to mind. But there are thousands of others of the same bent, ordinary men and women with a spirit of adventure that has carried them to new horizons, yet whose exploits--often as fascinating as those of better known aviators--are unheralded, unknown. Many of their achievements are both breathtaking and mind-boggling.

The exploits of some of these pilots are recounted in this chapter.

A FLIGHT THROUGH HELL

Claudio Tonnini is a guy who owns a truck repair shop. He puts in long, pressure-filled days. The pressure built up to the point where he felt a strong urge to find a way to escape the everyday burdens of business.

He happened to go for an airplane ride and that experience provided the perfect answer. Looking down from above everything seemed small and insignificant. He felt relaxed. He felt as if a burden had been lifted off his shoulders. Right then and there, he decided he would learn to fly.

Since he was a skilled master mechanic, Claudio decided to build his own airplane from a standard kit. When it was finished it was a thing of beauty.

A couple of years later, he decided to make a marathon flight to Ushuia, Argentina, and on the return flight to stop at Sao Paulo, Brazil, his birthplace to visit his mother. who still lives there. What follows is the story of that flight and the monstrous, unexpected obstacles he encountered and how he dealt with them.

Claudio Tonnini seemed a bit tense as he told me about his 18,000-mile flight in an airplane he built himself. "That's equal to three round trips across the Atlantic," he said, as if he could hardly believe it himself. His destination was Ushuia, a town at the tip of Argentina. Flying conditions there are almost always unfriendly, with constant gale-like winds.

The flight had taken place a few weeks before our meeting, but reliving the experience by talking about it put a harshness in his voice as he described his adventure.

Claudio Tonnini and his RV-4 which he dubbed, "The Purple Passion," the airplane he built himself and flew 9,000 miles to the tip of South America and back, winning him much recognition including the plaque he is holding.

The trip took him from his home base at Marlboro Airport (now closed) in New Jersey to Ushuia and put him through a wide variety of hazardous situations he never anticipated. At times, for example, the distance between airports en route was measured in hours not miles.

The flight took him over towering mountains and dense jungles. He made the trip in March, a month when the weather is usually unstable.

To get to his destination he had to fly 9,000 miles. To get back home he had to fly another 9,000 miles. That would be a very long flight in a jet airliner, but it is hard to imagine such a trip in a little two-place airplane. Not surprisingly, it turned out to be anything but a routine flight. His trip was filled with unanticipated nail-biting, sweat-filled hours. The most unforgettable occurred during his journey home. On the leg between Porto Alegre and Sao Paulo, Brazil, Claudio ran into the worst cold front the area had seen in years.

"I was flying on instruments at an assigned altitude of 11,000 feet when I encountered hail pounding viciously against the aircraft. Then I ran into pouring rain which was freezing on the airplane. Ice covered the canopy. I couldn't see outside." Claudio was sealed in the airplane as if it were a cocoon. And he knew ice on the airplane could force him down in the middle of nowhere.

But that was only the beginning of his problems. "In the middle of all this, my engine began to miss," he said, reflecting an air of terror. "My heart was pounding."

The tiny, two-place tandem RV-4 aircraft was taking a tremendous beating, as was Claudio. Both he and the aircraft were being put to the ultimate test.

It should be pointed out that while the term homebuilt may conjure visions of something amateurish, flimsy, and of questionable reliability, nothing could be further from the truth.

The RV-4 is a sturdy, excellently designed aircraft and Claudio, is a master mechanic. The craftsmanship in his homebuilt airplane is more like what you see in an expensive hand built automobile.

To add to his dilemma, Claudio had radio problems. "I lost communications with the Air Traffic Control Center," he said. "I called again and again and I got no answer. The ice which coated the antennas, prevented my transmissions from getting through.

"As I kept calling, I did get a response from an airliner in the area. The pilot relayed my message to the Center and then got back to me. But the Center didn't offer me much help.

"The engine continued to miss and run rough. I couldn't get full power. I lost 4,000 feet in a few seconds. I was over mountains that were 5,000 feet high. They were covered with tropical jungles. I tried everything I could think of. I switched fuel tanks. I put the electric fuel pump on. I pulled the carburetor heat knob out a little at a time (to get rid of carburetor ice, if there was any). I was afraid to do anything extreme.

"After I pulled the carburetor heat knob, I began to climb. But I couldn't get higher than 9,000 feet. I was assigned to 11,000. My normal cruise speed is 135 knots. I couldn't get over 80. If my speed fell much lower, I wouldn't be able to remain aloft. The weight of the ice as well as the effect it had on the air flow over the wing, could force me down.

"A nearby airliner I contacted asked the Air Traffic Control Center if I could get a lower altitude. I told the pilot to tell them I was going through hell. He got a message back that said there was no lower safe altitude."

For the next two-and-a-half hours conditions did not improve. The engine continued to run rough--but it kept running. It was touch and go. There was nothing Claudio could do to improve the situation.

Fortunately, he was not alone. Lady Luck was riding with him. In spite of all his problems and the long odds against him, he made it to Sao Paulo. When he arrived in the area controllers gave him a radar approach. "The approach to the airport is right between buildings," Claudio said. That could be a challenge even if the pilot wasn't exhausted from hours flying through hell. "But I had no problem," he said. "I landed okay."

Claudio is a native of Sao Paulo and his mother, who still lives there, was waiting for him, along with his sister and a friend.

"When I got out of the airplane I couldn't walk up to them," he related. "I walked away from them. I walked around for 15 minutes to calm down. Then I walked back and hugged my mother."

His engine problem, he discovered, was due to the fact that one of the two magnetos (ignition systems) was shot. Aircraft piston engines all have dual magnetos so that if one goes out, the engine will continue to run on the other, although it may run rough and you may not get full power.

That was only one of the problems Claudio encountered in his 18,000-mile journey. He had been told before he left that the winds in Ushuia often blow as high as 80 miles an hour. When he got there he found it was not far from the truth.

He had some evidence of that even before he arrived. As he approached Trelew, in southern Argentina, a little more than 300 miles from his destination, a member of the Aero Club there, whom he had contacted before the flight, called him from the tower and said, "Claudio, don't land here. There is a 35 to 45 mile-an-hour crosswind."

"I said, 'What should I do?' He said, 'Go to the Aero Club Airport.' " The club had bulldozed a strip out of the woods about four miles away. The wind was blowing right down the runway. "There were big stones all over the strip," said Claudio. It was not the kind of strip he would choose to put down on, but he had no choice. "I landed," he said, "and didn't have any damage."

By the time this happened, incidents like it were almost routine. When he tried to land at an airport 30 miles outside Buenos Aires, he got down to minimums and couldn't see the runway. He shot a missed approach and was directed to Buenos Aires' main airport. The situation wasn't much better there. But just as he reached minimums he broke out of the clouds. If he hadn't broken out, he would have had to shoot another missed approach and then make a second attempt to land. After his long flight, he had a limited supply of gas. If he had missed his second approach, he might not have had enough gas for a third try.

Would he do it again, he was asked, after he related his hair-raising experiences? It seemed like a foolish question. The response, however, was not what was expected.

"I could leave right now," he said. "The worst thing is when you get back. Getting used to normal life again is hell. I wish I could tell you what this trip means to me--what I feel. When I'm doing this I'm really alive. When I landed at Ushuia I was so happy I couldn't believe it. I wish I was a poet so I could describe all this."

This wasn't Claudio's first adventure in this airplane, which he named, "The Purple Passion." (It is painted purple with a dove on the side.) He had flown the airplane down to Sao Paulo a few years previously to visit his mother. On another marathon flight--in a single-engine Cessna--he was one of three pilots who flew from New Jersey to Moscow. (See "The Perils of a Flight to Moscow," Page 43).

Although he knew of no one who had ever flown a homebuilt aircraft from the United States to the tip of South America before, Claudio's achievement did not go into the record books. He didn't have his flight sanctioned by the National Aeronautic Association, the U.S. arm of the French organization that verifies flight records and makes them official. But at his home airport in Marlboro, they call him "Our Hero."

Claudio logged more than 150 hours flying time on his trip. In Brazil and Argentina he paid between $4 and $5 a gallon for gas. (This was in 1990). In Brazil, landing fees ranged from a minimum of $104 to a maximum of $158. In Argentina, he never paid a landing fee. "When I made my first landing in Argentina, I was called into the office," he recounted. "I wondered, what did I do?

"When I entered the office, the officer in there said, 'Claudio, what can I do for you? Any airplane flying south from here is under my command.' He gave me charts and marked them for me. Then he said, 'I hope the flame in you never goes out.' "

Everywhere Claudio stopped there were local reporters, photographers, and TV crews waiting to greet him. He assumes they were alerted by the international flight plans he had filed, although he had contacted some South American members of the EAA (Experimental Aircraft Association) who knew he was coming. They don't often see pilots from the United States landing in their communities, much less in aircraft they built themselves.

"After all that, would you *really* do it again? " he was asked once more.

"If nothing happened," he said, "it would be boring."

8/19/90[1]

---

[1] The date at the end of each story indicates the date when the column on which the story was based, originally ran in the *Sunday Star-Ledger*.

There may be some facts or figures in these stories that will raise your eyebrows. Gasoline prices is one example. Look at the date at the end of the story. That will put it in perspective and explain what at first glance seems like an error.

GLUTTON FOR PUNISHMENT

After reading the story of adventuresome Claudio Tonnini's stormy flight to the tip of South America, you may have thought that despite what he said, he would never do that again in a million years. You would be wrong.

It didn't take him a million years. He did an encore two years later. His second trip was no less memorable than the first. It had its own set of incredible incidents.

Here is the sequel to his story.

Some people never learn. Claudio Tonnini is one of them.

Two years earlier, when he flew from New Jersey to Ushuia, Argentina, he described some of the conditions he encountered as "hell."

You might think that someone who has been to hell and back would never dream of risking a return. You would think that Claudio would be happy to take safe refuge in his truck repair shop. That was not the case. He did it again. He undertook a second flight to Ushuia. That is what makes Claudio a true adventurer: his unquenchable spirit.

The first time he made the 18,000-mile flight, you'll remember, he did it in March. Now in March, much of Brazil and Argentina experience the most severe weather of the year. Claudio had plenty of evidence of that on his first trip when for two-and-a-half hours he battled the elements, flying over jungles and mountains through a steady, unrelenting downpour of freezing rain that might well have forced him down.

He arrived at airports, low on fuel, where conditions were below minimums and it was impossible to land. Certainly, after his first experience you would expect that if he even dreamed of repeating the flight, he would pick another month--any other month.

"Knowing what you know, how did you decide to do it again-- and in March?" he was asked. "I was under a lot of pressure," he replied. "My nerves were getting to me. I wanted to get away." He thought for a few moments. "It's a challenge. I guess I've got it in my blood," he replied.

The script was different this time, but the problems were no less grievous. Before he undertook this trip, Claudio installed a GPS (Global Positioning System) in his aircraft. The GPS can guide an aircraft to any point on earth and get it to the runway at an airport there within feet. It can also tell the pilot exactly where he is at any given moment.

Claudio planned to rely on this system which would greatly simplify his navigation chores and relieve him of at least that one burden.

It worked beautifully...until he left Buenos Aires on his southbound trip. Then, he inadvertently pushed the wrong button and wiped out the system's memory. That's like having everything on your computer wiped out. But it's a lot more significant when you're relying on a piece of equipment while you're in flight.

As it happened, there was a 35 to 40-knot crosswind on the leg where he lost his GPS guidance and that would blow him off course. He could only estimate how much correction he needed to compensate for the wind. If the GPS were working, it would have been no problem. It would compensate for the wind drift angle and steer the aircraft along its intended route. But now he didn't have a GPS. Claudio was off course and he knew it. But he didn't know how far off course and he didn't know exactly where he was.

His destination on this leg was Bahia Blanca. Argentina is not like the United States where there are usually airports every few miles. In some places down there it's 400 miles between airports.

Claudio had no idea where he might find an airport. He flew on, not quite sure of exactly where he was. Anxiety built up and he began to sweat as he flew through a kind of no man's land in the sky.

Then sheer luck tapped him on the shoulder at precisely the right moment. It was like a miracle. He spotted a small airport and he landed. He was greatly relieved to be on the ground, but he didn't know where he was. It turned out he was not that far off course. A fellow at the airport told him he could follow a road to Bahia Blanca. One problem solved. He had no trouble following the road and he found the airport, where he landed, gassed up and took off for Trelew.

Trelew had a turf runway. There had been heavy rains prior to his arrival and the runway was turned into thick, sticky mud. He landed and got bogged down and couldn't get out. His engine could pull him through the air at 135 knots with ease, but it couldn't pull him out of the mud.

They found ten men and pushing and shoving and rocking the airplane, they succeeded in freeing him.

His next move was to call the factory in Washington State which made his GPS He told them of his problem. "No problem," they said. "Just send it back and we'll fix it."

When he told them where he was, they said they'd explain how he could reprogram the unit. It was no simple task. He spent a half hour pushing buttons according to the instructions he had been given. When he finished, the system worked again.

Now he had something to celebrate. The Aero Club down there, some of whose members he had contacted before he left, helped him do just that. They arranged a barbecue in his honor. He wasn't sure if this was a good omen or not. The Aero Club at Martinique had staged a party for him also. But a couple of legs later, flying from Trinidad to Guyana he found himself in real trouble. He was 200 miles out when he encountered a downpour such as you only experience in the tropics. "It was black," said Claudio. "I couldn't see anything. When it rains there, it rains."

He decided he couldn't go on. He turned around and flew back to Trinidad. He landed safely, but the idea that nothing could stop him was destroyed.

There were other unanticipated problems. When he landed at Carolina, Brazil, on a flight from Belem, he was informed that they had no gas. That was not good news. He didn't have very much in his tanks either. They told him there was another airport 50 miles away that did have gas. Fortunately, he had just enough in his tanks to get him there.

When he arrived at Sao Paulo, Claudio was again greeted by his mother and sister and by the television cameras of the biggest TV station in the city. For a little while, Claudio was a hero again.

On his arrival at his final destination, Ushuia, there was a 20-knot crosswind. That's a calm day at Ushuia.

On his previous trip, he didn't even stay overnight, even though his wife's cousin lived there, because the winds which were bad enough, were forecast to get worse. This time, he stayed overnight and spent some time with his wife's cousin. She greeted him by asking, "Are you crazy, coming back here in that little plane?" But a moment later she told him, "You're just in time for my granddaughter's birthday party."

The flight north had its own memorable moments. When he arrived at Cayenne in French Guiana, the weather was zero-zero. "As I was coming in on final, the tower asked me where I was. They couldn't see anything. Neither could I. I couldn't see the runway. But I continued my approach, relying on the GPS. I never saw the runway until I was right over it. The GPS got me to the runway and told me what my altitude was."

The experience he'll remember the longest took place at a grass strip outside Buenos Aires. It was very hot and his fuel pressure was low. On takeoff, when he reached an altitude of five or ten feet, the engine quit.

"There was a house right at the end of the runway," he said. "Another three seconds and I would have crashed into it."

With lightning-like reflexes, he managed to get the airplane back on the runway and stopped. He pulled the airplane off the runway and started looking for the problem. He found that the electric fuel pump was not working. "I hit it with a screwdriver and it started working again," he said. "I was scared, but I started the engine and taxied back to take off again. This time it didn't quit. It had a vapor lock which precipitated the problem. The gas is bad there. They put a lot of alcohol in it."

The pump never quit again. Claudio doesn't quit either. After completing two 18,000-mile flights in his homebuilt aircraft, what would he do next? He was thinking about a flight around the world.

5/9/93

Note: *As of the date of this writing, he is still considering it.*

THE HAIR-RAISING RESCUE OF A SICK AIRCRAFT

John Neumeister, an airline pilot, stumbled on a real aircraft bargain in an unlikely place--Zaire. While he was there, he visited a local airport where he spotted a Grumman Widgeon sitting on the field. A Widgeon is a relatively rare old twin-engine amphibian aircraft, which is a favorite of many antique airplane buffs. It was like finding a buried treasure in a most unlikely place.

He had no way of knowing it at the time, but what he really found was the makings of a classic, hair-raising adventure.

This is the story of that adventure.

To say that John Neumeister didn't know what he was getting into when he spotted Grumman Widgeon N4122A in Kinshasa, Zaire, (now the Democratic Republic of the Congo) could be the understatement of the century. His story, which begins in 1976, has all the mystery of an Agatha Christie novel, the intrigue of a James Bond movie, and the adventure of a ride down the Colorado River in a rubber raft.

Neumeister, a Pan Am pilot, had gone to Zaire to visit his brother, Bill, a medic with a U.S. construction company putting in power lines.

John Neumeister with the Grumman Widgeon which he rescued from what seemed like a death sentence in Zaire.

During his week's stay he drove to the local airport out of curiosity. There, he spotted a Widgeon, sitting out in the broiling sun. It's an airplane that catches the eye because it's a little bit different. It's an amphibian and you don't see too many of them around. Widgeons were built in the decade from the early 40s to the early 50s. The airplane bore a U.S. registration number.

Neumeister learned that the aircraft had been sitting there for six years, but he couldn't find out who owned it.

Since it had a U.S. registration number, he tried to trace its ownership through FAA records. That should have been simple, but it turned out it wasn't because there was a disagreement over who was the aircraft's owner.

He pursued the issue. After a year of investigation, Neumeister confirmed the fact that the legal owner was someone named George Barnes. But he couldn't locate Barnes. He did, however, find friends of his. But they refused to reveal his whereabouts or relay any messages.

One story Neumeister heard was that Barnes was with the CIA and the aircraft had been flown to Zaire in connection with a CIA mission.

The title to the aircraft was in the name of Barnes' wife, but the registration was in the name of Nick Carter, an American aircraft dealer, who had supposedly sold it to Barnes.

Neumeister contacted Carter who claimed he still owned the aircraft. They agreed on a sale price of $5,000 which was very reasonable. Neumeister estimated that a Widgeon with the same 300-hp radial engines to be worth about $100,000 in the U.S. in good condition.

But this aircraft was deep in Africa. There was the problem of getting it out of there and back to the U.S. And then, too, it had been sitting under the hot African sun for six years.

Neumeister paid Carter $1,000 with the balance due when he got the aircraft back to the U.S.

During its long stay in Zaire the engines had been run up occasionally, but no one ever flew the aircraft. A mechanic in Zaire told Neumeister that a Belgian fellow paid him to work on the aircraft. In 1977, Neumeister met this fellow, a friend of Barnes, in Belgium, and he was told that Barnes, not Carter, actually owned the aircraft.

Eventually, Neumeister got to talk to Barnes by phone (he never met him) and he bought the airplane from *him* for $7,500.

Neumeister and a friend who is a Pan Am mechanic, flew to Zaire to ferry the plane back. It was now a year after he first saw the aircraft and it looked like he was on his way home at last. But he had a lot further to go than he ever dreamed. "We put a battery in the aircraft and it started right up," Neumeister recounts. But that didn't mean they could go anywhere. They would not be permitted to take off from Zaire without authorization. For $10 in cash they got a general to let them send a telex saying they had authorization. They had to list every airport up the coast of Africa so that no matter where they might have to land that airport would be listed on the authorization. Their plan was to fly to England and change both engines before flying across the Atlantic. That plan fell apart, however, when they blew an engine over Sierra Leone. They were able to put the aircraft down on the island of Sherbru near Freetown. "There was nothing there," said

Neumeister. There was only one flight a week into the island in a commuter aircraft.

"We spent the night in the airplane calling on 121.5, the emergency frequency, for help. Eventually, an Air Afrique airliner heard our message and they were good enough to relay it to my brother. He made arrangements for a pilot with a Cessna 180 to pick us up and fly us to Liberia. The next morning the authorities began interrogating us. They placed us under armed guard and the interrogation went on for two days, continuing even after the Cessna 180 pilot arrived. There was political unrest and riots in the country at that time. They wanted to make sure we were not part of an invasion force to take over the island."

Neumeister and his mechanic friend were not allowed to leave the country until they got permission from the president. When Neumeister was eventually able to get out of the country he returned to the United States, but the airplane stayed in Sherbru. It wasn't until a year later that Neumeister returned with parts for the damaged engine. But he soon discovered that the engine was beyond repair. He returned home once again and bought an engine for $6,000.

In the spring of 1978, he flew back to Africa aboard a Pan Am flight that also carried his engine. In order to mount the engine on the airplane, they needed a gantry but there was no such thing on the island. So they built one out of three pieces of steel salvaged from a burned out building in a convent.

With the engine replaced, he was able to fly the Widgeon to Liberia. Leaving it there, Neumeister again returned to the United States, this time with the propellers.

Back in the states, he bought another engine for $6,000 and had the propellers overhauled for $3,000.

With the new engine installed and the overhauled props mounted, Neumeister and another brother, Dave, took off for the United States. It was now May of 1978 and they still had a few problems ahead of them. In Mauritania, they weren't allowed to leave the airport because they didn't have a visa. They slept under the wing of the aircraft.

In Agadir, Morocco, there was no gas at the airport. They hauled 60 gallons of auto gas from a gas station in town back to the airport in five gallon cans.

At Heathrow Airport outside London, the customs agents were sure Neumeister was hauling drugs. They spent hours searching the aircraft, going so far as to remove the aircraft's side panels, before they were finally convinced there were no drugs aboard. Crossing the Atlantic turned out to be the first routine part of the trip. Neumeister's long and frustrating odyssey ended on June 11, 1979, three years after it began, when he finally touched down at Sussex Airport, his home base, in the pretty green hills of northwest New Jersey.

7/24/83

A RACE AROUND THE WORLD

*Circling the globe in an aircraft is a major accomplishment--
even if you're a paying passenger in an airliner.*

*Racing around the world adds another dimension, especially if
it's in a single-engine aircraft.*

*That would be enough for most adventurous aviators, but not for
Ken Johnson. Johnson accomplished all the above in an airplane he
built in his basement.*

*No one had ever raced around the world in a homebuilt
aircraft. One thing you can be sure of is that such a flight will provide
more than its share of suspense, surprises, anxious moments, and
unpredictable situations.*

Here is the story of Ken Johnson's flight.

W hat do you say when you return from an around-the-world
race in an airplane you built in your basement?

What Ken Johnson said, rather proudly, when he
landed back at his home base at Sky Manor Airport in Pittstown,
N.J., was, "We finished second."

That's not too shabby when you consider that some of the
contestants (there were
14) dipped into their
mattresses for amounts
in seven figures to buy
an aircraft in which
they thought they
could win the race.
(There were even a
couple of turbine
aircraft entered.)

The winners, it
turned out, were two
women (women don't
take second place to
male chauvinists

Ken Johnson, left, and Larry Cioppi, in front of the Glasair III,
Zephyrus, (God of the West Wind), which Ken built and the two
pilots flew in an around-the-world race.

anymore, in case you hadn't noticed). Marion Jayne and her daughter,
Patricia Keefer, of Roanoke, Texas, flying a Piper Twin Comanche,
were the winners. The last of that breed of aircraft rolled off the
production line in 1972.

So the aircraft which won the race was virtually a senior
citizen, as aircraft go, and second place was taken by an aircraft that

never saw the inside of a factory-a homebuilt Glasair III.

Johnson, along with his copilot, Larry Cioppi, made the flight in 85 hours flying time, averaging 214 knots (that's about 246 miles an hour). Since each aircraft in the race was capable of a different flying speed, each plane was handicapped so that the pilots were flying against their handicap, based on their aircraft's average speed. Entries came from Canada, Spain, India, Belgium, Switzerland, France and Norway, in addition to the United States. One of the biggest obstacles Johnson and Cioppi (and their competitors) faced was dealing with air traffic controllers in remote areas of the world. Controllers in such areas are not accustomed to handling any semblance of what might be considered normal traffic volume and they were overwhelmed by the 14 race contestants. Many of them don't expect to see that many aircraft in a week. Fourteen within a matter of hours was more than they could conceive.

Imagine arriving at your destination in a race, anxious to get your wheels on the ground, and when you call the tower for landing instructions you're told you can't land because an airliner is inbound. You're told to hold outside the airport area. The airliner might be 60 miles away and there would be plenty of time to land ten aircraft before the airliner arrives. This happened to them several times, costing valuable time. But they were not alone. Other contestants experienced the same frustrations.

That was only one problem. You don't fly around the world without experiencing more than one problem.

For Johnson and Cioppi the problems started early--on takeoff from the race's starting point, Montreal. It was raining when they were scheduled to take off and the temperature was 40 degrees. There was an 800-foot ceiling and the freezing level was 5,000 feet. Ice may be fine in a well-made highball, but it's not something you want on an airplane. It adds weight, slowing down the aircraft. It slows down the rate of climb and can prevent the aircraft from reaching the desired altitude. And ice on the wings can distort the airflow, destroying lift so that the aircraft might not be capable of remaining aloft.

Johnson's aircraft did not have deicing equipment, but he and Cioppi had a somewhat unorthodox method of dealing with that situation.

Before they took off, they coated the wings, tail surfaces and propeller with oil. Ice wouldn't stick to the oil which would stay on the airplane for about an hour. It would only take them minutes to get above the freezing level.

Having solved that problem, they were the first piston-powered aircraft to arrive at stop number one, St. John's,

Newfoundland. But when they got there, they faced a new problem. There was an airliner on the runway. They had to extend their pattern five miles, costing them valuable time. For all their frustration, they were still the first piston aircraft--single or twin-engine--to land.

Those were minor obstacles, compared to what awaited them the next morning. There was a 200 foot overcast. The cloud level was below the tops of the buildings. At the same time, there was a strong wind blowing at 30 knots. That's a rather unusual combination, since normally, when there is a strong wind, it's clear.

"We took off and we didn't see the ocean until more than three hours later," said Johnson. That was not a real hang-up, but they did encounter a serious problem flying through the clouds. The cabin was full of severe static electricity discharges. The door knob sparked. If they touched the panel, it sparked. With a full load of fuel, including an auxiliary tank in the cabin, sparks flying around didn't make for a comfortable situation.

Were they scared? "We didn't have time to be scared," said Johnson.

The static was being generated by the trailing antenna used for high frequency communications. But they couldn't make contact with anybody on the HF set. They slowed down to 120 miles an hour and the static stopped. In a few minutes they were between cloud layers and they were able to resume speed with no problem. But by then the static had done its damage. It blew their autopilot and they had to hand fly the airplane to Morocco, with a stop in the Azores.

They flew through a thunderstorm on the way to Marrakesh, but it was clear as they approached their destination.

"We could see the lights along the coast of Africa off in the distance," said Johnson. "And it was a great feeling when we saw the lights of Marrakesh. We landed at ten minutes to midnight, finishing second on that leg. The next morning we had to get up early for an agenda that included a visit to a flea market shop, a pilots' briefing, and a press briefing. In the evening our hosts took us to a place that reminded me of the Arabian Nights. It was highly decorated with carpets and tapestries. They brought out a whole lamb and you picked at it. Then we had entertainment. There were belly dancers, and there was trick horseback riding. The riders fired guns in the air as they galloped around at full speed. Everything was loud. We got back to our hotel at midnight and had to get up at 4:30 for a scheduled 7:35 departure."

At the airport in the morning they got ready to go. "We started our engines and asked for our IFR (Instrument Flight Rules) clearance to Istanbul. The controller said, 'I call you back.' Every five minutes we called again and got the same response. So did everybody else. We finally got off at 9:15. After that, every time anyone took pictures of us, we didn't say 'cheese', we said, 'I call you back.' "

One good thing did happen in Marrakesh. Ken fixed the autopilot.

"We took off from Morocco and flew over Algeria, Tunisia, Sicily, past the toe of Italy. We saw two volcanoes. The first was smoking, the second was covered with concrete. We flew over Greece and the Greek Islands and the mountains were beautiful," said Johnson.

"Coming in to Istanbul, the controller told us, 'Do not descend.' There was an airliner coming in. It was 40 miles out. We told them we were in a race. They vectored us around for seven or eight miles. When we landed, we had been in the airplane 11 hours and 40 minutes, including the long takeoff delay. And then, there was another delay when we landed. We sat there for 10 to 15 minutes waiting for them to give us taxi instructions.

"Taking off from Istanbul was worse than landing. We shut our engine off three times while sitting there waiting for clearance to take off. They let three airplanes off, but not in the proper order, and the rest of us just sat there.

"When we finally took off for Dubai, United Arab Emirates, we couldn't get permission to fly over Saudi Arabia, so we had to fly over Iran. That was May 7, my birthday, and Larry gave me a Hershey bar and a flashlight."

At Dubai, Johnson said they stayed in the second nicest hotel of the trip, the Jebel Ali. The nicest was on Okinawa, the Manz Beach Inn.

After Dubai, they took off for Pakistan and India where they landed at Agra, near the opulent Taj Mahal.

"We saw grinding poverty at Agra," Johnson said. "A hundred thousand people have no shelter. They sleep outside. There is a fence around the hotel to keep people out. We ate in the officers' club. The next day a lot of people were sick."

After takeoff from India, the pilots in the race were advised by Bangladesh controllers that if they flew into their airspace, they would be fired on. The race planes flew out over the ocean.

They went on to Ho Chi Minh City, Vietnam, stopping in U-Taphal, Thailand. In Vietnam, Ken's wallet was stolen along with his passport and Russian visa. The hotel called his room and said somebody at the desk had his passport. The fellow at the desk told him to come across the street. He said he wanted money. Ken gave him $20. He wanted more but Ken managed to get away without giving him any more.

At U-Taphal, the authorities wanted $600 for the use of the navigation system. Arrangements had been made in advance, to take care of that, but they pretended they didn't know. Airport authorities also tried to collect extra money in India.

The next stop was Okinawa where Johnson reported the food was good and you could drink the water. Then it was on to Sendai, Japan, 200 miles north of Tokyo. Approaching the airport they requested permission to descend from 11,000 feet. They didn't get it. When they got to the downwind leg for landing, they were still at 11,000 feet. An airliner was coming in so they were still refused permission to descend. When they finally did get clearance they went into a dive, hitting 335 miles an hour--beyond the airplane's red line (never exceed speed)--and they were on the ground in two minutes.

Their next stop was in Petropavlovsk, Russia, where it was rainy and cold and there was snow on the ground. "The people were nice and they were helpful," Johnson said. "But they had nothing and were trapped there with no roads or railroads, just a few old cars."

From Petropavlovsk they flew to Anchorage, 1,700 nautical miles, 1,200 of it over open ocean. "It was beautiful to talk to American controllers again," they commented. They then flew to Calgary and on back to their starting--and finishing--point, Montreal, Canada.

It's always good to get home after a long trip, but this was not an ordinary trip. They had seen a lot that most tourists never see.

Johnson's comment on arriving home: "This country is like a magical kingdom compared to the rest of the world." A sentiment shared, no doubt, by everyone else in the race.

6/12/94

FLYING A FLIVVER ACROSS THE POND

Crossing the ocean in a single-engine airplane is a challenge to an experienced pilot in a well-equipped aircraft. Doing it in an old, single-engine aircraft with a high time engine is something more than a challenge. Weather over the North Atlantic can be unpredictable and if you run into an unforecast situation, you can't turn around and land at the airport you just passed because you didn't pass any.

But that didn't stop Murray Cooperman. Read on.

Murray Cooperman loves adventure.

To Murray, adventure is flying a small, 22-year-old, single-engine Piper Tri-Pacer with a nearly run out engine across the Atlantic Ocean.

So you figure Murray is a guy with years and years of flying experience under his belt. Wrong. He took his first lesson four years ago (Oct. 1, 1976).

Well, you tell yourself, he must be a guy who took to flying like Bo Derek takes to bikinis. He must have gotten his license in the minimum time--40 hours. Wrong again. Murray didn't solo until he had 65 hours.

"That wasn't my fault," he said. "That was because every time I had a lesson my instructor had us fly to an airport that had a place to eat. We would eat and then fly home."

Murray Cooperman in the cockpit of the Piper Tri-Pacer he flew across the Atlantic.

To his instructor, eating took priority over soloing, according to Murray's account.

If his instructor loved to eat, Murray could keep pace with him. You would know that by looking at him. Murray is rather round around the middle.

At first glance, Murray, a graduate of the Kings Point Merchant Marine Academy, who makes major repairs on oceangoing vessels, may not look like your average adventurer. If he is on the full-blown side physically, he is even more so in personality. He is an extremely outgoing fellow. Ask him to tell you about his flight and he will talk for hours. As a matter of fact, you may not even have to ask him. He may tell you anyway. His story dwarfs the Perils of Pauline. It will certainly not make you want to fly across the ocean in a tired, 22-year-old, $4,500, single-engine airplane.

We won't bore you with all the details Murray related to us. But let us pass along Murray's account of the highlights of his adventure, starting with his arrival at the Faroe Islands in the Atlantic between Iceland and Scotland, one of many stops along the way.

"The weather was fierce," said Murray. "There was high wind and rain. Ice started forming on the windshield and wings. We descended from 5,500 to 3,500 feet and the ice melted."

Murray did not make this flight solo as he had planned. A few weeks before his departure from Essex County (N.J.) Airport, his wife and son asked him to take another pilot along with him. Finding another pilot who would want to fly across the ocean in that airplane would not normally be an easy job, but Murray had heard about Tommy Walker, an old-time air show performer whose act involved flying an airplane through the side of a barn, and he asked Tommy to join him on the flight. Tommy seemed like the kind of guy who would say, "Yes." He had given up air shows for more hazardous pursuits. He made a specialty of taking flights that nobody else would take because of the risks involved. Murray's invitation was a natural. In the course of their flight, however, when decisions had to be made, Murray and Tommy usually had divergent opinions and they discussed them rather heatedly.

When they arrived at the Faroe Islands, conditions were so bad they didn't have time for discussions. It was rough enough that neither of them thought they could consider landing.

"The airport was in a valley surrounded by 5,000-foot mountains," Murray said. "We were in a solid overcast with 60-knot winds and driving rain.

"We couldn't make a descent because of the mountains. I turned out over the ocean to descend. When we broke out we were four or five hundred feet over the water. But the cliffs rose straight out of the ocean.

"I flew along the cliffs and came to a fjord. The opening was about a half mile wide. I knew that if I flew into the fjord, I was committed. Once you got in, it wasn't wide enough to turn around and fly out.

"I didn't have many choices. I decided to fly up the fjord. At the end of it, there was the airport. The wind was 60 knots, but it was blowing straight down the runway. We made a perfect landing."

That incident was probably what Murray will remember

longest about his trip.

He will probably remember his birthday as well. That was on August 19 when they landed at Reykjavik. He recorded in his diary, "My birthday. 56 years old. I was just 34 years old when this airplane was built." The entry continued, "Crossing Greenland, the ice cap, to Iceland."

They had landed at Reykjavik at 2300 (11 p.m.). It was just twilight. The restaurants were closed so all Murray could get for his birthday dinner was a bottle of coke and a cheese sandwich.

It is only fair to report at this point that Murray was not totally inexperienced at ocean flying when he made this trip.

In July of 1977, flying back to the U.S. from Nassau with his wife, Jeanette, Murray made a slight miscalculation in his navigation, which he is still not able to explain. Instead of heading west toward Florida, he headed east out over the open ocean.

After a couple of hours when all he saw was water and no Florida, Murray suspected something was wrong. Jeanette wasn't concerned at all. She was sound asleep beside him.

Murray made some course changes, but after three hours and forty minutes, still no Florida. Jeanette was awake now and he told her they had 20 minutes of fuel left and he was going to descend. "At the last minute I decided to climb," said Murray. "I got up to 12,000 feet and I saw an island off in the distance. I set up a glide with the nose pointed at the island. As we got closer, I could see there was nothing there. I landed in an open field. I saw a black man with a dog come out of the jungle. I yelled, 'Me American pilot.' In perfect English, he said, 'You're on an outer island. You have nothing to be afraid of.'

"We were on the island of Cay Sal, 26 miles from Cuba. There were only five people on the island, two policemen and three trainees who were there to keep refugees and narcotics smugglers off the island."

There was no phone there, but they had radio communication. Murray tried to get a message through to seek help. It happened that his brother-in-law, a Civil Air Patrol pilot, was out searching for him and picked up his message. He landed on the island with fuel.

None of this discouraged either Murray or Jeanette from making other adventurous flights. Not long afterward they flew from Key West, Florida, to the island of Cozumel off the coast of Mexico's Yucatan Peninsula. That flight took five and a half hours over the Gulf of Mexico. Murray was so proud of Jeanette for her bravery that he gave her a gift of a thousand dollars.

He calls his airplane, the *Intrepid*, although that description might fit him and Jeanette better. It is the only airplane he has ever flown. He bought it for $4,500 before he took his first lesson.

The *Intrepid* has a 2,000-hour engine which means it is recommended that after it has logged that many hours the engine should be overhauled. When Murray left on his transatlantic flight (he visited Edinburgh, Paris, and Amsterdam and then had the airplane shipped back) the engine had 1870 hours on it.

"Weren't you a little bit concerned about that?" a somewhat less adventurous pilot asked.

"No," he said. "Danny Syrek of Syrek-Mee Aviation at Caldwell Airport, went over it. He said it was in good shape. If Danny says it's okay, it's okay.

"I had the radios you need to go over the ocean. I had confidence in my equipment."

Normally, Murray's Tri-Pacer holds 36 gallons of fuel. For his transatlantic adventure he had a 65-gallon auxiliary tank installed where the back seat was, which gave him a 13-hour range.

The Tri-Pacer, which was built by Piper in the 1950s, was one of the first General Aviation production airplane to have a nose wheel instead of the old tail wheel. The Ercoupe, built right after World War II, was the first.

11/2/80

THE DARING EXPLOITS OF TEST PILOTS

One of the greatest challenges pilots face is flying into the unknown.

This is all in a day's work for test pilots. That's their business. Whether it's taking a new airplane up on its first flight or breaking the sound barrier for the first time, test pilots are never sure of what they will face. They put their life on the line every time they climb into the cockpit.

These are pilots who must have extraordinary skill, cool nerves, a heightened sense of self confidence, and most of all, a driving sense of adventure--the desire to stare the unknown straight in the eye with impunity.

Stories about the raw courage of these men are legend. Some of them were recorded in a book by Richard P. Hallion titled "Test Pilots, the Frontiersmen of Flight." That book inspired this column.

One of the most unusual stories in the book is about a nerve-wracking incident experienced by test pilot Herb Fisher who flew over the "Hump" (the Himalayas) during World War II (as a civilian test pilot) to study icing conditions. He also test flew every Curtiss P-40 that came off the production line. The incredible incident described in this story is one I had heard many times from Fisher himself, an old friend, who passed away on July 29, 1990. It exemplifies what test pilots face when an emergency strikes suddenly and without warning.

P ilots may come in second only to fishermen in the realm of colorful tales--but not by much. Get a bunch of pilots together in the hangar on a rainy day or in some local watering spot after the moon has come up and the airplanes have come down and vivid imaginations can turn a relatively routine occurrence into a super macho experience.

There is one realm of flight, however, where any attempt to relate the actual facts might well understate the case. This is the experiences of test pilots.

Those who bear this job description must have tremendous resources of skill, knowledge, and judgment. But all of these qualifications put together are not always enough to overcome the challenges of the unknown which they face as a matter of routine.

The stories which these pilots have woven into the pages of aviation history are carefully chronicled in Richard Hallion's, *"Test Pilots, the Frontiersmen of Flight"*.

Hallion's book begins with the first "test pilots" around the year 1000. These were men who attached "wings" to themselves and jumped off towers or hills, proving that man still had a lot to learn about flight. The book pursues the often extraordinary exploits of test pilots through the historic first flight of the space shuttle.

The early pioneers of the air were often looked upon with a certain degree of skepticism. Glenn L. Martin, one of the greatest aviation visionaries of his day, was one of these.

Herb Fisher in the cockpit of one of the many aircraft he flew as a civilian test pilot during World War II.

Hallion relates how the family doctor wrote to Martin's mother in 1910, "For heaven's sake, if you have any influence with that wild-eyed, hallucinated, visionary young man, call him off before he is killed. Have him devote his energies to substantial, feasible and profitable pursuits, leaving dreaming to the professional dreamers."

Some idea of the stuff test pilots are made of can be gathered from the story of an attempt by Shorty Schroeder to set an altitude record in 1929.

He took off on February 6 in a LUSAC-11, an open cockpit biplane, and reached 30,000 feet (not a record) when his oxygen system failed and he passed out. When he regained consciousness he was in a spin over Dayton, Ohio. Somehow he managed to pull the airplane out of the spin, regain control, and land safely. Three weeks later he took off for a second attempt, this time with two oxygen supplies. He was at a record 36,100 feet when his main supply failed and in his befuddled state he could not locate the auxiliary supply.

Instruments in the aircraft indicated it fell 33,200 feet and reached speeds of more than 300 miles an hour before righting itself.

Schroeder, whose eyes were frozen and whose heart and internal organs had been severely stressed (three of the aircraft's four fuel tanks were crushed by the pressures), gradually recovered consciousness and with limited vision he made a safe landing.

By the early 1920s the parachute came on the scene. It saved the lives of many a test pilot. After one fatal accident in which the pilot's life might have been saved had he been equipped with a parachute, a sign went up at McCook Field in Dayton reading, "Don't forget your parachute. If you need it and haven't got it, you'll never need it again."

Very little phases test pilots. In September of 1942, when the U.S. was ready for the initial test flight of its first jet aircraft, the Bell XP59A, one of the aircraft's two jet engines would not start. The first test flight was made with only one engine.

One of the most unbelievable test flight stories in Hallion's book had its beginning and end at Curtiss-Wright Airport (now Essex County Airport) in Fairfield, N.J.

Herb Fisher, flying a series of electric propeller tests, would take off from Curtiss-Wright Airport, fly to an altitude of 35,000 feet over Allentown, Pa., and put the aircraft into a dive which would terminate over Long Island Sound in New York.

On the afternoon of August 15, 1948, he took off and climbed to 38,000 feet over Allentown and began his dive. When he reached 28,000 feet at a speed of 590 mph, a high pressure oil line, installed as part of a piece of test equipment, ruptured. Seventy-five gallons of hot oil spewed over the windshield, the canopy, and the engine. It penetrated the cockpit and coated Fisher.

"I couldn't read the instruments," he told me when he related the incident which was later described in the book. "They were covered with oil and my eyes were full of oil. I had oxygen, but I was still desperate for air.

"I opened the canopy and the turbulence blew my headset off. So I no longer had communications with anybody. Because the wind was whipping the oil around the cockpit, I closed the canopy. I couldn't see straight ahead at all. The only way I could see was to look back."

He could have jumped out, but he wanted to save the plane. "Since I knew I was near Curtiss-Wright Airport and I had landed there many times, I decided to try to land looking backwards.

"As the houses and buildings I recognized passed beneath and behind me, I judged my heading and altitude and lined up with the runway, which I couldn't see." This was a true blind landing.

Miraculously, Fisher brought the airplane down and landed without further damage to the aircraft or himself.

That was an extraordinary accomplishment. But for a test pilot that kind of experience is all in a day's work.

10/18/81

CIRCLING THE GLOBE NONSTOP!

Just when you think there are no new mountains to climb some fearless soul finds one.

Burt Rutan is such a soul. He never marches to anyone else's beat. He does things his way, and that way is always innovative and intriguing. He constantly creates new approaches to aircraft design that mark a substantial advance over conventional practices.

Rutan is the most imaginative aircraft designer of the 20th Century. He is a pioneer in designing aircraft fashioned of composite material. Many of his designs use pusher engines in the back of aircraft which are more efficient than the conventional tractor engines with the propeller(s) in front.

Those with the greatest sense of adventure are people who set goals never attained before. Often they are goals that had always been considered impossible. To Rutan the impossible is a challenge. One of the most incredible challenges he undertook was to produce an aircraft that could fly around the world nonstop. I first heard about this project from two old friends, Lee Herron and Diane Dempsey (later Lee and Diane Herron). They moved from New Jersey to Mojave, California, where they became good friends of Burt Rutan. They had built several of his kit planes.

They told me about his project, an aircraft called the Voyager, designed to meet the challenge of flying around the world nonstop.

It was shortly after the aircraft's rollout in December of 1986, two-and-a-half years before the actual flight, that I wrote the following column based on information Lee and Diane provided. When this column was written you could not find many people who thought the mission it was designed for was possible.

What is Burt Rutan up to now?

The latest project by the genius of aviation design is a 'round-the-world, nonstop, non-refueling flight. No, Virginia, it has never been done before.

I have details from two of Rutan's friends and neighbors, Lee Herron and Diane Dempsey, who not too long ago were "neighbors" of ours here in New Jersey. They were operators of the Airplane Shop Inc. at Essex County Airport, a leading purveyor of aviation collectors' items of World War II, and in some cases even earlier.

They left New Jersey last fall to set up shop under the name Aviator's World at Mojave Airport in Mojave, Calif., where Rutan's operation is located. (They have since retired.)

Herron and Dempsey are no strangers to Rutan. When they lived in West Orange, they built the first Rutan-designed VariEze to take to the skies. This aircraft has flown 70 miles on a gallon of gas carrying two people. It has achieved speeds approximating 200 miles an hour with a 62-hp Volkswagen engine. Today there are dozens of them flying all over the country.

The Voyager, the Burt Rutan-designed aircraft which flew around the world non stop, attracts throngs of visitors who view it every year at the Smithsonian National Air and Space Museum in Washington.

The aircraft built for the around-the-world flight, which rolled out earlier this month, is even more mind-boggling than some of Rutan's earlier creations.

Dubbed the *Voyager*, the aircraft was designed to carry five times its weight in fuel. It is a two-place aircraft with a wingspan of 111 feet-- comparable to the Boeing 727 airliner which originally carried 131 passengers. Its fuselage is about the size of Lindbergh's *Spirit of St. Louis*.

The aircraft has a smaller forward wing or canard, which is a trademark of many Rutan designs. Between the canard and the main wing are three streamlined bodies, the fuselage in the center flanked by two outrigger fuel tanks.

There are two engines on the *Voyager*, a pusher and a tractor, mounted on each end of the fuselage. Details on the engine will not be released until after test flights and a final determination on power plants has been made.

One of the more amazing features of the design is the aircraft's weight--with two engines--of 938 pounds. This has been accomplished through the use of special lightweight materials, another trademark of Rutan designs, in this case, resin-treated paper honeycomb and carbon graphite fiber, molded and oven cured.

Herron and Dempsey sent me samples of these materials. You could imagine them being used for model airplanes, but for people-carrying machines? Never. But that is the secret of Burt Rutan.

The Voyager will carry 8,400 pounds of fuel and, fully loaded, its 938 pounds will swell to 11,300 pounds.

With a full load of fuel the aircraft will be able to stay aloft for two weeks. It will need that much endurance because the 25,999 mile flight will take an estimated 12 days. Although the *Voyager* looks fast it actually is not. At gross weight it will have a true airspeed of about 130 knots. As fuel is burned off, instead of increasing speed, the speed will be intentionally reduced to less than 70 knots. At this weight and speed the aircraft will require less than 25 horsepower so one engine (the front one) will be shut down and fuel consumption reduced to about two gallons an hour.

Though it is a two-place aircraft the *Voyager* has only one seat. While one crew member is flying the other will be occupying what is described as an uncomfortable-looking bed.

The cockpit is about the size of a large bathtub so merely switching places will be something of an accomplishment. The crew for the flight which will probably not take place for about a year, will be Dick Rutan, retired Air Force fighter pilot and older brother of Burt, and Jeanna Yeager, 32, who holds several speed records in Rutan-designed aircraft. She tips the scales at all of 100 pounds, 67 less than Rutan.

Lee Herron and Diane Dempsey have designed a *Voyager* patch and they are having desk models of the aircraft made in 1/72 scale which will be signed by the pilots on each wing, so collectors will have a real memento of the event.

The actual aircraft is already spoken for. If the flight is successfully completed, it will hang in the National Air and Space Museum in Washington.*

6/17/84

*Note: *The flight was successfully completed on December 23, 1986, after nine-days aloft. The aircraft is on exhibit today in the Smithsonian National Air and Space Museum in Washington.*

FLYING THE OLD-FASHIONED WAY

Talk about aerial adventurers normally conjures up visions of daring flights. But there are adventuresome pilots who have no interest in tempting the fates. Yet some of these flights are no less adventurous than those of daredevil pilots seeking to stretch the bonds which restrain most of us.

Alan Lopez in one of these pilots.

Lopez has his own definition of adventure and he wrote a book about it.

His concept of adventure was to fly to every state in the country except Hawaii, plus every province in Canada. That in itself might not seem all that adventurous. But there is another dimension to his undertaking. He made the flight in a World War II era open cockpit biplane that was used as a trainer.

What made it an adventure is the fact that he did it with only one navigation instrument--a compass. His journey is somewhat different than the flights which put a pilot face-to-face with his mortality, but it is no less an adventure.

The spirit of adventure is alive and well, but few people have tasted it the way Alan Lopez of Princeton has. His personal adventure has taken him to hundreds of towns and villages across the land, few of which have ever been visited by tourists. He's met people who live off the beaten track, but close to the land. He's seen America from a perspective you don't get on a bus tour.

He didn't look up at the presidents who peer out on the world from Mt. Rushmore. He looked down on them. He's looked down on mountains and valleys, rivers and lakes, the broad stretches of farmland in middle America, the glaciers in Alaska.

There were times when he pushed through areas where the visibility was marginal, times when turbulence tossed his trusty little biplane around like a cork in the surf. At times he ran a race with a storm.

An adventurer never knows what he or she will encounter. That is the soul of adventure.

Lopez' World War II era Stearman biplane has no navigation equipment. Flying with a cockpit full of navigation aids and an autopilot is not his idea of adventure.

Instead of using modern navigation equipment, Lopez flew by dead reckoning, using only a compass and charts. Holding a compass heading will not always get you where you're going. If there's a crosswind blowing, the farther you fly, the farther off course you can get unless you pick up your check points (prominent landmarks) and follow them to compensate for the wind drift.

In addition to the lack of navigation equipment, the Stearman Lopez flew had no transponder which would have allowed controllers to identify him on their radar scopes. That prevented him from following major highways which normally go to major cities. Without a transponder he had to steer clear of the controlled airspace around big cities and go to the smaller airports in rural areas. Few people have heard of most of the towns where he landed.

Alan Lopez in the Stearman he flew to every state in the union and every province of Canada with no navigation aids other than a compass.

While he didn't have any fancy navigation instruments, Lopez did carry one vital piece of equipment on the trips that took him around the U.S. and Canada-- a knee board with a pad. He used this to record virtually every detail of his flight. A time was listed for every entry made. He describes the terrain he is flying over, prominent points of interest, the weather, the places where he stopped, the people he met, the little towns that never saw a tourist.

At times he brings in historical facts you won't find in a history book. His flights are something virtually none of us will have the opportunity to experience firsthand. But Lopez has made it possible for us to share his adventures by compiling all his detailed notes in a book he's titled, *Biplane Odyssey*.

The only thing you won't experience in this book is the feeling in the pit of your stomach when the turbulence gets testy or the weather begins to deteriorate. Every other detail is there, making the reader feel like part of the trip. The people he met in small towns were always ready to offer a friendly welcome and helping hand to a stranger. In Larned, Kans., population 5,000, he had supper with Doyle and Neva Holcombe who managed the fixed base operation (FBO) at the town's airport and raise corn on their farm.

When he landed at Baker Field in O'Neil, NE., he was greeted by a sign that read, "Welcome to O'Neil, Irish capital of Nebraska. Home of 4,000 friendly people (and two old grouches) 'Golfing*Camping*Swimming'."

In the Yukon, he met 81-year-old Herman Peterson who learned to fly during the late 1930s and still flies a homebuilt Smith Miniplane and a modified Luscombe on floats. Herman, for all his 60 some years of flying, enjoys considerable fame in the area, not as a veteran aviator, but for the fiddles he's crafted over the last 15 years.

In Kingman, Ariz., he gave a ride to an 82-year-old who was stationed at the field when it was an Air Corps base during World War II. The old gentleman breakfasted with Lopez in his motel and then drove him to the airport in his brand new Lincoln Continental.

He brought his own helmet and goggles, mementos of his old flying days and, when asked after they were airborne if there was any place he'd like to go, he responded, "Let's go buzz my girlfriend's house."

Lopez graduated from Princeton University in 1965 with a bachelor's degree in Russian studies. In 1968, he got a master's degree in European history from Columbia University. He ran a 150-year-old family pharmacy in Princeton for 18 years. He then turned himself into a flying Charles Kuralt.

The book details flights to Colorado and the Rockies, Montana, the West Coast, the Maritime Provinces of Canada, and the Yukon and Alaska.

Each trip begins and ends at Van Sant Airport in Erwinna, Pa., just across the Delaware River from Frenchtown, N.J. Van Sant is a turf strip long known as the home of old biplanes.

There is a chapter at the end of his book on orienteering, the art of navigating by compass and charts alone, which is the way Lopez flew all over this country and Canada. It's extremely interesting and you will be fascinated by it even if you don't fly.

2/27/00

NOVICE PILOT FLIES AROUND THE WORLD

The story that follows belongs in the archives of Ripley's "Believe It or Not." It's about an around-the-world flight. The pilot took off on his globe girdling journey shortly after he passed his private pilot's flight test. It's an unlikely scenario, but here is his story.

C all this one "Fools Step in Where Angels Fear to Tread." It has nothing to do with anything believable. But it is a true story.

It's a story of a fledgling pilot who flew around the world in a two-place training aircraft. He had a total of ten days of flying experience. He undertook the flight shortly after getting his private pilot's license which he accomplished in an incredible ten days.

Hans Tholstrup at LeBourget Airport in Paris on his around-the-world flight.

In the course of his adventure he fought monsoons, typhoons, and the greatest peril of all-- red tape. The man who did this is a 30-year-old native of Denmark, now an Australian citizen, Hans Tholstrup.

He didn't do it for money. (He's almost $6,000 in debt as a result of the trip.) He didn't do it for fame. He only granted a couple of interviews after the completion of his 153-day flight.

He did it because he met a fellow in Australia (a New Zealander) who claimed to be the first man to fly around the world without an autopilot or copilot.

"But he didn't really do it," said Tholstrup. "He had his aircraft shipped from Tokyo to Seattle on a boat. I decided someone should actually do it."

Because it's cheaper to buy an airplane in the United States than in Australia and cheaper to learn to fly here, this is where Tholstrup decided to embark on his great adventure.

He chose to make the trip in a two-place, Grumman American Trainer, the smallest aircraft in mass production, because he liked the looks of it, especially the wings. They looked to him like they were built to take it.

Tholstrup came to the United States and bought an airplane from the Smokey Mountain Flight School in Knoxville, Tenn., and he spent ten days learning how to fly it.

"I had about 40 hours when I got my license," he said. "Then I took about 12 hours of instrument instruction before I left."

That gave him a total of approximately 52 hours of flying time when he took off from Knoxville to fly around the world.

How much time did he spend planning the flight? None.

Did he have all the charts he would need? No. "Charts are expensive," he said. He took off with an outdated IFR (instrument fight rules) chart another pilot gave him.

And that's how he flew around he world--using charts he was able to scrounge from other pilots, almost none of them current.

Tholstrup took off with a 45-gallon auxiliary fuel tank in the seat next to him which, along with the 22 gallons in the wing tanks, gave him a range of 1,100 miles.

He had an inexpensive navigation/communications radio (the Narco 110 Escort), a Narco ADF (Automatic Direction Finder), a Narco transponder, and a high frequency (HF) radio. In addition, he also had a two-man inflatable dinghy, an extra emergency locator transmitter, food and water.

He got his clearance to cross the North Atlantic in Canada and flew via Greenland and Iceland to Norway.

When he landed in Norway after a nine-and-a-half-hour flight from Iceland which covered 940 nautical miles, he had only 10 minutes of fuel left in the tanks.

Tholstrup landed at Le Bourget Airport in Paris when the Paris Air Show was being held there, "because I didn't have taxicab money to get there from any other airport."

Flying over India took him through monsoons, and at one time, he was on solid instruments for four hours (even though he didn't have an instrument rating) before he was able to find an airport.

When he arrived in his home country, Australia, Tholstrup was broke. Grumman, the manufacturer of his airplane, came to the rescue with $3,000.

But worse troubles were in store for him. Flying over the Pacific, north of New Guinea, he lost four inches off the tip of one propeller blade. "The vibration was so bad I couldn't read any of the instruments," he said. Not a good thing to deal with when you're flying over the ocean. Incredibly a safe haven was within reach. "In a few minutes I came over the island of Manus, in the Admiralty chain. "I landed and sawed four inches off the other blade and took off and flew 30 miles further to my original destination, Mamote.

"There was an old American air base at Mamote served by a once-a-week flight. I had to wait ten days to get a new prop shipped to me."

The prop failure was probably caused during a takeoff or landing when he picked up a stone that put a nick in the blade deep enough to cause a hairline crack.

Again, flying over the Pacific Tholstrup ran into another problem. A typhoon blocked his path. He flew through it at altitudes from 7,000 to 300 feet. He made it to Guam with hardly more than a gallon of fuel in his tanks. When he landed, the airplane was covered with salt. "The typhoon sucks up the salt," he said.

As lucky as he was to make it, when he landed he didn't find a warm welcome. He was promptly advised by the U.S. Navy that he had no right to land at a military base without proper clearance. He was fined $100.

When he got to Russia, the airplane developed a fuel leak and he landed on an island just south of the Kamchatka Peninsula, 700 miles north of Japan. Once again he had landed on a military base. This time a Russian base.

The Russians fixed the leak in a couple of days, gave him 40 gallons of fuel that they drained out of a big aircraft and they sent him off with a lunch pack.

"They were very nice," Tholstrup said.

When he landed back at Knoxville, he had covered 33,000 miles in 331 flying hours. Nearly eight times more hours than he had logged when he began his trip.

10/26/75

AROUND-THE-WORLD FLIGHT
WITHOUT LANDING AT AN AIRPORT

Tom Casey did something nobody had ever done before. He flew around the world without ever touching down at an airport. That was fortunate because his aircraft didn't have any landing gear. It was mounted on floats.

His goal was to be the first to fly around the world in a float plane. His initial attempt failed, but he didn't give up. He tried again and on the second attempt, despite enough problems to fill a couple of volumes of the Encyclopedia Britannica, he made it.

As a result of events not included in his flight planning, it took him more than six months to complete the trip.

In 1924, four Army planes mounted on floats took off on the same mission and two of them made it home, becoming the first aircraft to circle the globe. But they switched from floats to landing gear on one leg of their flight. In all the decades since, nobody ever circled the globe solely on floats. So Casey holds the honor of being the first man to do it.

Tom Casey could have found a cheaper way of flying around the world. He estimates his trip cost him $ 250,000.

He might have found a faster way, too. It took him 188 days. It wasn't all flying. The 188 days included 27 days in a hospital in Saudi Arabia, where he had surgery for a herniated disc which resulted from his lifting five-gallon cans of gas in Alexandria, Egypt.

The surgery delayed his trip by six weeks and by then he was in the middle of a war zone. He left as quickly as he could.

The 188 days also included a 30-day delay waiting for permission to fly into Egypt and India. In the case of India, the delay wasn't his worst problem.

"I had to pay $10,000 in graft," Casey said. "Before I could enter the country I had to hire an agent and agree to the payment. The agent's job was to pay off all the officials."

These are only a few of the problems Casey encountered on his around-the-world flight. And even though the flight is over, his problems aren't. He still owes $150,000 in expenses connected with the flight.

As far as he is concerned, it was worth it because he did something nobody had ever done before. He was the first pilot to circle the globe in a float plane, taking off and landing on water all the way.

He made 55 stops in 20 countries. It wasn't easy. The problems described above don't begin to tell the story of the obstacles that beset his adventure.

I had written about Casey before, in July of 1989. On that occasion he landed on Sandy Hook Bay (in New Jersey) on an attempt to fly around the world from Seattle, which was the point of departure for the first around-the-world flight made by U.S. Army fliers 67 years ago.

Casey's first attempt came to a sad end in Iceland. After an overnight stop there, when he went out to the airplane in the morning, it was under water. It sank as a result of a hole mysteriously punched in one of his floats while it was tied up at night.

Tom Casey, the first man to circle the globe in a float plane.

Last May 20, the 63rd anniversary of Charles Lindbergh's flight, Casey tried again. He took off from Seattle flying the opposite way (west). This time he didn't get as far as he did on his first attempt. While he didn't know who the culprit was who ended his initial attempt, this time he knew. It was the Russians. Although he had been led to believe he would be permitted to fly to the Soviet Union from Alaska, permission was denied.

Casey didn't give up. He returned to Seattle and on June 14 he departed once again, flying in the opposite direction once more (east) on a course that would avoid Russia.

This time there were a few problems with the aircraft along the way and with the pilot as well. When he took off from Iceland the waves were five feet high. That would have stopped a lot of seaplane pilots, but not Casey. He took off under less than favorable conditions. He didn't know until he landed in Scotland, that on the rough takeoff he bent a strut support. It took three days for a new part to arrive from the U.S. It was installed and he flew on.

On the leg from Athens to Crete a wire to the alternator broke and he lost his electrical system.

In Jeddah, Saudi Arabia, a compression check showed that all but one cylinder were dangerously low. He believes it was the result of having received bad gas along the way. That is a risk adventurous pilots face when landing in countries where there is little general aviation flying.

The Soviets thwarted him once again by denying him permission to land just to refuel on the leg from Japan to Atta in the Aleutians. The denial forced Casey to fly 1,388 nautical miles, the longest leg of his trip. It took him 11 hours and 45 minutes, all but one hour of it at night.

But it got worse. Between Shemya and Kiska in the Aleutians he had an engine failure. He was 35 miles from land. The waves were 7 to 8 feet high. You simply don't put a float plane down in those conditions. Casey didn't have an option.

With a little luck and perhaps more than just a touch of skill, he managed to bend only one float support in landing. The aircraft stayed afloat with the nose pointing down, as if it were hanging its head in shame. Casey bounced around on the rough waters in that tipsy condition for 11 hours.

"The Coast Guard found me by satellite," he said. "It took them 4 1/2 hours. Then it took a fishing boat, the *Judy B*, 6 1/2 more hours to reach me. They took me aboard and eight hours later they hauled my airplane aboard." His engine was shot. Wipaire, the manufacturer of his floats and one of his major sponsors, shipped a new engine from Minnesota. It took eight days to get there and several weeks to install it.

But it wasn't all bad news. There were a few upbeat experiences along the way. In Saudi Arabia, Casey was the guest of Prince Bandar, the ambassador to the United States, who is a pilot. His father is the country's minister of defense.

"The Saudis never let me pay for a thing," Casey said. "They even picked up the bill for my operation (for the herniated disc) and hospitalization. In Seattle, the medical bills would have been more than $100,000.

"The highlight of the trip was in Thailand. I was greeted by 300 kids with a big banner that said, 'Welcome to Thailand, Uncle Tom. Happy Flying Around the World.' While there I was the guest of the Thailand Petroleum Co.

"The Thai Army, Navy, and Air Force were all very helpful to me. The Army and Navy provided me with charts and the Navy assisted me at several stops. The Air Force loaned me a survival suit and other survival gear."

Philips Petroleum, Casey's major sponsor, contributed $25,000 to the flight. There were some 25 secondary sponsors whose contributions were mostly in equipment.

One of these was Trimble Navigation Systems of Sunnyvale, Calif. Trimble provided Casey with a GPS (Global Positioning

System).

"This is a system that provides navigational information from satellites," said Casey. "It's the same kind of system that enabled the military to put a missile down a chimney or through a door in the Gulf War. It's incredibly accurate."

Casey predicts that GPS will replace the Loran system now widely used in aviation. (To a large extent that has now happened.) General aviation units like the one he used cost $6,000, but that figure will probably drop drastically when they get into mass production.

His airplane, the *Liberty II*, a Cessna 206, will be sold to help him pay off his debts. A group is planning to buy it to donate to the Museum of Flight in Seattle.

Now that the flight is behind him, Casey is planning a book that he'll do with a writer, and he hopes to lecture at schools and colleges to spread the word about the fun of flying (his trip was fun in spite of its problems) as well as aviation's capabilities and safety.

I've bumped into pilots here in New Jersey who, when they heard of his achievement, say, "I remember when Casey used to tow banners over the Jersey Shore and Philadelphia stadiums."

He's found more exciting things to do in an airplane since then.

3/3/91

PERIODONTIST AND POLICEMAN GIRDLE THE GLOBE

All kinds of people fly. Here is proof of it. A policeman and a periodontist teamed up to share an adventure--a flight around the world in the periodontist's single-engine Cessna 210 .

The two intrepid pilots had a dress rehearsal for this flight. A couple of years earlier they flew together in the same airplane from New Jersey to Australia.

That's almost halfway around the world and that inspired the periodontist to ask, "Why not go all the way?"

One day last spring, Edison police officer Bob Zuber received a call in his patrol car to investigate an accident on Route 1 near the Flea Market. He had no idea that responding to that call would make him a VIP in Cairo, Egypt. But that's just what it did.

The driver of one of the cars in the two-car accident, in which fortunately the injuries were confined to the cars, rather than their drivers, was a woman who was a native of Egypt.

Officer Zuber told her he was planning a flight around the world with periodontist Ed Galkin, also of Edison, in his friend's aircraft, and that one of their stops would be Cairo.

The woman was the wife of a retired general in the Cairo Police Force. Her brother, Mohammed, still lives in Cairo. "I'd like you to meet my family," she told Zuber.

When Zuber and Dr. Galkin arrived at Cairo International Airport last month at seven in the morning, eight days late because of equipment problems, Mohammed was at the airport waiting for them.

Police officer Bob Zuber, left, and periodontist Ed Galkin. aboard camels in front of a pyramid outside Cairo, Egypt.

He drove them to their hotel, an hour's ride away, in his Mercedes, and then had them to his home for a sumptuous lunch.

Mohammed introduced them to the captain of the Cairo Police Force who played host to them for a couple of hours.

"Everybody on the force knew Mohammed, the brother of

the woman who had been involved in the accident in New Jersey," Zuber said.

They were Mohammed's guests on a Nile River dinner cruise. He took them to the pyramids and the Sphinx and provided them with camels.

"We were in Cairo for four days and we were treated like family," Galkin said.

Mohammed, who had 200 families farming cotton for him, had a big going away party for them and presented them with gifts.

He drove them to the airport at two in the morning and stopped on the way to buy them fruit for the flight to Dubai.

They received royal treatment in other places as well, although not as a result of any motor vehicle accident.

When they landed in Cairns, Australia, near the Great Barrier Reef, at seven in the morning, the owner of The Flying Horseshoe Motel, a pilot and part-time employee of the Australian Civil Aviation Agency, was waiting for them even though they were 15 days behind schedule. Galkin and Zuber had met him on the previous flight they had made to Australia two years earlier.

He took them to his home for breakfast and then to his motel. They were treated like royalty during their four-day stay in Cairns. They went snorkeling and sightseeing.

On the flight from Honiara, Guadalcanal, to Majuro in the Marshal Islands, they met another friend--via the radio--from their previous trip. They were monitoring the emergency frequency when they heard a call, "2160 Sierra. Is this my friend, Ed Galkin from Woodbridge, New Jersey?" (Galkin's office is in Woodbridge.)

It was Fred Sorrenson, a 737 captain, who was ferrying a Cessna 310 from Honolulu to Australia. They had met him on their previous flight to Australia.

"Honiara is trying to reach you on high frequency," Sorrenson told them. The controllers were having trouble reaching them on their HF radio so Sorrenson relayed the message.

In New Zealand, Galkin and Zuber met aviation writer Peter Lert who was ferrying a French-built CAP-10 to the U.S. He was flying west to get there; they were flying east. New Zealand is about halfway around the world so it's six on one hand, a half dozen in the other.

Controllers all along the way knew of their adventure and often offered congratulations. At Darwin, Australia, controllers at the flight service station didn't want to accept their flight plan to Cairns because they knew they had just flown 13 hours. The controllers didn't realize there were two pilots. When they found out, they let them go.

The only bad weather they experienced was between Madras, India, and Singapore. For 40 minutes they both had to hang on to the controls for all they were worth.

"We'd drop 2,000 feet and go up 2,000 feet," said Galkin.

One thing encountered on the trip that they will never forget was the sign at Singapore Airport which said, "Carrying or using drugs is subject to the death penalty."

"They hanged 64 people," said Galkin. "Drugs are now a minor problem there. Two American boys in their 20s were picked up with five or six marijuana cigarettes. They were hanged despite pleas from the American government, their parents, Amnesty International, and others."

About 80 percent of their flight was over water and about 50 percent was at night.

"The prettiest night flight we made was from Honolulu to Oakland," Galkin said. "We were flying over a solid overcast and there was a full moon. It was so bright we could read the charts by moonlight.

"There were big buildups in front of us but as we approached them they opened up and we flew between them. It was like the Red Sea parting."

The trip was planned for 28 days. It took 32 because of equipment problems on the first half of the flight, but it could have taken a lot longer.

Zuber had to get home to attend his niece's wedding. So while the first half of the flight took about 28 days, in order for Zuber to get home on time, they flew the second half--from Australia--in 3 1/2 days, with only a one-day stop in Honolulu.

After two marathon flights from Linden Airport--to Australia two years ago and around the world last month, perhaps they should change the name of the airport to Linden International Airport.

11/20/88

PERILS OF A FLIGHT TO MOSCOW

In 1988, Moscow was not the ideal destination for general aviation pilots with a bit of wanderlust. This is the story of three pilots who found that out the hard way. But they are proof of the spirit which makes adventurers, people who don't turn away because there are a few bumps in the road.

One member of this intrepid triumvirate was Claudio Tonnini whose two 18,000-mile journeys to the tip of South America are recounted earlier.

The three pilots learned a few lessons along the way--at considerable cost.

I f you were thinking of flying yourself to Russia, we have a bit of advice for you. Don't!

We say this after talking to a trio of pilots who were the first to fly a private single-engine aircraft to Russia--with permission--Jerry Gordon of Edison, Seymour Gelzer of Jamesburg, and Claudio Tonnini of South River.

They relate a saga of misadventures such as you've never heard. Also, they may have set a record for the most expensive trip to Russia since Hitler's ill-fated excursion in World War II.

"Our fuel bill for 70 gallons at Narsarssuak, Greenland, was $540," said Gordon.

Our trusty $3 calculator tells us that's $7.71 a gallon. Did we hear you complain about paying $2?

They found out on the way back that $540 was a bargain. On the return trip they paid $749 for 63 gallons. There is a $250 surcharge for fuel on weekends!

Jerry Gordon, Claudio Toninni, and Seymour Gelzer, discussing plans for their flight to Moscow.

At Reykjavik, Iceland, they paid an $80 landing fee because they landed after hours. After paying the landing fee they had to leave because there were no hotel rooms available. They flew to Keflavik, about 15 minutes away.

When they landed there, both their transponders were inoperable. The next day they had to fly back to Reykjavik to have them fixed.

"The avionics man fixed one and said he'd have the other on our return flight," said Gordon. "Then we had to fly back to Keflavik because we left a credit card there.

"An old-timer at Keflavik advised us to fly up the coast of Iceland to Hornsfjordhur as a jumping-off point for the flight to Bergen, Norway.

"The 4,000 foot runway was full of rocks. We landed at 6 p.m. and the operator charged us a $50 surcharge for gas because he said we arrived late. We took off for Bergen at 7 p.m.

"Claudio was flying and when we arrived I complimented him on his smooth landing," said Gordon. But the nose gear didn't lock down when they landed and the prop hit the runway.

They pushed the airplane onto the grass. After the gear-up landing, they were taken to the police station and given breathalyzer tests. Claudio, who was the pilot, was given blood tests as well. They were all put through a whole series of sobriety tests.

"But they were very kind, sensitive, considerate human beings," Gordon said. "They asked us to use their phones to call our wives. After all our tests were finished they put us in their station wagon to drive us to our hotel. On the way they got a call that there was a stolen car directly in front of us."

The next day a big Sikorsky S-61 helicopter lifted the airplane, Claudio got underneath, and after a couple of tries he forced the nose wheel down and the main gear came down and locked.

"A stone had lodged in the nose gear door and prevented the nose gear from locking," said Gordon.

They paid $500 for the helicopter and $1,200 for the use of the facility and equipment to make repairs.

The intrepid flyers got a rebuilt prop in Oslo for $7,000, less $500 for their hub which wasn't damaged. Claudio, who had built his own aircraft, repaired the skin on the belly of the Cessna 210, put in new rivets, changed the antenna, and mounted the new prop.

They test flew the airplane for 40 minutes and found that it was quieter than it had been before and a vibration they had experienced had disappeared.

At two in the afternoon they took off for Helsinki.

When they arrived at their hotel in Helsinki after an uneventful trip they discovered that Claudio's attaché case with $2,700 in cash and all their papers were missing.

They took a $50 cab ride back to the airport and found the attaché case hanging on the baggage cart where it had been left.

The trio spent four days in Helsinki trying to get clearance to fly to Russia, even though permission had been granted before they left home.

The foul-ups and confusion could fill a book, but they finally got things straightened out and with a Russian "navigator" whom they described as a very nice guy who spoke fluent English, in the back seat, they took off for Moscow.

Crossing the border, Claudio spotted a MiG. "The navigator started gibbering on the radio like crazy," said Gordon. "The MiG came within a half mile and backed off."

After a 4 1/2 hour flight they landed in Moscow.

At the airport they picked up their guide, a girl who, judging from their pictures, could win any beauty contest. (They were allowed to take all the pictures they wanted, including video. The only restriction they encountered was a prohibition of taking pictures in the subway, which they said is beautiful.)

They stayed in what is known as a businessmen's hotel which they described as gorgeous, with luxurious accommodations.

On their arrival, they were hungry, but they soon discovered you can't get into any restaurant without reservations. They found a cab driver who said for 25 rubles he would get them into a restaurant. Although generally nobody would take rubles, only hard currency (dollars).

He dropped them off at an old four-story building that had a restaurant on each floor. The cab driver paid the guard at the door to let them in and agreed to return at 11 p.m. to pick them up.

None of the restaurants in the building would let them in. They didn't know what to do. They were standing outside one restaurant when a waiter spotted a pen in Jerry's pocket. Jerry gave the waiter the pen and they were admitted.

The restaurant, it turned out, was a hot singles spot. A 6'4" girl grabbed Claudio, who is about 5'4" and started dancing with him. It was a scene to behold, they related.

When they got ready to leave Moscow, they were told there was no gas at the airport, although they had been told there was gas available before they left the U.S. Their two-day visa expired and they were put in a detention section of the airport hotel and told they couldn't leave.

"We had to squeeze through a narrow door to get into that section of the hotel and they locked it behind us. The rooms were depressing. Worse than a jail cell," they said.

They wouldn't let them out the next day, but Jerry screamed and carried on until they released them and they took a bus and subway to Moscow.

After two days, they pulled the right strings and they learned there was indeed gas at the airport and they got it in a hurry. They took off from Moscow at 7:43 p.m. with a Russian "navigator" aboard, bound for Helsinki. On takeoff from Helsinki, they mistook the runway edge lights for center line lights and busted the propeller and an antenna once again.

But by now, you're probably tired of reading about busted props.

10/9/88

BRINGING HISTORY BACK TO LIFE

This is a slightly different kind of adventure story. It's the story of the recreation of the first cross-country flight made in a Wright Brothers-built aircraft in 1911. Nobody remembers the pilot's name today, but it was Calbraith Perry Rogers.

Rogers made the flight because of an offer of $50,000 by publisher William Randolph Hearst for the first aviator to fly coast-to-coast in 30 days or less. The flight took him 49 days so Rogers' bank account stayed the way it was.

Dr. James R. Lloyd, Jr., who earned his Ph.D. in metallurgy at Stevens Institute of Technology in Hoboken and works as a metallurgist for IBM, took off from a street in Hoboken in an aircraft which closely resembled Rogers'. His flight took longer than the original.

Rogers' aircraft had Vin Fiz painted on its side because Armour and Co. was his sponsor and they had come out with a new grape-flavored drink by that name. Lloyd had the same sponsor and his aircraft carried the same name, although the drink Vin Fiz had faded from the scene after 11 years.

James Lloyd had all of 150 hours flying time when he undertook the flight described in the following column.

It might not have created the excitement and anxiety of the *Voyager's* nonstop, non-refueled flight around the world, but the cross-country flight of the *Vin Fiz II* which began last Sept. 17, from Sinatra Drive in Hoboken, had its full share of adventure, surprise, frustration, nostalgia, and finally success, as the members of Detachment 490 of the ROTC and their guests learned last weekend at their 60th anniversary Military Ball sponsored by the Arnold Air Society at Ft. Hamilton alongside the Brooklyn end of the Verrazano Bridge.

Their guest speaker was Dr. James R. Lloyd, Jr., the man who flew *Vin Fiz II* from Hoboken to California to commemorate the 75th anniversary of the original *Vin Fiz* flight by Calbraith Perry Rogers, the first man to fly across the country.

Comparisons of the two flights, separated by three-quarters of a century, are interesting. Rogers was aiming to make the flight in 30 days to win a $50,000 prize. It took him 49 days and he lost the prize money. Lloyd, who wasn't chasing any prizes, expected to make the flight in 39 days. It took him 57 days.

Rogers' delays were caused mostly by crashes and the rebuilding of his aircraft. Lloyd's were caused by some of the worst weather to hit the East and Midwest in years. He experienced 26 days of unacceptable or marginal weather. Rogers made 58 miles an hour on 30 hp. Lloyd made 45 miles an hour on the same horsepower.

Rogers had 16 crashes, 6 of them major. Lloyd experienced no major crashes in his modified ultralight *Vin Fiz* look-alike, but he wiped out the gear four times, suffered one busted prop, and one engine seizure, which required the installation of a new engine in Texas.

One of his gear mishaps was one for the books. It was caused by wake turbulence from a Piper Cub. Lloyd was landing behind the Cub that unbeknownst to him, was shooting a touch-and-go. The Cub gave it the gun just as Lloyd was flaring. That did it.

That incident did not provide the only surprise on the trip. At one point when Lloyd was putting down on a golf course he suddenly noticed wires stretched across the fairway right in front of him. They were painted green so as not to be conspicuous.

It was too late for Lloyd to get over them. His only hope was to try to duck under them. He accomplished that, but in doing so he suffered some slight damage in landing.

"The police came out and they thought it was great," Lloyd said. "They filed a long accident report. It was the most exciting thing that happened in their town in a long time."

In the course of the trip, which duplicated Rogers' route, Lloyd met 150 people who remembered the original flight in 1911. He had each of them sign the fabric on the wing.

James R. Lloyd, Jr., and his wife, Susan, dressed in the garb of 1911, the year of the first transcontinental flight which Lloyd recreated in 1987, with his wife and a crew following him on the road.

One woman who remembered the flight was a little girl at the time and Rogers wrote to her afterward. "In Decatur, I met a 97-year-old man who said he helped Rogers start his engine," Lloyd related.

"We saw a lot of rural America and the hospitality we received was incredible. I'm a city boy," he said. "In a lot of areas where we landed a big town had a population of 600. At one place where we stopped everybody in the town came out to see us". They came in a school bus. But the town had only one school bus so the townspeople had to come out in three shifts.

"We saw farms so muddy the farmers couldn't harvest. Those farmers get one paycheck a year," said Lloyd. "And some years they don't get that."

His talk was illustrated by a selection of slides chosen from among the hundreds taken by his wife, Susan, who traveled along with him, although she drove and stuck to the highways and byways. The original flight followed railroad tracks, and a train with enough spare parts to rebuild the airplane three times, traveled along with Rogers. But many of those tracks are gone now so Lloyd's wife and crew followed on the roads.

"We met a lot of good people and a lot of bad weather," said Lloyd, summing up his adventure.

At the conclusion of his presentation, Lt. Col. Ed Roche, a professor of chemical engineering at the New Jersey Institute of Technology, one of seven colleges with students who are members of the 490th Cadet Corps. (The others are Stevens Institute, Rutgers Newark, Seton Hall, Fairleigh Dickinson, Montclair State and Kean Universities) presented Lloyd with a gift that could not have been more appropriate.

Roche, a close friend of Keith Ferris of Morris Plains, the renowned aviation artist, knew Ferris had done a painting of the original *Vin Fiz*. He obtained a print of that painting and presented it to the Lloyds.

The original *Vin Fiz* is now in the National Air and Space Museum in Washington. The *Vin Fiz II* will be on display in the terminal at the airport in Omaha, which is the home of Armour Meat Co. Armour sponsored both the original flight in 1911 as well as Lloyd's recreation of it.

4/5/87

Chapter 2
Featherweight Fliers
(The Ultralights)

Ultralights are the mosquitoes of the aircraft world. They are tiny (maximum weight 254 pounds), their little engines have a buzz that resembles the sound of an angry mosquito more than the roar of an aircraft engine.

They don't generally build ultralights in factories. They ship them in pieces (in kit form) and the buyer assembles them. Although they are flimsy-looking aircraft made of aluminum tubing with fabric stretched over it, they are sturdy enough for safe flight. Their range is about 100 miles. (They carry five gallons of fuel.) Their maximum speed is 63 mph.

You don't need a license to fly one and a growing number of people are choosing to enter the world of flying via ultralights.

They are purely recreational vehicles--a means of getting up in the air to experience the joy of flight for the sheer fun of it at a minimum cost.

Today's ultralights are a long way from the originals. Many of them resemble conventional aircraft rather than the basic aluminum tubing and fabric.

There is also a new category of aircraft, the Light-Sport Aircraft that fits between the ultralight and conventional aircraft. It requires a license to fly, but it has limited privileges, such as no night flights, no more than one passenger, and no more than 180 hp.

15,000 MILES IN AN ULTRALIGHT

Not all adventures in flying take place in conventional airplanes. Some would-be fliers opt for ultralights. Ultralights are not designed for adventure. They're designed for fun. But don't tell that to Rick Trader. He made a flight in an ultralight that would have strained the capabilities of pilot and plane in a conventional aircraft.

Trader flew 15,000 miles in an ultralight on a trip that took him to the rugged country of the last frontier, Alaska, and then on up above the Arctic Circle.

Trader is an unusual individual. His life has had more twists, detours, and obstacles than the plot of a prize-winning mystery novel. His background makes his adventure story all the more memorable. It's almost as unbelievable as his flight. Trader's flying adventure is a once in a lifetime tale.

This is his story.

Anybody in his right mind knows you couldn't fly a flimsy-looking ultralight 15,000 miles around the circumference of the United States, up to Alaska, north of the Arctic Circle, and back home to New Jersey.

Maybe Rick Trader is not in his right mind. He did it.

There are two schools of thought about his flight, according to Trader himself. One says, "He's crazy". The other says, "You've done something I always wanted to do."

"When I was a boy," he says, "I used to dream of flying through the air in a red American Flyer wagon. I dreamed of levitating." (Floating through the air without the benefit of any vehicle or visible means of support.)

His father, a merchant seaman who traveled all over the world, used to tell him stories about the exotic ports he had visited. "He'd take an encyclopedia and show me the places he'd been to," said Trader. "He said, 'Someday we're going to see your uncle in California and we'll go to Alaska.' "

But that never happened. His father died when he was 10 years old.

"I was never very good in school," he says. "My report cards always said, 'Doesn't pay attention. Underachiever.' " Getting through school was a struggle for him.

It wasn't until after he was out of high school that he discovered why he got bad report cards. He learned that he had a learning disability. He discovered that when he read a newspaper story about a dysfunction involving an inability to read properly resulting from an uncontrolled transformation of letters.

Trader immediately identified that condition (dyslexia) as the problem from which he suffered during all those years of bad report cards. He had never been aware of it before. In all his years in school it was never diagnosed.

After leaving school, Trader held a wide variety of jobs. He was a construction worker, sold newspaper subscriptions on the phone, worked in the extermination business, took baby pictures and sold insurance. Most of those activities never amounted to much. None lasted very long.

Rick Trader in the ultralight he flew up above the Arctic Circle.

"In 1981, when I was 31, I took a look at myself and didn't like what I saw," he says. "I started going to school for air conditioning and refrigeration."

But then his world, which was never very stable, fell apart completely. "I lost my job. I skidded on an icy road and banged up my car. My girlfriend (he was divorced) said, 'Don't darken my doorstep again.' I had no money.

"Everything happens for a reason," he said. "I had a few options. One was to start my own extermination business. I took that option. I got my first job and bought $300 worth of chemicals and equipment I needed. I covered the check I wrote for the equipment by running to the bank with the $300 check I got for the job and cashing it to deposit in my account.

"The business took off. After one month I went back to my girlfriend's house and put $4,000 on her kitchen table.

"I took some of that money and started taking flying lessons. But it was one of the most disappointing things I had ever done. It was so regulated. There were so many restrictions. It wasn't what I dreamed about when I was 8-years-old. I soloed and quit."

One of Trader's extermination customers was a very successful real estate broker. He was a man who had everything Trader always wanted but never had.

One day in 1989, when Trader went to his office, somebody pulled him aside. "Did you hear about John?" he asked. "He killed himself." The real estate broker he envied so much had been stricken with cancer and couldn't live with it.

"I was in shock," said Trader. "I asked myself, 'Why am I crawling under dirty crawl spaces spreading chemicals?' The government chases you. The DEP (state Department of Environmental Protection) chases you. I said, 'When am I going to do what I want?'

"About that time, a pilot friend of mine rented a Piper Cherokee and my girlfriend (not the one who told him not to darken her door again) and I flew with him down to First Flight Airport at Kill Devil Hills, N.C., where the Wright Brothers made their first flights.

"Down there I saw something that changed my life--ultralight aircraft. I talked to the guys who flew them.

"When I came home, I spent six months learning all I could about them. Then I bought a kit for a Kolb ultralight like one I had seen at Kitty Hawk. I didn't have the skills to put it together, but I found a guy in Florida who would build it for me.

"After it was finished, I didn't know how to fly it. Nobody wanted to teach me. Then I met Vince Vitollo who ran the Ultralight Flight Center in Jackson. He agreed to teach me.

"I wanted to see the world at treetop level. And I said someday I'm going to fly to Alaska."

Trader thought he ought to have a private pilot's license before thinking about such a trip. So he went to a flight school in Florida, got the rating, and began planning an ultralight flight to Alaska.

He modified the Kolb, a two-place model, by putting big tundra tires on it, installing a bigger gas tank, and adding a cargo pod underneath. (These modifications for his long flight exceeded the technical limits for an ultralight, but the basic machine was still an ultralight.)

On Feb. 12, 1991, he took off from Piney Hollow, a small turf strip in southern New Jersey, for a nine-month odyssey in a flying machine powered by a little two cylinder engine. Experienced ultralight pilots thought his proposed trip was impossible and they warned him against it. But that didn't discourage him.

He followed his flight plan which took him south to Florida, then across the southern tier of states, up the west coast to Washington State, into Canada and on up into Alaska.

In Alaska he flew through mountain passes that intimidate

pilots of more substantial certificated aircraft. On one occasion, he flew through a pass at 2,500 feet above the Alaska Highway, following the northern ridge where he anticipated getting lift.

"Instead," he said, "I got a severe sink. Within a minute I lost 1,500 feet. I managed to get over toward the south ridge, picked up lift and got back to 2,500 feet. Then I started getting sink again. I was fighting the rough air as best I could.

"It took 40 or 45 minutes to go the 15 or 20 miles through the pass. Cars on the highway were passing me.

"When I got to the end of the pass there was a convergence of four passes with moist air coming off the Gulf of Alaska. I got hit with an especially strong wind gust. I heard a whoosh and the aircraft seemed to stop dead. But the air speed indicator read 95 which is the red line. (Never exceed speed.) The nose cone twisted. The windshield pushed in on me. I pulled off the power and pulled the nose up to reduce speed. I looked up at the red handle for the ballistic parachute I carried. I was sure I was going to have to use it. I thought of all the people who said, 'I wish I was going with you.' I was hyperventilating. I had tunnel vision. I had no feeling in my arms or legs. I knew if I pulled the chute, I'd end up on the side of the mountain. I was never so scared in my life. I was holding the stick with both hands and I was saying, 'Please, God, get me out of here.'

"After I bled off the speed I glided through the pass and out over a lake. I had tears in my eyes. I flew for five or ten minutes over the lake, just long enough to recompose myself before I landed. I was totally drained emotionally."

If there were terrorizing moments of tremendous strain and pressure on his journey, there were also views of indescribable beauty.

"I flew low over rivers running through the woods," Trader said. "I saw beautiful towering mountains. I flew over fields and saw ducks and deer, moose, caribou, black bears, grizzly bears, eagles. You can't imagine how beautiful the wild flowers of Alaska are. Alaska far exceeded any expectations I ever had.

"I met so many wonderful people. They put me up, they bought me meals. I'll never forget them. A trip like this makes you realize you're only a flyspeck in this world. It gives you a feeling of insignificance."

Since he made the trip, Trader has established a foundation he calls, "In Search of Eagles," to help youngsters appreciate nature, wildlife, and ecology. He also wants them to get to realize the capabilities and potential of aviation. He speaks in schools and shows some of his collection of thousands of slides taken on the trip. He also pulls his ultralight behind his pickup truck and parks it in the school yard so youngsters can sit in it and work the controls.

The message he wishes to leave with students is: "Whatever you can conceive and believe, you can achieve."

His goal is to speak to a million youngsters in the next ten years about turning their dreams into reality.

10/31/93

FUN IS WHAT ULTRALIGHT FLYING IS ALL ABOUT

It often takes someone with a passion for a particular activity and a compulsion to convince other people to share that passion that provides the impetus for that activity to grow and flourish. The late Vincent Vitollo filled that role in promoting ultralight flying in New Jersey.

He had a rich and varied background in conventional airplanes before he became enamored with the little lightweight aircraft. He was an instructor during World War II. He flew business aircraft after the war when they were twin-engine piston planes and not the speedy business jets we know today. He worked for NASA.

There were 20,000 hours in his log book in conventional aircraft before he discovered ultralights and was completely captivated by them.

This column not only tells you about Vincent Vitollo, but it provides an insight into what ultralights are all about.

You would have no trouble finding pilots whose attitude toward ultralights is, "You wouldn't get me up in one of them." If you visit the Ultralight Flight Center in Jackson, the largest ultralight operation in New Jersey, you'll hear pilots saying, "I wouldn't fly a regular airplane. That's no fun."

Fun is what ultralight flying is all about. You can't go anywhere in them. They're slow. They have limited range. You're sitting out in the open in most ultralights. There is generally no room for baggage. Nevertheless, ultralights have been flown from coast-to-coast four or five times and the previous story in this chapter described a 15,000-mile ultralight flight.

The ultralight usually carries five gallons of fuel, good for about an hour or two of flight. Cruising speeds range between 40 and 60 miles an hour.

While ultralights don't go fast and usually don't go far, to their pilots that's not important. What is important is that these tiny flying machines provide an opportunity to get up in the air as free as a bird. And they do that without breaking the bank accounts of these enthusiasts and without having to comply with volumes of regulations.

Kits for ultralights start at about $5,000 and go up to somewhere around $21,000. You don't need a license or an FAA medical certificate to fly them.

Initially there were only single place ultralights. You put them together and taught yourself to fly them. Unfortunately, that didn't always produce the best results.

Today, there are two-place ultralights and there are qualified, rated instructors. At the Ultralight Flight Center in Jackson, a complete course, which includes basic, pre-solo, and advanced instruction, costs $800. When the course is completed, the student is granted a license by the United States Ultralight Association.

Vince Vitollo

"The new procedures have made a big difference," said Vincent Vitollo of Point Pleasant Beach, a 70-year-old great grandfather, who owns and operates the Flight Center. He estimates there are about 30,000 ultralights in the country.

Vitollo had a long career in aviation before he discovered ultralights. He took his first flight lesson at the old Westfield Airport (as I did) and later got his license on Long Island.

He returned to New Jersey to get his seaplane rating at the Mellor-Howard Seaplane Base on the Hackensack River followed by a multiengine seaplane rating.

During World War II he was an instrument instructor in BT-13s and after the war he flew for Atlantic Aviation. In those days Atlantic was flying twin-engine, piston-powered twin Beeches for corporations. He logged more than 20,000 hours before he stopped keeping track of his flight time. He has more than 5,000 hours of ultralight time.

Vitollo had his introduction to ultralights at the big Oshkosh (Wis.) Air Show 14 years ago. "They were nothing more than hang gliders with an engine and weight shift controls. I didn't go for that," he said. "The next year I saw the Weedhopper at Oshkosh. It had a stick and wing struts instead of cables. I said, that's more my style.

"I bought a Weedhopper kit. The fellow who designed it used to work for NASA and so did I. I knew him from my days at Cocoa Beach and Cape Canaveral. He sold me the kit for cost. It took less than a week to assemble."

At that time, Vitollo was living in Manasquan and running a die casting business. He owned a Piper Comanche based at Allaire Airport (now Monmouth Executive Airport). He had owned about a dozen airplanes, the first being a 38-hp Aeronca C-3 on floats.

His Weedhopper had a 20-hp engine. He put floats on it and flew it out of a lake behind his house. It had a one gallon fuel tank which could keep him flying for about one hour and carry him about 30 miles.

"I never intended to go into business." said Vitollo, "but people followed me and said, 'This is neat. Can you get one for me? Can you teach me to fly?'

"I got Weedhoppers for them and I taught a number of people to fly them. I sold more Weedhoppers than most dealers.

"Ten years ago, I acquired 19 acres in Jackson Township and cleared a 2,500 foot strip."

Today, Vitollo is a dealer, not only for the Weedhopper but for Challenger, Honey Bee, Pegasus, and an H-40 ultralight version of the World War II P-40 fighter.

While no FAA license or physical is required to fly an ultralight, instructors are required to have an FAA rating. The Ultralight Flight Center soloed its 500th student this year.

All kinds of people fly ultralights. Among those who fly from Vitollo's strip are a state supreme court justice, and two state senators.

Ultralights are limited to a weight of 254 pounds and must not carry more than five gallons of fuel. But these aircraft are not what they used to be. Many newer models have enclosed cabins. The old machines were open air aircraft. Some of today's models bear a close resemblance to certificated aircraft.

You start most of them by pulling a string but there are some today that have electric starters. And some carry radios and navigation equipment.

It's a far cry from the first ultralight Vitollo saw at Oshkosh in 1979.

Today there is a new class of certificated aircraft, Light Sport Aircraft, that are smaller and less powerful than the traditional certificated aircraft. Light Sport Aircraft cannot weigh more than 1,320 pounds, carry more than two people, or be capable of an airspeed of more than 120 knots. It's necessary to have either a private license or a Sport Pilot License to fly them. The Sport Pilot Licenses have a number of restrictions that the Private Pilot's License does not have. Sport Pilot Licenses are not valid for night flight and the pilot may not carry more than one passenger. One feature of the Sport Pilot License is that an FAA medical is not required if the pilot holds a valid driver's license.

10/10/93

Note: *Vince Vitollo died in an ultralight accident in March of 1999.*

ENGLISH GRANDPA TOURS THE COLONIES IN AN ULTRALIGHT

Ultralights are not the height of comfort. They have none of the speed with which flying is associated. Their pilots usually watch the cars below outpace them. They are the snails of the air. They have a short range. Fifty miles is kind of a long trip in an ultralight. In fact its fuel supply might not always stretch that far.

None of these things seemed to phase Peter Harris. He owns an English version of an ultralight. While these aircraft are somewhat primitive, the American versions are a generation or two ahead of the English aircraft Harris flew.

His aircraft has no controls. It flies by weight shift like a hang glider.

It is not exactly the machine most travelers would choose to tour the United States, but Peter Harris did it. Here is an account of his journey.

E nglishmen are not what they're cracked up to be. If you don't believe that, you obviously have not met Peter Harris.

Most Americans think Englishmen are stiff and stodgy and so very, very proper you could choke. Peter Harris is the antithesis of that. He's warm, friendly, outgoing, and very down-to-earth, even if he does find himself in this space because of his adventures off the face of this earth. Peter, 67, a retired importer of electronic components, had never been to the United States, but he had a yearning to see this country. As an ultralight pilot, he knew there was no better way to do that than in one of those tiny flying machines that race through the skies at 55 or 60 miles an hour, presenting an unparalleled view of the landscape below.

He owns an English version of the ultralight, a contraption called a Medway Raven. This machine, like most things English, is a bit different from an ultralight you would find in the United States. They do everything a little differently over there. They drive on the left side of the road, you know.

To start with, if you look for the stick in the Raven, you won't find it because there is none. You don't need it if you have no control surfaces, and the Raven doesn't. It flies by weight shift, like a hang glider.

There is a bar in front of the pilot. If the pilot wants to go up, the procedure is to simply push on the bar to pitch the nose up, the wing tilts up and the aircraft climbs. To descend, the pilot pulls the bar toward him and the nose pitches down. To turn left, the pilot shifts his weight to the left, warping the wing by providing more twist on one side than the other and that produces roll. The left wing drops and the aircraft goes into a left turn.

One other thing is different about the Raven. It's a delta wing, which means it's a big wide thing shaped like a "V."

Unlike virtually all U.S. ultralights, which are built from kits, the $14,000 Raven is factory built. It's powered by a two-cycle, 43-hp Bombardier Rotax engine. The aircraft weighs 330 pounds dry. It can carry two passengers, but Peter used the back seat to carry his personal belongings.

Peter started flying in England when he was 50. What he flew was not an airplane or even an ultralight. He flew a hang glider.

"Hang gliding is pure flying," he said when we talked to him at the Ultralight Flight Center in Jackson during a stop that stretched to several days when the center's owner, Vince Vitollo, invited him to be his house guest.

Englishman Peter Harris in the British ultralight in which he toured the United States.

Peter loved hang gliding and virtually nothing could stop him. Even when he broke his foot at it. "I was back flying in six months," he said.

He lived in the south of England where there were ridges perfect for hang gliding. But then he moved to Harlow, 25 miles north of London. The land there is flat. You can't do any hang gliding in that country. So he took to ultralight flying.

Peter who flies out of a former U.S. Marauder Base which was called Matching Air Force Base, has a flying buddy named Dave O'Gorman who also owns a Raven. They decided to come to America together and tour the country in two aircraft.

A pretty good salesman, Peter got Virgin Atlantic to fly the two ultralights to Orlando gratis, in return for which he put Virgin's logo on his flying machine.

Peter also has a cause which helped inspire his trip. One of his five children (and he has eight grandchildren) is a daughter who has had two hip replacements, two knee replacements, and an elbow replacement as a result of severe arthritis.

He wanted to use their flight to raise money for the English Arthritis Council. He got a hundred people to pledge donations based on the mileage flown.

When their aircraft arrived in Florida from England they assembled them at Gator Flying Park in Claremont and began their odyssey from Titusville.

They hadn't completed their first leg when misfortune struck. Dave had a problem and made an emergency landing. After he was on the ground he hit a ditch. He wasn't hurt but the injuries to his aircraft were fatal.

What to do now? They rented a van and Dave drove while Peter flew. The van could go faster than the Raven, but that was no problem. After a couple of weeks passed, Dave took to the skies again and flew some legs while Peter drove.

Few Americans have ever seen as much of this country as these two Englishmen and virtually none have seen so much from the perspective they had.

"It was a tremendous feeling when I flew through a pass at 8,000 feet and could see San Diego and the Pacific Ocean laid out before me," said Peter. He saw many breathtaking sights from the Raven. He flew over the Golden Gate Bridge, Yosemite National Park, Lake Tahoe. "They were absolutely beautiful," he said. He got up to 13,500 feet over the Rockies approaching Denver, another beautiful sight.

"I flew down the Hudson, past New York City's skyscrapers, around the Statue of Liberty. It was the most exhilarating experience I've ever had," Peter said.

They stopped at Oshkosh where they met Rick Trader whose 15,000-mile flight was described in the first story of this chapter. They also stopped at Old Rhinebeck, N.Y., where they saw the World War I and pre-World War I air shows. (See pg. 438)

The trip was not without its incidents. In Texas, they were in a restaurant when they saw a tornado approaching. They rushed out to the airport and found the Raven upside down. They held onto it for three-quarters of an hour in pouring, freezing rain. Fortunately there was very little damage.

In Las Vegas, the aircraft was stolen. Peter offered a $1,000 reward to anyone who found it. *The Las Vegas Sun* printed a story and photo and in four days it was found.

They were in Granby, Colo., on the Fourth of July, where the airfield is run by English people and where the only Raven in the United States is based. Peter and the pilot of the other Raven, a Welshman, were asked to fly over the town's Fourth of July parade in formation.

"Here," said Peter, "were a couple of Brits helping the Americans celebrate getting us kicked out of the U.S."

Perhaps the most memorable incident of their trip occurred in Lake City, Fla. They landed late in the day, and the people who operated the airport were gone. They wanted to camp out. Peter had a tent that he carried in a storage compartment in the center section of his wing.

They didn't want to camp on the airport property without permission, so they looked for somewhere else to camp. But the area was all wooded. They couldn't find an open field.

Finally they found a cemetery with high grass. They pitched their tent there and went to sleep. In the middle of the night lights suddenly shined in their tent and they saw red lights flashing. It was a police car. Two more police cars came with flashing lights. It looked like the police had a major case at hand.

"Who's in there?" one of the policemen shouted. "Come out with your hands up," they ordered. The two tired Englishmen stumbled out of the tent.

"They wanted to know what we were doing camping in a cemetery," said Peter. "We explained the situation to them.

"When the policemen realized we were just a couple of crazy Englishmen, they laughed, shook our hands, and went away. "

When we spoke to Peter (O'Gorman had returned to England) he had flown 10,500 miles and he still planned to fly back to Florida and over the Florida Keys which he heard were beautiful.

9/18/94

ON TOP OF THE WORLD

Imagine an airline pilot flying along at 21,000 feet and suddenly he spots what looks like a man sitting in the middle of some aluminum tubes with something that resembles a cloth wing on top of him. He might very well think he's delusional.

But if it were Sunday, May 24, 1981, it was no illusion. It was Jim Campbell in an ultralight.

Today, some ultralights have enclosed cabins. In 1981, they were little more than a hang glider with a lawn mower engine.

You wouldn't normally expect to find one of these machines even at 5,000 feet, but 21,000 feet where there is little oxygen and the temperature is way below zero? That's out of this world in more ways than one. That's tempting the fates. But Jim Campbell did it and he came back down to earth to talk about it.

Today, Campbell is editor-in chief of Aero-News Network, an online aviation newsletter.

I first met Campbell seven years earlier, in 1974. He was then a 17-year-old high school student who had a pilot's license and he was a member of the four-man cabinet of the National Association of Aviation Explorers. I wrote a column about him. The opening sentence said: "You never heard of Jim Campbell before, but chances are pretty good you'll be hearing about him again."

I will never do that again in my life."

That was Jim Campbell's comment after setting an ultralight altitude record of 21,210 feet in an aircraft known as the Pterodactyl No Pturkey.

Campbell, who's 24, had tried for the record the day before at the Lakehurst Naval Engineering Center. But after reaching an altitude of only 1,500 feet he abandoned the effort because, "the aircraft didn't feel right."

For the record attempt, Campbell carried a radio, oxygen, a parachute capable of lowering both him and the aircraft together and a special smoke grenade attached to the step to be used in case of any problem that would require abandoning the attempt. That's a bit of extra weight for an ultralight.

"It wasn't so much the extra weight as the effect on the balance of the aircraft," Campbell said. The aircraft itself weighs 160 pounds. The Pterodactyl No Pturkey, a modified version of the Pterodactyl Fledgling, is constructed of lightweight aircraft-type aluminum tubing with dacron covered wings and control surfaces.

After failing in the attempt Saturday, Campbell stayed up late into the night working with his calculator to try to determine safe limits for his assault on the record.

He decided that if he removed the radio, he could do it.

But the radio was necessary for Campbell to maintain contact with his chase plane which would remain in contact with the New York Air Traffic Control Center. Airspace above 18,000 feet is controlled and aircraft cannot enter that space without clearance and radio communications.

Jim Campbell

Campbell worked out a series of signals with the pilot of the chase plane, Jerry Dare, who was flying a turbocharged Beech Bonanza.

Campbell took off at 8:12 a.m. on Sunday, hours before the crowd at the Lakehurst Air Show would be turning out to see the Blue Angels, World Aerobatic Champion Leo Loudenslager, and the French dual aerobatic team, the French Connection.

His instructions were to be down by 11 a.m.

Campbell, who only two weeks earlier, on May 9, set the altitude record for ultralights at 17,380 feet on a flight from Hanover Airport to Hightstown (both in New Jersey), was aiming for 25,000 feet.

On the way up to the record of 21,210 feet, he experienced carburetor icing problems and at 13,200 feet, the engine quit. Not a comforting feeling. "Fortunately, I was able to start it up again on the first try," Campbell said.

"I was scared to death at 18,000 feet," he said. "Sitting there in the open in a hammock-type seat was frightening."

His major problem, however, wasn't fear, it was sub zero temperatures.

"When I reached 18,000 I was freezing, but I said I'll go for 500 more. The moisture from my breath froze my oxygen mask to my face."

Climbing at that altitude is a slow process. The aircraft would only gain 150 feet a minute.

Campbell was wearing long underwear, a snow suit, a heavy jacket, two pairs of socks, a Navy watch cap, and a helmet. In spite of all that clothing, his hands, feet, and face became so frozen that at 21,210 feet, he called it quits.

At that altitude the temperature was 51 below zero and the wind was blowing at 53 knots.

When he got back on the ground at 10:49, Campbell needed help getting out of the aircraft.

All the members of the Blue Angels and World Aerobatic Champion Leo Loudenslager signed the canard (a little auxiliary wing up front) of the aircraft.

"Anybody who wants to try for that record is welcome to it," said Campbell, who makes a living selling ultralights like the one with which he broke the record.

5/27/81

Note: *This piece did not run as a "Wings Over Jersey" column. It ran as a news story.*

Chapter 3

Soaring in Silence

They don't need engines, they don't need gas. They can soar to altitudes where you get frost bite. They can travel hundreds of miles. All without power. Those are some of the intriguing qualities of gliders, or, if you prefer, sailplanes.

Glider pilots travel on currents of air. Their pilots often watch and learn from hawks. Hawks know where the thermals (updrafts) are. They turn lazy circles in the sky while letting the air currents carry them to higher and higher altitudes.

Glider pilots often play Follow the Leader with hawks. The hawks will sometimes fly right alongside gliders while eyeing them suspiciously.

The most unusual quality of gliders is their silence. We don't usually think of aircraft as being noiseless vehicles, but gliders are as silent as snowflakes landing on a fir tree. Flying in one, the only sound you hear is the rush of the wind. It's an unusual and memorable experience.

Gliders normally are towed aloft by an airplane to an altitude of 2,000 to 3,000 feet, although they can also be launched by a motor vehicle or a winch.

Once aloft, the pilot must find a thermal in order to stay up there for an extended period before settling back down to earth.

A 1,000 KILOMETER (620 MILE) POWERLESS FLIGHT

The column which follows will tell you a lot about determination and persistence and how it led to the achievement of a goal few others in the world have realized.

It will tell you something else. It will tell you about the spirit of a pilot who says you can throw me a knockout punch, but that doesn't end my quest. It just means I have to start all over again.

This is the story of two men who waited patiently for three years, watching for the exact weather conditions that would afford them the opportunity to pursue a rare goal. Both men completed the mission. For one it was a triumph, for the other a tragedy, except that wasn't the way he looked at it.

One perfectly beautiful Sunday, two New Jersey men, Ken Kochanski and Bob Templin, did something nobody in the state had ever done before. They traveled 1,000 kilometers (620 miles) without burning a drop of fuel. That's no small feat, even if you're a glider pilot, which both of them are.

They had been dreaming of making such a flight for a long time. They spent three years planning for it. But when you undertake a task like that you never know what may happen, and Bob found out all about that.

"There are only two or three days in a year when such a flight would be possible," said Bob. "You need exactly the right conditions. Those conditions are a cold front that generates northwest winds of 20 knots at 3,000 feet that will last all day and must pass through before the flight, and unstable air that will create thermal development and just the right amount of clouds, not more than 50 percent cover and not less than 10 percent."

In the year before they made the flight there was not a single day when those conditions existed. You can only expect to find such conditions from April to June and for a short time in the fall.

Ken and Bob watched the weather channel on TV religiously to follow the movement of fronts and weather patterns. Then, one Saturday night, it looked like conditions would be right the next day. They declared their intention to make the flight, a necessary step because an official observer is required if a flight is to gain sanction and be authenticated.

Pilots are permitted to make three changes of direction in the course of a record flight attempt of this nature. The pilots are required to take a photograph of the point where they make their turn home. They must also carry a barograph which records altitudes and provides proof that they did not land somewhere along the way.

Both Ken and Bob own gliders that they keep at Blairstown Airport where their flights began and ended.

They got out to the airport at 8 o'clock in the morning and took off two hours later.

The trick in long distance glider flights is to follow ridges on a windy day. The wind bouncing off the ridges on the upwind side creates lift so they can gain enough altitude to make it to the next ridge. Where there are gaps between ridges long distance glider pilots have to find thermals to stay aloft.

They stayed together until they were about 70 miles out when they were forced to split up. Bob couldn't gain enough altitude to make it to the next ridge on the route

Bob Templin, left, and Ken Kochanski, who flew 1,000 kilometers in a glider.

that Ken was following, so he flew along a different line of ridges.

Ken photographed a road intersection where he made a turn and flew back over Schuykill County Airport, about a hundred miles, and then back to West Virginia where he made his third and last turn for home from a point just north of Winchester, about 230 miles from Blairstown.

Bob flew to similar points, although he followed a different route. Ken landed back at Blairstown at 6:30 p.m. after 8 1/2 hours in the air. Bob came in 15 minutes later.

There are only 183 people in the world who have ever flown 1,000 kilometers in a glider. Only 59 of them were U.S. glider pilots.

The flight put Ken in the 1,000 Kilometer Club, which is quite a distinction. He received a 1,000 kilometer diploma and an international ranking. Bob will not get either. He ran out of film and did not get a photo of his last turn.

Was he upset at doing something only 59 people in the country had ever done before and not getting official recognition for it? Not at all.

"It happens to a lot of people," he said. "It gives me an excuse for doing it again."

Both men are Gold Badge glider pilots which means they

have flown a 300-kilometer (186 mile) flight, have made a 3,000 meter (close to 10,000 feet) altitude gain, and have made a flight of five hours duration.

Both men hold power plane ratings but rarely fly gas guzzling aircraft.

Ken, a systems manager for Morgan Guarantee, got interested in gliding after watching a space shuttle glide to a landing on TV in 1981. "I said, if that thing can glide, I can glide." He went for a glider ride a couple of weeks later and he was hooked. He got his glider rating at Somerset Airport.

Bob, an ironworker, was a bird watcher. "I watched hawks fly down the ridges and I thought it would be nice to do the same thing" he said.

His father is a pilot. Bob started flying with him, then got his power rating and transitioned into gliders in the early 1970s.

Neither man is ready to rest on his laurels. Both have achieved two of the three legs toward their Diamond Badge which requires a 310-mile flight, a 5,000-meter (16,404 foot) altitude gain and a 300-kilometer (186 mile) closed course flight declared in advance.

Bob has said he plans to try the 1,000 kilometer course again. And Ken might just try it again, too, just to prove the first time was no fluke.

Bob Fitch, another glider pilot who now flies out of Blairstown, is one of the 59 Americans who has made a 1,000 kilometer flight, but he did not make the flight out of Blairstown Airport. (See next story)

Two other records were set on glider flights out of Blairstown on the same day as Ken and Bob's flights. Dave Michaud of Middletown achieved a record speed of 82 mph on a 500 kilometer (310 mile) out-and-back course to the tunnel 39 miles west of Harrisburg, Pennsylvania. A speed of 82 mph over a long course is not bad when you are flying without an engine.

And Ron Schwartz of Blairstown flew to 15,500 feet, an altitude record for a standard class glider.

4/19/92

Note: *Bob made his 1,000 kilometer flight again on April 4, 2000, and this time it was official. He also got his Diamond Badge in 1999. Ken Kochanski has fulfilled two of the three requirements for a Diamond Badge.*

WHERE'S GRANDPA? OUT SETTING RECORDS

There are many things you can do in the golden years after retirement. You can collect stamps, raise orchids, go fishing, take the grandchildren to the zoo.

Bob Fitch became a collector. What he collects are records. A glider pilot, he set more records in powerless craft than anyone else--grandpa or not--in his home state of New Jersey.

One of the records he set was a first.

His name is not a household word, but his accomplishments are no less noteworthy because of his anonymity.

W here's grandpa?

If the grandpa you're looking for is Bob Fitch, chances are he's up in the sky trying to set another record. He holds seven state soaring records, more than any other glider pilot in New Jersey.

The record he's proudest of is one that puts him in a class by himself--worldwide.

"I'm a one-of-a-kind," says Fitch, a tall, lean, 65-year-old father of four, grandfather of five. "I'm the only man in the world who ever flew a 1,000 kilometer (620 mile) flight in a glider he built himself." That record was sanctioned by the FAI (Federation Aeronautique International) in France, which oversees and sanctions aviation records worldwide.

"I'm the 16th U.S. pilot to fly a glider 1,000 kilometers," says Fitch. "There are 33 in the world." None of the others, however, made the flight in a glider they built themselves.

Fitch's flight, from State College, Pa., to Bluefield, Va., in 1981, took 11 hours. The seven state records he holds (an eighth was taken away from him by another pilot) were all established on flights from Blairstown Airport.

Although, Fitch first soloed an airplane in 1942, he never climbed into a glider until 1968. He was never one to rush things. It was five years after his first solo before he got around to getting his license and in the process he had to solo a second time because he waited so long to come back to flying.

Then after he got his license in 1947, he didn't fly again until 1965. By that time, "the kids were pretty well grown up and the house was nearly paid for," he says.

So he went to Lincoln Park Airport to get reinstated. There were no instructors available, but airport owner Ed Gorski (formerly

Amelia Earhart's mechanic) was there.

"You're an instructor, " Fitch said.

"Yes, but I haven't flown in years," Gorski responded.

After considerable persuasion, Fitch talked Gorski into going up with him. Gorski went around the pattern with him once. They came down, he got out of the airplane and said, "Okay, go."

Bob Fitch, a record-setting grandfather.

It was 1968 when a coworker (Fitch is a retired mechanical engineer) expressed an interest in glider flying. They went out to Elmira, N.Y., one of the nation's major soaring centers.

"We each went for two rides. It was fun. I asked my instructor, 'What does it take to solo?' He said, 'Two rides.' But it was late in the day and we had to go home."

The next time Fitch flew a glider was three years later. "I got something in the mail from Blairstown Airport. It said pilots could get a glider rating for $108. I went to Blairstown.

"One of my first rides was with Dent Brome, a TWA pilot who told me about the Aero Club Albatross, a glider club. I joined the club in 1971 and got my rating the next year. I flew out of Somerset Airport with the club and made a lot of new friends. Four of us got together and bought a kit to build a glider. We finished it in the spring of 1973, after nine months of work."

In 1975, the same group bought a second kit for $4,995. But the one other member of the group who was interested in competition flying was seriously injured in an automobile accident and the other two lost interest. So Fitch took over the project, which he finished in 1977. That was the ship in which he established the FAI record.

The glider he flies now, a German Glasfluget H301, known as a Libelle (Dragonfly) was purchased in 1982. He has continued setting records in that aircraft.

Here are some of the state records Fitch has set:

• 1976: Speed for 200 kilometer (120 mile) triangular course.

• 1978: Distance straight out. 165 miles. Also, second record on same flight for distance to a declared goal. Blairstown to Frederick, Md.

- 1980: Speed record. 300 kilometer (187 mile) triangular course.

- 1982: Speed records for 300 kilometer and 200 kilometer courses, breaking his own records.

- 1983: Altitude record: 16,700 feet, plus record for altitude gain.

- 1983: Out and return record. 376 miles to Hancock Airport in West Virginia and back

- 1984: Straight out distance record. 244 miles to Mt. Jackson, Va.

In the course of his 916 glider flights, Fitch has had an occasion or two when he did not reach his goal. In a glider, you can't run out of gas, but you can run out of lift. And if you run out of lift, you're not going anywhere.

On one occasion Fitch made Page 1 of a major metropolitan newspaper. A headline in the *Philadelphia Inquirer* read: "Glider Pilot Survives Landing on Cemetery."

"Where I landed," he said, "it was as good as Blairstown Airport. It was a clear area. There were no headstones or tablets.

"But the caretaker was very upset. He said, 'There are dead people here.' I said, 'I'm sure they won't mind.' He replied, 'Yes, but I do.' "

Which proves that you don't have to set records to make headlines. As a matter of fact, none of Fitch's records ever made Page 1.

5/12/85

GLIDERS GO TO WAR

Gliders were designed for fun. They're not much use as transportation vehicles, at least that's how it was until World War II.

World War II saw gliders used to transport troops behind the lines along with paratroopers. There were always heavy casualties as a result of glider crashes. Military gliders seldom made anything resembling a normal landing. Their return to earth was generally a crash--of varying degrees of severity.

Gliders were used on D-Day, in the invasion of Southern France, in the Netherlands, in Sicily, and in the Pacific. I had some firsthand experience with this method of transportation having flown as a member of a 4.2 mortar battalion, from Rome to Southern France in one of hundreds of gliders towed by C-47s.

This column presents a different face on the world of non-powered aircraft.

Walter Cronkite and I have one thing in common. We both did it--once. We both made one combat glider landing. He volunteered.

In his foreword to a new book on World War II glider operations, *Silent Wings at War, Combat Gliders in World War II,* by John L. Lowden, Walter Cronkite sums up that experience this way: "I'll tell you straight out. If you've got to go into combat, don't go by glider. Walk, crawl, parachute, swim, float--anything. But don't go by glider."

Glider operations which were a new military innovation in World War II, have received relatively little attention from those who have written about that period in history. John Lowden, a much decorated combat glider pilot, makes up for that. His book is an accurate account of that aspect of the war from a personal, firsthand point of view. It's also a well-researched history of glider operations in every theater of the war.

In reading Lowden's book, it came as a complete surprise to find a chapter on the landing in Southern France, on August 15, 1944, some two months after the landing in Normandy. That was not one of the most auspicious actions of the war.

I was even more surprised to note also that the book mentioned the outfit I was in, the 83rd Chemical Mortar Battalion. These battalions were small units made up of four companies so they understandably did not garner a lot of coverage. The battalions were attached to larger outfits, very often assault units. Little mention has ever been made of the highly effective 4.2 mortars we used.

In the Southern France invasion, one company in the battalion, D Company, made the invasion in gliders. The other three went in by sea. I was in D Company.

As we approached the coast of Southern France we saw a black puff of smoke in the air, a good distance in front of us. We were to be dropped at a relatively low altitude so the gliders could hit the drop zone fast and not give time to enemy troops to organize opposition. When the C-47 pilots saw the puff of smoke (antiaircraft fire) they climbed a couple of thousand feet.

As we were approaching the drop zone, the glider pilots saw that there were poles planted throughout the relatively open area where we were to land. As we got closer they

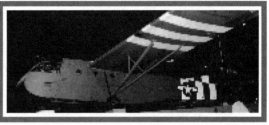

A World War II combat glider, one of the few left in the world, on exhibit in the Air Force Museum in Dayton, Ohio. It now hangs from the ceiling. The stripes were used to indicate it was a U.S. aircraft in the D-Day invasion at Normandy.

could see wires radiating from the poles. The glider pilots believed the Germans attached mines to those wires. They were, therefore, understandably terrified of the idea of putting down in the fields that were our designated drop zones. That left them with virtually no alternatives. When they were low enough to see the wires, they were too low to go anywhere else. But they were afraid to set off the mines. They had to make instant decisions and they had little choice. They crashed into trees in the woods surrounding the fields. Some hit the sides of stone barns. Some of the gliders had jeeps in them with men sitting in those jeeps. The results were tragic.

The four of us in our glider were extremely lucky. Our pilots set us down at the edge of a vineyard alongside a road. Damage to the glider was slight. We were able to lift the hinged cockpit to unload our cargo. Beside the pilots there were two "passengers" (I was one.) and 25 rounds of ammunition.

Lowden carries an account of the operation in Southern France that he got from a British glider pilot who explained that the poles were hastily erected and easily knocked down and there were no mines. Many gliders farther back in our group did land in our designated drop zone. Once they saw a glider landing between the poles and there was no explosion, others followed.

According to an account of a glider pilot on a flight in

advance of ours, some of the tow planes increased their speed to 150 miles an hour which the loaded gliders (some with jeeps in them) were not stressed for. Some came apart in the air and disgorged their contents.

There are accounts in the book of pilots of the C-47 tow planes dropping their gliders over open water, turning and hightailing it for home. There are also accounts of gliders being dropped at several thousand feet instead of several hundred (which happened to us), that would have enabled them to hit the ground fast, giving the enemy less time to respond. Apparently that happened to other flights besides ours.

We talked to Luttrell (Lut) Maclin (See page 166) of Ringoes, a World War II glider pilot, to get his reaction to some of these stories and others in the book. He was familiar with all of those stories. Maclin was aboard the liner, *France*, en route to England on D-Day. He participated in the recovery of some of the gliders used in that action. Combat gliders were built for one mission. Few survived combat landings in condition to be reused, but a few were salvaged.

The gliders that were recovered were launched using a system in which the tow rope was attached to a rope strung between two poles about 18-feet high. Tow planes, generally C-47s, swooped low and with a stinger (hook) protruding from the tail, snatched the gliders in a manner similar to the way banner towers pick up their airborne advertising.

One unusual glider mission took place when American troops took Templehof Airdrome in Berlin. The runways were so full of bomb craters they were unusable. Three gliders were dropped carrying bulldozers especially designed to fit in a glider. Lut piloted one of those gliders.

The bulldozers filled in the craters and a couple of days later C-47s landed and pulled the gliders out.

Lut is commander of the New Jersey chapter of the National World War II Glider Pilots Association which has almost 35 members. At 79, he is still an active general aviation pilot. He didn't get his civilian pilot's license until the early 70s after his children were out of college.

He took up aerobatics after he passed the three score and 10 mark and participated in several competitions taking third place in a couple of them.

Before he enlisted to become a glider pilot, Lut spent eight years as a financial writer for the *New York Herald Tribune*, After the war he worked on Wall Street for several major firms.

It's been a long time since my own experience in military

gliders, but I saw things in that landing in Southern France which will stick with me until my final flight. And there was very little enemy opposition to our landing.

John Lowden's book is an accurate and engrossing account of that aspect of World War II. *Silent Wings at War, Combat Gliders in World War II,* is published by the Smithsonian Institute Press.

6/28/92

THE KID AND THE OLD MAN

There was this 14-year-old kid who soloed a glider after 4 hours of instruction back in 1965. A year later he made headlines all over the country when he and his big brother, Kern, flew from New Jersey to California and back in a $300 Piper Cub they rebuilt in their barn over the winter. The kid, Rinker Buck, was 15 then, not old enough to solo an airplane. You have to be 16. His big brother, the pilot, was 17.

Their trip had all the ingredients that inspire the writing of wonderfully readable books. As a matter of fact, Rinker did write a book about his youthful adventure with his brother--32 years later-- titled, "Flight of Passage". It is a remarkable tale, filled with tense moments and laced with humor.

Rinker, who had been a foreign correspondent for Life Magazine and more recently the winner of the AOPA's Max Karant Award for his outstanding series in the Hartford Courant on the tragic John F Kennedy, Jr., accident, has published three books.

While this glider story begins with excerpts from a column about teenagers, it winds up with a tale about a senior citizen who was the heartbeat of soaring in New Jersey in the early days, Gus Scheurer. Which is to say, that the appeal of the free spirit of gliding reaches out to young and old alike.

R inker Buck, a freshman at Delbarton School in Morristown, had four hours of instruction before he soloed. He took his first lesson only a few hours earlier.

Teenager Rinker Buck, ready to take off after he earned his single engine certificate.

On Labor Day, at Somerset Airport, Rinker Buck, 14, made his first solo flight. No, he wasn't doing anything illegal. It's true you have to be 16 to solo an airplane. But Rinker soloed a glider, and that's perfectly legal at 14.

Flying, however, was nothing new to Rinker. His dad, Tom Buck, is a veteran pilot, and though Rinker had no instruction in an airplane, he had a lot of time flying with his dad. His older brother, Kern, who soloed four different airplanes 16 times on his 16th birthday, got his pilot's license a few weeks ago, and one of his sisters (there are 11 children in the Buck family) is a student pilot.

Rinker still has quite a wait before he can get a glider pilot's license. You have to be 16. By then he should be a veteran.

Gliders, incidentally, are one way to beat the high cost of flying. Since you have no engine you don't have to buy gas or oil and you'll never need an engine overhaul.

9/26/65

One way to get an introduction to soaring is by joining a glider club. The Aero Club Albatross is one of the oldest glider clubs in the country.

The club charges an initiation fee of $100 and a $40 flight fee per year. Club dues are $10 a year. After that you can fly all you want and all you pay is a $4 tow fee for a tow to 3,000 feet. (Note: This was written in 1965.)

Gus Scheurer ready to go up for a glider flight.

If you should happen to find some nice thermals up there, you may be able to stay aloft for hours and you don't have to worry about added costs because once you've paid your tow fee that's it.

There's no instructor's fee for club members either. The club is a nonprofit organization.

Aero Club Albatross was founded in 1929. At 66, its president and founder, Gus Scheurer, of Cedar Glen City, near Toms River, is one of the oldest glider pilots in the country.

Gus first soloed a glider in Germany in 1922. In those days a glider was just an open framework with a pair of wings.

It was launched by a catapult device that was really a big sling shot.

Gus's license was International Glider License Number 55. He founded Aero Club Albatross just a few years after he came to this country. At 66, he's still a very active glider pilot.

This summer he returned to the scene of his first solo flight, Naberu, Germany, where soaring enjoys great popularity. In order to learn more about the most modern methods of glider construction, he worked in the Wolf Hirth glider factory there for three weeks.

Most of the towing for the aero club is done by Al Schillberg who used to run the old North West Jersey Airport back in 1945 and 1946, but these days towing gliders into the wild blue yonder is an extra curricular activity for him.

His major occupation is as an electronics technician working on the Forrestal Research Project at Princeton University, a project engaged in work on nuclear heating.

If you're a rated pilot and would like to get a glider rating, you need two hours of dual and ten solo flights. That's all there is to it. They say if you try it once, you're hooked.

9/26/65

THE BIRTH OF A HEAVENLY IDEA

This story has a very special distinction for me. In more than 38 years of writing an aviation column I've run across many touching stories about pilots who have gone out of their way to help others. These are special people and each story left me with great respect for the pilots who made personal sacrifices to aid people in need of help.

Of all those stories, however, I was more moved by the one that follows than any other. This story explains what made it possible for quadriplegic Ray Temchus, to become a glider instructor.

Although it was almost two decades ago that the idea was born and the two people who gave birth to the idea are no longer active, the program they established to teach handicapped people to fly gliders, is still going strong.

The story of how this came about is the story of two dedicated people, who turned a heavenly idea into a remarkable reality.

It started one day in April of 1980 at the Aviation Week exhibit at the Flemington Mall sponsored by Airborne Arts which ran a glider school at Sky Manor Airport in nearby Pittstown.

Mary DeAngelo, a glider pilot, was at the mall helping out. She talked to people about flying, she explained the workings of a glider, with an enthusiasm that was contagious As she was talking to someone, she noticed a woman in a wheelchair staring at the glider which Airborne Arts had put on exhibit inside the mall.

Mary walked up to the woman and pushed her wheelchair right up next to the glider. "I watched her reaction when she looked at it," Mary said. "Her whole countenance changed. She touched the glider and said, 'All my life I've wanted to fly. But I've been imprisoned in this wheelchair for 25 years,' the woman, a victim of multiple sclerosis, said. 'I'd just love to get in that glider and fly away.' "

There were tears in Mary's eyes as she told the story.

The woman's long-standing dream of flying had never been fulfilled because both her father and her husband considered airplanes to be dangerous.

Irv Soble, a United Airlines pilot who did some voluntary glider instructing for Airborne Arts, was helping out at the exhibit also. Mary brought him over to the woman.

She told him, "I want to fly that airplane."

Irv replied, "I'd be glad to take you for a ride."

"I don't want to go for a ride," the woman said, emphatically.

"I want to fly it."

Since she had no use of her legs, Irv told her he'd look for a hand-controlled glider. If he couldn't find one, he told her, he'd make one.

Irv wrote to *Soaring* magazine, published by the Soaring Society of America. They printed his letter and responses came from all over the world, from disabled people who wanted to fly, from people with ideas about hand controls, from people who congratulated Irv and Mary for their interest in helping disabled people learn to fly.

Mary D'Angelo-Soble and her husband Irv Soble, founders of Freedom's Wings. In the glider are Jay Donovan, front seat, who lost the use of his legs in an accident and instructor Carl Fishler.

And that was the beginning of Freedom's Wings, an organization dedicated to getting disabled people out of wheelchairs and into gliders.

The woman in the wheelchair who started it all, never got to realize her dream. Her family's objections squashed it. Nevertheless, she was responsible for a great many other disabled people realizing their dreams.

We met a number of these people at Sky Manor Airport.

Denny McMains is a book designer who has been confined to a wheelchair since a 1948 bout with polio. He has flown a glider with Carl Fishler of the Bell Telephone System, a volunteer who has helped Irv with Freedom's Wings instructing chores.

Jay Donovan, was a power plane student when he lost the use of his legs in a motorcycle accident 11 years ago. He has made three flights and has gotten to handle the controls again after 11 years. Jay is employed in the records and identification department of the New Jersey State Police Headquarters in Trenton.

Don Wilkens, a junior studying electrical engineering at Rutgers, has been in a wheelchair for three years as a result of a diving accident in which his neck was broken. He lost the use of both legs and has no strength in his left hand.

Irv plans to design a headrest device which will enable Don to operate the speed brakes with his head.

Flight instruction given by Freedom's Wings is free. If the students can afford to make a donation toward their flying time, those donations are accepted. Disabled pilots pay $25 a year to the organization--if they can afford it.

The Kiwanis Club of Phillipsburg has raised $10,000 toward the purchase of a two-place Schweitzer 2-33 glider for Freedom's Wings.

Irv hopes to get other Kiwanis Clubs all over the world to contribute toward the purchase of portable hand controls for disabled students and pilots in their areas.

A second glider, a single-seat I-26, has been donated to Freedom's Wings by Joan Fitzhugh, a psychologist and glider pilot.

The only limitations now on the organization's activities are its limited funds. All officers are volunteers who donate their time and efforts, but there are a lot of expenses related to running a flight training operation.

The group's logo is an empty wheelchair with a glider soaring above it. There is a story behind that logo.

One day, Doug Angel, who operates Sky Dive East, a sky diving operation at Sky Manor Airport, met Irv in the airport's restaurant and told him about one of his sky diving students, Jim McGowan, who was a paraplegic. McGowan, a six-foot-three giant of a man, has played basketball from a wheelchair and serves as chairman of the Committee for the Disabled of the Pennsylvania Governor's Council.

"We took him up," says Irv, "and he went crazy. He was ecstatic. I never saw anybody so enthusiastic about anything. The big thing was that he escaped from his wheelchair.

"We knew of a disabled pilot, Bruce McGhie, flying out of Wurtsboro, N.Y., who had a hand controlled glider. We asked him if we could fly his glider with Jim. He said, 'Sure'.

"We got Jim in the back seat of a Tri-Pacer and flew him to Wurtsboro.

"When we landed and taxied over to the glider parking area, we saw an empty wheelchair. Soaring above it was Bruce McGhie in his hand-controlled glider."

And that was what inspired the Freedom's Wings logo.

10/11/81

Note: *There is a nice footnote to this story. Last New Year's Eve, Irv Soble and Mary DeAngelo, who founded Freedom's Wings, were married. Mary is now Mary DeAngelo-Soble.*

Chapter 4

Hot Air Can Get You Places

Man first took to the skies more than a century before the Wright Brothers flew their fragile, powered aircraft over the sand dunes of North Carolina. The vehicle which first carried men aloft was a hot air balloon.

They lit a smoky fire underneath a big cloth bag and filled it with hot air. They never realized, however, that it was the hot air that made the balloon light enough to lift off the ground carrying people up with it. They thought the smoke gave them the lift.

A lot of pilots still travel through the air today on a big bagful of hot air. Malcolm Forbes, the flamboyant publisher, crossed the country in a hot air balloon, making numerous stops along the way.

Hot air balloonists today heat the air in their colored "vehicles" with propane burners. They can't steer their balloons. They must go where the wind takes them. Headwinds are one thing balloonists never have to worry about. They travel with the wind.

Ballooning is the most colorful form of flying there is. Go to a balloon festival sometime and see for yourself. Those inflated gas bags come in every color of the rainbow and in an infinite variety of designs and patterns. And some of them even have unusual shapes.

WHERE OTHERS FEAR TO TREAD

Some balloon pilots have had truly unforgettable experiences. A few of them are recounted in this chapter.

Before apartheid was eliminated in South Africa, Soweto was the largest all black city in the country. It was a closed city. Strangers were not welcome.

No one, black or white, could enter the city without a permit. Permits were difficult to get. It was virtually impossible if you were white. If you were smart, you didn't even apply for a permit.

The people of Soweto were not particularly enamored of the white people who kept them subjugated. Whites would not find a friendly welcome there.

Richard Michalski wasn't intimidated by the warnings he had received about staying out of Soweto. He managed to enter the city-- and he did it without a permit. He never even applied for one. Here is how it happened.

--—

R ichard Michalski is a man possessed with an urge to go where others fear to tread. This has taken him to some unusual places. He is, for example, probably the only white man ever to enter the all-black city of Soweto, outside Johannesburg, South Africa, without a permit.

The reason Michalski was able to do that is that he didn't enter through the gate. He dropped in out of the sky.

Michalski, you see, is a balloon pilot. He was in South Africa to compete in the first World Hot Air Balloon Championship.

There were 14 entries from 14 different countries. Michalski was there at the invitation and sponsorship of Sealy Posturepedic of South Africa, but he represented the United States in the competition. And he won!

But that victory, as satisfying as it was, was not his most memorable experience in South Africa. His visit to Soweto claims that distinction.

"I wanted to land there," said Michalski, "because everybody warned me to stay out. I remember the warning: 'Whatever you do, stay out of Soweto.' "

That's all they had to tell Michalski. To him, it was an invitation.

"I took off from Baragwaneth Airport, two miles from Soweto. The wind was blowing toward the city. That's why the authorities were concerned."

It was two weeks before the competition and Michalski was carrying a passenger, a white South African woman, on a promotional flight.

"She was really scared when we came down in Soweto," he said.

"A thousand children came running up to the balloon. I carried a small American flag, so they would know I was an American.

"The children spoke Zulu and Swahili. One boy spoke a little English. And several adults spoke English.

"They were very much interested in America. They wanted to know did we all have a lot of money and did we all drive big cars."

Michalski kept his balloon inflated and took dozens of the youngsters for tethered rides. He was especially impressed with how polite the children were. When his chase crew arrived (they let them in, in order to get him out), the children all pitched in to help deflate, pack and load the balloon in the truck.

Richard Michalski

Soweto isn't the only offbeat place Michalski has floated into. A couple of years ago, he came down in the middle of a nudist camp in Pennsylvania.

He was told that if he wished to remain, he would have to disrobe. Michalski was prepared to accept their hospitality, but he was carrying a woman passenger and she took a dim view of the invitation. So they packed up in a hurry and got out of there.

"Actually," said Michalski, "they stared at me more than I stared at them."

But he's used to attracting attention. When he landed in Durban, South Africa, in the competition, a large flock of ostriches came running to gawk at him, he said.

Another unusual landing was on the roof of a home center store in upstate New York. He was doing a promotion for them and he thought that would attract a lot of attention.

Nobody thought he could do it, and of course, anybody who knows him knows that's all the incentive he needs.

He made a careful check of the wind and picked a takeoff point a mile away, calculated to take him right over the store. (In

a balloon, of course, you go where the wind takes you.) In this case
(based on his calculations), it took him right where he wanted to
go.

In addition to winning competitions (he also won a Hound and
Hare competition in Albuquerque, N.M., in 1974) and in staging
shopping centers and store promotions, Michalski and his balloon have
been the feature attraction at birthday parties and bar mitzvahs.

Where will his balloon take him next? Right now he's looking
forward to a competition in Australia under the sponsorship of Avion
Balloons of Spokane, Wash., for whom he is a dealer.

After Australia,   he'll   head for Japan for some informal
ballooning. Occasionally he flies without having a special mission or
challenge, but just for the fun of it.

12/18/77

THE BALLOON THAT DISAPPEARED

A hot air balloon is a pretty tough thing to lose. They're usually seven stories high or more when inflated and they're brightly colored. They're not hard to spot.

But this is a story about a balloon that got lost. Among its passengers was a frail, if gung ho, World War I Ace whose guns had downed five enemy aircraft almost seven decades earlier. How could this happen? Read on.

Few events hold the fascination of a balloon festival.

It is a happening that borders on the surreal. Long strips of colored fabric stretched out on the ground leap to life as they are inflated to reveal their true nature and form, that of a hot air balloon.

At a balloon festival there are dozens of balloons and when they rise from the ground it's like a field full of giant toys springing to life.

Mass balloon ascension

The sight of them is one that evokes the special brand of excitement that a wonderful new toy elicits from a child. This is an excitement that stirs the blood of seniors as much as children.

To augment the visual excitement, sound is added in the form of the spasmodic roar of propane burners heating the air in the balloons' cavernous innards.

As the balloons gather enough hot air, the battalions of them at a balloon festival gently rise skyward with baskets of people dangling below them. It's exciting because it all seems so unreal. It's like something you might see in Technicolor on a wide screen, but not in real life.

There are three aspects of ballooning: the beauty of the slow, silent flight experienced by those carried aloft in the baskets, the uplifting feeling of witnessing a balloon ascension, and the adventure of being part of the chase, or recovery crew that helps pack the balloon into the basket after the landing to return to the point of departure.

World War I ace A. Raymond Brooks, facing the camera, waiting for liftoff on his first hot air balloon flight in 1986.

At one balloon festival from the campus of a New Jersey county college (now Raritan Valley Community College) I inadvertently became part of a chase crew.

When the okay to fly was given, we helped Cindy and Rich Stoneking, both balloon pilots, prepare their all-red balloon for the flight.

We had flown with Cindy at an earlier balloon festival a couple of years prior to this. On this occasion Rich was going to be the pilot. He had two passengers, Lori and Jeff Riner. The balloon flight was a surprise birthday gift from Lori to Jeff.

At the last minute, an unusual passenger joined the flight, a 90-year-old World War I ace, A. Raymond "Ray" Brooks. Since his World War I fighter days, Brooks had flown in everything from a Breezy, a flimsy-looking, open air flying machine, to the supersonic Concorde. He had even flown in a hydrogen balloon--in 1921. But he had never been on a free flight in a hot air balloon.

They were just about to takeoff when Rich agreed to take Brooks aboard to add that experience to the vast variety of flying machines he had flown in. Brooks was boosted into the basket and when the balloon lifted off it had three passengers instead of just two

As soon as balloons take off, their chase vehicles take to the roads to follow them until they descend to a landing.

A balloon's route of flight is entirely dependent on the wind, of course, and they only fly when there is not much of a breeze blowing. So they don't move very fast. Trying to find roads to follow the balloon is sometimes a bit of a challenge for the chase crew even though these sky chariots don't move very fast.

When Cindy climbed into the chase vehicle to follow the balloon, she made a terrible discovery. She didn't have the keys. She knew exactly where they were--in Rich's pocket up there in the balloon. It was obvious, as the balloon drifted away, that the chase car was not going to do much chasing.

I volunteered my station wagon for the mission. However, it wasn't on the launching field where all the other chase vehicles were, but in a parking lot a good distance away.

When Cindy, the chase crew, and I got to the car, we jumped in and took off in search of the red balloon. If Cindy had left from the launch area immediately after takeoff, she could have followed the balloon easily. But by this time it was nowhere to be seen.

The balloons had drifted eastward with a westerly wind. We drove in the direction of the balloons we could see, all of which had taken off after Rich. We stopped from time to time to ask someone if they had seen a red balloon. Nobody had. They had seen dozens of balloons in all colors of the rainbow, but no red balloon.

The missing balloon, which had taken off from a group of baseball fields on the grounds of what was then Somerset County College, with a cargo of four souls, had drifted off into the great unknown.

We turned down one street and up another. We retraced our steps. We passed some balloons returning with their chase crews. But we could find no trace of Rich and the red balloon.

Our search went on and on as we drove up and down main roads and back roads. We drove over the same areas again and again. We saw yellow balloons and gray ones, and balloons of all colors, but no all-red balloon.

At one point, after we had searched the areas over and over where other balloons had landed, we stopped and asked some locals if we could use their phone. We called the inn where the pilots were to attend a banquet after their flights.

Cindy and Rich had agreed in advance to use the inn as a message center if the need arose. We called, but there was no message. We drove on.

We continued to drive back and forth over the roads east of the college, watching the sun sink lower and lower, casting a pretty orange glow in the sky.

A cloak of darkness spread over the land and still we hadn't found the red balloon. A pall of frustration and concern held us in a tight grip. Where were they? Where else could we look? By now we were very concerned about what might have happened to them.

Then we met another search crew heading back with their balloon loaded in their van and they said they had seen a red balloon stretched out in somebody's front yard. We headed in the direction they indicated, but looking for a 75-foot high balloon that has been deflated, under cover of darkness is not the easiest job in the world.

We drove up and down streets in the area pointed out. Still no red balloon. The frustration was now overshadowed by growing concern.

We stopped at another house to ask if we could use their phone to call the inn again. We explained to the lady who answered the door that we were searching for a red balloon.

"A red balloon?" she said. "It landed just on the other side of the bridge over Route 287. The pilot had the keys to the chase car with him" she went on, "so they couldn't come out to get them. My husband drove him back to the college to get the chase car."

She drove down the street with us and over the bridge to make sure we found the balloon. And there it was, stretched out on the grass and the three passengers, including our friend, Ray Brooks, the 90-year-old World War I ace, enjoying the hospitality of the family they dropped in on.

A few minutes later, Rich arrived with the chase vehicle and the balloon was repacked and loaded into the trailer.

It is traditional to break out champagne after a balloon landing. The Stonekings had cheese and crackers and melon to go along with the champagne. We had a wonderful party under the stars.

And so the adventure ended, with raised glasses, smiles, praise for the pilot, exhilaration of the passengers, and much to talk about in years to come.

9/21/86

COWBOY IN THE SKY

The balloon flight described in this column was a very special one for a whole host of reasons. The pilot was a bit different, the balloon was historic and the circumstances surrounding the flight were atypical.

It was, in short, a memorable experience and rereading the account of this flight, after many years brought it all back to life. I trust the account which follows will bring the experience to life for you.

You wouldn't normally go out to an international airport to embark on a hot air balloon flight. That, however, is exactly what I did a couple of weeks ago. And if that was a bit unusual, the flight which followed proved to be memorable in more ways than one.

The airport was Dayton (Ohio) International and it was part of the Dayton International Air Show and Trade Exposition. When you talk about an air show having everything, you're talking about the Dayton show. You don't normally see balloons at an air show. And it's not often you see an air show at an international airport.

Our balloon ride took place on Friday, the second day of the four-day event. Thursday and Friday are trade show days, Saturday and Sunday are air show days.

A notice was posted at the media center inviting those who were covering the show to sign up for balloon rides.

Late in the afternoon the balloonists assembled in their headquarters hotel for a briefing. Daughter Amy and I, having signed up late, were among the few not assigned to a balloonist when the match ups were completed.

The question was then asked if any of the balloonists in the room could take two passengers. A hand in the back of the room went up.

We looked at the body attached to the hand. Surely, this was a mistake. This character couldn't be a balloonist. He wore a cowboy hat, cowboy boots, blue jeans. He had the lean look of a cowboy. You could picture him on a horse, but not in a balloon.

At the end of the briefing we met with the man in the cowboy outfit. His name: Gary Rosenberg. A Jewish cowboy?

He was indeed a cowboy. Not just any cowboy mind you, but a member of the sheriff's posse of Santa Fe, N.M. He had a big sheriff's posse badge to prove it. And yes, he was also a balloonist.

He had driven his pickup truck with his balloon in the back and his crew chief, Carlos Vasquez, up front, 1,500 miles to get here.

The official U.S. Bicentennial Balloon, acquired and flown by Texas cowboy/ sheriff's posse/balloonist Gary Rosenberg of Santa Fe, New Mexico, photographed after a flight which originated at the Dayton Air Show in 1987.

The truck, which served as his chase vehicle, bore a bumper sticker reading: "Some people can chase rainbows. I chase balloons."

For some people ballooning is a sport. For Rosenberg it is a sport, a love, and a living. He earns his daily bread as the operator of Wind River Balloons of Santa Fe, carrying passengers at $150 a person. "It's a ma-and-pa operation," he says, "without the ma."

In the parking lot outside, a caravan of balloonists formed with police escort for the 15-minute trip to the airport.

Here we met David and Joe Kelsey of Dayton, who had been passengers of Gary's in Santa Fe. They were to be part of the crew. David, a Princeton graduate, is a retired Air Force officer.

On the way to the airport, Gary revealed that his was a very special balloon. We would see, he said, when it was inflated.

As the air filled the 80-foot-high balloon and we could read the inscription we saw what he meant. It read: "The Air and Space Bicentennial 1783-1983".

This balloon was especially crafted by decree of President Reagan and was named, "Freedom." It made its first flight from Cape Canaveral, Fla., on the same day the Challenger made its first flight into space.

Since then, it has had a distinguished history, having been flown by the late Ben Abruzzo, one of the three balloonists who made the first successful crossing of the Atlantic in a helium balloon. It also carried Scott Crossfield, the first man to fly at twice the speed of sound, and several other astronauts.

In 1984, the government put it up for sale and Gary bought it with the provision that when he's through with it, the balloon will go to the National Air and Space Museum in Washington.

When flight time arrived, we rose slowly and ever so gently, drifting just a bit as we floated aloft. "Fly gently" is Gary's motto. He had it inscribed on the back of his shirt.

Airliners were taking off to the northeast, into the wind, as we floated in the opposite direction with the wind.

We floated over Vandalia and had a bird's-eye view of the air show parade on Main Street with the sound of a marching band drifting up to us. Then we floated across the Miami River.

The quiet, the peacefulness, the serenity of a balloon ride are indescribable. The occasional roar from the short bursts of the propane burner interrupt the silence of the flight.

"If you talk to passengers after a balloon flight, they never remember the noise, only the quiet," said Gary.

As we descended, we floated just a few feet above the trees. You felt like they were going to scrape the bottom of the basket. There was something almost unreal about it. Then we touched down, feather-like, in a field alongside a pond behind a home.

When the balloon was repacked, the sun had set, and the beautiful pink sky had faded into darkness, revealing the twinkling stars above us, Gary instructed Amy to kneel on the ground in front of him with the crew behind her. And then, by flashlight, he read the balloonist's prayer in honor of her first balloon flight.

> *The winds have welcomed you with softness,*
> *The sun has blessed you with his warm hands.*
> *You have flown so high and so well*
> *That God has joined you and your laughter*
> *And He has set you gently back again.*
> *Into the loving arms of Mother Earth.*

And then, Carlos poured some champagne on her head.

8/9/87

MALCOLM FORBES, BALLOONING'S BEST FRIEND

No one did as much for the world of ballooning as the flamboyant publisher, Malcolm Forbes. His enthusiasm for ballooning attracted a lot of positive press.

He was noted for the creation of highly unusual balloons, many times larger than anyone had seen before.

But size was not the most distinguishing facet of his balloons. It was the shapes. He had balloons fabricated in the shape of the Sphinx, an elephant, a Faberge Egg, Sulleyman the Magnificent, and his chateau in Normandy, Chateau de Balleroy, among others.

His shaped balloons were flown all over the world and they garnered great publicity every time they flew.

Forbes himself was a balloonist. He was the first man to cross the country in a single hot air balloon. He made many stops, the last of which was frightening. He splashed down in the mouth of the Chesapeake Bay. It could have been a disastrous end to his long flight, but fortunately, he came down in shallow water.

I met Forbes twice, although I knew Dennis Fleck, who headed his Forbes Balloon Ascension Division, for a long time. A brief description of our meetings will close this chapter.

The spirit of Malcolm Forbes is alive and well. There were those who saw it floating over the lush green countryside of Somerset County a few days ago.

He would have been 72 this past Monday. Dennis Fleck, who heads the Forbes Balloon Ascension Division, thought the occasion should be remembered in a special way. So he dreamed up a most appropriate means of accomplishing that.

Forbes was famous for many things, not the least of which was his sizable collection of special-shaped balloons. The first was the "Chateau," a balloon that dates back to 1983. It was a huge replica of the 40-room, 18th Century Chateau de Balleroy in Normandy, France, that he bought in 1970.

The chateau, incidentally, was not far from where Forbes was shot in the leg during World War II while serving as a sergeant in charge of a machine gun section. It left him with a purple heart, a bronze star, and slight limp for the rest of his life.

The chateau balloon was like nothing anyone had ever seen before. To watch this gigantic replica of a chateau floating through the sky was a sight to remember. It made headlines all over the world.

Airborne chateaux don't enjoy the longevity of the land-based variety and the huge balloon began to show its age. It began to get mildewed and Forbes decided to build a new airborne chateau. When he died in February 1990, the project was put on the shelf. Several months later, the decision was made to finish it. The new chateau was delivered a couple of months ago.

Denny Fleck conceived the idea of flying both chateaux (the old one was still flyable) in commemoration of Forbes' birthday.

So one evening a few days before his birthday, they flew from Fleck's Yellowstone Balloonport in Whitehouse. It was an event Forbes would have loved.

Forbes, the world's best known balloonist, became involved in the sport in 1972.

Forbes' two "Chateau de Balleroy" balloons, an old, worn one, and a new replacement, were flown together to celebrate his birthday five years after his death in 1990.

"I used to pick him up at 5:45 every morning," said Fleck, who was then his chauffeur, "and drive him to his New York office. He was always at his desk by 7 o'clock.

"One morning, he said, 'We're going to take a detour. I want you to take me to Princeton.' He gave me directions. 'Turn here, go up that road.' It was foggy that morning. We finally came to an open field where a balloon guy was waiting.

"He said, 'We can't fly.' (Because of the fog.) Malcolm was impatient. 'Can't we see it?' he asked. The balloonist agreed to inflate it and tether it to a tree.

"Malcolm was intrigued. 'What do you have to do to fly one?' he asked.

"'I'm an instructor,' the balloon guy said. Malcolm said to me, 'Let's get our licenses.' We started right there, with the balloon tethered. Then the fog lifted and we made a free flight.

"When we got to the office, he ordered a balloon. He also ordered two banners saying, 'Forbes Magazine,' and 'For High Ups in Business.' That was in June. By November, we had our licenses.

"The following April, we went to the Kentucky Derby where they stage a Hare and Hound balloon race, which we entered.

"Malcolm was giving a TV interview in the balloon during the race and he became so distracted he didn't pay attention to his flying. The next thing I knew, we were falling out of the sky. I said, 'Quick, we've got to get some heat on'.

"We gave it everything, but we came crashing down on top of a big tree. The balloon was torn, but the heat began to take effect and we took off again and came crashing down on the other side of the tree.

"One of the judges came up in a helicopter and said, 'I think you've taken second place. I have to measure it.' (The winner is determined by how close they land to a target put down by the hare). We did get second place," said Fleck.

It was at the Kentucky Derby that Forbes met Ed Yost, who invented the modern hot air balloon, and he talked to him about making a cross country balloon flight.

"It had never been done," Fleck said. "By October we were out in Oregon with a balloon he named Chateau de Balleroy.

Malcolm Forbes flying his balloon, "Chateau de Balleroy," over eastern Virginia on the last leg of his record-breaking transcontinental flight on November 6, 1973.

"There were 22 people in the crew. It took 22 flights to cross the country and many of the crew members were given the opportunity to fly one leg with him.

"He set six world records on that trip. One of them was an endurance record of 13 hours, five minutes, and another, a distance record of 312 miles. On those legs, he flew solo," said Fleck. The flight ended in Chesapeake Bay. His son, Robert, was with him. (Robert was not a balloonist. Forbes' youngest son, Tim, is.) They were drifting out toward the ocean so they put down in the bay. Fortunately, the water where they put down was only three or four feet deep.

Forbes always liked to do what nobody else had done. Balloons normally fly from open fields out in the country. He made many flights from the center of world capitals.

"He flew the Sphinx from a park in the middle of Cairo," said Fleck. "He took off in the Bust of Beethoven from downtown Munich. He flew the Golden Temple from a soccer stadium in Tokyo.

"One of the largest balloons ever made was the Santa Maria. It was three times larger than Christopher Columbus's vessel. He flew it from the center of Seville and landed in the middle of a bull ring. The bow touched the wall on one side of the ring and the stern touched the wall on the opposite side."

In 1974, Forbes attempted to fly the Atlantic in a hot air balloon. The takeoff was from California. The plan was to climb to 40,000 feet and get into the jet steam. If all was going well, they would continue on across the ocean. If not, they would land on the east coast.

But a launch accident wiped out the flight. Only an instant release, designed by Fleck, that separated the gondola from the balloon, averted what would likely have been a real disaster.

Incidents like that never fazed Forbes. Not even a little bit. Several years later, he fractured three ribs in a motorcycle accident. Nine days later he was flying the Sphinx at the New Jersey Festival of Ballooning at Solberg Airport when the balloon's crown popped and hot air started leaking. They threw the propane burners overboard to lighten the load. The huge paws which retained hot air, helped slow the descent and although they crashed, no one was hurt.

It is not likely that ballooning will ever find another Malcolm Forbes. But it'll never lose his spirit.

8/25/91

MALCOLM'S FLYING ELEPHANT

Who else but Malcolm Forbes could make an elephant fly? And what an elephant! He (or she) stands 90 feet tall and 90 feet long. Can you imagine how many peanuts it would take to keep an elephant of such proportions happy?

Malcolm Forbes' flying elephant.

Fortunately, Malcolm doesn't have to spend any money on peanuts. His elephant is a balloon that thrives on air--hot air.

Malcolm's elephant was seen by the good people of Thailand, Malaysia, Singapore, and Brunei earlier this year. But it has never been seen in the United States until now.

This weekend that situation will be corrected. Malcolm's elephant will be the star of the New Jersey Festival of Ballooning which will be held at Solberg Airport in Readington.

It is scheduled to fly in the Hound and Hare races which will be launched each evening of the show between 6 and 7 p.m., weather permitting. Participants in the race will be eligible to win two tickets from TWA to anywhere in the world the line flies.

Can you imagine an elephant winning the race? If you can imagine that, how about Malcolm Forbes winning two free tickets to anywhere TWA flies?

At last count, there were 65 balloons registered. So the elephant will face a lot of competition.

7/14/85

A FEW PERSONAL RECOLLECTIONS
(Excerpted from the column of 6/25/95)

For all his wealth and celebrity he was an outgoing guy, easy to talk to. One time as I was driving to Somerset Airport, he landed his balloon in a field in Bedminster near his son Steve's home. I recognized Denny Fleck, who ran the Forbes Balloon Ascension Division, and stopped.

Fleck introduced me to the boss who proceeded to chat away as if we were old friends.

It was the same when I met him the night he was inducted into the Aviation Hall of Fame of New Jersey in 1985. When he was introduced to my wife, Esta-Ann, he kissed her hand as if he were paying homage to the queen.

That was Malcolm Forbes.

6/25/95

LANDING WITH TWO PASSENGERS MISSING

Losing passengers in the course of a flight is not an activity most pilots would want to have anything to do with. But there are exceptions. The story which follows is an account of one of those exceptions.

It is the story of a balloon which took off with six passengers (I was one of them) and landed with only four. I was one of the four.

This flight was a little different. When we landed, the pilot raised a paper cup of champagne along with his passengers and said, "Here's to taking off with six and landing with four."

Not too many pilots ever offer a toast to the loss of two passengers. To those who know Jack Grinton of Bedminster, this was quite in character.

The last time I flew with Grinton, in July of 1977, he had a huge skull and crossbones painted on the side of his balloon (by noted aviation artist Keith Ferris). And at that time, he had only a single passenger, me.

The flight on which he lost two passengers departed from Solberg Airport just before 7 a.m., a few hours before the gates opened for the New Jersey Balloon Festival. The five souls aboard, in addition to Grinton, when we lifted off were Roseanne Quigley of Old Bridge, Jamie Thackaberry of Central Valley, N.Y., Ruben Soto of Brooklyn, N.Y., the fellow pushing these typewriter keys, and a teenager who acts as a third hand when the guy at the typewriter needs a third hand and who takes out the garbage cans on Mondays and Thursdays.

At 6 a.m., when Grinton and his crew began preparing his aircraft for flight, Solberg Airport was colorful, but quiet. The long lines of striped tents looked pretty in the early morning light, but the long lines of humanity that stretched outside them the night before were gone. Rocky Aoki, the major-domo of the Benihana restaurant chain, drove up in a stretched limo. He was apparently going to do some early morning flying, along with about a dozen other groups preparing to go aloft to enjoy Central Jersey's splendid scenery in the early morning sunlight.

It takes about an hour to prepare Grinton's balloon for flight. First you have to pull it out of the big bag it's packed in and stretch it out full length on the ground. That's a lot of pulling and stretching. It's 90 feet, or some nine stories high, when inflated. Then you have to pull the passenger compartment--they call it the gondola--out of the trailer.

The next step is to start a gasoline-powered fan to blow air into this long piece of fabric stretched out flat on the ground. After they've blown a lot of air into it, they light the propane burners and blow hot air into it.

Then, slowly, it stands upright and you can see that this is a hot air balloon.

The previous evening 67 of these big bags of hot air took off in a "race" chasing a bloated elephant full of hot air that stood nine stories high. That was part of the annual New Jersey Festival of Ballooning. There were something like 20,000 spectators waving goodbye and cheering the balloonists onward and upward. This morning, only the ground crew is there to wave goodbye to us as we lift off.

Grinton takes us up to 4,100 feet and two among us, Soto and Thackaberry, decide to say goodbye. Soto climbs up on the rim of the gondola, stands there for a few moments and jumps off backwards.

Balloonist Jack Grinton, left, with members of the West Point Parachute Team, Ruben Soto, center, and Jamie Thackaberry, just before liftoff.

Not to worry, he has a parachute. Soto is a master sergeant with the Special Forces based at Ft. Bragg, N.C., and serves, on detached duty, as an instructor with the West Point Cadet Parachute Team. He has made 125 jumps, but this is his first from a free flying balloon.

After his departure, Thackaberry, a sergeant first class, making his 418th jump, goes over the side in a similar fashion. He has done this once before, last year, from Grinton's balloon.

They are using "squares," a chute that is like an air foil, that they can steer to a landing with great accuracy. We watch them land and then we drift on down to a field in Neshanic Station.

Two pretty young ladies come running across the field to meet us because they heard we serve champagne when we land. They are, of course, correct. But as far as this occasion is concerned, it is a first. No popping of champagne corks. Grinton has installed an in-flight champagne dispenser, similar to what bars use to pour mixers. This is the first time he is using it.

The chase vehicle, with which we have been communicating on a CB channel, arrives shortly with the two passengers who took off with us and landed on their own. They help us initiate the new champagne dispensing system. They do a creditable job. Then we repack the balloon, put it back in the van and it's back to Solberg.

What's an experience like this worth? We couldn't put a value on it. But Grinton does. He says it's worth $150. And he finds a lot of people who agree with him.

He also has something a little bit different to offer--a first class balloon flight. That doesn't entitle you to a seat. It's standing room only, whether you're on a regular or first class flight. There are no seats in the gondola.

The first class flight is known as the "Gourmet Express." Patrons are picked up at their home by a limousine. Dom Perignon 1955 is served by a white-gloved maitre'd prior to departure. The limousine and a catering truck chase the balloon and on landing a table is set and a seven-course meal is served including liver pate, Beluga caviar, a choice of Steak Diane or Veal Oscar, served with two wines.

There is a candelabra, flowers and a serenading violinist. A perfect way to tell your girlfriend or wife you think highly of her. However, you can't do that unless you find two other guys who feel the same way and are willing to share your high spirits with you. The Gourmet Express, at $400 a head, is for a minimum of six.

Do they get many lovers on this heavenly trip? The pilot blushes just a little. "It's mostly corporations," he says.

7/28/85

Chapter 5

Making a Splash!
(Seaplanes)

Seaplane pilots are in a league of their own. They combine the joys of flying and boating and, from their point of view, pilots who fly only land based planes are missing half the fun. They could be right.

Seaplane pilots can land on remote lakes where they can enjoy truly great fishing in places the rest of us will never see, places of awesome beauty and extraordinary peace and quiet, where the only sounds are the songs of the birds, the strange sounds of insects, the breeze rustling through the trees, and maybe a fish jumping out of the water.

To seaplane pilots, splashing down on the water is something special, something you can't compare to a mundane landing on a strip of concrete or macadam.

Alaska is the kingdom of the seaplane. There are more of them up there than any other state in the union, by far. There are all kinds of little towns in Alaska you can only get to by seaplane.

This chapter will give you a little taste of what it is that makes seaplane pilots think they have discovered something special...something awesome.

A FLOCK OF SEAPLANES
DESCEND ON MOOSEHEAD LAKE

The big event for seaplane pilots each year is the fly-in to Moosehead Lake in Greenville, Maine, where the Seaplane Pilots Association holds its annual get-together. Pilots fly in from far and wide on the first weekend after Labor Day.

There are flying competitions, seminars, guest speakers, and a big banquet. It's a birds-of-a-feather event. And it's special because it's shared with others who harbor the same passion for water flying. It's the place where the seaplane fraternity reunite with old friends they only see there and it's the place where they discover new friends with new stories about water flying experiences.

I have enjoyed that experience many times over the years. This is an account of one of the Moosehead events I've attended.

Greenville, Maine—It's a bit early for skiers, but they had a full house up here at the Squaw Mountain Lodge at Moosehead Lake.

They came from Florida and Louisiana, from Minnesota and New Jersey, and across the border from Canada. There were even several people who came from Germany and a Concorde pilot from France. Up here the first weekend after Labor Day belongs not to the skiers, but to seaplane pilots. This was the eighth year seaplane pilots have congregated here from all points of the compass. It's like the swallows returning to Capistrano.

They came together to have a good time, to compete in spot landing contests, water bombing competitions, and other competitive events. They saw some unusual seaplane films, including one on the first aerial crossing of the Atlantic in 1924 by two Army Douglas World Cruisers. Four aircraft had begun the trip, but two were lost, although their two-man crews survived.

And they came to listen to the unrestrained sound of a rock 'n roll band that could make a four-engine jet on takeoff sound like a whispering giant.

They come in such numbers now that Squaw Mountain can't accommodate them all. These are all people who fly for the love of it.

This is the seaplane event of the year and they come here in all sorts of water birds. Each year, some unusual seaplane is here that not many people have seen before. This year it was a rejuvenated twin-engine Grumman Albatross, which is being used by the Smithsonian Institution for research on coral reefs in the Bahamas.

There were a lot more unusual aircraft. Jim Moore of Ho-Ho-Kus, N.J. a commodity broker who holds a jet rating, flew up in a Spencer Air Car, a homebuilt amphibious aircraft named for its designer, who was responsible for the post-World War II Republic Seabee that it closely resembles.

Gathering at the Seaplane Pilots Association annual convention at Moosehead Lake, Maine.

Moore is rather high on this aircraft. There are nine of them flying and he owns two of those, for a total of 22 percent of the world fleet. In spite of his love for them, he is willing to part with one and he gave demonstration flights on Moosehead Lake to prospective purchasers, including a 72-year-old New Hampshire judge who is still an active seaplane pilot.

We flew over the lake with Charles Byran in an aircraft owned by Dr. Wayne Choper, a Highland Park dentist. The view, looking down on the lakeshore with its picturesque coves lined with seaplanes, and the feathery white wake of seaplanes taking off and landing, was breathtaking.

The big event is the Sunday night banquet. There was room for 400 and it was a sellout with lots of pilots looking for tickets that weren't available.

Guest speaker at the event was John Baker, president of the Aircraft Owners and Pilots Association, which now handles administrative functions for the Seaplane Pilots Association. (The AOPA and Seaplane Pilots Association have gone their separate ways since this was written.)

Baker, who was in rare form, talking to people who understand his language, made the point that pilots are generally "lousy salesmen," failing to communicate to their friends and neighbors a true picture of what flying is all about.

"Unfortunately, too many people still think of pilots as Sunday afternoon thrill seekers. That concept went out with the passing of the barnstorming days of the twenties and thirties. But the impressions linger on.

"Today," Baker pointed out, "general aviation flies more miles than the airlines and carries as many people.

"Because pilots are lousy salesmen, they rank high among the nation's most misunderstood minorities.

"General aviation contributes billions to the national economy, hundreds of millions to our balance of trade, provides employment to hundreds of thousands of workers, and helps to keep the wheels of industry turning by providing the fastest, most efficient transportation available.

"And on top of all that, flying is fun. For those who are opposed to general aviation, we have no answer, only pity." Baker said.

He pointed out that it's nice for controllers to hear a thank you. He recalled an old saying about controllers that was once considered apt, but apparently has been forgotten. "We're here because they're there."

The flight to Greenville in my Piper Arrow (460 miles in three hours and 20 minutes) was my second flight since the air traffic controllers' strike. The first, was my trip to Oshkosh, Wisconsin, for the Experimental Aircraft Association Convention. I, like a good number of other land lubber pilots, landed at the Moosehead Lake Airport.

On both flights I found the system to be working smoothly and the controllers to be courteous, efficient, and helpful. Their attitude helped make my flights smooth--and safe.

9/20/81

A TOUCH OF NOSTALGIA AT A SEAPLANE GATHERING

The annual Seaplane Seminar at Lake Piseco in the Adirondack Mountains at Speculator, New York, is the second biggest gathering of the water loving pilots in the east after the Greenville, Maine, fly-in.

You never know quite what you may run into when you attend one of these events. And on one occasion what I ran into was a bit of nostalgia that took me back more than 25 years.

In the following column I shared that nostalgia with the readers of my column.

The old, fire-engine red Taylorcraft is just a shadow of a memory now. It was the first aircraft I ever owned and that was 28 years ago. I didn't buy it. I won it. By putting down some $120 in advance (that was quite a bit of money then) toward flying lessons, I earned a chance to win the airplane. The number on my ticket was 28.

The flight school held a dinner-dance at which they were going to award the airplane. They asked an elderly lady attending another affair in the catering complex that night to draw a number from the hat. And bless her soul, she pulled number 28 and I became an airplane owner. I was still a student pilot.

Taylorcraft 43489 wasn't exactly new, although she looked shiny enough to have just rolled out of the factory. Actually, the fabric on her had seen better days. The coat of high gloss enamel that covered it was probably sturdier than the fabric underneath.

The log book said the engine had something like 6,000 hours on it, which seemed like quite a lot to me, so I asked the fellow who ran the flight school and gave the airplane away, how long the engine was good for. Without a moment's hesitation, he said in a deep authoritative voice, "It'll last forever."

All this came to mind a couple of weekends ago at Lake Piseco, in Speculator, up in the Adirondacks where a reborn Taylorcraft made an appearance at the annual Seaplane Seminar co-sponsored by the FAA and the United States Seaplane Pilots Association, which is headquartered on the Hackensack River in Little Ferry, N.J.

The old Taylorcraft of the 1940s, a two-place, side-by-side aircraft is being manufactured again. There were a few changes. The new bird wasn't red. It was a kind of ivory color. The fabric was good and tight and the engine didn't have 6,000 hours. It had a shade over a hundred hours on it. Under the cowl, the old 65 horsepower putt-putt was replaced by a 100 hp engine.

The desire to fly her again, just for old time's sake, was irresistible, even though she was a water bird mounted on floats, and I'm not seaplane rated.

The man who owned her, wearing a perpetual smile and an old-fashioned peak cap, seemed to be giving everybody rides. So I asked and he said, "Sure."

His name was Mike Hart and he runs Hampton Airfield in North Hampton, N.H.

I told him I wasn't seaplane rated, but he said, "Don't worry about it. It flies itself, " and with that I climbed into the left seat. I fired her up and taxied slowly away from shore and then, under his direction, I opened the throttle and held full back pressure. The nose went way up as we built up speed.

In a few seconds Mike said, "Relax the pressure and she'll fly herself off. I did and she did. With relaxed pressure on the yoke the airplane had a slightly nose high attitude and in just seconds we were off the water and reaching for the sky.

Landing wasn't much more complicated. I glided down toward the water, cut power, and flared, held a little back pressure, as Mike advised, and we settled back down as easily as we took off.

There were a lot of seaplane enthusiasts up there for the weekend. According to FAA Accident Prevention Specialist Ward H. Shandoff, Sr., who played a major role in running the event, there were 550 registrants (and probably a couple of hundred more who were there but didn't register). Of those who registered, 333 were pilots, 192 were seaplane rated.

Sixty-one seaplanes put down on the lake and another 47 land planes put down at Piseco Airport.

Just about every kind of seaplane and amphibian you can imagine was there. It's really rare to see such an assemblage of seaplanes.

Those who were in attendance could not only admire their presence, but they were able to witness demonstrations by experts of how to handle the craft under all kinds of conditions.

There was a lot to be learned and there was a lot of fun as well. They held a water bombing in which contestants had to drop "bombs" (actually bags of flour) on a target in the water from seaplanes flying at 200 feet.

The event created a moment of excitement when one "bomber" narrowly missed an aircraft parked a couple of hundred feet from the target.

Sharon Clark, a right pretty lass from Louisiana, demonstrated how it should be done, as well as what good bombers women can be, when she hit the target and took first place honors.

New Jersey pilots have to come to places like Lake Piseco to see seaplanes because they can't see many back home. In spite of all the water the state has, it's virtually impossible to get landing rights in any lake, river, bay, or inlet. The entire state has only one licensed seaplane base.

New Jersey's a great vacation state, but it doesn't offer much to the seaplane pilots like those who left a pretty fair amount of green stuff up in them thar hills in the Adirondacks.

6/17/79

LEARNING TO FLY SEAPLANES

A lot of pilots have a curiosity about flying on floats. Chances are they've encountered a seaplane pilot some place or other where they were exposed to a brand of enthusiasm that's rare. It makes you want to go out and learn right now.

It took me a long time, however, to get around to it, but the time came when everything seemed to fall into place and I embarked on the road to a seaplane flight school on the Connecticut River. There is a runway right alongside the seaplane base, which is great for land based pilots, but as it turned out, it was not a day to fly, it was wet out there, so we left our wings in the hangar and traveled up to Connecticut on wheels instead of wings. A little wet weather might ground land plane pilots, but it doesn't always faze the seaplane crowd.

Learning to fly a seaplane involves takeoffs and landings, including rough water takeoffs and smooth water takeoffs and there's a big difference. And it involves learning how to navigate the waters under various wind and water conditions. So if the ceilings are low, it doesn't matter. You don't have to get up very high. If it's raining, who cares? While the weather kept my Piper Arrow grounded, it didn't stop the water birds from flying and it didn't stop me from learning to fly one.

And so it was that on one rainy summer weekend, I learned to fly a plane on floats.

Last weekend, you may remember was the kind of weekend you would like to forget. The rains came. And they came. And along with the rains, low ceilings and poor visibility. It was the kind of weekend that turns bustling airports into something that resembles a ghost town.

But seaplane bases, now that's something else again.

Several weeks ago when I spoke with Bill Zambarano, who runs the Goodspeed Airport and Seaplane Base, at East Haddam, Conn., and agreed to take his $195 guaranteed seaplane course, he had said, "If the weather's bad, come anyway. Even if you have to drive. We'll be flying."

One of the reasons for going to Goodspeed is that the airport and seaplane base are together. You can climb out of your land plane and climb right into a seaplane. So I could fly up there in far less than half the time it takes to drive.

Another reason was that an old flying friend, Don Morrison, who used to live up the river apiece in Springfield, Mass., invited us (my wife and me) to spend the weekend at his home in East Haddam to enjoy his big swimming pool and the two acre pond on his property. We could barbecue steaks at poolside. All around it was the kind of offer you couldn't refuse.

And then Saturday dawned with predictions of thunderstorms and showers all day. So we drove.

That meant waking up at five in the morning for a three hour drive instead of getting up at seven for a one hour flight to get us to Goodspeed by nine a.m.

Well friends, it didn't rain, it poured. The ceiling wasn't a thousand feet, it was 400. And while that might mean scrawling "canceled" next to a land plane student's name, it meant no such thing at the seaplane's base. Water, after all, is what seaplane pilots thrive on.

So, we went to work. First a thorough briefing on what seaplane flying is all about--taxiing, dealing with the wind, how to do a preflight inspection for a seaplane. It seemed like that part of the course was going to last forever.

Then, happy day, we are ready to fly.

Step one is pumping out the floats, which is a jolly lot of fun in a pouring rain. There are seven or eight compartments in each float. You remove the inspection cover and pump out each one. Some floats are known to take on some water sometimes and they are known to perform better when the water is on the outside and not the inside.

On to the checking of box wires, bracing wires, struts, and water rudder cables.

And at last, into the airplane. For the $195 guaranteed course, the airplane is a 1947 Taylorcraft, similar to the one I won many years ago and for which I still nourish a twinge of nostalgia.

When I looked at the beautiful green Skyhawk on floats the nostalgia was swamped and we switched to the $295 guaranteed course, which normally requires five to ten hours of flight time for the average pilot.

Before you start the engine of a float plane you go through a check list known as CARS (for Carburetor heat off), Area clear (no boats in front of you), Rudder (water rudder down for idle taxi), and Stick back.

You always hold the stick all the way back in a float plane (except for step taxiing) or you might find yourself doing a somersault which isn't at all pretty in an airplane.

Once the engine starts in a float plane, you're on the move. You can't put on the brakes. So you have to keep heads up all the time.

Most taxing is done at idling speed with the stick or yoke all the way back and the airplane heading into the wind. Generally this is how you taxi a seaplane.

A second kind of taxing is the "plow" taxi.   This requires a little power. It is the least desirable kind of taxiing.

When you're plow taxiing you're kicking up a lot of spray, which is not good for the prop, the nose is high, which is not good for visibility, and you're carrying power, but at slow speed, which is not good for cooling.

There is one other disadvantage I forgot even before taking the flight test--which I managed to pass. (Quick check of notes reveals the other disadvantage is that the plane is more susceptible to the wind when plow taxiing.)

Plow taxi is used to check the mags.

Step taxiing is the third type of taxi in a seaplane. This is a high speed taxi used when there is a long distance to cover. You pick up the water rudders before you start.

Step taxi means you get the airplane up on the step, that is, in a level position, skimming the water. You start with full power, stick back, The spray line from the floats moves back as you develop a little speed, and as it does you ease the back pressure on the stick and let the nose come down. Now the float is in a position where it offers the least resistance to the water, so you cut back a little on power to keep from taking off.

If you keep full power, the aircraft will indeed break loose from the water and take off. And then you may find yourself shouting, "Hey look, I'm flying!"

8/19/79

Chapter 6

Whirlybirds
(Helicopters)

Helicopters are the most versatile flying machines there are. Anything a bumble bee can do, they can do. They can fly backwards and sideways. They can land on a dime. They can take off straight up. No runway needed.

Their versatility has helped save thousands of lives. Helicopters can land on a highway where there has been a serious accident with critical injuries and fly the victims directly to hospitals. They have been invaluable in saving people from the ravages of fire and floods.

Helicopters have been used to rescue seamen whose vessels were capsized by a storm or driven onto rocks in high winds.

They are used regularly in police work and have been instrumental in the apprehension of criminals who might otherwise have escaped. They have helped nail drug traffickers. And hundreds of thousands of motorists are indebted every day to helicopter traffic reports which warn of roads closed by accidents or backed up because of construction so that alternate routes can be sought.

Thousands of tourists have taken breathtaking helicopter tours of natural creations such as the Grand Canyon, and over other exotic places such as Hawaii and Alaska.

While they have a myriad of uses, helicopters are still basically a means of transportation. Executives save priceless hours of travel time by using helicopters. They are also useful in selecting construction sites and in aerial photography. Helicopters lift heavy equipment such as air conditioners to highrise rooftops. Television news watchers see live pictures from helicopters almost every day.

The following stories should give you some insight into the many uses of helicopters.

LIFESAVING FLIGHT REVIVES PERSONAL MEMORIES

The stories of many of the lifesaving missions flown by helicopters are often touching. In one emergency case involving a newborn infant, the pilot knew exactly what the tension and suspense was like. He had lived through a similar experience himself. There were no helicopters available when potential tragedy tapped him on the shoulder. His story is one of those which can arouse the emotions of the most dispassionate individual.

"My first born son was stillborn," the helicopter pilot said. "He was purple when he was born. The medical staff in the delivery room at Peapack Valley Hospital in Westwood worked feverishly to revive him. After ten minutes he was breathing with the aid of a machine.

Chuck Howard in the cockpit of a Port Authority of New York & New Jersey helicopter.

Courtesy of Chuck Howard

"We had to get him to St. Joseph's Hospital in Paterson as quickly as possible because they had the infant life support system there to keep him alive.

"They put him in an ambulance and I followed in my car. There was construction on Route 80 and traffic was backed up. I kept wondering if we were going to make it in time. You can't imagine the tension, the anxiety, the helpless feeling that overcomes you in a situation like that."

A few years later, there was an occasion when the Port Authority of New York & New Jersey helicopter facility at Teterboro Airport received a call from the Westchester Medical Center stating that they had an emergency situation. They had to transport a 6-week-old infant to the Pennsylvania Medical Center in Philadelphia for open heart surgery. They had contacted every commercial and government helicopter operation in the area but were unable to find a 'copter available to fly the mission immediately.

Luckily, the Port Authority had a helicopter on the ground.

The chopper is used on such missions only when all efforts to find a commercial or government 'copter have been exhausted.

One of the pilots on duty was Chuck Howard. Chuck was the father of the little boy who had been stillborn. He was assigned to fly the mission.

"My mind flashed back to my own experience," said Howard. "It was like reliving it all over again.

"When we arrived in Philadelphia we had trouble finding the hospital. Air traffic controllers guided us to the facility."

The next day, Chuck Howard conceived the idea of preparing a directory of all landing places for all hospitals in the tristate area. Some hospitals have helipads, but for many, nearby fields are used in emergency situations.

More than a thousand copies were printed by the Port Authority and distributed to police and medevac units, the Coast Guard, the New York Fire Department, air traffic control towers, and all Port Authority facilities.

On another occasion, a 13-year-old boy was set on fire by another teenager. He was taken to St. Peter's Hospital in New Brunswick. It was a touch and go situation. If the boy were to have a chance, they had to get a surgeon from the burn unit at St. Barnabas Hospital in Livingston as quickly as possible.

The State Police helicopters were grounded by bad weather. Harry Gaynor, president of the National Burn Victim Foundation in Orange, called the Port Authority helicopter facility. They had a helicopter available and they could get off the ground from their base at Teterboro. They picked up Gaynor and Dr. William Fuller at St. Barnabas and flew them to St. Peter's. Dr. Fuller worked intensely for hours. He was successful and the boy's life was saved.

One of the pilots on that mission was Michael Pignataro. He was a helicopter pilot in Vietnam. Four of the five Port Authority 'copter pilots are Vietnam vets. While Pignataro was flying in Vietnam, a 50-caliber bullet tore off his foot. His leg was amputated below the knee. He fought his way back to flight duty with an artificial limb. He still astounds seasoned helicopter pilots with his skill.

The National Burn Victim Foundation will honor him as the Pilot of the Year at their annual awards banquet to be held in September.

Probably no other helicopter in the country flies missions as varied as the Port Authority's. It flies mercy missions and police missions. It is used for executive transport and missions to attract business to the area.

Last spring, a Port Authority helicopter played a key role in the second biggest drug bust in New Jersey. The Drug Enforcement Administration was preparing to make a major drug bust in Jersey City and they needed aerial photos to plan the operation. They contacted the Port Authority Police (the 17th largest law enforcement agency in the United States). The PA helicopter was pressed into service. Since it flew traffic missions frequently in that area it would not attract special attention. They obtained the needed photos which helped the DEA seize 3,315 kilos of cocaine with a wholesale value of $50 million and busted one of the largest drug rings in the metropolitan area.

After a bank robbery at LaGuardia Airport a few years ago, the PA helicopter located the suspect hiding in tall grass. It hovered above him blowing down the tall grass to expose him until he was captured.

When structural damages to bridges in New York threatened their closing, engineers inspected the damage from the air using the PA helicopter. Scaling the bridges' towers and cables would probably have taken weeks.

On several occasions the PA helicopter has been used to avoid major traffic tie-ups. A few weeks ago, protesters attempted to close down the Holland Tunnel to gain attention to their cause. The PA helicopter was used as an aerial communications center. It directed police to areas where protesters were congregating and the police were able to head them off and avert a major traffic tie-up.

A similar incident occurred recently at the George Washington Bridge. With the help of the PA helicopter, police were able to prevent the bridge from being completely closed down.

The helicopter has been used frequently to take executives seeking plant sites on aerial inspections to show them available locations and the outstanding transportation facilities--highway and air--close to the Port-owned Newark and Jersey City port facilities.

The Port Authority operates 28 facilities in the greater New York metropolitan area. Fast transportation between these facilities is often required. The helicopter provides it. It also transports PA executives to and from meetings, saving hours of valuable executive time.

PA helicopters have transported drug and bomb sniffing dogs in emergency situations. Their pilots participate in the regular emergency drills conducted by the National Burn Victim Foundation to be trained and prepared in the event of any mass casualty incident.

A New York newspaper did an investigative story recently to determine how the Port Authority helicopter was being used. The resulting story that appeared in the newspaper that prints, "all the news that's fit to print," did not mention any of the uses described in this column except executive transport inferring that this was the only way the helicopter was used.

The story reported that an employee of the PA had been transported to New York by helicopter to file retirement papers, creating the impression that this was the way the helicopter was normally used. There was no mention of the fact that the employee was given permission to occupy an empty seat on a flight scheduled for other purposes.

Two newspapers outraged by this report, picked up on it. One New Jersey daily ran an editorial referring to the article in the New York newspaper, which did not find a single justifiable use of the helicopter and didn't report that the flight in question was not for the purpose of transporting an employee to file retirement papers.

7/19/92

THE ONLY ESCAPE FROM A FLOOD

Floods are among the most frightening and devastating of natural disasters. As waters rise, routes of escape are cut off. At the same time rescue workers and medical personnel are unable to get to the scene. But for helicopters it's not a problem. And when someone is trapped by rising waters, there is no more blessed sight than a helicopter.

Here is an account of one flood which took place only a few miles from where I live and one in which public officials had called for the closing of the airport which served as a command post for the rescue operations when this devastating flood hit.

Normally, there would have been no one in the office at Central Jersey Regional Airport in Manville at 3:15 in the morning on Friday, Sept. 17, when the phone and a beeper went off at the same time.

However, as a result of circumstances arising from the flood, there *was* someone there at that uncanny hour. When Rich Reinhart, chief pilot for Taft Air, the airport's charter service, headed home to his wife and two-week-old baby daughter in Neshanic Station at 5 p.m. on Thursday, Hurricane Floyd barred his way.

Roads were flooded all over the place. Reinhart had talked to his wife on the phone and he knew that the electricity in his house was out. Understandably, he was anxious to get home. He knew his presence was sorely needed.

He tried desperately to find a way to get there. But there was no way. Everywhere he turned he found the roads flooded. He had no choice. He was forced back to the airport and he slept on the couch.

At 3:15 a.m. the phone and the beeper awakened him. It was the Coast Guard. "Do you have jet fuel?" they asked. "Can you dispense it now?"

In less than an hour, two Coast Guard helicopters based at Atlantic City International Airport came in to refuel at the airport. At 7 a.m. a third helicopter landed. Reinhart, who was not familiar with the fuel truck which dispensed the precious fluid, had to learn fast.

The helicopters airlifted 12 workers from a flooded Elizabethtown Water Company's water-treatment plant. They brought them to the airport which was on high ground and dry. Later, they brought five of them, who were key technicians, to another Elizabethtown plant so that they could keep that one running.

One 'copter picked up a 33-year-old woman who was semiconscious. They airlifted her from a bowling alley parking lot to Robert Wood Johnson Hospital in New Brunswick. Ambulances couldn't get her to the hospital. The helicopters brought in families who were picked up from the second floor of their flooded homes.

Another 'copter surveyed the area and directed rescue workers in boats to areas where people were in most danger. Each 'copter carried a rescue swimmer in a wet suit. These men were lowered by hoist in areas where people needed help.

Ginny Fasanella, who lives in a house adjacent to the airport, and is a member of the American Red Cross in Somerville, received a call asking for her help in setting up a shelter in Bound Brook High School. Bound Brook was the hardest hit community in the area. Its main street was virtually wiped out.

Fasanella's home, next to the airport, was high and dry, but because of flooded roads she couldn't get to the school. Her husband, Dan, and two children, Danielle, 15, and Danny, 10, all Red Cross trained and certified volunteers, were stranded in her mother-in law's house in the middle of nearby Manville.

She walked over to the airport. There she saw families gathered around with no place to go after they had been plucked from their flooded homes. She went home and brought food and drink for the homeless families and crayons for the children.

She was at the airport when the Coast Guard received a call that a man was ill in a car on Route 206. A helicopter went out and picked him up. He was a resident of Warren on his way home from a vacation in Virginia. They brought him to the airport. Fasanella took him to her home to be more comfortable. Having been an EMS worker, she recognized the symptoms of a heart attack. She advised the Coast Guard and they medevaced him to the Robert Wood Johnson Hospital. She heard later that he was doing well.

At 9 a.m., Central Jersey Regional Airport ran out of jet fuel. The airport had been fueling from a truck that held 2,000 gallons. The helicopters had to go to Somerset and Princeton Airports to refuel. Time that might have been spent helping people in trouble was spent in transit.

Two 6,000-gallon, federally-approved tanks which had cost the airport $150,000 dollars, had been on site for two years, but were never installed. The town of Hillsborough and the state had issued permits for their installation, but because of protests from a small, vocal group of neighbors, both the town and the state revoked the permits they had issued. So as a result of protests from a few neighbors, when the flood emergency struck, the tanks were empty.

"We refueled three helicopters twice," Reinhart said. "We had 540 gallons on hand and by 9 o'clock we had dispensed it all. If our two 6,000 gallon, double-walled tanks, which met all government standards, had been installed, the Coast Guard might have been able to help more people."

It was only a quirk of fate that had Reinhart at the airport when the emergency call came in at 3:15 in the morning. If the approved tanks had been installed, they wouldn't have needed to reach anyone at the airport. They are self service units which are able to dispense fuel 24 hours a day with the use of a credit card.

The mayor of Manville, who has called for the closing of the airport because of the constant protests from the same small group of neighbors, said, after it was pointed out what a vital role the airport had played in the emergency, "It's a shame the airport is trying to use this as justification to stay open. It's not the time or the place."

10/10/99

HELICOPTERS SERVE STATE POLICE WELL

State police use helicopters in a variety of roles. They have been used to track criminals, make drug busts, provide security. But one of the most important roles has been their use for medical evacuation or medevac missions.

The following column was written shortly after the New Jersey State Police Medevac Unit was launched a quarter of a century ago. Since then the unit has flown thousands of missions and saved countless lives.

Even when it was brand new it performed a wide variety of missions as this column indicates.

An elderly man had wandered away from a nursing home in Lincoln Park and had not returned. He was not in the pink of condition and there was grave concern for his well being.

A search of the area was undertaken, but it turned up no trace of the man.

One of the New Jersey State Police Medevac helicopters was called in. This was one of three helicopters which went into service on July 1 in the state's first organized Air Rescue Medical Evacuation program.

In a short time the helicopter spotted the old man in a swampy area not far from the nursing home. It was an area only accessible by helicopter. If the Medevac unit that had gone into service only a few weeks before, had not been called upon, it is very likely that the old man would not have been found in time to rescue him from the swamp.

This is only one example of the type of missions this unit was designed for.

"We have performed blood and organ relays," said Lt. Robert W. Hoy, commander of the New Jersey State Police helicopter unit that includes the new Medevac unit.

In one case when a special type of blood was needed quickly, it was transported by one of the unit's helicopters in about five minutes. Using the roads it would have taken about 45 minutes to deliver.

Medevac helicopters will be used to reach seriously injured accident victims, particularly in cases where traffic jams would prevent an ambulance from reaching the scene quickly.

Helicopters make it possible to take seriously injured victims to major medical centers immediately, bypassing local institutions which might not have the equipment or staff to deal with life threatening injuries.

Medevac units are also used to transfer premature infants to specially-equipped nurseries where they will have a better chance of surviving the first days and weeks of life.

The Medevac unit has commenced operations with two Jet Ranger helicopters equipped to carry two litter patients and one attendant, and one helicopter that can carry three litter patients and two attendants.

Medevac pilots are required to have Emergency Medical Technician training so that they are competent to provide emergency first aid treatment on the scene in the absence of medical personnel.

There are currently four pilots in the Medevac unit with such training.

Trooper Charles Homeijer of Boonton, one of the four pilots in the unit, described the emergency equipment carried in the 'copters. It includes fold away litters, oxygen tanks, and portable suction units.

A veteran of the Vietnam conflict, in which he flew helicopters for more than a year, Trooper Homeijer has been in the State Police ranks for seven years and has been flying State Police helicopters for two-and-one-half years. Troopers are required, incidentally, to have at least two years of general service before they are eligible to fly helicopters.

The New Jersey Medevac unit was in the planning stage for 13 months before it became a working reality, according to Lt. Hoy. It took the combined efforts of a number of state agencies to get it organized.

Under present regulations only a member of a first aid squad or a police officer can put in a request for a Medevac helicopter.

The 'copters operate from the Helicopter Bureau's secondary base at the State Police maintenance facility in Bedminster Township. The headquarters are at Mercer County Airport.

Lt. Hoy is anticipating a substantial increase in the number of calls in the months ahead. He bases this on the experience of a similar unit which has been in service in Maryland for some time. Last year, according to Lt. Hoy, the Maryland unit answered 2,000 calls.

9/3/78

THE EYE IN THE SKY

If you've ever found yourself stuck in traffic on your way to work, you very likely have a healthy respect for helicopter traffic reporters. One of the best known is George Meade, an ex-Vietnam War 'copter pilot. George covered the traffic scene for New York's radio station WOR from Helicopter 710 *for many years.*

George used to do morning and afternoon traffic reports. On one occasion I joined him on his evening rounds. It was the kind of experience you don't soon forget. The following column was an account of that flight.

L iftoff was at 4:46 p.m. Before you could say, "There's an accident inside the airport (LaGuardia) near 94th Street, ambulances and emergency vehicles are on the scene," we were soaring along over New York City doing a cool 70 miles an hour.

And there, spread out before our wondrous eyes, like something unreal, something out of another world, was this sprawling complex of buildings and highways and bridges that eight million people call home and millions more call unbelievable.

I was flying with George Meade, WOR's loquacious traffic reporter in this glass bubble with a huge fan on top, known to millions of radio listeners as *Helicopter 710.*

Down below as we flew over Queens, Manhattan, New Jersey, the Bronx and Brooklyn were dozens of arteries, leading in and out of the island of Manhattan with some 600,000 cars carrying 850,000 people who wanted to get home after another day's work.

George Meade flying Helicopter 710.

Some of those arteries showed a pretty healthy circulation. Some looked like terminal cases. It's the humanity locked into those terminal cases that looks to George for salvation, much as a seriously ill patient might look to their doctor for a miracle.

George can't produce miracles, but he can tell you, as he did when I was flying with him, not to take Route 46 to the George Washington Bridge because it's backed up, but to take Route 80 instead. The driver who saves a half hour of bumper-to-bumper traffic can be pretty thankful for that advice.

Immediately after lifting off from the Butler ramp at LaGuardia Airport, George spotted the accident within the airport boundary mentioned above.

Then we flew over the Grand Central Parkway, over the Triborough Bridge, down the East River, past Gracie Mansion, where the mayor of all the city lives, and then over the stately west tower of the 59th Street Bridge.

As we approached the Wall Street area, George pointed out a particular building on our right. "Look at the roof," he said. "There's a replica of an old World War I Spad sitting there on an astroturf runway."

That is what you see when you look down on 77 Water Street.

We flew over the Statue of Liberty so low you felt like you could reach out and touch that gentle lady's face.

Then up the Jersey side of the Hudson River for a look at the Holland Tunnel entrance (not too bad) and the Lincoln Tunnel (not too good) and over the George Washington Bridge ("Take the lower level. It's better.")

On the way up the river we cross over to fly right above the brand new Cunard *Princess*, tied up at the pier where she was christened by Princess Grace earlier that afternoon.

George likes to pepper his air time with descriptions of unusual sights and with little anecdotes and stories. He enjoys getting a chuckle in whenever he can.

"This job could get boring," he says.

But it never does. George is full of enthusiasm for what he's doing and he communicates it. He generates a feeling of excitement for his traffic reports.

"If I tell a little joke and there's somebody down there who laughs, and feels that I told that joke just for him, then I'm achieving what I want to achieve," says George.

"I don't think I should take this job too seriously. I have a job to do for all the people down there on the roads during rush hours, but I think I ought to offer a touch of entertainment, too."

There are less than 50 traffic helicopters in the country, but only in relatively few cities does the pilot do the reporting also. In most cases, it's a two person job, a pilot and a reporter.

This month, incidentally, if you tune in from 4:30 to 6:30 in the evening, you won't hear George. You'll hear "Fearless" Fred Feldman. George is flying the morning shift from 6:45 to 8:45 and you can hear him if you tune in the John Gambling Show, America's Number One radio wake-up show.

The late Fred Feldman was George's predecessor. He flew helicopters in Korea and also flew military jets. He was the second helicopter reporter in the nation and the first in the east.

After we fly over the George Washington Bridge, we come over the south Bronx with Yankee Stadium looking like a big blue flower blooming in the middle of a scarred battlefield.

From the Bronx we fly out over Queens past Shea Stadium, the old World's Fair grounds, and over the Brooklyn-Queens Expressway.

The second time around, the Cunard *Princess* is sailing down the river looking as pretty as the lady who christened her.

The third, and last time around, the sun is setting and the World Trade Center Towers look sort of eerie from the east, sticking up out of the mist with a red ball of fire between them.

Up the river one more time and then back to LaGuardia Airport where George settles *Helicopter 710* on the tiny dolly from which we took off a short two hours ago.

"You have to have the greatest job in New York," I tell George. He smiles. He knows it.

4/10/77

AIR TRANSPORTATION FROM THE FRONT DOOR

Flying is the most efficient form of transportation because it takes travelers directly to where they want to go. Aircraft don't have to take circuitous routes around lakes, or mountains, or even big cities.

But helicopters are the most efficient of aircraft since they can fly point-to-point. They don't need airports or runways. That can eliminate the need to drive to the airport, which can be a long way off. Many major corporations have helipads right outside their headquarters. The executive can walk outside his office and be in the air almost immediately. It saves top level executives hours of valuable time. These are the men who keep our economy humming.

The following column written in the 70s, when the advantage of replacing the limousines on the road with the limousine of the air--- helicopters---was just beginning to be recognized. It illustrates some of the uses to which businesses put helicopters.

Though helicopters make headlines most frequently because of their use in dramatic rescue operations, their most rapidly expanding use is as a business tool. In an era when corporate operations are far-flung and key executives must move around a lot and still make the most efficient use of their time, the point-to-point capabilities of the helicopter are a strong selling point.

Public Service Electric & Gas Company, the state's largest utility, provides a good example of how the helicopter serves industry. PSE&G is building a huge nuclear generating station in Salem, near the very bottom of the state, about 119 air miles from corporate headquarters in Newark.

The company's engineers are based in Newark, but naturally, their presence is frequently required on site. Driving takes close to five hours round trip. Using the company's Gazelle helicopter it's a 45 minute ride from the downtown Newark heliport on the Passaic River, two short blocks from corporate headquarters, to the construction site.

Public Service has nine generating stations throughout the state. Each has a licensed heliport so if it is necessary to get personnel to any of them in a hurry, they can fly by helicopter and land right on the site.

Public Service also uses its helicopter in aerial site surveys. The company has long been active in trying to attract desirable new industry to the state. Helicopter tours for executives considering a location in New Jersey are most effective.

PSE&G flies its Linden-based Gazelle about 500 hours a year.

Before purchasing the 'copter in 1974, the company's aviation administrator, Doug Benner, conducted an exhaustive feasibility study and economic analysis to determine the value of such an investment to the overall corporate operations. The results of those studies have been substantiated many times over since the helicopter went into service.

Another corporate Gazelle based at Linden Airport is owned by Purolator, that makes its headquarters in Piscataway and has its product division, that manufactures filters, in Rahway.

Corporate executives frequently have to travel from New Jersey to other corporate facilities in Pennsylvania.

"It's a three-hour drive from Piscataway," says the company's chief helicopter pilot, Ron Beam. "And even if we used a fixed wing aircraft, we couldn't save much time because the nearest airport is at Hazelton, 45 minutes away from our plant. With the helicopter it's possible to land right at the plant.

"Not only are personnel transported in the Gazelle, but frequently important papers and documents must be delivered as quickly as possible and the helicopter is pressed into service for that purpose."

Helicopters are very often an indispensable tool. Schiavone Construction of Secaucus is working on subways in Manhattan and Queens and by using helicopters, executives of the company can get to the work sites in five or ten minutes instead of an hour or an hour-and-a-half on the road.

At the same time the company is doing highway construction work in New Jersey and is working on a water treatment plant in Parsippany. Executives can get from one site to the other in minutes.

"It's the most flexible and productive means of transportation we can use," said George Reinstra, chief pilot for Schiavone.

9/26/76

Chapter 7

Big Fat Little Blimps and Their Big Sisters
(Lighter-Than-Air Flying Machines)

They're big and fat, but they can turn a playboy's eye. They're slow as a snail, but they can capture the attention of a racing fan.

What's their secret? Maybe it's because nothing that big should be able to float through the sky, with people in it.

Maybe it's because no flying machine should be able to move so slowly. Or maybe it's because those big fat flying machines are such avid sports fans. They never miss any of the big sporting events.

I speak, of course, of blimps, specifically the Goodyear blimps. Two decades ago, when the following column was written, if you saw a blimp floating by, it had to be a Goodyear blimp. There wasn't much competition.

Today, there are a number of companies producing blimps. But there's still something special about the Goodyear blimp.

Back in the 20s and 30s, the skies played host to the blimp's big sisters, the dirigibles.

These were huge, sleek, lighter-than-air machines that could, and did, fly across the Atlantic carrying dozens of passengers. There were state rooms, dining rooms, and a passenger lounge. Ninety-seven passengers were aboard the German dirigible Hindenburg when it exploded while landing at Lakehurst, N.J., on May 6, 1937. Twenty-two crewmen and 13 passengers died in the disaster. This brought the era of giant dirigibles to an end. The blimps, however, survived and they are still part of the flying scene today.

SHE'S NOT BEAUTIFUL, BUT EVERYBODY LOVES HER

Everybody, it seems, wants to go for a ride in a blimp. Companies that operate these unlikely aerial chariots are constantly besieged with requests for a ride. Since there are generally only six seats in these flying whales, the number of people who have flown in one is not overwhelming.

If you happen to be an aviation writer, you probably have a better chance of wangling a ride than the average guy who buys Goodyear tires, especially if you plan to write a column about it. And so it was that one day I got to ride in one of those lumbering airborne whales.

For those who have not been so lucky, the column which follows includes an account of my flight, which I shared with those who could not experience it first hand.

There is little doubt that it is among the most familiar aircraft in the world. It's been seen on TV by millions of sports fans.

Is it the fastest? No. It's among the very slowest.

Is it trim and attractive? Negative. It looks like a pregnant pig.

Well, is it big? Yes, indeed.

Does it carry a lot of people? Six.

Is it jet powered? No. It has two small piston engines.

Is it safe? Yes. It's the safest type of aircraft in the world.

Is it something new? No. It's 60 years old.

If there's anyone out there who hasn't guessed what we're talking about, we'll tell you.

It is, of course, the Goodyear blimp, more properly blimps. There are three of them that tour the United States and a fourth based in Europe.

Millions have craned their necks to watch these overblown flying machines gliding over New York City, Boston, Chicago and Los Angeles, and dozens of other cities. Hundreds of millions more have had a bird's eye view of major sports events from these blimps, as well as watched them on their TV screens as they drifted over sports stadiums.

In the 60 years Goodyear has been operating blimps, they have carried more than a million passengers without ever scratching one. You couldn't say that for roller skates, or rowboats.

As aircraft go, the blimps are monsters. They are nearly 200 feet long, 59 feet high, and 50 feet wide. Each of the blimps has an electric sign, that just about everybody in the world must have seen by now. It has 7,500 bulbs in red, green, blue and yellow, that flash messages and cartoons via a computer that triggers some 40 million on and off instructions in a six minute show that is visible up to a mile away.

You may wonder what it's like to fly in one of these machines. I did, too, until the *Enterprise N1A* was based in New Jersey several weeks ago.

Through the courtesy of Captain Mike Fitzpatrick of Newport, R.I., a seven year veteran of blimp flying, I had the opportunity to find out.

It's different.

It's not like an airplane in which you have to get up a good head of steam before you can become airborne. The blimp lifts right up without much forward speed.

It's not like a glider. The blimp has two engines out there and they let you know they're there.

It's not like a hot air balloon. You

A Goodyear blimp flying over the Reading (Pa.) Air Show.

can steer a blimp and you have a seat (although there are no seat belts). You don't stand up in a wicker basket and go fancy free wherever the wind chooses to take you.

As we took off from Teterboro Airport we slipped slowly through the sky over Giants Stadium at an altitude of only a couple of hundred feet. The scoreboard screen flashed a big "Welcome." That sure can make you feel wanted.

Then we headed for the Hudson River.

To demonstrate what flying the blimp was like, Captain Fitzpatrick pointed the nose of the big bag of gas down at a very jaunty angle. He held it there for what seemed like a very long time.

"How much altitude do you think we lost?" he asked.

We shrugged.

"If you were in an airplane, you would have lost 300 feet," he said. "We lost 30 feet." Things happen very slowly in a blimp.

"Come on up here and try it," Fitzpatrick said. So I slid into the pilot's seat.

The two directional controls are a huge set of rudder pedals to turn the nose right or left, and to the right of the pilot, a large upright elevator wheel to point the nose up or down.

I decided to play with those controls. I pushed the left rudder pedal and it felt like nothing was happening. But eventually the nose did begin to turn.

We were approaching the Hudson and Fitzpatrick said take her down river, so I pressed the right rudder pedal. Slowly, ever so slowly, the nose moved right.

The two engines turning the props out there were 210-hp Continentals. "The same engine that's on the Cessna Skymaster," Fitzpatrick said.

If you open them wide, you might do 50 miles an hour.

That's top speed. Cruise is 35. There's one thing to be said for that. You can't beat it for sightseeing over New York.

We floated over lower Manhattan peering down on the rooftops and the traffic below from an altitude of only a couple of hundred feet.

I turned north and there below us was a big "100" painted on the side of a white building with a smaller "Avenue of the Americas" beneath it. It's kind of hard to get lost with guideposts like that. A little further north and there's Washington Square Arch at the foot of Fifth Avenue, with the park stretched out on both sides of it.

Then past Madison Square Garden which looks like a big round layer cake.

We look down at the web of roads converging into the Lincoln Tunnel and I recall the times I have been stuck in the same spot on one of those roads for a half hour or more.

A little further uptown we fly directly over the carrier *Intrepid*, looking straight down at the flight deck. Then, back across the Hudson to land.

Captain Fitzgerald slips back into the pilot's seat. On the first try the wind shifts a little and we are not straight into it. He opens the throttles, points nose up, and around we go for another try. Yes, they do go-arounds in a blimp.

The second time around it's a perfect approach. All kinds of humanity is down there waiting to grab the ropes that hang from the nose.

It takes a crew of 23 to keep this thing going. There are five pilots, 16 ground crewmen and a public relations man for each blimp, plus a crew bus, a tractor-trailer and a van.

Goodyear never charges for the use of the blimp. It gets

Goodyear so much exposure, it's got to rank as one of the best public relations and advertising promotions ever conceived.

11/13/83

THE MYSTERY OF THE HINDENBURG'S FATE

The world of aviation has been intrigued for years by two great mysteries, the disappearance of Amelia Earhart over the Pacific, and the fire that destroyed the dirigible Hindenburg as she was mooring at Lakehurst, N.J., after a crossing of the Atlantic. Oddly enough, both incidents occurred in 1937, just a couple of months apart.

The Hindenburg was destroyed by flames on May 6 and Earhart disappeared on July 2.

Many books have been written about both. The books about Earhart's disappearance on the leg of her around-the-world flight that would have taken her to tiny Howland Island in the Pacific, are filled with all kinds of wild theories. It is generally believed today that she missed the island because she could not establish radio communications with the Coast Guard cutter Itasca. They could hear her, but she couldn't hear them. They heard her report that she was low on fuel.

There were a great many theories about the Hindenburg's fate as well. One was that the airship was sabotaged. Dr. Douglas Robinson, a New Jersey psychiatrist, who is an expert on dirigibles and has written several books about them, does not go along with the sabotage theory.

The following column detailed some of his opinions on the Hindenburg disaster and offers a good bit of information on the huge lighter-than-air ships of the thirties.

Though it's been 47 years since the era of the giant dirigible came to a blazing end at Lakehurst, there is still talk of a revival and there are still those who contend that it was sabotage that caused the destruction of the *Hindenburg*. Articles, books, and a television drama have been devoted to that theory.

Dr. Douglas Robinson, a Pennington psychiatrist, scoffs at that idea. And when Robinson talks about dirigibles, he's worth listening to. He is probably the leading authority on lighter-than-air-craft in the country--maybe the world.

It is Robinson's belief that if there had not been a rather blistering argument between Dr. Hugo Eckener, Germany's leading dirigible authority, and Capt. Ernest A. Lehman at the conclusion of a propaganda flight by the *Hindenburg* a year earlier, the Lakehurst disaster might never have occurred.

The flight was made at the request of Hitler's propaganda minister, Joseph Goebbels, to drop leaflets and aim loudspeakers at the ground exhorting the Germans to vote for Hitler.

Lehman, who was in command, made a downwind takeoff and in the process severely damaged the lower vertical fin of the *Hindenburg*. The airship flew its mission for two hours in spite of the damage, and when it landed, Eckener was waiting and was furious. The result of the argument was that Eckener, who hated the Nazis, was kicked upstairs and stripped of authority and Lehman, who courted the Nazis, was named director of operations.

How could that have affected the disaster at Lakehurst?

"Just prior to the outbreak of the fire during the Lakehurst landing, the *Hindenburg* made a sharp turn into the mast which could have snapped a bracing wire, and that could have slashed open a gas bag," said Robinson.

"Eckener was a very conservative man. If he had been in charge of operations and training, chances are such a sharp turn would not have been made."

Most of the witnesses to the disaster were in the landing area,

The giant dirigible Hindenburg going up in flames on May 6, 1937 at Lakehurst, N.J.

but Robinson spoke to a Princeton couple who saw it all from the gate some distance away.

"They saw a blue flame shoot across the top of the *Hindenburg* just prior to the fire and commented about it. That probably would have been static discharge," Robinson commented.

"The *Hindenburg* was tail heavy when she came in," he said, a pretty good indication of a gas leak in the tail.

Lehman was aboard the flight and although he walked away from it, he died two days later.

"I talked to Capt. Max Preuss, who was in command, and he believed sabotage caused the fire. But that theory exonerated the crew."

Up until the *Hindenburg* accident, commercial airships carried 354,265 passengers without any injury. Thirteen passengers and 22 crewmen died in the *Hindenburg* fire.

Robinson, who has written three books on lighter-than-air

(LTA) craft and will have a fourth published next spring by the Smithsonian Institution Press with a co-author, is a visiting lecturer on LTA craft for the National Air and Space Museum. He is fluent in German and has gone through all the flight logs of the German Navy airships of World War I, several of which were used to bomb England.

His interest in dirigibles began in 1923 when he was just five years old.

"The *Shenandoah* flew over our house in Weston, Mass., and I never got over it," he said.

"My father, who was a law professor, was violently opposed to my interest in aviation and wouldn't tolerate anything connected with aviation. But in 1939, when he was in Europe for four months, I soloed a glider. Two years later, when I was in Harvard Medical School, I got my glider license."

Robinson now holds a Silver C Soaring Badge and owns a Schweitzer 134 sailplane, that he flies regularly out of Sky Manor Airport in Pittstown.

He also owns a 1952 Cessna 170B, that he bought in 1965 and keeps at Twin Pines Airport near his home.

His first writing effort on the subject of lighter-than-air craft came when he was in prep school. A friend loaned him the official British list of German zeppelins that had attacked England. He wrote a term paper on it. He was 17.

At 19, he went to Europe and made his way to Friedrichshafen, home of the zeppelin works. There he met Harold G. Dick, an American who worked for Goodyear as a liaison man in Germany from 1934 to 1938. Dick took him on a tour of the *Hindenburg* sister ship, the *Graf Zeppelin II*, which Herman Goering, who hated airships, later ordered destroyed.

His forthcoming book, *The Golden Age of the Great Passenger Airships, Graf Zeppelin and Hindenburg,* is based on eight notebooks of correspondence (and sketches) with Dick.

Robinson's first book, *The Zeppelin in Combat*, is based on microfilm copies of the World War I German Navy archives that are in the National Archives in Washington, D.C. It was first published in England in 1962 and after two subsequent editions there, was published in the United States in 1980 by the University of Washington Press.

He traveled to Germany to talk to some of the men who flew in those ships, including an old nightclub operator in Heidelberg who survived a 12,000-foot fall in a dirigible set afire by British incendiary ammunition fired from a British plane.

His second book, *Giants in the Sky,* contains a lot of information on Count Ferdinand Zeppelin, founder of the Friedrichshafen Zeppelin works, much of which appeared previously only in German publications. *Giants* was published in England in 1972 and the United States in 1973. His third book, *Up Ship,* written with Charles Keller, is about the U.S. Navy rigid airships from 1919 to 1935. It was published in 1982 by the Naval Institute Press.

As an expert on dirigibles, does Robinson agree with those who think rigid airships will make a comeback? In a word, "No."

"Economically, dirigibles are not viable," he said. "They were subsidized in their day. Peter Brooks, an English author, has pointed out that if the *Hindenburg* came back, it would carry 100 passengers across the ocean while a 747 was making seven round trips carrying 350 passengers or more on each trip."

12/9/84

Chapter 8

Look Out Below
(Sky Diving)

To most of us, airplanes are vehicles to get us places. But there are those who look at them as something to jump out of.

If you visited a jumping school, you would be surprised at the number of students you would find there. You might also be surprised at the makeup of the student body. While you might think of this as a sport for big, bruising macho men, you would probably find more women than men. And most of those women look as if they wouldn't weigh a hundred pounds if they were holding ten pounds of groceries.

Parachute jumping has really become an archaic term these days. The proper terminology is now sky diving.

A book about general aviation wouldn't be complete without a story or two about people who jump out of airplanes. So here are a few.

40 YEARS OF JUMPING OUT OF AIRPLANES

Leaping out of airplanes is not exactly a sport everyone would jump at. But there are a lot of people who think it's the way to go.

It's not a sport with the leisurely, deliberate pace of golf. But if a hole in one has its kicks, so does jumping out of airplanes.

President George Bush the First did it in 1944 in the Pacific with a little encouragement from the Japanese. He did it again in Texas to celebrate his 75th birthday without even the encouragement of his wife.

So if you're ready to say people who jump out of airplanes are crazy, remember, you're talking about our 41st president.

Not all jumpers have been presidents, but here are a few rousing stories about some lesser known aficionados of the sport. The following story is about a jumper who stayed with the sport for 40 years.

If someone says to you, "I've climbed down a couple of trees I never climbed up," it's a pretty good bet you're not talking to a tree surgeon.

Put your money on the space marked "Parachute jumper" and the odds are you'll come up a winner.

Dick Mascuch is congratulated by jumpmaster Mindy Mihalik after a jump in celebration of his 40th Anniversary as a parachutist.

The odds are pretty good also that anyone who has been jumping out of airplanes for 40 years has seen the top of a tree from a bird's perspective once or twice.

So we asked Richard Mascuch (ma-shoo) of Morristown if he ever landed in the tree tops.

"It has happened," he answered, rather sheepishly.

Dick Mascuch made his first parachute jump on Nov. 24, 1942, at the parachute school in Ft. Benning, Ga. He served as a member of the 551st Parachute Infantry as a Rifle Platoon leader.

A week ago Saturday, Mascuch came out to Sky Dive East, the parachute center at Sky Manor Airport, to celebrate the 40th anniversary of his first jump.

He celebrated by donning a white jump suit (so that's where the name came from) with a patch reading "POPS" on it, to make his 277th jump.

"POPS" is not a reference to his being a father or grandfather. It stands for Parachutists Over Phorty Society, an elite group of parachutists who have passed their 40th birthday and have made at least one jump. Mascuch, since he is 62 and a grandfather, is quite eligible. There are about 1,000 members in the group. Dick is No. 38.

"I know one fellow who made his first jump at 56," Mascuch said. "And didn't quit till he was 76. He was a retired schoolteacher."

Mascuch is a real youngster by comparison and he is not quite ready to quit, although he doesn't jump very often these days.

"When you haven't jumped in awhile and you come out to make a jump, you ask yourself, 'Why am I doing this?' But the minute you leave the plane you know. It's fun."

It wasn't all fun when he was initiated into the fold. His outfit was formed in the Canal Zone and went on to see service in Africa, Sicily, Italy, and France. They jumped into southern France as part of the First Airborne Task Force.

Mascuch, who held the rank of first lieutenant and saw service in the Battle of the Bulge in Belgium, came home with two purple hearts. After his discharge in 1946, he didn't don a parachute again until 1964. "I wanted to make a free fall," he said, "so I went out to Kupper Airport in Manville."

It was fun, so he stayed with it. His log book shows nine jumps into the Atlantic Ocean and one into Greenwood Lake which stretches across the New York-New Jersey border.

He made seven jumps out of a glider when he was in the military and he was part of the first mass parachute jump from gliders in history at Ft. Bragg, N.C.

He's also made a couple of night jumps.

Today, he jumps for fun.

"It's nice to come down with guys you know," he says. "It's lots of fun. I enjoy being at the airport with younger people sitting around in the sun. You find out some guys are doctors, roofers, iron workers, artists, stock brokers." And there are a lot of women jumpers.

At Sky Dive East, 1,300 people made their first jump this year. A first jump course takes four hours and costs $125. After that each jump is $25 including equipment, the airlift, etc. Student jumpers all have radios so they can receive instructions from the ground.

When he's not jumping, Mascuch's favorite pastime is ice skating. He and his wife, Olga, have skated in many shows at the South Mountain Arena in West Orange, starring such champions as Peggy Fleming, Janet Lynn, and Dorothy Hamill.

If you saw the smile on his face when he hit the drop zone on his 40th anniversary jump, you'd understand why Mascuch doesn't pack it in.

The entry in his log book showed it to be his 277th jump.

Did he ever, in all those jumps, use his emergency chute?

"Never."

11/28/82

GREAT-GRANDMA LIKES TO JUMP OUT OF PLANES

There's something inspirational about senior citizens doing things associated with youth. I am always fascinated by the sight of white haired couples figure skating at the Rockefeller Center Skating Rink in Manhattan with the grace, skill, and nimbleness, that would do credit to people less than half their age.

There are more extreme examples than that. You wouldn't think, for example of parachute jumping (of course, they call it sky diving today, but this is written by an old-timer about an old-timer) as an activity for a great-grandmother.

But Gertrude Box would disagree with you.

Gertrude was no youngster when she took up parachute jumping and she didn't think she should pack away her chute just because she was a great-grandmother.

For her, that is the best time to do the things you like to do. There are less responsibilities and obligations.

Gertrude Box has seven children (one son died), 17 grandchildren, and nine great-grandchildren.

She also has a lot of hobbies, not the least of which is sky diving. You might not expect a great-grandmother who will turn 73 next month to be jumping out of airplanes. But that's only because you never met Gertrude Box.

We met her last weekend at Skydive East that now operates out of Alexandria Airport in Pittstown. Sky diving is one of her favorite hobbies, but she also enjoys flying (she's an active private pilot), scuba diving (she's gone scuba diving from Alaska to Florida), motorcycling (she owns two motorcycles), water skiing, surfing, and swimming. She holds two New York State swimming records for her age group.

She goes dancing a couple of times a week with her 80-year-old boyfriend. (She's divorced.) Before World War II she was a swimmer and dancer in the Jones Beach (Long Island, N.Y.) Shows.

How did she get involved in such a string of activities that the average macho guy couldn't handle?

"My father wanted a boy," she told me, "and I spent my life trying to make it up to him."

He never had a chance to have a son because Gertrude was his first born and Gertrude's mother died in childbirth.

Her father, who lived to 83, was a minister, a high school principal, and a swimming and track coach, so she probably inherited her love of sports from him.

She follows in his footsteps in one other way. She has played the keyboard for church services and weddings for 57 years.

Gertrude's passion for sky diving was born when she was 15 and used to go out to Zahn's Airport on Long Island. She wanted to jump then, but that was not an activity her good father would smile upon.

So she had to wait until she was 51, three years after her father died and the year after she was divorced, after 25 years of marriage, to realize her girlhood dream.

Gertrude Box preparing to board jump plane.

She learned the delicate art of jumping out of planes at Lakewood Airport when that was one of the busiest jumping centers in the country.

"I made 20 jumps--three in one day--in five years," she said.

The same year she took up jumping she got her private pilot's license at Zahn's Airport in Amityville N.Y.

But in 1989, a son, who was a physician, died of AIDS, and she gave up most of her activities. "But life goes on," she said, and she gradually got back into her old activities.

In the spring of 1993, she called Skydive East because they have an accelerated free fall course. They were a bit reluctant to take her on when they learned she was in her 70s. But Gertrude is persistent and they finally told her to come on out and she could join a ground school class.

"I had to do all the things the 20-year-olds do," said Gertrude, "like jumping off a platform forward and backward, rolling on the ground to the right, to the left, and backwards. I wasn't winded."

"She was better than 90 percent of our students," said an instructor. She was good enough that they let her jump that day.

"Jumping's wonderful," said Gertrude. "It's addictive. After that first jump all I knew was that I wanted to do it the rest of my life."

Being a student was kind of a reversal of form for Gertrude. She was a teacher for many years. She taught music in Brooklyn and in the Bronx (Ft. Apache) for more than eight years and she taught high school equivalency in the Rikers Island (N.Y.) Prison for more than eight years.

She holds 11 teaching certificates from early childhood education through school district administrator.

Gertrude is currently working on a doctorate in sociology. The subject of her dissertation is "The Sociology of Parachute Jumping."

She already holds an E.D.D. (doctor of education). Her dissertation for that degree was on Motorcycle Education. "They gave me a hard time on that," Gertrude said. "It took four years to get approval. But I'm persistent. It took me five years to write it.

"Those who take the Motorcycle Foundation rider course are less likely to be killed," she says. "Those who just get on a motorcycle without any kind of training are the ones who get hurt."

Gertrude also has a masters degree.

She graduated from high school at 16 and by the time she was 18, she had finished two years at New York University.

She belongs to a number of parachuting organizations including POPS (Parachutists Over Phorty Society) "The president of that organization is a woman," she says.

She is also a member of SOS (Skydivers Over Sixty). That organization has 213 members worldwide.

Her accomplishments are not limited to sky diving or motorcycling. She was the first woman in the Jones Beach Power Squadron. She owned a 21-foot Stegercraft for five years. Right now, she's thinking about buying an airplane.

Gertrude is very conscious of keeping in good shape. One way to accomplish that, she thinks, is to watch your diet. She eats only natural foods. No prepared foods or junk food. "I never eat cake. I never eat pie," she says. Her diet is heavy on fruits and vegetables. Although she does eat some meat. "I've never been sick a day in my life," she says.

"I haven't had a drink in 50 years," says Gertrude. "I've weighed 94 pounds for 50 years."

So Gertrude expects to continue her sky diving activities for a long time to come. "I'll probably be able to parachute until I'm a hundred," she says, confidently.

11/27/94

HE CAN'T WALK, HE CAN'T TALK. BUT HE SKY DIVES

In the course of 38 years of pursuing human interest aviation stories, I have encountered my fair share of inspirational tales.

Even among such stories, the one that follows is unique. It is one story I will never forget.

J oe Hughes is 40. He has a trim attractive, vivacious wife, Janet, and two loving daughters, Samantha, 9, and Abby, 7. But Hughes can't return their affection by embracing them. He has no use of his hands or his arms. They are limp.

It is difficult for him to tell them he loves them because he speaks haltingly and with great difficulty. The average listener would be unable to understand him. His wife, is able to interpret what he struggles to say.

He cannot walk. He cannot stand without help. His legs tremble when he is sitting in his wheelchair.

There is one thing he is able to do. He can smile. And that smile is almost always there, and never more so than when he talks about his parachute jumps.

Joe Hughes, bottom, in a tandem jump with his instructor, Pete Fiddler.

They are not something that happened before his affliction. It happened recently, first in June and for a second time on his 40th birthday, Aug. 1, when his second jump was a gift from his family.

They were tandem jumps on which Hughes was strapped to his instructor, Pete Fiddler. His wrists, his knees, his ankles were strapped together so they wouldn't flap around in the wind since he has no control over his arms or legs.

They took off from Newton Airport, home of the Sky's the Limit Sky Diving Center, in a Cessna turboprop Caravan with a dozen other jumpers. At 13,500 feet, Fiddler and Hughes, joined together as one, exited the airplane. For about one minute they were in free fall dropping toward the earth at approximately 125 miles an hour.

A small drogue chute opened to hold their descent to what it would be for a single jumper. After a minute of free fall Fiddler tapped Hughes on the head to alert him that he was about to open the parachute. When the chute opened they were at 5,000 feet--about one mile up. They drifted down to a soft, controlled landing and Hughes wore a smile from ear to ear.

Hughes, who lives in East Hanover with his family, hasn't been able to work for the last year-and-a-half. He was a very successful executive representing an Omaha financial firm and he had his own office in Parsippany.

In January of 1999, he first felt a weakness in his right hand. He thought it was related to an injury he suffered playing ice hockey. He is an avid hockey fan and loved playing the game just for fun.

The doctors did a battery of tests over a period of four months. Their diagnosis was not good news. He had amyotrophic lateral sclerosis -- Lou Gehrig's disease. His family was devastated. Joe took it better than anyone else, according to Janet. "He was hoping he could fight it," she said.

Hughes first thought about making a parachute jump in June, by which time his affliction was quite advanced. He and one of his friends from the days when he was a student at Montclair State University, Mike Archambault of Parsippany, had discussed it. Hughes began thinking about it again. He went on the internet (he can use one finger) and contacted five sky diving schools asking if they would jump a handicapped person.

Theresa, the office manager at Sky's the Limit, responded that she thought it would be no problem. Instructor Pete Fiddler, she e-mailed, had jumped three handicapped people previously.

Janet was petrified at the idea. She thought it was dangerous. "But I saw Terry's e-mail response about the school jumping handicapped people and some pictures," she said, "and Joe is tough to say no to. He was very persuasive in business. My mother used to say he could sell the leaves off the trees."

There was ample evidence of that. He convinced three people who had never jumped before that they should jump with him. One was John Thorn, a recruiter and resume writer. Thorn had an office in the same building as Hughes. They met there and became fast friends. A second was Archambault, his friend from college. And the third was Lee Connor, his physical therapist.

"He couldn't have done it without Lee," Janet said. "His arms were very stiff. Lee worked for hours to stretch his arms. Neither she nor John had any intention of jumping."

Hughes changed their minds. "He told us we were going to jump," said John. "He is still the motivator and the one in charge," Janet said. "He's been a natural leader always. He inspires confidence.

"The minute he left the airplane he knew he wanted to do it again," Janet said. "He wasn't nervous, he was so excited. When he landed he said it was the best thing he ever did." Janet now shares his excitement. "When the chute opened, it made his back feel good," Janet said. "He has chronic back pain. When it opened he felt like he could stand up."

Hughes first came to Newton Airport on June 29. He went through two hours of briefings. He wanted to know everything. He didn't want any surprises. When the briefings were finished they got him into a jump suit and harness and they lifted him into the airplane to join 15 other people, including Archambault and Connor. Thorn had jumped on a previous flight because Hughes wanted to hear all about it straight from the horse's mouth before he jumped.

A cameraman with a video camera on his helmet jumped just ahead of Fiddler and Hughes. He photographed them exiting the plane and then he showed them in free fall, including a close up of Hughes's face. He wears a huge grin as he descends in the free fall. It is an awesome sight on video.

At Sky's the Limit jumpers have the option of having a video taken of their jump. The price of the video is $85.

The day we met Hughes and his family at Newton Airport he was hoping to make yet another jump. The weatherman dampened that idea.

But there is no way to dampen Hughes' spirit, no way to erase his smile. And no way to comprehend his courage.

8/26/01

Note: *Joe Hughes died on October 23, 2002.*

PILOTS WHO JUMPED FOR THEIR LIVES

There is a club called the Caterpillar Club. It's a very exclusive club. In order to be a member you must have jumped for your life from a disabled airplane.

More than 25,000 members of the club have written accounts of how they earned their membership. There is file cabinet after file cabinet stuffed to capacity with those records. There are probably more hair-raising stories in those files than anywhere else in the world. Each one is the story of a life saved by a parachute.

The stories in this chapter that have preceded this one are about people who jump for fun. This story is about people who jumped for their lives.

There is a very unusual museum in Trenton that's kind of a well kept secret. Few people know it exists. Actually, it's not a public museum. It's tucked away inside a large (60,000-square-foot) factory on East State Street where 150 people come to work every day.

The museum is the repository of thousands of gripping aviation stories. They are the firsthand accounts of aviators who experienced the ultimate in aviation emergencies, the necessity to jump for their lives. The files in this museum are crammed with 25,000 such stories, a majority of them from World War II flyers.

Here in this museum are the applications for membership in the Caterpillar Club. To be eligible, the applicant must be an American pilot who made a verifiable jump for his or her life.

There are those who have earned entry into this exclusive circle more than once. Charles Lindbergh, who made the first solo flight across the

Richard Switlik

Atlantic, jumped for his life four times. Jimmy Doolittle, who led the daring raid on Tokyo early in world War II, earned the distinction twice.

The late Fay Gillis Wells, the celebrated aviatrix and

later foreign correspondent, became the club's first woman member in 1929.

Although there are 25,000 members of the club, it is estimated that only one in four aviators who are eligible ever applied for membership. The vast majority are military aviators.

The custodian of these precious historical records is the Switlik Parachute Company Inc., of Trenton. In 1939, the Air Corps designated Switlik, one of the world's leading parachute makers, as keeper of these records.

Dick Switlik, son of the company's founder, Stanley Switlik, took me on a tour of the plant and the museum within its walls. As he pulled club membership applications from the files at random, they revealed a stream of chilling stories, descriptions of an aircraft being blown into three parts and the airmen jumping from a section that was floating down.

One letter said, "When I jumped, I left my shoes in the plane. My leg was in one of them."

Another letter Switlik found in the files was written by a Navy pilot shot down by antiaircraft fire at the Bonin Islands in the Pacific on Sept. 2, 1944. It was signed by George H. W. Bush. He was wearing a Switlik parachute when he jumped.

"His airplane (a TBM-1C Avenger) was built in Trenton," said Switlik.   "It was made by Eastern Aircraft, a division of General Motors, in a factory across the street from Mercer Field. The aircraft were towed across the road for test flights."

Switlik showed me a copy of a book titled, *Flight of the Avenger: George Bush at War*, by Joe Hyams. It was inscribed, "To Richard Switlik, with thanks for my life. Best wishes, George Bush. 7-2-91. A grateful card-carrying member of the Caterpillar Club."

The club was formed in 1922 after two emergency jumps at McCook Field in Dayton, Ohio. There was a problem in coming up with a suitable name. It was resolved when M.H. St. Clair, a member of the Cook Field parachute unit, got some literature from his brother-in-law who was with the Caterpillar Tractor Co. It carried an emblem used in their ads, with a wavy looking creature with "caterpillar" written in it. Since parachutes were then made from the finest silk and the silk worm enclosed itself in a cocoon from which it eventually broke out and flew away, it was deemed that Caterpillar Club would be an appropriate name. A couple of years later, St. Clair went to work for Switlik as an engineer. He stayed on for 20 years.

The Caterpillar Club records are only a small part of the aviation heritage in the Switlik Museum. Those records are hidden in filing cabinets, but lining the walls and tables in the museum are dozens of products of the company that were part of aviation history and mementos of some of the people who used them.

There is a huge blowup of a photo of Amelia Earhart wearing a parachute harness boldly inscribed, "Switlik," as she is greeted by the Mexican Consul General upon landing at Newark Airport after a flight from Mexico City.

There is also a photo of pioneer aviator Wiley Post, who was killed, along with humorist Will Rogers, in a crash in Alaska in 1935. Both men were wearing Switlik parachutes.

Most of the Doolittle Raiders wore Switlik chutes. A number of them visited the factory in 1944 to help celebrate the 250,000th parachute manufactured by Switlik. In those days--during World War II--Switlik employed 1,500 people.

The company, founded in 1920, no longer manufactures personal parachutes. It still makes chutes, drag chutes for military aircraft, cargo chutes for heavy equipment such as Jeeps, mortars, and artillery pieces, but that is not a major part of production today. It now manufactures life vests (such as those required on airliners for about 50 airlines around the world), life rafts, and G-suits for military pilots.

A couple sailing around the world survived for 66 days in a Switlik raft after their boat was capsized by whales 1,200 miles off Costa Rica.

They've had some unusual orders over the years. "In about 1979," recalls Dick Switlik, "the Air Force ordered G-suits for monkeys. We made 21 of them. We don't know why or if they were ever used."

They made a chute with a silver-coated fabric to block radiation. Gary Powers was wearing it when his U-2 spy plane was shot down over Russia.

Switlik has made chutes for nuclear bombs, to stabilize them while the aircraft that dropped them got away. During World War II they designed and made a special suit with an internal harness used to pick up secret service agents dropped in China. The suits came with a cable that was stretched between two trees and the agents strapped themselves to it so an aircraft could swoop low and snatch them up, the same way aerial advertising banners are picked up, and then they were reeled into the aircraft.

Dick Switlik is 74 today. He's seen his share of excitement. But he's not ready to quit. He's still very active. His three sons are officers of the company. Richard, Jr. is Vice President, Marketing; Gregory is Vice President, Legal Administration; and Stanley is Vice President and Chief Engineer. Dick, who jumped from a parachute tower when he was 17 to prove that it was a safe and effective training aid, is in his office every day. He comes to the plant because he loves it. "It's my life." he says.

11/22/92

Chapter 9

Bottoms Up
(Aerobatics)

As I've pointed out previously, airplanes are basically vehicles of transportation. Their principal use is to get people from one place to another for business or pleasure and to do it faster and more efficiently than any other means of transportation. With an airplane you don't have to go miles out of your way to get around a lake or take winding roads across mountains. You just fly straight over them.

But airplanes can be more than transportation. For some people they are a way to get away from it all and look down on the beauty of the earth, its majestic mountains, snaking rivers, picturesque lakes. It provides a sense of freedom and perspective that is unique to flying.

Airplanes can also be pure fun, perhaps never more so than when looping and rolling through the skies doing aerobatics. But aerobatics can be serious, too. As a sport they are one of the most highly competitive in the world.

Aerobatics is an internationally recognized sport with world championships held every two years in a different country. It is also a spectator sport. Air shows that feature aerobatic performers attract huge crowds. Millions have seen the Air Force's Thunderbirds and the Navy's Blue Angels, military precision aerobatic teams, perform in air shows.

There are also solo performers whose skill is incredible, many of whom have won championships in competition.

The stories that follow describe the exploits of some of the greatest aerobatic pilots in the world as well as a few of lesser fame whose accomplishments deserve recognition.

CHAMPION OF CHAMPIONS

Leo Loudenslager was the greatest competitive aerobatic pilot this nation ever produced. He won the National Aerobatic Championship seven times and the World Championship in Oshkosh, Wis., in 1980.

I met Leo when he was building his first aerobatic aircraft, a Stephens Akro, in the basement of his home in Sussex, N.J., not far from Sussex Airport which was his home base for years. For some three decades Sussex had an annual air show that over the years featured many of the world's top aerobatic performers. He took me to his home to see the work in progress.

Leo was a very intense man. He was a perfectionist and highly competitive. He thrilled audiences at air shows all over the country.

In all his years of aerobatic flying, he never scratched an airplane or himself.

In 1997 near his home in Tennessee where he had moved to from New Jersey, he was in a motorcycle accident. As he was coming over the crest of a hill he was in a head-on collision with a van.

Leo suffered a spinal injury which left him paralyzed. After a few weeks he succumbed to his injuries.

The following column recounts how Leo, who became such an outstanding competitor, discovered aerobatic flying and the problems he had finding his way to the top. It includes an account of his first National Championship competition.

In 1964, Leo Loudenslager watched aerobatic ace Duane Cole perform at the Reno Air Races and immediately it rang a bell. "If you can do that," he said, "you've got it all."

Eleven years later Leo Loudenslager proved he had it all.

A few weeks ago, Leo returned to his home base, Sussex Airport, from Sherman, Texas, as the National Aerobatic Champion. He flew against the country's best and he topped them all.

As a result, Leo, who flies for American Airlines, will go to Kiev, Russia, next summer with the U.S. aerobatic team to compete in the World Championships.

This will come just five years after Leo entered his first competition, a local event at Brookhaven, L.I., in which he finished first.

His next competition was in September of the same year, 1971, at Oak Grove Airport in Fort Worth, Texas. This time he was competing against the nation's best for a spot on the U.S. team that would fly in the world championship competition.

He placed as third alternate and was named an assistant judge. As a result he went to France with the team in the summer of 1972. But he didn't fly. That year the U.S. won the team competition and brought home the cherished Nesterov Cup.

In the Nationals later that year, Leo placed fifth among the world team members.

He went back to Oak Grove in 1973 to practice, but he had problems with the engine pump and he found metal shavings in the engine. Leo and his partner, Jim Roberts, tore down the engine and put it together again, but then they ran into more mechanical problems.

Nevertheless, Leo competed, and after the first event, the known or compulsory maneuvers, Leo was first.

Leo Loudenslager with the aerobatic aircraft he built in which he set new records.

He didn't do as well in freestyle and lost his lead. In the final event, unknown maneuvers, in which competitors are handed a routine just before takeoff, he slipped a bit further. He finished sixth and was dropped from the team.

He came back to try again in 1974. This time he was leading when they disallowed his last maneuver because he went over the time limit.

There was a very high wind that affected his time. That knocked 400 points off his score, enough to make the difference between first and fourth place.

Early this year, Jim and Leo stripped his airplane, a Stephens Akro that he spent three-and-a-half years building, and in the process they discovered a cracked spar in the wing.

They found a fellow in Ponder, Texas, who could build a spar for them.

After five months, the aircraft first flew again on Sept. 1. However, it wasn't ready to fly aerobatics until mid-September. The Nationals started on October 20.

After the compulsories, an event that he had won only a couple of years before, Leo was seventh.

In the freestyle he recouped in a big way, receiving the highest score ever achieved. When it was all added up, Leo Loudenslager was National Champion.

Lest he forget, there are signs all around his home base at Sussex Airport, reading, "You're Number One."

11/23/75

THE WINNINGEST PILOT

In 1984, Lt. Col. Mel R. Jones, wrote a book titled, "Above and Beyond, Eight Great American Aerobatic Champions". One of those champions, was Leo Loudenslager.

One chapter in the book, titled "Winningest Pilot," is devoted to Loudenslager. It describes some of the difficulties Leo had to overcome before he made it to the top. It is a worthy and more detailed addition to the account of his travails presented in the previous column.

The book also refers to some of the other outstanding American champions worthy of mention. This column, written nine years after the preceding column adds to the story of Leo Loudenslager and also includes some background on other aerobatic champions.

Every summer at the Sussex Air Show thousands of spectators thrill to the breathtaking performances of some of the world's greatest aerobatic pilots. Some of the performers have come all the way from California.

But there is one pilot who can virtually roll out of bed and he's there. Sussex Airport is his home base. I speak, of course, of Leo Loudenslager.

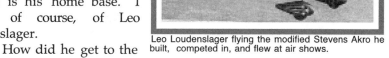

Leo Loudenslager flying the modified Stevens Akro he built, competed in, and flew at air shows.

How did he get to the top in this demanding sport? What drives him to perfection? The story is told in a new paperback called, *Above and Beyond, Eight Great American Aerobatic Champions.* The chapter on Loudenslager is titled, "The Winningest Pilot."

The other pilots whose stories are told in this book by Lt. Col. Mel R. Jones (Retired), are Bob Herendeen, Charlie Hillard, Gene Soucy, Tom Poberezny, Henry Haigh, Kermit Weeks, and Betty Stewart.

Loudenslager's single-minded determination to reach the top is told in the story of how he put in an eight-hour shift as an airman at Travis Air Force Base in California and then worked nine hours at a gas station to earn money for flying lessons, usually getting only three hours sleep a night and going without sleep on the night he had ground school.

After he got a job as an airline pilot in 1966, he put in 12 hours a day. On those days he wasn't flying he was building the airplane he would one day compete in.

And then there were the disappointments--the year in which the world championships were held in Russia and the Soviets turned the contest into what one writer described as, "a well-oiled propaganda machine."

"The contest was so blatantly rigged through manipulation of scoring devices, Soviet protests, and delaying tactics, that Henry (Henry Haigh, one of the U.S. team members) observed that 'it was like watching one contest and then seeing the scores for another contest posted,' " Leo, who was then U.S. National Champion, finished 23rd.

The only American to win any medal in the world competition in Kiev was Betty Stewart, a pharmacist and relative newcomer to aerobatic competition. It was only the second time she had competed in the Unlimited category.

In the 1980 World Championships in Oshkosh, Wis., Betty won the gold medal in the first two events. She invited her brother to come to the closing events. Then she suggested that he invite her parents to come. Though she had been flying for 13 years and had won a bronze medal in world competition in Russia, her father, a professor of mechanical engineering, and her mother, had never seen her fly.

After they agreed to come, a mix-up in the third event in the competition threatened to disqualify her from flying in the fourth and final freestyle event. It wasn't until takeoff time for that event that Betty learned that the protests filed on her behalf had been accepted. She flew and was awarded a gold medal for that event and would be permitted to fly the final freestyle.

Betty took the silver medal in the final event and it was enough to win her the World Championship.

The stories of 57-year-old Henry Haigh and 31-year-old Kermit Weeks are combined in a chapter titled, "The Trend Setters." It's interesting to note that aerobatic competition, one of the most physically demanding of sports and one requiring a tremendously high degree of skill, still has active competitors in their late 50s.

Gene Soucy and Tom Poberezny are two top competitors who have flown in air shows together for years, and their stories are combined in one chapter.

The next air show you see will have a lot more meaning to you if you've read "Above and Beyond", and understand what these pilots go through before they reach championship status.

12/2/84

SWEET LITTLE LADY, A KILLER IN THE COCKPIT

In 1970, when the U.S. aerobatic team went to England to compete for the World Championship, that title had never escaped from behind the Iron Curtain.

But in that year, it all changed, due in no small part to a diminutive, middle-aged lady from Florida named Mary Gaffney. With her help, the United States became the first nation to take the championship to the west.

Mary Gaffney captured the Women's World Championship, contributing to the team victory. (Today, the women compete on an equal basis with the men.) Mary achieved this distinction in a day when no one could dream of a woman airline pilot, much less an aerobatic champion.

She stands just a shade over five feet tall. She looks like a sweet little middle-aged lady who could do miracles with a pair of knitting needles while sitting in the old rocker on the back porch.

Her name is Mary Gaffney and she's the 1970 Women's World Champion of Aerobatics. Right now she's in France preparing to defend that title.

Mary Gaffney and her Pitts aerobatic biplane.

Mary is part of the seven-member United States Aerobatic Team that will defend its team championship in competition between July 18 and 31.

A couple of weeks ago they loaded seven little aerobatic airplanes into the belly of one giant C-5A and flew the little birds to Europe.

Part of the team stopped off in New York long enough to talk to a luncheon meeting of the Aviation/Space Writers

Association at the Overseas Press Club.

Until 1970, only Iron Curtain countries had won the World Championship title--Czechoslovakia in 1960, Hungary in 1962, Russia in 1964 and 1966, and East Germany in 1968.

But at a place with the unlikely name of Hullavington, England, in 1970, the United States team took it all and brought the Nesterov Cup and the title out from behind the Iron Curtain for the first time.

Mary Gaffney, who played an important role in accomplishing that feat, told the aviation writers about how shocked the foreign competitors were when they learned that such a tiny, meek-looking lady was a member of the United States team.

"In Russia," she said, "girls are ineligible for competition after they pass 40. I didn't get into competition until I was 40. Mary is 46 now and she plans to do a lot more competing. She's logged 16,000 hours and she holds just about every rating they ever dreamed up--and in addition she's an FAA designated flight examiner.

She and her husband run a flight school at Tamiami Airport outside of Miami.

In addition to her World Championship, she has taken the Women's National Aerobatic Championship for the past five years running.

The team this year includes one other woman, Carolyn Salisbury, a promising newcomer who is still in her 20s. Carolyn is a California x-ray technician who learned to fly in 1966 and has logged a grand total of less than 400 hours.

One other newcomer will compete this year, 25-year-old Tom Poberezny, a protégé of one of the team's veterans, Gene Soucy.

The other members of the team are Professor Art Scholl, another veteran competitor who heads the Department of Aeronautics at San Bernardino Valley College in California; Charles Hillard, a world championship competitor since 1966, and Bill Thomas, first alternate, filling in for Bob Herendeen who is unable to compete.

7/9/72

Note: *Mary Gaffney successfully defended her Women's World Champion of Aerobatics title in 1972.*

KING OF THE AIR SHOW CIRCUIT

All aerobatic flying is divided into two categories-- competitive flying and air show performances. Most top aerobatic pilots cross from one side to the other. When it comes to air show performing, one man stands pretty much alone. There are many greats, but there is only one Bob Hoover.

Hoover has probably performed at more air shows than any other pilot. He has thrilled millions of spectators. But that is not what he is best known for. The name Bob Hoover is most often associated with a routine he's done hundreds and hundreds of times that no other performer has duplicated.

Most performers go up in aerobatic aircraft and do loops and rolls and hammerheads and spins, and occasionally, the tumbling maneuver called a Lumchovak.

Hoover performs in a twin-engine Shrike Commander, an airplane not built for aerobatics, but for transportation. That, however, is only half of Hoover's uniqueness. The more arresting half is his unduplicated routine described in the following column.

In his 50 years of flying, he's thrilled untold millions of fascinated spectators. If you asked professional air show performers which of their colleagues they have the most respect for, with hardly an exception, the answer would be, "Bob Hoover."

There is no air show routine that leaves quite the same indelible impression on the spectator as the power off aerobatics Hoover has performed hundreds of times in the twin-engine Shrike Commander.

It is a routine in which Hoover cuts both engines, feathers (stops) the propellers, then does a loop and a roll and lands, power off, with such precise control over speed and touchdown point that he is able to roll, with no power, to the exact spot from which he departed. No one who ever saw that routine will ever forget it.

Bob Hoover

Hundreds of thousands remember him doing the routine at the old Reading (Pa.) Air Show year after year.

"It started," said Hoover, "when I was testing P-38s in Africa during the war." (World War II) It was easy to do in a P-38. In the Shrike Commander I had to do it more gently. I had to cut down on the Gs and the speed."

Hoover was in New Jersey recently as a guest of the Magic of Alexandria Balloon Festival in honor of his 50 years of incomparable air show performances.

Alexandria Airport in Pittstown, where the balloon festival is held, is owned by the Fritche family, who observed the 50th anniversary of their facility at this year's event.

While Hoover is world renowned for his amazing air show performances, there is much more to him than his memorable Shrike Commander routine. He was, for example, chosen by Chuck Yeager to be his backup pilot for the Bell X-1 mission in which Yeager became the first pilot to break the sound barrier.

Yeager refers to Hoover many times in his autobiography. They used to dog fight each other when both were test pilots and neither could outdo the other. In the autobiography Yeager calls Hoover one of the two best pilots he ever met. The other was Bud Anderson who flew in combat with Yeager.

Hoover was also a combat pilot. He flew 59 missions. On the 59th, Feb. 9, 1944, two weeks after his 22nd birthday, he was flying a Spitfire out of a base in Corsica. The target was a German convoy off the coast of southern France.

Hoover was jumped by a flight of Focke-Wulf 190s. A German pilot, just a few months older than Hoover and a veteran of the Battle of Britain, attacked from an angle from which Hoover did not think he was vulnerable. But he was hit. It was the German pilot's 17th victory and he got three more Spitfires that same day.

Hoover's airplane started to come apart and then caught fire. He bailed out. The Germans plucked him out of the water a few miles off Nice, and he spent 15 1/2 months in a German prison camp.

After the war, he served as a test pilot at Wright Field near Dayton, Ohio. He evaluated many captured German and Japanese aircraft.

Later, test flying an F-84, he had a fire on board, and then his engine failed. His ejection seat wouldn't work. He crawled over the side, jumped and went into the tail, which broke both his legs. They thought he went in with the plane. But he got his chute open and he landed in the California desert 15 miles from where the aircraft went in.

"A farmer found me just before dark," he recalled. Hoover was lucky. "It was November and it gets very cold in the desert at night."

On another occasion he was testing an F-86 with an irreversible flight control system. There were two systems. If one failed, it would automatically switch to the other. But both failed.

He had no elevator or stabilizer. (Unlike most aircraft, the stabilizer on an F-86 moves.) They were both operated by the failed electronic system. The nose pitched up on takeoff and then dipped and recovered just before it hit the ground. It repeated that maneuver several times and each time he wound up with a bit more altitude.

Using the rudder and aileron that were mechanical, Hoover was able to turn toward the ocean. Over his headset he could hear the pilots in the escort planes shouting, "Bail out, bail out. You'll never make it." (He learned after he landed that a pin had been removed from the seat and he could not have ejected if he wanted to.)

With the throttle and speed brake he gained some pitch control. He had to maintain a relatively high speed so the stabilizer remained in a level position.

Hoover managed to get the aircraft back to Edwards Air Force Base where he got into ground effect and put it down on the sandy soil of the dry lake bed at 240 knots in what he described as "the smoothest landing I've ever been through."

8/21/94

DON'T LET THEM TELL YOU, YOU'RE TOO OLD

The aerobatic pilots we've talked about up till now are people who, for the most part, are well known. This column is about an aerobatic pilot nobody ever heard of. But he earned his way into this column because he typifies the spirit that makes people want to fly.

As we've mentioned previously, aerobatic flying is the most strenuous sport there is. Participants are subject to extreme G forces (gravitational pull) both positive and negative. You need to be in first class physical condition to tolerate the punishment those G forces inflict on the body.

It's generally not a senior citizens' sport, although Bob Hoover, about whom we wrote in the previous story, is 85 as of this writing (2007). But he started when he was young and just didn't quit until he was 78.

The subject of this column started aerobatic flying when he was pushing 70, an age at which many aerobatic pilots have hung up their goggles.

He pursued the strenuous sport far enough to enter several competitions--and to carry home some trophies.

There are those who think a man who had 69 candles on his last birthday cake ought to find something better to do with his spare time than flying upside down. James L. Maclin of Ringoes would not agree with them.

James L. (Luttrell "Lut") Maclin

"I am the most enthusiastic aerobatic pilot in the state of New Jersey," says the 69-year-old Maclin.

If you talk to him for five minutes, you know he's not kidding. He bristles with enthusiasm.

Maclin took his first flying lesson in 1942, courtesy of Uncle Sam. He was training to be a glider pilot, but for his first taste of the wild blue yonder they put him through primary training in Piper Cubs and Aeroncas.

He wound up flying the CG-4A, a glider that could carry 13 fully equipped infantry men and a crew of two, or a jeep or light artillery piece. (Maclin's experiences as a World War II glider pilot are recounted in the story "Gliders Go to War" in Chapter 3.)

A financial writer for the old *New York Herald Tribune,* before enlisting, Maclin hung up his wings in 1946 and became editor of publications for Merrill Lynch and later Paine Webber.

He took early retirement and then taught economics at Trenton State College for five years.

Flying came back into his life in 1978, after a lapse of 36 years, when a neighbor took him for a ride in his Breezy. A Breezy is a homebuilt aircraft that makes one of the old ultralights look like a sophisticated machine.

The fuselage is an uncovered frame (bare tubing) with a wing and a pusher engine. The pilot, and his passenger behind him, sit out in the wide open.

The Breezy in flight

"My neighbor let me fly it. He even let me land it. And that was what did it," says Maclin.

He went out to Princeton Airport and learned to fly all over again.

"I started from scratch." he says. "I went to ground school in the Delaware Valley High Adult Education Program.

"While I was learning, I bought a Citabria."

A Citabria, for those not up on such things, is a high wing tandem, two-seat tail dragger, which means that the aircraft has a tail wheel rather than the nose wheel that is common in most production model aircraft today.

It is an aerobatic aircraft, but it has limitations since it carries a standard engine that precludes flying upside down. Since he likes flying upside down, Maclin recently traded his Citabria for a Decathalon, a beefed up version of the same aircraft with a modification that makes it possible to sustain inverted flight.

Although he got his license after a lapse of 36 years, he wasn't satisfied with that. He wanted to learn aerobatics.

So at 67, he took his first aerobatic lesson. That was two years ago. Since then he has flown in several internationally sanctioned aerobatic competitions. He usually finishes somewhere in the middle of the pack.

He performs what is known as the Sportsman's Sequence, which is made up of a series of aerobatic maneuvers including loops, Cuban 8s, reverse Cubans, hammerheads, snap rolls, slow rolls, and barrel rolls. In competition, the routine must be performed in a tightly confined area known as the "box."

There are five judges. The high and low judges' scores are thrown out and the three middle scores are averaged.

Maclin is a member of Chapter 94 of the International Aerobatic Club at Vincentown, known also as the Mid-Atlantic Aerobatic Association.

"They call me 'tail slide.' " Maclin says, "because I was doing a hammerhead one time and didn't pull it out soon enough."

A hammerhead is a maneuver in which the aircraft is put into a vertical climb and just before the airspeed bleeds off completely, the pilot kicks rudder, the aircraft falls off to one side into a vertical descent. If the aircraft loses flying speed before the pilot kicks the rudder, it will slide back on its tail.

As we were getting ready to leave after a stimulating conversation with Maclin, he said, "You didn't ask me about my cap." The words, "Silver Eagle" were printed across the front.

"That's an organization of World War II glider pilots who are still active pilots," he said. "We have 70 members. The number is dwindling as our members flunk the physical."

The Silver Eagles meet annually at the convention of the Glider Pilots Association composed of WW II veterans.

Maclin has flown to the organization's annual meetings in Dallas and Atlanta in the Citabria with his wife.

The organization is preparing for its 12th annual reunion at the MGM Grand Hotel in Reno, Nev., next month.

There are 28 Jerseyans in the organization but there are probably a lot more glider pilot veterans who don't know about the group.

Two of the group's national officers are Jerseyans. Tipton Randolph is secretary and Eugene Soden is treasurer. Both men are residents of Freehold. Randolph flew in four glider operations in Europe, including Normandy and Southern France.

I remember the latter operation that took place on Aug. 15, 1944, rather vividly, since that was my one experience with a combat glider landing.

I am not eligible to join the Glider Pilots Association, however, since I was a "passenger" as a member of a 4.2 mortar battalion, and not one of the pilots.

8/15/82

Note: *"Lut" Maclin died on March 10,1997.*

A VIEW OF AEROBATICS FROM THE COCKPIT

Watching aerobatics is an exciting experience. It's exciting enough to attract millions every year to air shows all over the world.

But watching it is like petting a kitten compared to facing a collection of tigers in a circus ring.

I've been in the cockpit numerous times while aerobatic pilots demonstrated loops and rolls and I've done a few loops and rolls under the watchful eye of an instructor. But one experience stands out above all others. That was a flight in a two-place Pitts in which 747 captain and aerobatic instructor Jim Chaudoin took me through what is known as the Intermediate Routine.

Jim operated out of Sussex Airport which for years was the home base of aerobatic champion Leo Loudenslager who told me many times about the physical punishment aerobatic pilots take in competition. Jim Chaudoin gave me a pretty good demonstration of what he was talking about.

I've watched the wiry little Pitts biplanes whirl and spin and loop through the skies with a vengeance, a hundred times. Last weekend, the role was reversed. Instead of standing on the outside looking in, I was on the inside looking out.

I flew into Sussex Airport which is kind of the unofficial aerobatic center of this part of the firmament. Here is where champion Leo Loudenslager is based. There are probably more aerobatic aircraft of all kinds at Sussex than any other airport within range of a tankful of gas. And here is where American Airlines 747 captain Jim Chaudoin of Sparta spends most of his time when he's not in the flight deck of the giant airliner. Jim devotes many of his non airline hours teaching aerobatics. Aside from his Pitts S2A, he uses a Stearman, a Citabria, a Decathalon and a Cessna Aerobat 150.

Two other aerobatic instructors, Marilyn Hubbard and John Neumeister (see story "The Hair-Raising Rescue of a Sick Aircraft" in Chapter 1) help Jim out.

"Our course is informal," Jim said. "The student proceeds at his own speed. The object is for them to have fun while learning."

A primary aerobatics course runs 13 hours and includes some intermediate maneuvers. In the curriculum are such choice items as loops, rolls, spins, stalls, stall turns, Cuban 8s, snap rolls, and Immelmans. The course costs $700.

"The average student is a 500-hour pilot who wants to improve his flying and have fun at the same time," said Jim. "We have quite a few female students. I usually take the girls, Marilyn takes the guys.

"Come on. Let me show you what it's all about," he said with a healthy dash of enthusiasm.

We pulled the Pitts out of the hangar, got strapped into chutes, and then into the little biplane, and off we went into the wild blue yonder.

"I'm going to take it up to 4,000," Jim said over the intercom, "and then fly parallel to the runway. The runway is 3,100 feet and the aerobatic box (which is used to limit the area of flight in competition) is 3,000 feet, so that's a good guide."

On the way up, Jim invited me to take the controls and do some 360s. The airplane hardly needed any help from me to do what I wanted it to do. You put it in a turn and it stays right there.

At 4,000 feet Jim took over and did some warm-up maneuvers--a barrel roll, loop, snap roll. Then he broke into a routine that included eight maneuvers.

We started off with a stall turn with a half roll on the way down, then half of a Cuban 8, an Immelman, a snap roll, a one-and-a-half turn spin, a split S, a half roll to inverted on a 45 degree climb, and a vertical dive with a quarter turn on the way down.

Let me tell you, it's a lot different up there looking down than it is from down here looking up. The earth gets to spinning like a top. Sometimes you look up to see the earth and down to see the sky.

Sometimes your bottom leaves the seat. And sometimes the flesh on your face feels like it's being pulled off.

When we got down and I hit the ground again, I had sea legs. I wasn't sure if it was me or the ground wobbling. But in just a couple of minutes, it all settled down and I could walk a straight line.

You call that kind of experience fun, you might ask? Hell, yes. There's nothing you can do that's going to get the blood flowing like it's heading for a waterfall.

It's only for crazy kids, you might think. Well, Jim Chaudoin is a World War II vet, two years from retirement.

And Henry Haigh of the U.S. Aerobatic Team won the U.S. Aerobatic Championship last year at 54. He's definitely not a kid. But it's nice to know there are some older guys with a little of the kid left in them.

7/6/80

IN RESPECTFUL MEMORY OF JIM'S LAST FLIGHT

Jim Chaudoin, the aerobatic instructor I wrote about in the previous column, was a man who epitomized much of what the spirit of flying is all about.

Jim died of cancer in June of 2001. I wrote a column about his passing that I felt was imbued with the essence of the emotions that hold pilots in their embrace.

I hope this tribute to Jim Chaudoin transmits that feeling.

Jim was a big man. He stood 6 feet 4 1/2 inches. And he flew a tiny little airplane--a Pitts biplane. He had graduated to that pygmy of an aircraft from a jumbo jet.

Jim and that airplane were like blood brothers. He was part of the airplane and the airplane was part of him. Their home was Sussex Airport. They were always together, and they had a lot of friends there.

On June 11, after a long battle with cancer, Jim went west. That's how pilots describe the departure of their compatriots from this earth. There was a terrible emptiness in the air at Sussex Airport that day. A big part of the spirit of the little country airport was gone. Most of his students felt that Sussex would never be the same because there just aren't many Jim Chaudoins in this world. He had a great reservoir of patience and he cared about helping his aerobatic students, especially if they encountered hurdles. On June 23, a cloudy Saturday, 12 days after Jim made his last and longest flight into the heavens, 125 of

Jim Chaudoin in his Pitts Special.

Jim's students and friends gathered at Sussex Airport in the maintenance hangar he knew so well, to pay tribute to him.

Pat Tipton, who had been his hangar mate for ten years, as well as one of his students, spoke at the memorial service at the invitation of Jim's wife, Jodie. He recalled his first flight with

Jim. "I can still hear Jim's big confident airline captain's voice, describing each maneuver, demonstrating it, and then patiently talking me through my own ham-fisted attempts. His voice still flies with me today."

Another student, Angelo Cilaroto, who has performed in the Sussex Air Show a number of times, and who has finished third in the Advanced category of a U.S. National Aerobatic Championship competition, told us, "He had an uncanny way of making his students confident."

Angelo was the last one to see Jim before he passed away. Forty-five minutes after Angelo left his hospital room, Jim was gone.

At the memorial service, Pat Tipton recounted a little of Jim's colorful background, which could fill a book. A graduate of Butler High School, in Butler N.J., he enlisted in the Navy in 1942 and was trained as a radio man, but eventually he got into the flight training program and earned his wings. After his discharge in 1946, Jim spent three years building all the flying time he could get in the United States and abroad. He'd go anywhere to build time.

For awhile he was based in Rome and flew cargo to Palestine while also serving as a ferry pilot for David Ben-Gurion, who later became Israel's first prime minister.

After three years of flying all the jobs he could find abroad, he returned to the United States and in 1949 got a job as copilot for Northwest Airlines. Responding to rumors that Northwest was going to be furloughing pilots, Jim and four of his pilot companions went to Chicago for interviews with several airlines and they wound up being hired by American Airlines.

When he retired from American in 1982, he had logged 33 years as an airline pilot, 31 of them at American.

On one flight, in 1954, Jim was flying copilot in a DC-6. One of the flight attendants on the flight was Jodie Zobel, an especially attractive girl from Arizona who was known as the singing stewardess of American Airlines.

"Jim asked her for a date," Pat related, "Jodie's memory of their first date ended with Jim asking her to marry him." Jodie didn't take the bait. But Jim hung in there.

Eventually Jodie said yes and in 1957, they were married and settled in Sparta. Two years later, their only daughter, Michelle, known to everybody as Chelle (pronounced Shelly), was born. She grew into a beautiful girl, glowing with personality, who inherited her father's love of flying. She got her license and Jim checked her out in a Stearman and a host of other antique and aerobatic airplanes.

Then tragedy struck. An aircraft in which Chelle was a

passenger, was in a midair collision and she was killed. Jim and Jodie established a memorial scholarship in her name.

Jodie has been at the Sussex Air Show, year after year, at a stand under the tower accepting donations and distributing photos of Chelle in the cockpit of the Stearman along with a poem she had written, titled, "Forgotten Flight," about the beauty and joy of flying that she gave her father as a Christmas present. It began, "All the colors of the horizon melt into the earth," and ended with the words, "No other time could be so perfect. If this moment lives forever, I will live forever, Love, your daughter, Michelle."

They have awarded three $1,000 scholarships every year since her untimely death.

Two years after the tragic accident, Jim retired from American Airlines.   He went into the business of aerobatic instruction and competition with all of the dedication that he poured into everything he ever did. Jodie kept the books and the schedule. If Jim and his Pitts were an integral part of each other, so it was with Jodie and Jim.

Pat Tipton illustrated that in his eulogy. "I've known Jim and Jodie for the last 10 years as a hangar mate and as one of the strays they seem to keep taking in and treating as their own," he said.

"It is difficult to describe Jim's love of aerobatics and his dedication to it. He had an eagerness to share his passion. One time he asked me if I would like to go up in his Pitts with him, and he would do the intermediate routine (described in the previous column).

"We buckled up and away we went. When I climbed out after the flight, I felt as if I had been in a washing machine for a couple of hours. Jim was radiant.   He had introduced one more person to the exciting world of aerobatic flight."

Jim's career was full of anecdotes and memorable stories. Tipton retold some of them for the benefit of Jim's students, colleagues, and friends.

One involved a passenger on a flight from Los Angeles to New York that ran well into Christmas Eve. One of the passengers was actress-singer Shirley Jones. Jim talked her into coming to the cockpit to sing Christmas carols for the passengers over the airplane's intercom.

"One time, Jim did a barrel roll in a cargo version of the 707," Tipton continued. "His copilot was a fellow named Dave Hoover who later became an air show pilot.

"When asked in an interview at Oshkosh about how he learned aerobatics," Tipton said, "Dave responded, 'Captain Chaudoin taught me in a 707' ".

7/22/01

Chapter 10

The Gutsiest Pilots
(Handicapped Flyers)

In a split second one's life can change drastically. A happy, healthy individual can suddenly become immobile---permanently paralyzed!

Usually it's the result of an accident. First, there's a numbness, no feeling in the limbs. Maybe the arms. Maybe the legs. Maybe both.

And then the doctor pronounces the sentence. The patient will be a paraplegic, wheelchair bound, for the rest of their lives.

The stories that follow are accounts of individuals who know the feeling that comes with hearing those words. But these are people who did not let their disabilities put them down. Many of the heroes of this chapter became pilots after they became paraplegics or were otherwise seriously disabled.

We can all learn a lot from the courage of these people displayed.

PAT CAN'T WALK, BUT HE CAN FLY

When an accident that was not his fault left him without the use of his legs just a short time before he was to finish his work for a master's degree, it would have been understandable if Pat Kelly folded, if he felt he had been dealt a bad hand and decided to retire from an active life and spend the rest of his days sitting around in a wheelchair.

The deal fate handed him was particularly tough for Kelly because he had been an athlete. That was now history. He would never again sense the challenge and excitement of athletic competition.

If he decided to spend his life watching television from a wheelchair, you couldn't fault him.

But that's not what he did. He got a job. With the money he earned he pursued a lifelong dream, one that went back to his boyhood. He took flying lessons and he got a pilot's license.

Somebody had once said he wasn't the greatest athlete in the world. But when Pat Kelly played slotback on the Pequannock High School football team in his senior year in 1972, he carried the ball five times and scored three touchdowns.

He was on the school's ski team for three years and in 1971 he finished seventh in the North Jersey High School Ski Association Meet at Great Gorge in a competition that included racing, free style, and jumping.

Paraplegic Pat Kelly pulls himself up the wing so he can pull himself into the cockpit.

After he graduated from high school he went to the University of Utah where he earned a bachelor of science degree in psychology.

Then he went on to Emory University in Atlanta, where he was a student in anesthesiology in a two-year course for a master's degree in medical science.

On April 6, 1976, just two months away from that master's degree, in one terrible instant, his life took a detour.

Kelly was on his motorcycle, stopped at a red light, when a car traveling in the opposite direction ran the red light and struck another car which spun around and landed on top of him.

A student nurse in yet another car rushed to jack up the car on top of Kelly enough to reduce the pressure on him.

Kelly suffered six broken ribs, punctures of both lungs, a broken pelvis, a badly broken leg, and a broken lower back.

He also suffered deep lacerations on his right buttock and some second degree burns. .

He was paralyzed from the waist down.

Kelly underwent three operations. In one, they inserted two ten-inch steel rods on either side of his spine. In another, they did plastic surgery on his buttocks. In the third, they operated on his bladder.

He would never ski again. He would never play tennis or golf, sports he took up after high school.

But on March 12, 1982, he became a licensed private pilot.

"I was always interested in flying," Kelly said. "I used to stand at the end of the runway at Lincoln Park Airport and watch the airplanes take off and land.

"It gets your blood going. It gets your adrenaline flowing, like skiing or riding a motorcycle," he said.

In July of 1978, Kelly heard of a program at Epps Flying Service at Peachtree-DeKalb Airport in Atlanta, where an aircraft was equipped with a hand-operated rudder bar so paraplegics could learn to fly.

Kelly knew then that he would learn. But it wasn't until September of 1980 that he was able to start lessons.

He had found a job in Atlanta by then and was able to pay for one lesson a week. He is administrative director of the Anesthesiology Department of the Emory University Hospital.

Except for the fact that he uses a hand bar to control the rudder instead of the usual rudder pedals, everything about Kelly's training was similar to that which any other student undergoes.

When the FAA examiner flew with him on his flight test, he prefaced the flight with a statement that Kelly would receive no special treatment or consideration. He passed his flight test with flying colors.

He developed some special techniques for overcoming his disability. He uses a mirror on a handle to do his preflight inspection. It's something like the mirror a dentist uses to look at hard-to-see areas in your mouth, except it's a bit bigger. Kelly uses it to check his oil, the fuel in his tanks, and the upper sets of magnetos.

He flies a low wing Piper Cherokee.

He can fold his wheelchair and pull it up into the aircraft without help.

On weekends he usually takes friends for rides. Friends who can walk, but can't fly.

6/6/82

QUADRIPLEGIC BECOMES A GLIDER INSTRUCTOR

Ray Temchus spent a year in Vietnam. Thousands of GIs came back from there crippled, maimed, or emotionally scarred. Temchus was one of the lucky ones. He came back unharmed. In his world everything was coming up roses. He had a good job. Life was good.

And then it happened, like a bolt out of nowhere. A freak accident left him with a broken neck.

Suddenly, he was a quadriplegic. He had no use of his legs. Almost no use of his right hand and limited use of his left hand.

He was lucky to have survived. Some people might have questioned what kind of luck that was.

For Ray, there weren't questions as much as challenges. He didn't ask why, he found ways to accomplish things many able-bodied people couldn't master.

He had been a pilot before his accident. He is still a pilot, but now he flies gliders instead of powered aircraft. And he's not just a pilot, he's an instructor. He teaches other disabled people to fly gliders.

This is the story of an extraordinary man who demonstrated how to overcome adversity and has helped others do the same.

A few weeks ago, on Oct. 15 (1988), Ray Temchus of Scotch Plains, established a first in the world of aviation. He became the first quadriplegic to earn a glider instructor's rating.

The story of that achievement goes back to 1983 when Temchus met Irv Soble, the United Airlines pilot we wrote about in Chapter 3, (The Birth of a Heavenly Idea), who founded Freedom's Wings, an organization that provides handicapped people with an opportunity to learn to fly gliders. Temchus met Soble at an Air Show at Sky Manor Airport in Pittstown, where he

Ray Temchus

conceived the idea for that organization. It wasn't until a year later, however, that Temchus, who was confined to a wheelchair, went back to Sky Manor Airport, where Freedom's Wings was based, to learn more about the program.

Temchus wasn't new to flying, but he had never flown a glider before his accident in 1975 left him a quadriplegic. Temchus first started learning to fly when he was stationed at Ft. Sill, Oklahoma, during a 3-year hitch in the Army, including a year in Vietnam.

After he left the service he had a good job as a supervisor in a pharmaceutical plant when tragedy struck on a street in Westfield. He was driving a truck when he hit a patch of water in the street from a backed up storm sewer and he lost control. The truck flipped and Temchus was thrown through the windshield. He suffered a broken neck.

He spent a year-and-a-half in the hospital and when he was discharged he had no use of his legs and he did not have full use of his hands. Nevertheless, just four days after his discharge, he went back to work.

In 1984, he took his first flight with Freedom's Wings. But it wasn't until two years later that he soloed. It would have happened much sooner, but the organization's experiments with hand controls for students who had no use of their legs were not especially successful.

In 1986, they acquired a Grob G-103 Aero, a German-made glider that had hand controls that worked well. A month later, Temchus soloed and in another month he had his private glider license.

Last December (1987), he earned his commercial license. His crowning achievement, an instructor's rating, came a month later.

That achievement brought about the realization of one of Irv Soble's original objectives: to train handicapped people to fly so that they could teach other handicapped people.

What made Temchus' achievement possible was not just the hand controls, but dual hand controls. He could not teach another disabled person to fly unless they both had hand controls.

Bill Smela, who was the Fixed Base Operator at Sky Manor Airport, and an excellent mechanic, developed a set of dual hand controls for the Grob. He got FAA approval, and installed them.

There are only three Grobs with hand controls in the country, but Freedom's Wings has the only one with dual hand controls and consequently is the only glider in the country in which a handicapped person can teach another handicapped person to fly.

Temchus' first passenger after he got his instructor's rating was the man who gave him his first flight in a Freedom's Wings aircraft, Larry Spencer of Morris Plains, a World War II glider pilot.

Spencer is one of the volunteer instructors who helped keep expenses down so that handicapped people who want to learn to fly pay only what they can afford. Freedom's Wings subsidizes the balance with funds from contributions, grants, and fund raisers.

Temchus' first student was Iris Helfrich, a substitute teacher afflicted with MS.

To get to the airport (Freedom's Wings has moved to Van Sant Airport in Erwina. Pa., just across the Delaware River from Frenchtown) Temchus drives a specially equipped van with hand controls.

It's a long ride from Ray's home in Scotch Plains to Van Sant Airport, about an hour-and-a-half each way, but he knows firsthand what it means to handicapped people. They find ways to get to the airport to fulfill a dream--to get buckled into a glider and go soaring into the skies where they can control the aircraft and experience a superb sense of freedom that most able-bodied people have never known.

11/6/88

A HANDICAPPED AIR SHOW PERFORMER

Steve Soper created the ultimate test for a handicapped pilot. He became an air show aerobatic performer.

But he didn't do the standard aerobatic routine in a high powered biplane or a competition aircraft. He did something akin to what Bob Hoover did with the Shrike Commander. He performed his aerobatics in an airplane designed for transportation, not aerobatics.

His performances could stand on their own, even though he could not. Talking to Steve sets you thinking about determined people achieving goals. Reading his story should do the same.

Steve Soper took the accomplishment of a handicapped pilot one step further than just getting his medical back. He carved himself a career doing something most able-bodied pilots can't do. He became an aerobatic performer at air shows.

To add a little extra to that, he did something few aerobatic pilots did. Instead. of performing in a high powered single-engine aircraft specifically designed and built for such specialized flying, he performed his aerobatics in a twin-engine Cessna Skymaster with one engine in front and one in back, an airplane built for business and pleasure flying, not for aerobatics. He gave it a new mission.

Talking to Steve makes you think about dreaming the impossible dream.

People who fly are not fainthearted. This was graphically illustrated by Soper to tens of thousands of spectators at the New Jersey Festival of Ballooning at Solberg Airport a couple of weeks ago.

He was not a newcomer to the balloon festival. Three years ago he flew in the air show that is part of the festival. At that time he did his routine in a Pitts Special, a biplane designed specifically for aerobatics.

Steve Soper in his wheelchair in front of the Cessna Skymaster in which he performs at air shows.

Shortly after that show Soper was taking off from a ranch in Montana when the engine quit. That marked the end of the Pitts. Steve was pretty busted up, too.

Unlike the airplane, however, he was down, but not out. He had a crushed vertebrae that kept him in the hospital for two months.

When he came out, part of him didn't work anymore. His legs. He was a paraplegic.

"I never thought flying was out," he recounted from his wheelchair before his performance at the show. "But I thought I was retired from air shows and would have to get a real job."

Steve had a lot of time to think and one of the things he thought about was the Ercoupe. That was an airplane that came on the market immediately after World War II. It was designed with simplified controls--no rudder pedals. There are still some of them around. You don't need the use of your legs to fly it. But it's a small two-place aircraft. There's no place for a wheelchair, and the aircraft is not approved for aerobatics.

"Then I thought about the Cessna Skymaster. I had worked on that aircraft as a mechanic. It has a big door and lots of room."

The Skymaster is a rather unusual aircraft. It is a twin-engine plane, but instead of having one engine mounted in each wing, in the conventional fashion, it has one engine in front and one in back.

Steve spent four months hunting for the right Skymaster. When he found one that met his specifications, he had to get a set of hand controls.

"There are a lot of companies that make them," he said. "I had no trouble finding a set. I got one at Union Aviation in Sturgis, Kentucky."

His hand controls consist of a bracket that attaches to the rudder pedals. A bar that extends from the bracket curves to the right. There is a metal ring at the end of the bar. Steve slips his hand through the ring and by moving his arm he moves the bar that controls the rudder pedals. At the same time he uses his right hand to control the throttles.

Steve is the only paraplegic performing aerobatics in the Skymaster. As if that weren't enough to demonstrate his indomitable spirit, there was an unscheduled event at the New Jersey Festival of Ballooning Air Show at Solberg Airport that further demonstrated it.

After Steve had done a loop and a couple of other maneuvers, he lost oil pressure in his front engine. Flying past the flight line with thousands of spectators watching, he shut down that engine and circled for a landing.

An oil line had broken.

Steve's major concern was getting it fixed so he could perform the following day. A mechanic got right on the job and, with the help of Steve's wife, Genny, who went underneath that engine, reaching into tight places, to pull wires into place, and Glen Akins, a friend who is part of his crew, they had the airplane ready for the following day's performance.

The Skymaster is an especially beautiful airplane to watch in aerobatics. Because of the rear-mounted engine, it has twin tail booms extending back to the horizontal stabilizer and the rudder. In flight it looks different than a conventional airplane. It somehow reminds me of a swallow in flight. Looping and rolling in the skilled hands of a seasoned aerobatic pilot like Soper, it is truly a thing of beauty.

When Steve landed after his performance he was greeted by a rousing round of applause from the tens of thousands of spectators who were fortunate enough to witness him and his Skymaster performing a ballet in the sky.

Part of that applause was for the skill Steve demonstrated and part of it had to be for the spirit that put him back in the air after his accident and then had him performing after a mechanical problem that might have grounded someone with less spirit and guts.

8/6/89

DOWN, BUT NOT OUT

You never know what can happen from one minute to the next. The subject of this column could confirm that. He owned a thriving photo business. He was an active pilot. And then...

The story of what happened to him is frightening. The way he dealt with it is inspiring. But let his story speak for itself.

Mike Sciullo was a relatively healthy man when he went to bed one night in October 1992.

"I didn't have an ache or a pain," he said. "I finished work, went home, and went to bed."

When he woke up, it was eight weeks later. He had been in a coma all that time. After he finally regained consciousness, he learned that both his hands and feet had been amputated.

"My intestine and bowels had tied a knot in each other" he said, "and they burst. That poisoned my system and caused septic shock which attacks all organs, including the kidney and heart. That can cause them to shut down.

"I was in the hospital for 14 weeks and in a rehabilitation center in Pomona for five weeks. I was so weak when I came to the rehabilitation center, I couldn't roll over in bed. I couldn't feed myself.

"Five weeks later, I walked out of there with two new hands and two new feet. (His left hand was replaced with a hook. And the stump of his right hand was fitted with a device that acts like a thumb and permits him to grab things.)

"Four days later, I came back to work," Sciullo said. He owns the Atlantic Photo and Imaging Center, a photo processing plant in Atlantic City that does retail and specialty work for ad agencies and makes large (3 x 10 foot) prints.

Mike Sciullo, who lost both hands and feet, but flew again.

Sciullo was a private pilot with more than 2,500 hours when he was struck down by the rare malady. He had owned four planes over the years. But there wasn't much chance that he would see the inside of a cockpit again.

Then one day an old friend he knew from the years they both flew out of Bader Field in Atlantic City, called him up and asked, "How would you like to go flying?"

His friend owned a Cherokee 180 that was based at Hammonton Airport, not far from Bader Field. He hardly gave Sciullo a chance to respond when he said, "I'll be there in an hour."

"Wait a minute," Sciullo replied, "I can't even get in an airplane."

"I'll be there anyway," his friend said.

"We got out to the airport and he put a plastic milk crate on the ground for me to step on to get up on the wing. But try as I did, I couldn't get up. I was exhausted from trying. I sat on the wing to rest. My friend said, 'Shimmy up the wing.' I tried it and got up to the door.

"With his help it took me almost an hour to get into the seat. It was February and it was cold, but I was sweating trying to get in that airplane. After I finally got my backside in, he swung my legs in and then he climbed over me to get into the left seat.

"We spent an hour in the cockpit talking about how I could handle the controls," said Sciullo. "We talked about how I would work the throttle, the trim tab, the instruments. I practiced until we knew what I could do and how I would do it.

"I couldn't use the toe brakes because I have no feeling in my feet. But the airplane had a hand brake.

"I couldn't turn the radio knobs, but I later fitted plastic tubing over the knobs to make them longer so I could turn them. The tubes were easy to slip on and off.

"One of the things I was concerned about was using the rudder pedals. But when you push one pedal down it pushes the other one up, so using them was easy.

"After we had gone over everything thoroughly, we started the engine.

"I taxied out to the runway and I had no trouble. When we finished our takeoff check my friend said, 'Take over.' I took off, flew around the pattern and did a touch and go. After that we flew to Easton on the eastern shore of Maryland.

"There was a strong crosswind, so my friend took over and landed. Then we went to have some crab cakes for lunch.

"Getting back in the airplane was much easier this time because we knew how to do it. On that trip I got in almost three hours of flying time.

"Almost every Sunday after that my friend called me up to go flying. We flew to Philadelphia, Bridgeport, and Rehoboth Beach,

Del. I made the landing most of the time.

"My friend was a retired civilian employee of the Coast Guard. He was a very easy going guy. He loved to fly. He would fly every day, if he could.

"His name was Bob Cornett, Jr. He died last year and I haven't flown since.

"I don't know if I can ever get my medical back, but I would like to," said Sciullo. "I'm 74 and I work five days a week. Sometimes seven. I know that people who have become disabled have gotten their medical certification back if they could demonstrate their competency to an FAA flight examiner.

"In order to apply for a reinstatement of my medical certificate, I have to submit all my medical records to the FAA flight surgeon in Oklahoma City. Those records are extensive and I've had trouble trying to get them, but I'm going to keep trying.

"I don't know if I'll ever succeed, but I know from all my hours of flying with Bob Cornett that I can fly safely. I'd be very pleased if I could get my flying status back, and I know that Bob Cornett would be just as pleased."

7/18/99

Note: *I spoke with Mike Sciullo a couple of years after this was written. He had still not flown since Cornett died and the press of business kept him from devoting the time and effort that would have been required to try to get his medical certificate back. "But I'm pleased," he said, "that I proved I could do it."*

Chapter 11

Mercy Flights

At any hour of the day or night there are general aviation (private or business) aircraft winging their way through the skies carrying seriously ill patients and family members to hospitals and treatment centers that may give them relief from suffering and sometimes a remission of their afflictions. In some cases they fly patients to distant hospitals for organ transplants that must be performed within four hours after the harvesting of the organ.

There are dozens of organizations that provide such services using volunteer pilots who donate their time and the use of their aircraft to help people who have suffered the ravages of life-threatening illnesses. In some cases these illnesses have drained their life savings leaving them with no funds to travel to institutions which may be able to help them.

There is no charge to these passengers. Volunteer pilots not only offer their time and their aircraft, they pick up the fuel cost as well.

Companies that own business aircraft in which they carry some of the world's top corporate executives, make empty seats available to transport patients to treatment centers.

There were many heartwarming stories associated with such flights over the years. This chapter contains a number of them.

TIME WAS RUNNING OUT

Every mercy flight story I've written was a moving experience for me. But of all the mercy flight stories I've written over the years, the one which will always stand out above the others is the one which follows.   It is a story full of high suspense and heartbreaking frustration, while a young life hung in the balance.

One of the elements that makes this story so memorable is its ending. I was left with the feeling that this was a real miracle .... with a little help from some charitable pilots.

T he charter operator kept an airplane and a crew on standby 24 hours a day, seven days a week, for 14 months, waiting for the call that might save a young life.   It was a painfully long wait.

Chuck McKenna, left, and framed photo, bellow, of Allison McCartney with letter of thanks to McKenna.

For Allison McCartney, a student at Pope John XXIII High School in Sparta, it seemed a lot longer.   Allison's life depended on that flight.

Allison was a freshman in 1986, when she learned she needed a heart-lung transplant.   Doctors told her she had a year to find a donor.

While she was waiting for that all-important call, Allison continued to attend classes, half days, in a wheelchair.

When they found a donor, Allison would have to be on the operating table in Presbyterian Hospital at the University of Pittsburgh, within four hours.

She carried a beeper just in case they couldn't reach her by phone.

Allison waited patiently for the call that might save her life.

Months dragged by and it didn't come. The year the doctors gave her passed --- and there was no call.

Then, late in the evening of a snowy day in the winter of 1987, after 14 months of waiting, the call came. It came to Allison, it came to Chuck McKenna, president of MacDan Aviation, a charter operator, in his office at Teterboro Airport. He had kept one of the airplanes in his charter fleet on standby all those months. The call came also to the Sparta Rescue Squad.

McKenna called the ground crew at his Essex County Airport facility and asked them to have the twin-engine Piper Seneca ready to go when he got there.

Allison arrived with her mother in the Sparta Rescue Squad ambulance, at almost the same time as McKenna. Within an hour of the call, they were airborne.

McKenna was the pilot, Brian Madigan, the chief pilot for MacDan Aviation, was the copilot.

It was Madigan who brought Allison's plight to McKenna's attention. He is a good friend of Father Kieran McHugh, principal of her high school. Father McHugh knew that the only way to get Allison to Pittsburgh in time was in a general aviation aircraft. And he knew that Madigan was a pilot.

He asked Madigan if he knew of someone who could assume the responsibility of having an aircraft and a crew available on an instant's notice. Madigan was aware that McKenna had offered his services in such cases before. As soon as he heard the story, McKenna volunteered.

On the flight to Pittsburgh they bucked an 80-mile-an-hour headwind. Allison, along with her mother, was in the back seat. "She was animated and in good spirits, all the way," McKenna related.
Time was of the essence. As a Lifeguard Flight (a recognized mercy flight), the FAA gave them priority handling and a direct route. But because of the strong headwinds, the flight took two hours instead of the normal hour and 20 minutes.

They landed in a heavy snowfall. But in spite of everything, they were still within the time limit.

An ambulance was waiting with its lights flashing, to speed Allison to the hospital. But when they disembarked and walked to the ambulance, the ambulance driver greeted them and said they weren't going to do the operation. There was a problem with the lungs.

They reboarded the airplane and flew back to Essex County Airport. That was how the 14-month wait for a lifesaving operation ended. But it was not the end of this story.

One afternoon a couple of months later, the phone rang again.

They had found another donor. This time, the weather was good, the flight was smooth, and this time, it wasn't a false alarm. The operation was performed and it was successful.

I chatted with Allison over the phone from McKenna's Teterboro office the other day. She spoke with unbridled enthusiasm about the activities she had been involved in since her operation two years ago.

She ran cross country with her high school team in practice sessions. "I was always last." she said, "but I loved it." She ran the 100-yard dash in one meet with the track team, but she pulled a hamstring in her dance class--she was taking tap, jazz, ballet, and lyrical dancing--and that ended her running.

She was full of enthusiasm about being in the chorus of a production of "How to Succeed in Business Without Really Trying."

Allison is working part time now in the Sparta Group Home Center for Humanistic Changes, which is working to help retarded adults find a place in society.

She talked about her anticipation of entering Allentown (Pa.) College in September to study theater.

And she talked about her graduation from Pope John XXIII High School last spring. She invited eight people to her graduation--people who had played an important part in helping her get there. Chuck McKenna was one of those she invited, along with people who had helped raise money for her operation.

"Father McHugh called them all up to the stage," Allison said. "1 didn't think he was going to do that. It was like, 'This Is Your Life '.

"It was an overwhelming experience to have all those people come up," she said.

As for Chuck McKenna's reaction: "No one could ever pay me enough for the pleasure I got from that," he said.

3/17/91

CORPORATE ANGELS

Hundreds of company-owned jet aircraft crisscross the nation daily carrying top executives on high level missions. Many of those aircraft also carry people not affiliated with the company. They are patients suffering from cancer for whom specialized treatment has been recommended to help them in their battle against the disease.

Airline travel would be difficult in many cases. And often the cost of transportation to treatment centers is a serious consideration.

Hundreds of the nation's corporations have joined together under the banner of an organization called Corporate Angel Network to make unoccupied seats on their aircraft available to patients who need transportation to specialized treatment centers.

The column that follows describes the origin of the program and it provides an example of how it works.

Hundreds of business jets fly to every corner of the country every day carrying the captains of industry whose responsibility it is to keep their companies profitable, their stockholders happy, and the nation's economy on the right track.

On many of those flights there is another precious cargo. It could be your next door neighbor. Corporations across America offer unoccupied seats in their aircraft to cancer patients traveling to treatment centers. There is no cost to the patient or a family member accompanying them.

Under the banner of the Corporate Angel Network (CAN), a nonprofit organization based at Westchester County Airport in White Plains, N.Y., more than 550 companies across the nation are part of the network that makes empty seats available on their flights.

Batya and Sam Margalit walk toward a Corporate Angel Network (CAN) jet waiting to fly her to Washington for treatment at the National Institute of Health in Bethesda, Md.

To the patients they serve, the companies in CAN are truly angels. Batya Margalit of Flanders could tell you something about that.

Nineteen years ago, ten days after she gave birth to her third child, Batya was diagnosed with melanoma, a skin cancer. She had major surgery and considered herself cured.

Then, last March, she was in an auto accident and her right ribs were bruised. X-rays showed there were no broken ribs, but they showed something more devastating, spots on her right lung.

"I had X-rays taken two weeks before the accident and they didn't detect the spots," recalls Batya. "The automobile accident was a blessing."

When her cancer was diagnosed, her doctor sent the records to the Memorial Sloan-Kettering Cancer Center in New York, one of the nation's leading cancer hospitals. They recommended that she go to the National Institute of Health in Bethesda, Md.

The NIH is doing a great deal of advanced research on cancer treatments and Batya was placed on one of its experimental protocols. She is one of the patients on a new procedure in which aggressive white blood cells are cloned, grown in test tubes for 40 days and then reindexed.

The treatments require her to go to Bethesda every third week, where she remains for five or six days. They do not do chemotherapy treatments there. They specialize in immune treatment. During her stay in the hospital Batya receives IVs and injections.

At first she was treated with Interleukin 1. That did not prove effective so she was switched to Interleukin 2. That was helpful. The reactions are severe, but the results have been good so far.

"I had three tumors in my lung," she says. "The two smaller ones have disappeared. The larger one has shrunk. I also have a tumor on my liver. So far that has not responded, but they are hopeful that it will."

Before she contacted the Corporate Angel Network, Batya's husband, Sam, drove her to Maryland which is a long drive. She also flew on commercial airlines.

"One time we got caught in traffic and I missed my flight by 10 minutes. I couldn't get on the next flight. It was full. They put me on standby. I had to stand around and wait without knowing what I would do if I couldn't get on. But I did get on that flight."

On Corporate Angel Network flights, patients have to make arrangements in advance so they can be matched up with business flight schedules. Most of the time Batya can't do that on the flight home because she never knows exactly when she is going to be discharged. She usually gets only a few hours notice.

Her husband, a principal engineer for Honeywell, who diagnoses and analyzes problems with highly sophisticated electronics equipment aboard business jets, usually drives down to pick her up. But she has flown on the airlines.

"One time I had a note from the hospital saying I needed help," she says. "They did provide an electric cart to take me to the gate. When I got there I told them I didn't feel well and I needed help with my things. They pointed and said, 'Go over there.' I couldn't get any help.

"The people in the Corporate Angel Network couldn't be nicer. They take my bags. They offer me something to eat or drink. They are friendly and polite.

"On one flight an executive took me in his limousine. When he got out he told his driver to take me anywhere I wanted to go."

Batya has gone on nine flights with five companies. Her first flight was from Trenton Mercer Airport. She has also flown from Morristown and Teterboro Airports, and she has landed at Newark on a return flight she was able to arrange.

She is usually on flights to Reagan National Airport in Washington, D.C.,[2] but she has also flown into Dulles.

CAN was founded in 1981 by Priscilla Blum, a recovered cancer patient who served in the Connecticut chapter of the American Cancer Society. A pilot herself, Priscilla flew out of Westchester County Airport. She was aware that corporate aircraft took off with empty seats every day. She suggested a plan to make those seats available to cancer patients traveling for treatments. The idea did not inspire much enthusiasm. But she formed a partnership with Jay Weinberg, another recovered cancer patient, and they went to work to set up an organization. They got office space donated by Westchester County.

That first year, CAN arranged 50 flights. Today, with a full-time staff of three and 65 volunteers, they average 100 flights a month. Since its inception they have arranged 10,000 flights for cancer patients.

Their passengers have ranged from a 13-day-old baby who needed a bone marrow transplant to a 92-year-old woman who drove herself to the airport.

CAN patients must be able to walk unassisted up the steps into the aircraft. They cannot be on any life support systems. Children may travel with both parents.

---

[2] *After 9/11 Reagan National Airport was closed to business aircraft. The airport was opened to this traffic on Oct. 18, 2005 with regulations which still keeps a lot of general aviation traffic from using Reagan National Airport.*

Patients constantly reaffirm the fact that the organization's name describes its mission perfectly. They are angels.

One of CAN's mottos is: "All angels have wings. Ours just happen to come with jet engines."

Names of the 500 companies that provide this service are normally not revealed. They prefer to remain anonymous. But to many people who owe their lives to CAN members, they are not anonymous at all.

12/6/98

EVERYTHING THAT COULD GO WRONG, DID

Mercy flight pilots never know what to expect. On some of their missions time is of the essence. There is usually a four-hour window between the time a donor organ is harvested and the time it is transplanted. That's one reason for general aviation mercy flights. Transplant patients can't wait around until the next scheduled airline flight. It will be too late.

General aviation volunteer pilots are on call 24 hours a day and can be at the airport and ready to go on short notice.

There are times, however, when everything doesn't go quite as planned. The unexpected sometimes injects its ugly head into a critical situation. There are times when there are misunderstandings, missed cues.

This story depicts just such a case.

Their beepers may go off at any time of day or night and somebody's life may depend on it. They are not physicians or law enforcement officers. They are pilots who volunteer their aircraft, their time, and fuel to help seriously ill people.

In some cases the beep may indicate that a critically needed organ has become available and the patient has a limited time frame in which to reach the hospital where the transplant will be performed. The patient cannot rely on airline schedules.

John Rochelle of Chester, a custom builder, and Ray Bersch of Watchung, are two of the hundreds of volunteer mercy flight pilots. In less than two years they have made more than two dozen such flights.

There are a number of organizations that recruit pilots to volunteer their equipment and services. Most pilots apply to one of them. Rochelle and Bersch, who have been flying together for 15 years, have been approved for such flights by three organizations, AirLifeLine in California, the largest such organization, Angel Flight in Blue Bell, Pa., and Volunteer Pilots Association in Hickory, Pa.

When a call comes in they never know what's waiting for them. On June 24 they got a call from Angel Flight asking if they could fly a cancer patient to Columbus, Ohio, for a special cancer treatment at Ohio State University Hospital.

They took off from Morristown Airport in Rochelle's Cessna 210 at 7:30 a.m. with the patient and her husband. The flight took three hours and 15 minutes. They waited five hours and flew them back. It was a routine mission. But not all missions are routine.

Another time, John and Ray were on a call to fly a 15-month-old boy to Pittsburgh for a liver transplant. The little boy had been waiting a year.

Last Feb. 27 at 5:30 p.m. John got a call from AirLifeLine. A liver was available. They had four hours to get the boy to Pittsburgh.

When he got the call, John tried to contact Ray, but he couldn't reach him. So he promptly assumed some of the copilot's duties. He checked weather and filed a flight plan from their base at Morristown to Teterboro, where they were to pick up the little boy and his parents and fly them to Allegheny County Airport in Pittsburgh.

After what seemed like hours, John finally got through to Ray who rushed to Morristown Airport to fuel and pre-flight the aircraft. But when he got to the airport the aircraft wasn't there. John has two partners in the aircraft and one of them was obviously out flying. A frantic call to John's mobile phone went unanswered.

Ray tuned his hand-held transceiver to the tower frequency just in case the aircraft was in the area. Ray's mobile phone rang. It was John. While they were trying to develop an alternate plan, Ray heard the airplane call the tower. It was inbound.

There was a great feeling of relief, but their problems were just beginning. First, John, whose office is a half hour from the airport, didn't arrive. In the meantime, an airport security officer rushed up to Ray and said the tower was trying to contact him. The tower had been advised that the patient pickup was to be at Newark International Airport rather than the originally planned Teterboro.

The only reason the security officer knew where to find Ray was because he had talked to the tower when he was looking for John's aircraft. If it were not for that call, John and Ray would have flown to Teterboro and waited in vain for the little boy and his parents to show up. And the clock was running.

Ray couldn't understand the change in plans. He and John knew nothing about it. He drove to the Morristown operations office to try to contact the person at Newark who called in the message delivered by the security officer.

Nobody knew who it was. He called Teterboro where they had been scheduled to pick up their passengers. No one there knew of any change in plans.

Once in the air and identified as a Lifeguard flight, as all such flights are, they were cleared to land on Runway 22 Right at Newark Airport. The tower reported a 27 knot crosswind with gusts to 50. That would strain the aircraft's capability. Traffic was held because of the urgency of their mission and in spite of the wind, they got down safely.

Three police cars with their red lights flashing in the darkness were waiting for them when they taxied in. The family was there, but the police thought they were supposed to take a Learjet air ambulance which was sitting on the ramp. But the Learjet operators wanted $4,000. The original fee they asked was $6,000, but even $4,000 was out of the question.

John and Ray learned that the family of the little boy didn't speak much English and in their excitement and confusion they had the police take them to Newark Airport instead of Teterboro. To them, airport meant Newark. They never heard of Teterboro. In addition to that, they had another infant with them, which John and Ray didn't expect. The family was not about to be separated.

They were fighting time. They faced a flight into headwinds reported to be up to 70 mph with possible turbulence.

John contacted the hospital to tell them of the delay because time was critical and they had wasted a lot of it. They told him they had a little extra time. He instructed the parents as best he could on how to hold the children in their laps during takeoff and landing. They were given a priority takeoff.

Because of the headwinds, their ground speed was cut to 49 knots at one time. They arrived at 11:30 p.m., and in spite of everything, they arrived a half hour ahead of their original schedule. An ambulance showed up shortly to take the little boy to the hospital. At 2 a.m. they were in the air on their way back to Morristown after a nerve-racking experience.

They received the good news sometime later that the little boy's operation was successful. Most of the time the pilots never hear about the final result of their mission.

8/31/97

PHARMACIST HEALS WITH WINGS

A pharmacist's normal working days are devoted to filling prescriptions that may ease pain, clear up infections, and cure a wide variety of ailments.

This is the story of a pharmacist who used a different approach to helping sick people. It came about as a result of a personal tragedy.

The great kindness shown to him during his trying days, caused him to develop a strong sensitivity to other people's troubles. And he did something about it, using his airplane.

Three years ago, Mountainside pharmacist Richard Reich had a new pilot's license, a beautiful new airplane, and he was the perfect picture of a happy man.

But that picture was blotted out in one awful instant. A hit-and-run driver struck and killed his eight-year-old daughter.

The blow was not an easy one to overcome. But sympathy and concern from friends and neighbors--and even strangers--helped the family return to their normal life pattern.

Ever since that experience, Richard Reich has been extremely sensitive to the tragedies of others. He thought constantly about how he might help other people faced with tragedy.

And it was his airplane that provided him with the answer.

Last fall a little boy in Clifton was badly burned when his pajamas caught fire as a result of playing with matches in bed. He suffered second and third degree burns on 90 percent of his body. Doctors at Passaic General Hospital struggled against great odds to keep him alive.

It was touch and go for awhile, but they won their battle. He would survive. But the little boy was severely scarred. Now he faced an even tougher battle, the long and painful struggle for rehabilitation. That meant dozens of skin grafts and reconstructive procedures.

Reich had been a Shriner for 14 years. The Shriners, in addition to operating 22 crippled children's hospitals throughout the country, support three of the outstanding burn centers in the world, one of which is in Boston.

When a bed became available for the little boy, the question arose as to how to get him there. He was in no condition to make the long journey in an ambulance.

Reich was contacted by the Shriners about flying him up there in his Cessna Stationair. He rigged a stretcher in the six-place, single-engine aircraft and the next morning the little boy was brought to Caldwell Airport by ambulance and placed aboard Reich's airplane along with a doctor, a nurse, and the Recorder of the Shriners Salaam Temple in Livingston, Whitney Agre.

Reich filed a special Lifeguard IFR flight plan that gave him priority going into Boston. Forty miles out he contacted the tower and told them he would like to make a very gradual descent from 9,000 feet. They told him he was cleared to land. All other traffic would be held till he was on the ground.

Two weeks ago, while he was celebrating the Jewish High Holy Days, Reich received a call to transport a badly burned 13-year-old Plainfield boy to Boston.

He left his family--his wife and three daughters--to fly Gregory Hicks from Morristown Airport to Logan Airport in Boston.

The cost of care per patient at the burn center averages between $40,000 and $50,000, according to Reich. The entire amount is picked up by the Shriners. And in some cases the cost runs into six figures.

For Reich, these two missions were only a beginning.

While on a trip to Nassau with the New Jersey Pharmaceutical Association, Reich met a fellow pharmacist-pilot-plane owner who had kicked around the idea of using general aviation aircraft for emergency medical purposes.

His newfound friend, Richard Peckman of Maplewood, owns a pharmacy in Jersey City and a Piper Cherokee Six based at Morristown Airport.

Peckman had discussed with one drug manufacturer the practicality of flying drugs and medical supplies in emergencies.

The two pharmacists found a common ground and in July they held a fly-in to Atlantic City where they held an organizational meeting of the New Jersey Flying Pharmacists.

Their fledgling group has 25 members including 20 pilots with airplanes.

Reich and Peckman both keep lists of all pilots and aircraft. Any time an emergency arises in New Jersey that requires the use of a general aviation aircraft to save a life, they will find an aircraft and a pilot.

Both men love to fly for the sheer beauty of the experience. But both are also keenly aware that general aviation is a practical means of transportation that cannot be matched by any kind of ground transportation.

Over the years they have made dozens of flights to help people who otherwise would have no way to get to distant hospitals or treatment centers.

And they both are dedicated to seeing an increased use of general aviation aircraft in New Jersey to save lives.

9/29/74

THE FICKLE FINGER OF FATE

Coincidence--sometimes known as the Fickle Finger of Fate-- works in mysterious ways. A chain of events that may come about entirely by chance, can trigger triumph or tragedy.

Like a fine Persian rug where a myriad of colors and patterns are interwoven to form a single work of beauty, the story that follows, details an incredible series of coincidences woven into a suspenseful story that solved a serious problem for an elderly couple, who, for a time, seemed alone in the world.

I f Ed Roth's son hadn't played football on the Montvale team with John Lambiase's son five years ago....

If Ed Roth didn't get tired of driving 6 1/2 hours from New Jersey to his second home in Vermont every weekend....

If John Lambiase hadn't had a heart attack followed by open heart surgery, the circumstances that fit together to solve what seemed for a time to be a problem without a solution, would never have existed.

The story starts in New Bern, N.C., where an elderly couple from New Jersey, Olav and Engelborg Ellefson, had driven in October to investigate the

Ed Roth in the cockpit of his twin Cessna 310 with his friend, Nancy Pederson, who flew with him on a Mercy Flight to New Bern, N.C.

possibility of settling in the area that had attracted many other retirees from New Jersey.

While there, 65-year-old Mrs. Ellefson developed an aneurism (an abnormal expansion of an artery) in the brain. It left her blind.

After several days in intensive care to stabilize her condition, she underwent brain surgery. Her husband remained by her side, living in an apartment nearby provided by the hospital.

After weeks of painfully slow recovery, though still seriously ill, and very weak, doctors granted permission for Mrs. Ellefson to be moved back to her home in Atlantic City.

But how could she be transported?

An ambulance would be too costly--several thousand dollars--much more than the Ellefsons could afford.

Mrs. Ellefson was too ill to travel by commercial airliner. Besides, there is no airline service at New Bern and no scheduled service into Atlantic City.

That would mean transferring her to three separate aircraft, a charter to a major terminal in North Carolina, an airline flight, probably into Philadelphia, and a charter or commuter flight into Atlantic City. For one in Mrs. Ellefson's condition that was entirely out of the question.

An air ambulance was the only answer, but that is very expensive and was not an option.

Enter John Lambiase.

John, a pilot, who had been chief of the Teterboro weather station for years before retiring and moving to New Bern 18 months ago.

After recovering from a heart attack and open heart surgery, he became an active and dedicated volunteer at New Bern's Simmon-Knot Hospital.

When Olav Ellefson came to the hospital to see public relations director Beth Dickinson seeking help getting his wife back home, John Lambiase happened to be in her office.

Lambiase had a lot of friends in aviation and he thought he could find someone willing to lend a helping hand.

He started making phone calls to people in the aviation business. But it wasn't easy to find help. Operating an aircraft today is expensive and profit margins among commercial operators are, for the most part, down.

Lambiase did get some offers to make the flights at a discount from regular rates. But even at that, the cost would be prohibitive. The only answer was a mercy flight, for which some individual would be willing to donate his aircraft and his services.

After several dozen calls, Lambiase remembered his friend Ed Roth of Pinebrook, whose son had played football with *his* son.

Roth, who owns a body shop in East Orange, has a twin-engine Cessna 310 based at Essex County Airport. Lambiase remembered him as a generous, outgoing guy, always ready to lend a helping hand to anyone who needed it.

He had learned to fly ten years earlier after he became tired of driving 6 1/2 hours each way between New Jersey and his second home in Stowe, Vermont, every weekend.

When Lambiase called Roth and explained the problem to him, Roth said, "Sure," right off the bat.

The following Sunday, he and his friend Nancy Pedersen, a

student pilot, flew to New Bern from Essex County Airport.

An ambulance brought Mrs. Ellefson from the hospital right up to the aircraft. They boarded her through the baggage compartment door onto a fully reclining seat. A registered nurse accompanied her on the trip.

Her husband had driven back in advance to be in Atlantic City when his wife arrived.

The flight back was made on a Lifeguard flight plan, that provides priority routing and handling. It took an hour and 52 minutes to Atlantic City.

"The tower even called the hospital to make sure the ambulance would be at the airport when we arrived," Roth said. And the ambulance was there waiting.

And so it was that a rather odd chain of circumstances provided a happy ending to the difficult situation that faced an elderly couple who were total strangers to Ed Roth until that telephone call from his old friend, John Lambiase.

1/2/83

Chapter 12

The Old-Timers

In the early days of aviation, flying was full of excitement, adventure, and romance. It was the era of the daring young man in his flying machine. He, or she, with white scarf, helmet and goggles, was everybody's hero.

The sound of the old rotary engines made one's heart beat faster. The sight of a biplane lifting off was an exhilarating experience. And seeing it float gently back to earth left the spectator with a very satisfied feeling.

Our ties to the pilots who can recall those days are getting fewer and fewer as the old-timers pass on, but they and their stories and recollections are worth preserving.

This chapter is devoted to conversations with some of those old-timers whose flying activities began back in the glory days. They were a lively bunch with some colorful stories and they cast a light on what it was like way back when.

THE SPIRIT OF THE OLD DAYS

Pilots of the early days of aviation were a fun-loving, hell-raising bunch. They loved to tell stories about their flying escapades, and there was never any shortage of them. You could generally count on their stories being a bit embellished, perhaps a bit exaggerated, but that just added to their allure. They were part of a very elite group. Very few people had flown back in the 20s, the 30s and the 40s.

The stories in this chapter consist of interviews with pilots who flew back in those days. They shed light on what flying and fliers were like then. Some of these pilots flew over a period that spanned half a century. Some were still active pilots into the 80s and 90s.

Homer Clapper was one of those whose flying career spanned more than 50 years. His story provides a bit of the flavor of the old days.

"My dad was a railroad man," Homer Clapper said. "He liked to keep his feet on the ground. There was no way he was going to go up in one of those newfangled machines. But one day, surprisingly enough, I got him to agree to go up with me.

"In those days, back in the 30s, there was a solo license. You could go anywhere you wanted to, but you couldn't carry passengers.

"I helped my dad get into the cockpit, buckled him in and off we went for a nice sightseeing flight. I'm sure he enjoyed the flight, but he wasn't about to admit it.

"When I landed, I saw a CAA (Civil Aeronautics Administration, predecessor to the FAA) man standing there waiting for me. I knew why he was there. He was going to nail me because I wasn't licensed to carry a passenger. I got out of the plane and helped my father out and before the CAA man had a chance to say anything, I said, 'Hey, I want you to meet my father. He was a pilot in the war'.

Homer Clapper, the personification of the carefree, devil-may-care, old-time pilot.

(World War I).

"The CAA man was overwhelmed to meet 'a World War I pilot.' They were all considered heroes. People were in awe of them. The subject of my solo license, which I expected was going to get me in real trouble, never came up."

That story gives you a pretty good idea of what the old-time pilots were like. They could think fast when they had to. And occasions when they had to were quite frequent. They were a rather loose breed.

Old-timers can reel off dozens of stories like that. Homer Clapper is one of those pilots. He soloed in 1936 at the old Hadley Airport in South Plainfield (the original eastern terminus for the first night air mail flights). He got his solo license in 1939 at Franklin Lakes Airport. Both those airports are dim memories now. But there's nothing dim about Homer Clapper. He tells his stories with relish and gusto. And as much as a listener might enjoy hearing his stories, it's obvious he enjoys the telling more.

One of the stories he likes to tell is about why it took him three years between his solo flight and his solo license.

He was an engineering student at Rutgers when he soloed. His family was in Pittsburgh. He didn't tell them about his aerial activities. They would object to that vehemently. Nevertheless, they had their suspicions. He was an only child and the idea of him flying didn't appeal to them. They said that as long as they were paying his tuition, they didn't want him to fly. Being an obedient son, he quit.

When he graduated in 1938 and got a job at Wright Aero in Paterson, he started flying again at Franklin Lakes Airport. He didn't bother to tell his parents. That would only worry them.

"I went back home to Pittsburgh to visit them," he related, "and while I was there, my mother took a phone call from New Jersey. The caller asked for Homer Clapper. That was my father's name also, so my mother asked him, which one?"

"The one who flies," the caller responded. "There's an airplane there and I want him to fly it back."

Homer's obsession with flying began when he went for his first airplane ride in 1930 with Col. Robert Copsey who later became director of the New Jersey Division of Aeronautics. They flew in an open cockpit biplane out of Newark Airport.

"Col. Copsey lived across the street from us on Parker Road in Elizabeth," Clapper said.

After he got his solo license Clapper became president of the Wright Aero Flying Club, which was based at Murchio Airport in Paterson. (Like Hadley and Franklin Lakes Airport, Murchio was closed years ago.) The club had 13 airplanes.

More than a half century after he got his solo license, Clapper is still flying. He owns a twin-engine Cessna 310.

His first airplane was a used Stinson Station Wagon that he bought in 1947. His next was a Cessna 180. That airplane had one of the first Narco Omnigators, a radio which, at that time, was a giant leap forward over the equipment used previously. He picked the airplane up at the factory in Wichita. It figured in another of Clapper's colorful old-timer tales.

He was at the Reading (Pa.) Air Show, which, in its time was one of the premier air shows in the country. When it came time to fly home the weather was bad and nobody was flying. Clapper didn't feel like enjoying Reading's hospitality for another night, so he filed an instrument flight plan.

He was based at Totowa-Wayne Airport (also now closed) but he filed for Teterboro because it had a better instrument approach. Three FAA men came with him.

Some time later, one of those FAA men saw Clapper taking a written exam at Murchio Airport. It was the instrument written. Although he was a proficient instrument pilot he had never bothered to take the test and get his rating. The three FAA men had flown in severe instrument conditions with a man who didn't have the credentials to fly under such conditions, much less carry passengers--and FAA passengers at that.

"The FAA man told me, 'You better pass'. Well, I got a good grade. When I took the flight test, not one, but three FAA men flew with me. It was an all day test. We flew to Albany for lunch. Then to Harrisburg for dinner." Homer went home with his rating.

He has his share of stories about emergency situations, also. Some of them you wouldn't want to hear. But his lobster story is a classic.

"I used to fly up to Portsmouth, N.H., when I did business with the navy yard up there," he relates. "The guys there used to get me two washtubs full of lobsters, one cooked, one live. I used to buy about 100 lobsters. They were around 39 cents a pound.

"One time I took off from Pease Airport at night in the wintertime. When I got in the air, I couldn't see anything. There was ice on the inside of the windshield. (In icing conditions ice forms on the outside of the windshield, not the inside.)

"It was from the steam coming off the cooked lobsters," he said. "I couldn't get it off. It was a clear night. You could see forever." With the ice on the windshield, however, Homer couldn't see anything.

"I called air traffic control and told them I need an instrument clearance right away and they should provide clearance from other traffic. They said, 'Right away?' I said I haven't got time to explain. I asked them to get me to Providence.

"I landed by opening the little ice window on the side and looking out through it. When I got on the ground I had to weave back and forth to see. The guys in the tower said, 'Having trouble tonight?' I said, yes. They said, 'What is it, brakes?' I said, yes.

"After I parked, I went up in the tower and told them my problem. I asked if they could suggest somebody who could help me out. They suggested I talk to the sergeant at the National Guard facility.

"I went to their facility and asked a sergeant there if I could borrow some blankets to cover the lobsters. I traded him some lobsters for the loan of the blankets."

Clapper has put his fertile brain to work in a number of successful businesses. For five years he was president of Reeves Industries, which made the first in-flight motion picture systems for airliners and developed Cinemax.

He set up Tradewinds, an airline that flew out of San Juan to a whole host of Caribbean Islands. He developed a shuttle valve for airliners that is used on some jet engines to prevent the loss of oil in case a filler cap is inadvertently left off.

He currently runs an international aircraft parts business. He also instructs select students for multiengine and instrument ratings. He holds all the instructor ratings.

Clapper was listed in *Who's Who in America*. "But I haven't answered them in ten years," he said. "They probably think I'm dead."

At 74, he is still very much alive.

7/8/90

KNUTE ROCKNE'S FATE

*Sometimes the difference between life and death is paper thin.
And that difference respects no one, king or pauper, idiot or genius.*

*In the story that follows, an old-timer reveals how the fact
that if one of the top aircraft designers of his time, Anthony Fokker,
had listened to a 14-year-old kid, the great Notre Dame coach, Knute
Rockne, would likely never have been killed in a plane crash.*

*The teller of this tale was the 14-year-old whose advice the
expert wouldn't listen to. When he related this story, which very few
people are aware of, although the fact that Rockne was killed in a
plane crash is widely known, that kid, Jerome Murray, was an old-
timer who could look back on decades of achievements. But none of his
many achievements stands out like the story of what he told Anthony
Fokker when he was a teenager.*

If Anthony Fokker, the highly respected Dutch aircraft designer
of the '20s and '30s had listened to a 14-year-old kid, the
legendary Notre Dame football coach, Knute Rockne might
never have been killed in a plane crash.

That is the opinion of Jerome Murray of Budd Lake. He was
that kid more than six decades ago.

Rockne lost his life in a Fokker Trimotor aircraft when a spar
broke and a wing snapped off.

In his boyhood years, Murray lived in Garden City, Long Island,
N.Y., and he used to hang around Roosevelt Field a lot. Tony
Fokker had his plant there before he moved it to Teterboro Airport.

Jerome Murray, who, as a teenager, foresaw the tragedy that took Knute Rockne's life, shown holding some of the instruments he developed later in life.

"One day," Murray relates, "I was in Fokker's hangar and I said
to him, 'Why don't you varnish the inside of that wing before you
cover it?' He threw me out of the hangar."

The wing spar in the plane in which Rockne was killed, broke
because of dry rot. Murray still thinks that varnish would have

prevented the dry rot. All the Fokker Trimotors, one of the most widely used transport aircraft of its time, were grounded after that accident and it was the end of the line for that aircraft.

Murray has had a lot of other ideas since those days, most of which he has patented, including the electric carving knife, the jetways for boarding jetliners, and the rotating TV antenna. "They sold 38 million of those antennas," said Murray. "I got 75 cents apiece." He sold the jetways to a bridge company.

At 81, he holds 60 patents and he's in his laboratory in Landing every day working on new ideas.

A graduate of the Massachusetts Institute of Technology, with a degree in aeronautical engineering, Murray's early career was all in aviation. In 1935, after getting his degree, he went to work for Curtiss Airplane Engine Co. at Roosevelt Field, originally Curtiss Field. His first job was drafting. That's what they assigned new people to.

He only stayed there a year and then he went to work for Ford, flying the Ford Trimotor. He had soloed in 1926, at the age of 15, in an OX-5 Jenny.

At Ford, he flew as co-pilot for six months, and then he got his own Trimotor. "I flew parts from Dearborn to the Buffalo plant. Dealers bought airplane ride tickets for 50 cents and gave them to prospective customers. We'd fly them.

"Ford put six airplanes on a barnstorming tour that covered the country. I drew the southern states, Florida, Georgia, and Louisiana," he said. "An advance man lined up farmers' fields for us to fly out of and set up the promotion with dealers. That was in 1936 and '37. It was a good promotion,"

After a couple of years with Ford, Murray went to Bridgeport (Conn.) Airport where he was field manager. He only stayed there a year, but during that time he became acquainted with Igor Sikorsky, who invented the helicopter.

"He started out building new wings for Jennys," said Murray. Then he built airplanes. He was a very intelligent man. A very nice man. He was experimenting with helicopters, and he always wore a Chesterfield coat and a derby when he flew helicopters.

After a year, Murray left Bridgeport Airport and started a mechanics' school. He had a mechanic's license. Two years later, World War II broke out and he sold the school.

"I got a commission as a first lieutenant," he said, "but I was a hydraulics specialist and they kept me from accepting the commission because they wanted me working in hydraulics. I joined the Weatherhead Corp. which made all kinds of hydraulic equipment.

"There were few hydraulic engineers around, so I did work for the Army and Navy on loan. I went overseas to both Europe and the Pacific. When I left the country I was given a temporary commission so that if I was captured, I couldn't be shot as a spy.

"I did some work for the British and I got to fly the Spitfire. I also flew the P-51, P-47, and P-40 while working on hydraulic problems."

A major problem early in the war was the fact that synthetic rubber used in aircraft melted in the heat of North Africa. "Chemists solved the problem in 90 days," said Murray. "I've always felt that chemists never received the credit they deserved."

Murray knows something about that problem because synthetic rubber, while it melted at very high temperatures, cracked at very low temperatures. He worked on that problem and went up to Alaska looking for minus 40-degree temperatures.

In the early '70s Murray served as a consultant to NASA, working on space flight programs. He was a consultant on navigation for the Apollo program and worked with Frank Borman. "While I was working for NASA I got to fly one of their T-37s," he said.

Murray has logged 18,000 hours in all kinds of aircraft.

One of the current problems Murray is working on is a system that would allow aircraft carriers to recover their aircraft while sailing downwind instead of into the wind as they must do today. That would permit them to pick up their aircraft while sailing away from the enemy.

The system would be based on the wind tunnel theory and would generate a wind of up to 150 knots directed at the landing aircraft.

The project in which he is most involved right now is the Rotorcam engine, a project he has been working on for about 20 years, which appears to be nearing acceptance.

Although it is much smaller than a conventional four-cylinder engine, Murray claims it develops as much power as an eight-cylinder engine. It can run on any fuel, regular gasoline, diesel, kerosene, propane or a mixture of all of them. It would be suitable, he claims, for general aviation aircraft.

Emission tests, he says, show that without a catalytic converter, emissions are lower than the California standards which are the lowest in the country.

Though he's been working on it for nearly 20 years, Murray is a patient man. He believes that all good things come to those who wait.

His achievements have won him induction into the New Jersey Inventors Hall of Fame at the New Jersey Institute of Technology.

He enjoys his work. To him it's not work. "The fun of doing these things is more important than money," he says. "I make money without working."

And his highly successful career really started with an idea that was rejected.

1/2/94

CHEWING GUM AND GUTS

What we call air shows today were known as flying circuses in the early days. Today, audiences thrill at the skill and precision of aerobatic pilots. In the early days they went to the flying circuses to see daring performers face and defy death. Sometimes the grim reaper won. These performances attracted huge crowds of spectators.

Bill Rhode, a New Jersey aviation historian, who died on January 2, 1998, at the age of 82, was a part of that era. As a kid, he worked for the Gates Flying Circus, based at Teterboro Airport, washing mud off planes, running errands, doing odd jobs, not for money, but for airplane rides.

He later became a parachute jumper and after that he enjoyed a long career as a flight instructor as well as a historian. He wrote several books, one of which was about the Gates Flying Circus, a subject he knew first hand.

This column sheds some light on what the old flying circuses were like.

Those were the good time days. They were the days of the Model T and the Charleston and bootlegged booze. The times were positively shocking. Girls wore one piece bathing suits and skirts climbed up above the knees.

Bill Rhode, who worked for the Gates Flying Circus in 1928, and later taught thousands of students to learn to fly, and became an aviation historian and author.

And in the midst of all this wouldn't you know, people were flocking out to cow pastures where they could go for a ride in a wood and fabric flying machine for a dollar. And they joined that very select group of people who could say, "I've flown in an aeroplane."

It was a fitting time for aviation to make its debut. It was a natural part of an age like the roaring 20s and of men who didn't know the meaning of fear.

They were pilots known as barnstormers. They swept back and forth across the country bringing thrills and excitement to hundreds of thousands of spectators, usually landing in farmers' fields just outside of small towns.

Among their numbers were fearless wing walkers--men who would stand on top of an aircraft wing while it did loops and rolls. Some of them would switch from one flying crate to another in mid air or transfer from a speeding car to a low flying aircraft via rope ladder.

Most of these men were part of the flying circuses. The most famous of them was the Gates Flying Circus that was based at Teterboro Airport in northern New Jersey. That organization expired in 1928 after new government regulations pertaining to aircraft standards put curbs on stunt flying (called aerobatics today). The flying circus had enjoyed a dazzling seven year existence.

When they folded, the Gates Flying Circus left behind a colorful chapter in the history of aviation in this country.

There was a kid, back in those days, who hung around the Gates organization at Teterboro and would work his butt off all day so he could earn himself an airplane ride.

That "kid," now a flight instructor, pursued his love of aviation by assembling what is probably the best collection of aviation books, periodicals and newspaper articles in the country.

His basement is a treasure chest of aviation publications, some of them one of a kind.[3]

His name is Bill Rhode and he just added one more book to his collection. This one is called, *Bailing Wire, Chewing Gum, and Guts,* the story of the Gates Flying Circus, and it has Bill's name on the cover because he is the author.

Bill had plenty of source material available to him and he has drawn on it heavily to present, in considerable detail, the triumphs and tragedies of those aviation pioneers.

He describes how newspapers went wild over the barnstormers and many of them sponsored their shows.

After Lindbergh's flight, the fever got so hot, Chambers of Commerce all over the country called hurried meetings to try to get airports for their area before they were left behind by other cities.

There were incidents of stuntmen--and even one girl--dangling from aircraft by a rope, unable to get themselves back up. There are stories of airplanes, busted up in pastures and put back together again with "bailing wire, chewing gum and guts," so the pilots could meet contractual obligations. And there are stories of a lot of good men riding to their deaths.

---

[3] *While Bill was in Florida, a homeless man took up residence in his house and started a fire that burned up his priceless collection of old aviation books, magazines and newspaper clippings.*

At one time, Ivan Gates, founder of the circus bearing his name, found himself losing so much money printing posters featuring the names of star wing walkers who got killed before he could use the posters, that he decided to use the name Diavalo on his posters--a term sometimes used to refer to the devil or in this case dare devil--to describe all wing walkers.

Rhode's book also includes a couple of dozen photographs of the men and machines of this era--including shots of wing walkers transferring from one aircraft to another in flight, dangling by their feet beneath the belly of a biplane and performing other stunts that might tempt you to question their sanity.

1/23/72

THE WING WALKER WHO SURVIVED

If you wanted to live to a ripe old age back in the days of the flying circuses of the '20s, the last job in the world you would want would be that of a wing walker. They didn't last as long as an ice cube in the sunshine of the equator. They had an excess of guts, but they were somewhat lacking in other departments.

One man came along, however, and changed that. He also put his good sense to use in other aerial pursuits after the government closed down the flying circuses.

He was a leader and innovator in his day and his story is well worth recounting.

There was a day when the biggest show on earth wasn't held under a big top. It was a day when dancing elephants were not the big attraction. Those were the days when the big top was the wide open sky and the big attraction was those daring young men in their flying machines.

One of the biggest of these flying circuses was the Gates Flying Circus headquartered at Teterboro Airport in the 1920s. Its greatest attraction was a daring and carefree young man named Aron F. Krantz, a wing walker, parachute jumper and pilot, known as "Duke" Krantz. He was good-looking, dapper, and sported a thin, waxed handlebar mustache.

At a time when pilots were heroes and idols, Duke Krantz was the Clark Gable of the flying set.

A Gates Flying Circus poster with "Duke" Krantz's photo in the center.

File photo

Krantz, who died in 1974, loved partying. Some of the best parties thrown in the area in those days were those of George Lambros who ran a seaplane base on the Hackensack River near Teterboro Airport.

George was a lively piano player. He would play and sing and everybody would join in lustily, inspired by the consumption of generous amounts of spirits. Even in that atmosphere, Duke stood out. He was an imposing figure. The stories about him are legendary.

But there are always new ones. We collected some we hadn't heard before during a visit with his son, Ron, of Franklin Lakes. Ron was an Eastern Airlines pilot for 24 years and served as an aviation safety inspector with the FAA at Teterboro Flight Service District Office working in Air Carrier Operations until his retirement in 2006.

Duke came to the United States from Sweden in 1917. He had 12 brothers and sisters and he was one of the last to come over.

The family settled in Illinois and went into farming. It didn't take long for Duke to discover that farming wasn't for him. In 1918, he joined the Air Corps. He became a sergeant and he requested flight training. His commanding officer, Col. (later major general) Carl Spaatz, looked down on him, a Swede who couldn't even speak proper English. His request was rejected.

When his enlistment was up, Krantz left the service and went to work for the Post Office in San Antonio. The Gates Flying Circus came to town and Krantz, who was fascinated by it, asked Ivan Gates for a job.

"What can you do?" Krantz was asked.

"I can do tricks on my motorcycle," he replied. He was hired. He did a warm-up act performing such stunts as standing on his head while holding the handlebars and sitting backwards while riding. He hadn't had a chance to do much warming up when the circus's wing walker was killed.

Krantz asked for the job and that was the start of his flying career. The careers of wing walkers were normally very short. So Gates printed posters reading, "Death Defying Diavalo," a term that could apply to any wing walker. (As explained in the previous story, the word diavalo was sometimes used to refer to the devil.) Krantz's career, however, was not brief. He developed a leather belt system using guy wires and snaps that he could put on without the crowd seeing it. The pilot could do loops and rolls and he was in no danger of tumbling off. He lasted so long that Gates eventually put his name on the posters.

The pilot was Clyde Pangborn, a leading barnstormer, who, along with Hugh Herndon, became the first to fly across the Pacific nonstop.

Pangborn taught Krantz to fly. He let him take the controls before he climbed up on the wing and after he climbed back into the cockpit.

One of the many achievements in Krantz's career was setting an endurance record.   After that event he met his old Air Corps Commander, Col. Spaatz, who held the record previously. Krantz reminded him that he was the Swede he wouldn't permit to fly.

Ron says one of his dad's stunts was changing planes in flight on a rope ladder.   One day, during a thunderstorm, the rope became charged with electricity.   When his dad grabbed it, he got a tremendous shock. The immediate instinct was to let go. But his feet had already left the aircraft. He hung on.

He was a parachute jumper before they had packed chutes. They were carried in baskets.   After a show in New Orleans, a Frenchman asked him to test a new parachute. He was unable to steer the chute and landed in Lake Pontchartrain. The chute settled over him and he couldn't get out. Pangborn, who was the pilot, circled low over some fishermen and yelled to them, "Help him. He's drowning." They saved his life.

After a night show in Havana in which Krantz used flares, General Fulgencio Batista, the Cuban dictator, invited him to the palace and gave him a gold watch.   After a show in California, Bing Crosby invited him home for dinner.

When new government regulations forced the Gates Flying Circus to close in 1928, Krantz found a new career as a pilot for the *New York Daily News* and he provided the paper with many scoops.

He was right under the *Hindenburg* with a photographer when it exploded at Lakehurst, in 1937. They landed and got pictures and prepared to takeoff. The military tried to block the runway, but Krantz gave his aircraft full throttle and lifted off. He landed at North Beach Airport (now LaGuardia Airport) and the *Daily News* was on the street with pictures before most people knew what happened.

He got photographs of the *Morro Castle* when that ship burned off Asbury Park and he flew over the huge French Luxury liner, *Normandy*, to get pictures when it burned at the dock in New York.

Krantz was with the *Daily News* from 1930 to 1939 and his activities as their pilot often made the news. When Dick Merrill and Harry Richmond, two well known pilots of the time, were flying film of King Edward VIII's coronation back from England they were forced down in Newfoundland. Several days of searching failed to turn up their whereabouts.

Krantz was in a bar where a ship captain took a shine to him and told him where he ought look for the pair. Duke followed his advice and flew to the spot the captain had suggested. And sure enough, he found them right where the captain had suggested he look.

"He scooped everybody," says his son, who added that his

father was the first to use an airplane to gain an advantage over the competition.

Today, major corporations use business aircraft for that purpose all the time,

With their airplanes--and the *News* had a variety of them over the years--he forged a special brand of journalism.

2/28/99

HE LIVED WHAT HE WROTE

Arch Whitehouse's career as an aviation writer had a somewhat unconventional beginning. His first aviation story was written at ringside during a major boxing event. But his story didn't have anything to do with the event he was covering. It was about a lean young fellow who, as he wrote, was flying across the Atlantic headed for Paris--one Charles A. Lindbergh.

What inspired him to write about that flight rather than the action taking place before him? Well, he had some background in aviation. He was a World War I gunner. He had been credited with shooting down 26 enemy aircraft. On one flight his aircraft was badly damaged over enemy territory in a fight with a red, enemy Albatross. In spite of severe damage they were able to get back to our lines and land safely. They later learned that the pilot of the red Albatross was the highly esteemed German pilot known as the Red Baron and he claimed them as his 42nd victory.

Whitehouse was one of the most prolific aviation writers. In addition to hundreds of articles, he wrote more than a dozen and a half nonfiction books and a half dozen novels about World War I aviation. Having been a World War I aircraft gunner, a fact in which he took great pride, he was very much concerned with presenting accurate accounts of that era rather than the glamorized and inaccurate accounts that found their way onto the silver screen.

With the advent of Word War II he became a war correspondent and in that role flew on several combat missions. His writing career spanned a half century.

The date was May 27, 1927. The place, New York's Polo Grounds, home of the New York Giants baseball team. On that date, however, the ball field was converted into a boxing arena. The main event was a heavyweight bout between an Australian boxer named Heeny and the American titleholder, Gene Tunney.

Sitting ringside was a young New Jersey sportswriter named Arch Whitehouse.

Before the bout, ring announcer Joe Humphries, barked into the microphone, "Ladies and gentlemen, I ask two minutes of silence for a young man who tonight is flying from New York to Paris."

The fight got underway and the crowd shouted and screamed.

Sportswriter Arch Whitehouse didn't see what was going on in the ring. He didn't hear the noise all around him. He was pounding away at his typewriter. But he wasn't writing about the fight. He was writing about the fellow who was flying across the ocean solo.

He wrote about how the pilot must feel, what it must be like on that long, lonely flight, and what his chances were.

Arch Whitehouse holding a model of a World War I fighter.

"I thought he would be very lucky if he made it," said Whitehouse.

The next day, Arch Whitehouse's story about the first solo flight across the Atlantic (Lindbergh's flight) ran on the sports page.

That Lucky Lindy story brought him tremendous response.

"How did you know so much about flying?" he was asked.

He knew, he explained, because he put in 1,300 hours as a World War I aerial gunner and then he became a pilot flying the Avro Trainer and the Sopwith Pup and Sopwith Camel.

After that story came out, a news dealer on Broad Street in Elizabeth, told Whitehouse that he ought to write for the pulp airplane magazines that were then enjoying great popularity.

"I said I wouldn't be caught dead writing for them," Whitehouse recalls.

"Don't be silly," the newspaper dealer replied. "They pay $25 a story."

"I was making $24 a week as a sports editor," said Whitehouse. "I went home and sent a couple of stories to 'Flying Ace.' Three days later I got a check for $100 with a request for more. I did send more and I got $100 a story.

"Then I began reading copy at the magazine every Friday. I got $150 a month for that.

"My wife convinced me to quit my $24-a-week sports editor job. Everybody thought I was crazy. But the first year I made $8,000-- at a penny a word."

In 1939, Whitehouse hit the big time. He sold his first story to *The Saturday Evening Post*. It was called "Spitfire Squadron," and he got $600 for it. It was later made into a movie called, "A Yank in the RAF."

Whitehouse wrote more than a dozen stories for *The Saturday Evening Post* and another of them was made into a movie called, "Bomber H for Harry." He never saw that film because when it was playing he was in England as a World War II war correspondent covering the 8th Air Force.

During that tour of duty Whitehouse flew on a B-24 Liberator mission over Norway and a B-25 raid over France just before D-Day. After the war, Whitehouse resumed his writing career. To date he's written a half dozen novels, and a dozen and a half nonfiction books. He's published seven collections of short stories, an autobiography and a number of juvenile books.

His *Years of the Sky Kings* is one of the most vivid, detailed accounts of the aerial warfare of World War I ever published (Doubleday, and in a paperback edition, Curtis Books).

Whitehouse had a reputation as an authority on World War I aviation which went back 40 years.

Back in the '30s, Howard Hughes produced a movie with a World War I theme that he wasn't too confident about. A pilot friend of Hughes suggested that he ought to get Arch Whitehouse's opinion.

Hughes came to New York, met Whitehouse and took him to a little offbeat movie house in the Bronx where he screened the film for him.

"I said, 'Howard, it will never go,'" Whitehouse recounts. "I told him, 'It's a silly story and it's technically all wrong.'"

Hughes never released the film.

At 77, Whitehouse is still pounding his typewriter at a pretty good pace. He knocks out 3,000 words a day, seven days a week. He is presently working on two books at once.

He rises at 8, has breakfast, and by 9, he's at his typewriter. At 1 o'clock he quits, has a glass of milk and goes for a walk along the country streets near his home in Montvale. He walks four miles a day, every day of the year.

"I walk," he says, "because it's the only place you can think. I write tomorrow's chapter while I'm walking."

3/4/73

FIRST PILOT TO CARRY A TRANSATLANTIC PASSENGER

Being Number Two can put you on the road to obscurity. Clarence Chamberlin could confirm that. Two weeks after Lindbergh's celebrated, never-to-be-forgotten flight across the Atlantic, Chamberlin did the same thing. He flew a bit farther and he carried the first passenger to fly across the Atlantic. But few people have ever heard of him. In fact, there are a lot of aviation history books that don't even mention him.

Even if he did not achieve the recognition he deserved, Chamberlin earned a place in aviation history. The column which follows tells why.

L ast Tuesday was his birthday. He was 82.

The occasion brought back memories of another birthday many years ago--in 1918.

Clarence Chamberlin

On that particular birthday Lt. Clarence Chamberlin was in Hoboken awaiting orders to ship "Over There" to join America's flying forces of World War I.

But on that birthday, his 25th, Armistice was declared. The young lieutenant's dreams of fighting in the skies over Europe came tumbling down.

Chamberlin did get to Europe--to Germany, as a matter of fact--although it was some years later and in a somewhat more unusual fashion than shipping out of Hoboken.

Two weeks after the Lone Eagle, Lindbergh, stunned the world by flying solo across the ocean to Paris, Clarence Chamberlin carried the first passenger, (Charles Levine), across the Atlantic.

They flew 3,906 miles in 43 hours and some minutes, landing in Eisleben, Germany.

A week or so ago, the prestigious Wings Club of New York paid tribute to this outstanding aviation pioneer by making him a life member.

In connection with that event, Doris Renninger, manager of the club, wrote to Chamberlin asking for some background material.

His response was full of colorful anecdotes, wry humor, and some beautiful nostalgia, and we pass some of it along to you here, courtesy of Mrs. Renninger and the Wings Club.

He tells about his first exploit after resigning his commission in 1919.

This took place in 1920. Chamberlin bought the first Bellanca GM ever sold. It was a two-seater with a 45-horsepower engine. And having become the proud owner of this fine aircraft, he joined the Franco-American Aeronautic Exhibition Company.

The group's first show was to be in Glens Falls, New York.

Chamberlin was to get a thousand dollars a month and 50 percent of the money from the passenger flights he flew.

On his first passenger flight, Chamberlin relates, he ran out of gas. He landed in some bushes and nosed over.

"Neither of us was hurt," he writes, "until my passenger unfastened her safety belt and fell out on her face and got a few scratches.

"Great crowds came," he says of the exhibition, "but most crossed lots or sneaked through fences, but very few came through the pay gate."

The outfit folded and no one got paid.

"It took me all summer to rebuild my ship to fly back to Roosevelt Field."

Before he crossed the Atlantic in the Bellanca, Chamberlin set several world records in it, "to demonstrate this new air-cooled engine and put it on the map." Among these was an endurance record of 51 hours.

But Chamberlin did more exciting things than that.

"I flew the first plane from the deck of an ocean liner, the *Leviathan*, to interest the Shipping Board in equipping liners with catapults so planes with mail could be shot off in mid-ocean to cut delivery time in half, also to help get money to build aircraft carriers.

"From 1935 to 1936," Chamberlin wrote, "I barnstormed with four 29-passenger Curtiss Condors, carrying about a half million passengers to make America more air minded and help cities build airports."

Chamberlin established the first New York to Washington airline with one Loening Amphibian, operating from a float at the Battery in New York and a Navy field in Washington, D.C.

In 1935, he operated the first New York to Boston service. That ran five days a week, and on Saturdays and Sundays he hopped passengers out of Teterboro Airport in New Jersey.

"I made so much more money hopping passengers that I canceled the airline and organized a barnstorming tour with four Condors," wrote Chamberlin in his letter to the Wings Club.

He was one of the first operators at Teterboro Airport and one of the first of the famed and distinguished aviation pioneers associated with the history of that field to be voted into the Teterboro Aviation Hall of Fame, (now, The Aviation Hall of Fame of New Jersey).

11/16/75

HE KNEW THE LEGENDARY PIONEERS

Addis Kocher was both a witness to aviation history and a part of it. He worked on the airplanes of many of the greatest of the early aviation pioneers and he has no shortage of stories to tell about his experiences with those pilots whose names appear in the pages of aviation history.

He spent 41 years working for Bendix which developed many aircraft instruments and systems.

Kocher probably knew more of the big name people of the Golden Age of aviation than anyone else I've ever interviewed and he had a close relationship with them because he worked on their aircraft. He has a fine collection of stories about those aviation icons. Here are some that he related to me for my column.

"I was the janitor in the back room when history was being made," he says rather modestly. "Most of the time you didn't know you were watching history in the making."

That's the way Addis Kocher describes a career with the Bendix Aviation Corp. that spanned more than 40 years.

During those years, Coke, as many of his close friends called him, met virtually every one of the pilots who made history in aviation's pioneering days and he worked on most of the airplanes in which they made that history.

Kocher checked out the electrical system in "Wrong Way Corrigan's" 1929 Curtiss Robin.

When Coke finished checking things out, Corrigan said, "Mr. Kocher, if I make this flight that I'm planning, I'm going to make you famous."

"I said, 'Maybe I don't want to be famous.' "

Corrigan, of course, achieved

Addis Kocher, who worked on the airplanes of some of the most famous aviators in history, including Jimmy Doolittle and Howard Hughes.

more than his share of fame when he took off from New York claiming he was flying to California and landed in Ireland. He had been denied permission to fly his old crate across the ocean. Somehow, however, he landed in Ireland instead of California after he couldn't get permission to cross the ocean in his flying flivver back in 1938. That earned him the name, "Wrong Way Corrigan."

That was only one of the memorable events in Coke's colorful career. Back in 1933, when Eddie Rickenbacker headed Eastern Airlines, he wanted to show movies in one of his DC-3s. Kocher installed a generator on one of the engines to run the projection system. They showed the first movies shot in the interior of Africa by Mr. and Mrs. Martin Johnson. It was an experimental flight.

"We had no idea then that someday they would be showing movies on commercial flights," said Kocher.

In 1942, Kocher was at a meeting of the Institute of Aeronautical Science at which Jimmy Doolittle was the guest of honor. Doolittle left the meeting early. Later that evening, Jimmy's wife, Joe, said, "Jimmy left early tonight, Addis, because he was going to Wright-Patterson Air Force Base in Dayton, Ohio, but he couldn't tell me why."

Addis found out later. "He was going to pick up his orders to bomb Tokyo," he said. Again, aviation history was being made right under his nose.

Addis knew Doolittle quite well by then. In 1932, when he was still new with the company, (he was hired on a temporary basis in 1931), Bendix developed the first wing deicer and Coke installed it on Jimmy Doolittle's Lockheed Orion at Newark Airport.

A few years later Bendix developed an improved design for the vacuum pump and it was shipped to California to be installed in Doolittle's Orion. When the engine was fired up it pumped oil into all his instruments. They replaced the instruments and Jimmy flew from California to Caldwell Airport, where Kocher was waiting with his tool box. He had written the instruction manual for the pump.

"Jimmy buzzed the airport six times before he landed, and when he climbed out of the airplane, he called me every name in the books," said Kocher. He said, 'What's wrong with you? Can't you even defend yourself?'

"While he was pacing up and down screaming at me, I said a silent prayer. 'Dear God, if I only had that piece of hydraulic tubing that runs through the pump to the firewall.'

"Jimmy unzipped a storage compartment in the airplane and pulled out that piece of tubing. He handed it to me. I had the cowling taken off. I held the tubing up and Jimmy saw that it was too short. They had switched lines when they hooked it up and installed it backwards.

"I've never been so sorry in my life," Jimmy said. "What can I do?"

He wrote a letter to the general manager and vice president of Bendix. The letter said, 'If you don't give this guy a raise, I'll hire him away from you.'

"I had been working for Bendix for a year and a half. I was earning $18 a week. I had not received a raise and I had not had a vacation. You had to work two years to a get a one week vacation. I got a $4 raise."

Kocher worked on airplanes flown by Howard Hughes, Igor Sikorsky, Roscoe Turner, and Guiseppe Bellanca. But the two men he admired most and spent the most time with were Jimmy Doolittle and Wiley Post.

Doolittle he describes as, "a very humble man," and Wiley Post as, "the most honest person I ever knew, and such a sweet guy."

In 1933, after he completed his around-the-world solo flight, Post had a contract with TWA to make the first stratospheric flight across the United States. "I had to put an auxiliary Bendix supercharger on the Lockheed Vega so he could climb from 22,000 to 32,000 feet.

"He had the first pressurized suit. I inflated it for him in the Standard Oil hangar at Newark Airport, which was run by Ed Aldrin, father of astronaut Buzz Aldrin."

Kocher recalled the elder Aldrin coming into his office at Bendix in Teterboro and saying, "Coke, I want you to meet the latest product of MIT." It was his son, Buzz. "Five years later," said Kocher, "he walked on the moon."

Coke met Amelia Earhart, only once, when he overhauled the starter on her red Lockheed Vega at Newark Airport after her solo flight across the Atlantic. It was a Bendix product, of course, as were all the products and equipment on all the historic aircraft Coke worked on. He describes Earhart as, "very polite, very intelligent."

There have been a great many books written about what may have happened to her on her last flight when she failed to arrive at Howland Island in the Pacific in 1937.

"Amelia Earhart is in about 850 feet of water within 10 miles of Howland Island," says Kocher. "The *Ixtaca*, (a Navy ship), was transmitting to her from Howland Island, and was getting a signal from her of 4. Tops was 5. So she had to be very close. But they asked her to change frequencies twice and she never did. So she apparently never heard them."

It's Kocher's opinion that a recently published book, *The Sound of Wings*, by Mary S. Lovell, originally published in England but now published here by St. Martin's Press, is the most accurate account of what probably happened. He calls it, "a no-nonsense book." "A lot of the previously published theories originated in Hollywood," Kocher says.

Kocher was born 83 years ago in Boonton and still lives there. He's lived in the same house since 1937.

His father was an engineer who graduated from ICS, the International Correspondence School. He worked for Thomas Edison from 1907 to 1910 and later had his own business.

Kocher went to the Stevens Institute of Technology for a year and worked part time at Radio Frequency Laboratories in Boonton. "They had seven Harvard-trained electrical engineers," he said. He then went to MIT where he got his degree.

After he graduated from MIT, Coke worked for his father, who made automatic lubrication systems for automobiles. "You pulled a lever on the dash and the whole car was lubricated," he says.

Ten engineers worked for his father. When the Depression struck, he had to lay off all but one. "He fired me," says Coke. "He said I can only keep one man and you don't have the experience."

Two weeks later, in September of 1931, Coke was hired by Bendix. He was with them until he retired in 1973, as research director.

During those years, Kocher was in charge of building the first 25 autopilots for both the DC-10 and 747. He was also in charge of building the first autopilot for the supersonic B-58 Hustler bomber.

He's proud of the fact that, "I triple-checked every installation I ever made." He never cared how much pressure was put on him to get it done now.

"I worked all night long for 300 nights for Bendix," he says. "Today, people complain about working an hour overtime."

Kocher sums things up this way. "If in your lifetime, you had three teachers who inspired you to do much more than you would have done otherwise, you're a fortunate person."

His three are Henry B. Wilson, founder of the Wilson School in Boonton, a prep school now in Mountain Lakes; Leslie H. Backer, a professor of chemistry at Stevens Institute, and Harold E. Edgerton, who died on January 4. He was the man who took the famed photos of the splash of a drop of milk and a bullet passing through an apple.

Three-and-a-half hours with Addis Kocher passes like the wink of an eye and it leaves you with the feeling that you haven't finished chapter one of a very long and fascinating career.

1/14/90

A PIONEER AIRPORT REPORTER

Newark Airport, now Newark Liberty International Airport, was the first commercial airport in the country. History was being made there on an almost daily basis. A kid named Mannie Berlinrut was there, witnessing it, reporting it for newspaper readers, and recording it for history.

Newark, which opened in 1928, was the first airport to have a paved runway. It was the first to have a control tower (the original tower has been preserved), and the first to have a weather station. It was the first commercial airport to have night lighting. Hadley Field in New Jersey, which served airmail planes had night lights in 1924.

In those early days of aviation in the late '20s and the '30s, virtually every one of the great names of aviation history from Billy Mitchell, to Lindbergh, put down at Newark Airport and Mannie met them all. Today, at 90, he has a lot of memories to look back on.

"I touched the hand of aviation history."

So spoke Emanuel "Mannie" Berlinrut, 90, of Long Valley. A soft spoken man, he said it with an obvious sense of pride and accomplishment, and the listener felt embraced by the aura of nostalgia in his words.

There was a time, from 1928 to the attack on Pearl Harbor on Dec. 7, 1941, when more aviation history was being written at Newark Airport than any place else in the world. And Mannie was there recording it. During those days he was a reporter for the old *Newark Sunday Call*. His beat was Newark Airport.

He knew Lindbergh and Amelia Earhart, Eddie Rickenbacker, Wiley Post, and Whitey Conrad, the nation's first air traffic controller, who worked in the Newark Tower, Richard Aldworth, the World War I pilot who became the airport's first

Mannie Berlinrut

manager, (they called them superintendents then), and the legendary Donald Douglas. He also met millionaire aviator Howard Hughes at Floyd Bennett Field, and Orville Wright in his home town of Dayton, Ohio, at a dinner of the Aviation/Space Writers Association, which Mannie helped found.

His 13-year career as an aviation writer came about as a result of a strange series of circumstances.

While he was still a student in Newark's West Side High School, Mannie got a job as a copy boy on the *Sunday Call*. He worked every Saturday from 6:30 p.m. to 2:30 a.m. and took home $2 for his efforts.

He went to the Newark College of Engineering, (now the New Jersey Institute of Technology), for a year, which was long enough for him to decide that engineering was not for him. Mannie then got himself a full time job at the *Call* as a feature writer at $35 a week.

Students at the Newark College of Engineering had built a huge white arrow against a black background on the roof of one of the college buildings. It pointed to Newark Airport as a guide to pilots. A public relations woman at the school asked Mannie if he could get the *Call* to take a picture of it.

The *Call* sent a photographer to photograph the six boys who built the arrow. He had them meet at Newark Airport where he stood them in front of a Ryan Brougham, an aircraft similar to Lindbergh's *"Spirit of St. Louis."*

"The photographer insisted I get in the picture," said Mannie. He was reluctant but finally gave in.

After that picture was taken all the boys were taken on a flight and Mannie went along. It was his first ride in an airplane.

But Mannie had flown before--in a glider. Some kids from East Orange had built a glider and formed a glider club. The glider had Waco wings that the boys built from plans and a plywood fuselage. The pilot sat on a board out in the open.

To launch it, they got an old car, jacked up the rear, put a drum on the rear wheel, and put a rope on it that they used as a winch. The "pilots" cut loose as they approached the car, at which time they had an altitude of about 200 feet. They then circled and landed. The glider was flown over land now occupied by the Lyons Veterans Hospital in Basking Ridge. Mannie flew the glider three times. He became president of the club, the Associated Glider Club of New Jersey, but he never got a pilot's license.

"When I was hired full time in July, 1929, the reporter who had been covering the airport left to take a job in New York. The editor remembered the picture of the boys in front of the Ryan with me in it, and he said, 'Your beat is the airport.' "

Mannie not only covered news being made at the airport, but he also began writing a column under the byline E.B. Berlinrut and it ran until he went into the service in 1942.

While covering Newark Airport he established close relationships with many of the early aviation greats. When Amelia Earhart landed in Newark after a coast-to-coast flight in her Lockheed Vega in 1936, Mannie was the only reporter there. "It was a Saturday," he said. "The only other person waiting for her was her husband, George Putnam.

"When she landed, she was very tired after an 18-hour flight, but she stood on the seat with her head sticking out of the hatch on top of the cockpit and chatted with me. I took notes because I knew I was going to write a story about the flight and she asked me to send her a copy. I did, and when she got it, she sent me a delightful letter. I later gave it to the Overseas Press Club for a charity auction. I don't know who bought it or where it is today."

Mannie recalled that when she and her husband left the airport, she did the driving.

He was a close friend of Donald Douglas, president of Douglas Aircraft, the company that produced the DC-3, the first highly successful airliner. He went to work for him after he was discharged from the service. Mannie has a warm, personal, handwritten letter from him signed, "Doug."

He remembers Lindbergh offering to drive him from the airport to the *Sunday Call* building on Halsey Street, Newark, in a fancy Lincoln that was given to him by Henry Ford. When they stopped for a red light, people recognized Lindbergh and they rushed the car. "One man pushed a baby through the window," Mannie said. "It was frightening."

One day Mannie spotted Wiley Post in the Standard Oil hangar, one of four hangars on the field at the time, working on the *Winnie Mae*, the airplane he flew around the world with Harold Gatty and the airplane in which he and humorist Will Rogers were killed a few years later.

"I introduced myself," Berlinrut said, "and asked him what he was doing. He was a bit testy that day, but at first he answered my questions quite courteously. He said he was getting ready to do some high altitude tests and he was checking the engine. I asked him if he was checking for anything special and he said he was checking his valve clearances. I didn't know what that meant so I asked him. He blew up. 'Look,' he said, 'I've got a lot to do. I can't stand around and explain how an engine works to somebody who doesn't know the first thing about it.'

"Later on, he apologized. But he was right. His time was valuable and I was wasting it. I had done a lot of reading about aviation, but not about engines. I had taken one year at the Newark College of Engineering, and while I didn't do particularly well, I was surprised at the knowledge I had picked up."

In 1931, Richard Aldworth, a World War I pilot who was recalled as a colonel after Pearl Harbor, became the first superintendent, (manager today), of Newark Airport. Berlinrut and he were close friends. Aldworth, in turn, was a close friend of General Billy Mitchell, who fought for the development and financing of military aviation, a position on which he banged heads with the top Amy and Navy brass, who did not support the idea of aircraft as a military weapon. In 1921, he offered to set up a test to determine if aircraft could sink warships. The brass considered that a foolhardy idea, but agreed to let him conduct the test using obsolete warships.

They put every obstacle they could conceive in the path of those tests. Aldworth was one of Mitchell's squadron leaders on those demonstrations and they sank every warship, including a battleship. The successful tests, however, had little effect on the opinions of the brass who witnessed it.

Mitchell persisted and became more outspoken than ever, which led to his being court-martialed. He was stripped of his rank of major general and suspended for five years. He retired and went into seclusion. But he did come out to Newark Airport one day to visit his old friend Richard Aldworth, who took him on a private tour of the facility. Aldworth asked Berlinrut to join them, and that's how he met the legendary Billy Mitchell.

A highlight of that tour came when Aldworth took Mitchell into a brand new DC-3. Mitchell stood at the door to the cockpit for a long time and then said, "That will never do. Never." Aldworth was stunned. He didn't know what Mitchell was talking about.

"Too many gadgets," said Mitchell. "A man can't fly in rough conditions and watch all those gauges."

After World War II, in which aircraft played such a key role, Mitchell, who died in 1937, had his rank restored posthumously and was awarded the Medal of Honor.

One time, Berlinrut found himself part of the news. He was at Newark Airport when New York's feisty mayor, Fiorello LaGuardia, landed there in a DC-3 after a flight from Washington. All the passengers debarked except LaGuardia. He refused to get off the plane.

He pointed at his ticket and it said, "New York." He insisted that they take him to New York. There was no LaGuardia Airport then or JFK. They flew him to Floyd Bennett Field in Brooklyn.

Berlinrut and a number of other members of the press were taken along to provide LaGuardia with publicity. Berlinrut was the only passenger on the plane when it flew back to its base at Newark.

During his years as an aviation editor and columnist, Berlinrut did meet one man who was already history. That man was Orville Wright. He came out of seclusion in 1944 to meet with a group of writers at Wright Field in Dayton, Ohio.

"Wright, who was hard of hearing, singled me out for a leisurely chat about the changes that had come about in aviation," Berlinrut wrote later. "In due course, I realized that he thought I was the son of an old acquaintance, Emil Berliner, who designed and built helicopters in 1914." Orville Wright died shortly after that meeting.

Later that year, when Richard Aldworth was critically ill with Hodgkins disease in San Antonio, he asked Mannie to come down and visit him. Mannie got himself a ride in a rare P-41, an unsuccessful outgrowth of the P-40 Warhawk, and he experienced a hair-raising flight. They got lost in bad weather at night. The instrument panel lights went out. The pilot didn't have a flashlight and couldn't read the instruments. They were prepared to jump when the pilot spotted a hole in the clouds. Directly below they could see an airport.

"He put us into a screaming dive," said Mannie, "and we landed at what turned out to be an emergency landing field in Palestine, Texas. It was the middle of the night and nobody was there."

In the morning two volunteers showed up. They got gas for them, and as soon as they were refueled they took off and flew on to San Antonio.

Mannie spent several hours talking to Aldworth and they flew home.

The next day, Richard Aldworth died.

3/25/01

Note: *Mannie Berlinrut died on Oct. 13, 2005, at the age of 95.*

Chapter 13

Those Wonderful Old Airplanes

The Tin Goose, the Pan Am Clippers, the DC-3, the Pitcairn Mailwing, the Piper Cub, and so many more airplanes of the past, contributed mightily to the colorful history of aviation. They made news way back when, and their legacy lives on today.

Most of these old birds are museum pieces today. But some of those in the columns that follow are still flying in spite of their age. It is an incredible experience to see them on the ramp of an active airport instead of in a museum. I had the privilege of flying in several of those aircraft. Those were unforgettable experiences.

THE TIN GOOSE

Henry Ford didn't just build Model T automobiles. He also built airplanes. The Ford Trimotor, one of the biggest and most popular airplanes of its day, was built in Detroit by the man who became famous and rich by devising the automobile production line.

The Ford Trimotor, better known by its nickname, the Tin Goose, (it was all metal), first flew in 1926 and was built into the early '30s. Ford built 200 of them.

As a transport aircraft it carried anywhere from 12 to 15 passengers.

There are still a few of these aircraft flying today. They give rides in one at the big AirVenture show in Oshkosh every year. It's an experience flying in an old aircraft like that. It makes you feel like you're a part of history.

I had the opportunity to fly in one a number of years ago.

The captain spoke to the passengers in a calm, confident tone. "This airplane," he said, "shakes like an airplane. It smells like an airplane. It sounds like an airplane."

The Ford Trimotor

Then he fired up the engines and taxied out to the end of the runway.

Before shoving the throttles forward for takeoff, he leaned back and held up a sign for the passengers in the cabin behind him. It said, "Don't just sit there. WORRY."

The captain smiled and turned back to his work. His passengers smiled and checked their seat belts. They were all VIPs, mostly local elected officials. In a few moments we were airborne.

This was a flight in an aircraft you might sooner expect to find in a museum than in the skies over New Jersey and, as a matter of fact, that's exactly where it's going as soon as the museum it's going to is finished.

This was a flight in an old Ford Trimotor originally operated by American Airways, (a predecessor of American Airlines). American Airlines purchased this ship and rebuilt it in preparation for presentation to the Smithsonian's National Air and Space Museum in Washington, D.C., when that facility opens.

Until the museum is ready, American Airlines pilots Jim Adkins and Floyd Mace, both from Nashville, are flying the venerable Tin Goose, as it is affectionately called, around the country.

Last Sunday, they paid a visit to Caldwell Airport in Caldwell, (now Fairfield), and on the first of several flights, they carried Mayor Stephen Szabo, a private pilot himself, and a number of his associates, on a flight over Essex, Passaic, and Bergen Counties.

This particular Tin Goose was built in 1929. American Airlines found it at a Mexican airport where it had been abandoned. A Mexican family had set up housekeeping in it. Originally, this airplane cost $55,000. It cost $105,000 to rebuild it. The old Tin Goose has three new engines in it for its junketing around the country. When it goes to the museum the original engines will be restored.

There are 13 seats in the 35-year-old airplane and for a ship of its years it's a very stable and smooth-flying craft. Not very fast by today's standards, (it cruises at 110 miles an hour), but it flies smoothly.

The pilot had informed his passengers before takeoff that they couldn't get a view from today's jetliners like they'd get from the Tin Goose, and he was right. This is a high wing airplane so you have a good view from any seat--with no wing sticking out. The landing gear is hanging out there. They didn't know anything about retractable gear in 1929--but it doesn't spoil the view. In fact, it sort of adds to it--in a quaint way.

As we flew over the open country surrounding Caldwell, Joe Bierce, president of the town council, spoke about how enthusiastic he and other town officials are about the development of Caldwell Airport. "We feel it is a strong factor in attracting new industry to the town," he said. "We're anxious to see the airport grow and prosper."

Down below, we looked at the partially completed Route 80. Paterson slipped by beneath us and the George Washington Bridge hove into view, and then we were right over Teterboro Airport.

When we landed back at Caldwell and taxied to the ramp, hundreds of spectators were lined up to see us come in. The old Tin Goose attracted one of the biggest crowds to come out to Caldwell in years. When it comes to airplanes, old age is an asset.

4/26/64

OLD AIRPLANES NEVER DIE

The old Tin Goose was not the only trimotor craft of its era that I flew in. More than a quarter of a century later, I flew in an aircraft that looked like the Tin Goose's twin, but was built about a decade later. This was the German Junkers Ju 52. Of the thousands built, only a handful are sill flying.

Noted aviation writer Martin Caiden bought it and named it Iron Annie, a name under which it gained considerable notoriety He flew it to air shows all over the country and some of his fame rubbed off on the old airplane.

Caiden sold it back to its original owner, Lufthansa Airlines, and eventually, when Lufthansa brought it back to these shores for a tour, I was fortunate enough to have an aerial tour of New York in this living piece of aircraft history.

Though it looked like a twin of the Ford Trimotor, it had its own colorful history.

I sat in one of the aircraft on line waiting to take off from Newark International Airport and watched aircraft from all over the world touch down as we waited to depart. A LOT Polish Airlines aircraft landed, and after it, an aircraft bearing the blue and yellow logo of Lufthansa German Airlines

The aircraft I was sitting in had the name Lufthansa on its side but it was a little different than the aircraft I saw landing and the other aircraft lined up for take off. Every seat was taken, but there weren't 200 or 300 seats in this aircraft. There were exactly 16.

Lufthansa German Airlines Junkers Ju 52.

We were served by a crew of four, pilot, copilot, flight engineer, and cabin attendant.

There were a few other differences between this aircraft and the others on line waiting to take off. Instead of jet engines, this aircraft had piston engines, three of them, turning propellers.

The other aircraft had smooth skins. This aircraft had corrugated metal skin. In this company it looked like a washed out stray cat that somehow got into a line of sleek racehorses.

But this aircraft, the Ju 52, was one of the grandparents of all those sleek-looking aircraft waiting to take off and streak through the skies to destinations all over the country and around the world.

The aircraft I was in was built more than a half century ago. It was one of some 5,000 of these aircraft built in Germany. Today, there are just five still flying. This one, owned and operated by Lufthansa German Airlines, now bears the name *Berlin-Templehof*, the airport that dates back to 1933, and gained its greatest fame as the terminus for the Berlin Airlift of 1948-49 that kept Berlin supplied after all land routes to the city through East Germany were closed by the Russians who controlled that territory. Of the other four Ju 52s, three are in Switzerland and one is in South Africa.

This airplane bore the identification D-AQUI, its original designation. It's had a lot of other names and designations since then. To say it had a checkered career would be an understatement. It has flown under German, Norwegian, Ecuadorian and American registrations. It has borne more than a half dozen different names. In the 30s when they were built, employees dubbed the Ju 52, "Auntie Ju."

D-AQUI was originally named *Fritz-Simon*, and went into service with Lufthansa on April 10, 1936. I never could find out who Fritz-Simon was. None of the crew had the slightest idea. After a few months it was in an accident with another aircraft and it was sold to Norway where it was repaired, fitted with floats, given the name *Falcon*, and put into service with the BNL Airline.

In 1940, Norway was occupied by the German Army, which requisitioned the aircraft and several months later it was transferred back to Lufthansa, which flew it on floats within Norway bearing the name, *Kurt Wintgens*. I never found out who he was either.

When World War II ended in May 1945, the aircraft was taken over by the Norwegian Air Force. It then went back to the Norwegian airline that flew it under the name, *Akkeladden*.

In 1947, corrosion was discovered and the Norwegian Air Force rebuilt the aircraft replacing about 60 percent of it, and it then went into service with SAS, (Scandinavian Airline System), flying along the Norwegian coast on floats.

It was taken out of service in October 1956, and the following July it was transported by ship to Quito, Ecuador, where it once again had a name change to *Amazones*. It was put back on wheels and was in service until 1963.

For the next seven years it sat exposed to the elements until a former U.S. Air Force pilot bought it for $5,200 and brought it back to the States. It was a wreck, but he restored it, although he never got it certified for flight.

Five years later, aviation author and novelist Martin Caidin bought the aircraft for $52,000. He gave it the name, *Iron Annie,* got it certified, and flew it to air shows around the country, including the big one at Oshkosh, Wis. Caidin overhauled the aircraft in 1976 at a cost of close to a quarter of a million dollars and then sold it back to Lufthansa, its original owner. On Dec. 28, 1984, it touched down in Hamburg, Germany, after a 16-day flight from Florida, up the east coast, to Greenland, Iceland, and Scotland. Its average speed on that trip was 111 miles an hour.

Lufthansa spent more than a year rebuilding the aircraft at its Hamburg maintenance base.

This past summer, D-AQUI was disassembled and loaded aboard a Russian Antonov An-124, which is the equivalent of our giant C-5A military cargo aircraft, and it was flown to Canada where it was reassembled for a tour of the United States. This tour will end in January in Seattle.

The present interior looks more like the 1980s than the '30s. It has leather seats, a plastic headliner, and overhead racks that can hold a jacket, but not much more. We were thankful for those racks because on the day we flew in it the thermometer was way up there and one modern convenience the old Junkers doesn't have is air conditioning.

After a briefing by a cheerful male cabin attendant, we taxied onto the runway for takeoff. The three engines roared into action and, after a surprisingly short run, we were airborne. The Ju 52 requires only 1,300 feet for takeoff. Takeoff speed is 80 miles an hour. It felt like riding a big Cub.

We flew over the Verrazano Bridge, circled the lady in the harbor, (the Statue of Liberty), and then flew up the Hudson at 1,000 feet, remaining below the TCA, (Terminal Control Area), so that when we passed the World Trade Center towers, they were higher than we were.

The Ju 52 is the perfect aircraft for sightseeing because it gives you plenty of time to see the sights.

We flew over the George Washington Bridge and came back down the river to circle the Statue of Liberty once again, and then back to a landing at Newark Airport.

Turning to look back at her as I walked to the terminal, I stopped for a moment. Here was a piece of aviation history, not in a museum, but sitting on a ramp at Newark International Airport after flying a full load of passengers.

The aircraft had once been offered to a museum in Oslo, but the offer was turned down because the aircraft was too big. How fortunate. If they had accepted, I would never have had the opportunity to fly in her.

9/20/90

EVERYBODY'S FAVORITE OLD AIRPLANE

No airplane evokes as much nostalgia as the trailblazing DC-3 which made air travel an acceptable, reliable, means of transportation. Almost seven decades after it first appeared on the scene there are still many of them at work all over the world.

During World War II, as the C-47, she did yeoman work, hauling supplies and personnel, dropping paratroopers behind the lines, and towing gliders into combat zones.

It was an aircraft that bridged the gap between a somewhat risky and adventurous means of travel to the point where air travel became a new and accepted means of public transportation.

Even her appearance was a giant advance over her predecessors, with the exception of the Boeing 247, which was smaller and couldn't survive the competition from the Douglas-built aircraft.

The DC-3 almost died before it was born. Its predecessor was the DC-1. On that aircraft's initial takeoff, it lost both engines. The pilot lowered the nose to gain speed and the engines came to life. He raised the nose and they quit again.

Lowering and raising the nose, the pilot skillfully managed to coax the aircraft around the pattern to a safe landing. The problem, they found, was that the carburetors were installed backwards so that when the nose was raised the floats cut off the flow of fuel.

If that DC-1 had crashed, it is very likely there never would have been a DC-3.

My first ride in a DC-3 was at a special event at Newark Airport in 1937, if I recall correctly, when I would have been 13 years old. United Airlines offered local rides for $5.

The column that follows was based on a book by Peter M. Bowers, a highly respected aircraft historian and author who died in April of 2003.

She is the grande dame of airplanes. At age 50, the mere sight of her will quicken the pulse of those who remember when she was the queen of the fleet.

Thousands of pilots who knew her intimately could spend hours recalling stories about her, and they would relish every moment.

She is known to pilots around the word by various names - the DC-3, the C-47, the Dakota. She was the first true airliner. And in World War II she was the workhorse of the skies. Her service in war and peace is legendary.

The story of this remarkable aircraft has been captured between the pages of a book, *The DC-3, 50 Years of Legendary Flight,* by Peter M. Bowers, an aeronautical engineer, (he designed the popular Fly Baby homebuilt), author, (he has written a number of books prior to this one), and a regular contributor to the aviation newspaper, *Western Flyer,* now *General Aviation News,* to which he still contributes, and a highly regarded aviation historian.

Bowers, who is obviously a dedicated researcher, has written a comprehensive history of the DC-3, illustrated by hundreds of photographs, many from his own collection, gathered over a period of 45 years, and others which he went to some lengths to acquire for his book.

The story of the DC-3 begins when United Airlines placed an order for 60 Boeing 247 airliners. Jack Frye, vice president/operations for TWA, realized that by the time he could get delivery of this aircraft United would control the skies. He, therefore, submitted specs for a tri-motor aircraft to compete with the 247.

In 10 days, Douglas aircraft submitted a proposal designated the DC-1, (Douglas Commercial number one). It was a twin-engine aircraft, not a trimotor. But it would seat 12, instead of the 10 the 247 would carry. It was faster and had a range of 1,000 miles-- more than twice that of the 247.

The first DC-3 to fly. Its maiden flight was made on December 17, 1935, 32 years after the Wright Brothers' first powered flight.

The one big question in the minds of the people at TWA was takeoff performance with one engine out at high altitude airports from which TWA operated. With three engines, the loss of one meant the loss of one-third of the available power. With two engines, the loss of one meant the power was cut in half.

Douglas was able to convince TWA that the DC-1 could hack it. And when the airplane was built the capability was proven.

Less than 10 months after the contract was signed, and less than five months after the Boeing 247 took to the air for the first time, the DC-1 made its first flight on July 1, 1933. It was not exactly a happy occasion. It lost both engines but amazingly the pilot got it down safely. The cause was traced to improper installation of a new type of carburetor.

On Feb. 19, 1934, Jack Frye and Eddie Rickenbacker of Eastern Air Lines, set a new coast-to-coast record of 13 hours and two minutes from Glendale, Calif., to Newark in the aircraft. They carried the last load of mail prior to the cancellation of the airlines' mail contracts.

Only one DC-1 was ever built. It was put into scheduled service in Spain following the Spanish Civil War. It made a belly landing after losing both engines in Dec. 1940. That was nothing new for this airplane, but this time it was scrapped. And that was the end of the DC-1, granddaddy of the DC-3

The designation of the first production model was changed to the DC-2. TWA placed it in service on August 1, 1934. They flew it coast-to-coast via Chicago, Kansas City, and Albuquerque. Flying time was 18 hours westbound, 16 hours 20 minutes eastbound.

The first flight of the DC-3 version took place on December 17, 1935, 32 years to the day after the Wright Brothers' historic first powered flight at Kitty Hawk.

Douglas built 10,655 of these aircraft. The registry of civil aircraft in the United States, published on May 30, 1985, showed 612 were still active in the U.S. and there were hundreds more in service in countries around the world.

No other aircraft has a story to match that of the DC-3 and it is well told and well illustrated in *The DC-3, 50 Years of Legendary Flight* published in soft cover by Tab Books.

7/13/86

THE FLYING CLIPPER SHIPS

I never set eyes on one of the great Boeing 314 flying clipper ships that pioneered transoceanic routes before World War II. And as it turns out, I never will.

After the war they were obsolete and all remaining examples of those historic aircraft were destroyed. Not one of these unusual aircraft was preserved for a museum.

Those colorful, pioneering aircraft were part of one of the most glamorous eras in air travel history. They had facilities no other aircraft ever had--dining rooms and passenger staterooms. They pioneered dozens of routes around the world.

It constantly saddens me to think that no one had the foresight to preserve this important part of aviation history so that I, and thousands of others, could get a glimpse of what flying was like in the days of the great flying boats.

Here is a column that provides some of the background of these wonderful aircraft.

I t started because a Fokker Trimotor built at Teterboro could not get to Key West on time. There was a hurricane coming. Runways were flooded and covered with debris. A fledgling airline named Pan American Airways had an air mail contract with the U.S. Post Office which required mail to be delivered to Havana by Oct. 19, 1927.

The Boeing 314 flying boat

Pan American World Airways photo

Juan Trippe, president of the airline, tried for an extension, but his request was refused. Either the mail would be delivered on time or there was no contract. The future of Pan Am depended on it.

Trippe had an idea. If they could get a seaplane, they could make the flight. The manager of the base at Key West heard that a Fairchild FC-2 on floats had landed at Miami with an oil leak on a flight to Haiti. They called Miami where, incidentally, there was a Fokker Trimotor that was unable to get to Key West. They reached the pilot of the Fairchild, but he was not anxious to fly the mail to Havana. An offer of $145 changed his mind.

That was Pan Am's first flight off the water. In the next

decade, Pan Am would make hundreds of flights across both the Atlantic and Pacific in one of the most colorful periods in airline history, flying huge seaplanes.

The dining room of the Boeing 314 Clipper.

Under Juan Trippe, a wily businessman who was born in Sea Bright, N.J., in 1899, Pan Am was to become the U.S. flag carrier and the pioneer of international airline flights. They did it without using runways. They used flying boats and landed on water.

The first airline flights across both the Atlantic and Pacific were made in those huge flying boats, called Clippers, a term still used to identify these aircraft.

It's a fascinating story that is told in a new book, *Pan American Ocean Clippers* by Barry Taylor, published by Tab Aero.

The routes across both oceans were surveyed by Charles and Anne Morrow Lindbergh flying the one-of-a-kind Lockheed Sirius, a low-wing monoplane on floats built especially for this mission. Lindbergh flew Pan Am flying boats on a number of pioneering flights establishing new routes through the Caribbean and Latin America.

Pan Am's earliest flying boats were built by Sikorsky. These were later replaced by M-130s built by Glenn L. Martin, and then, by the late '30s, these were replaced by the Boeing 314, one of the most comfortable and luxurious aircraft ever built. The 314 not only had staterooms, but a bridal suite as well, and dining rooms in which meals were served on real china.

A host of dignitaries flew on this aircraft, including Winston Churchill and Franklin Roosevelt. Roosevelt flew to the Casablanca conference with Churchill and Stalin on the 314, marking the first time an American president made an overseas flight.

In addition to their deluxe accommodations, (printed passenger lists were distributed on board as they are on ocean liners), the flying boats had tremendous range. They could fly more than 4,000 miles and made flights that lasted (non stop) 23 hours.

The 314 could carry as many as 74 passengers, but seldom did. The number of passengers depended on the distance to be flown. Where more fuel was required, fewer passengers could be accommodated.

The cost of a flight to Europe was $375 or $675 round trip. That's the equivalent of about $7,000 to $8,000 in today's money, or about twice the cost of flying the supersonic Concorde.

10/28/90

Note: *Pan American Airways, which pioneered most of this nation's international air routes and introduced some of the nation's outstanding air transport aircraft, including the Boeing 314 flying boat and the Boeing 747, went out of business in 1991.*

THE ONE AND ONLY SPRUCE GOOSE

Only somebody like Howard Hughes would undertake the task of building an aircraft as massive as the Spruce Goose--and building it out of wood.

Members of Congress and virtually all of the high-ranking military brass thought he was crazy. In that regard they were just a little ahead of their time.

The Spruce Goose is an aircraft that still baffles aviation experts. Many said it would never fly. It did, with Howard Hughes at the controls. It didn't go high, (70 feet), and it didn't go far, (about a mile), but it flew.

It was designed to carry more than 700 troops plus a Sherman tank. It was far larger than a 747.

Everybody, the aircraft manufacturers, the military, and government officials, said building such an aircraft was impossible. That aroused Howard Hughes' interest and he undertook the project.

I f there were an Oscar for airplanes, what airplane would you vote for? The *Spirit of St. Louis*, the *Wright Flyer*, the *Concorde*, or maybe the *Spruce Goose*?

The latter has certainly been the center of more mystery and controversy than any other aircraft.

The largest aircraft ever built, it made only one flight and then was hidden from public view for almost 40 years.

A large part of its mystery and the intrigue surrounding its creation, was linked to the man who designed and built her, Howard Hughes.

Much of that mystery is swept away in a fascinating new paperback, *Howard Hughes and the Spruce Goose,* by John J. McDonald, published by Tab Books.

The idea for this aircraft was not Hughes'. Credit for that

The *Spruce Goose* on its one and only flight

belongs to another genius of the World War II years, Henry J. Kaiser.

Kaiser, who achieved fame for turning out Liberty ships in record-breaking time, conceived the idea of 5,000 mammoth flying ships that would be free from the perils of enemy U-boats.

He took his idea to all the major aircraft manufacturers of the time and all of them scoffed at it. The military also rejected his idea and so did high government officials.

Kaiser went to Howard Hughes. Initially, Hughes was not interested. But in subsequent talks, when Kaiser related that all the major aircraft manufacturers said it was an impossible dream and Air Corps brass told him he was crazy, Hughes agreed to undertake the task.

There were seven concepts for the aircraft, the first three of which were twin-hulled craft. A contract for the project was signed by Kaiser, president of the Kaiser-Hughes Corp., in November of 1942.

Kaiser, who had hoped to have the ship flying in 10 months, withdrew from the project 16 months later when construction had hardly begun and cost overruns were enormous. In 1947, there were highly emotional Senate hearings on the project. (The aircraft cost the government $18 million and senators claimed it would never fly.) In November of 1947, just before the hearings were to resume, Hughes made its one and only short flight to prove them wrong.

For years, after it came out of hiding, it was on display at Long Beach, Calif.

12/20/81

Note: *It can now be seen in a museum in McMinville, Ore.*

THE TIGER MOTH

The Tiger Moth is a kind of anomaly. It looks like a World War I flying machine, but actually, it was a World War II trainer. Built by de Havilland, many of England's fighter pilots had their first taste of the sky in this airplane.

It wasn't especially pretty, it crawled through the sky at a less than breathtaking 90 miles an hour, but old aircraft collectors love them. The first Tiger Moth flew in 1931 and more than 7,000 were built in England, Canada, Australia, and New Zealand.

I had the good fortune to go for a ride in one and immediately I knew where Snoopy was coming from, dreaming of being a World War I ace. As a result, the column I wrote about that experience was addressed to Snoopy.

Dear Snoopy:
I know a lot of people think you're a mad romantic and a dreamer when you tell them about your exciting exploits in the helmet and goggles days of World War I. But, be assured, if you are a romantic, you have at least one admirer who appreciates your dream and shares it.

A few weeks ago, I donned helmet and goggles and climbed into the front seat of a gleaming, open cockpit Tiger Moth biplane.

Kurt and Susan Hofschneider in the cockpit of the Tiger Moth he helped rebuild and make famous.

This, of course, is an airplane that looks like a World War I relic, but was actually used to train British pilots during World War II.

Paul Jordan, a Seaboard Airlines captain, was in the rear cockpit doing the flying. I could communicate using a gossport--a tube into which you talk and which you can hear from the other end through your helmet.

Kurt Hofschneider, who shares ownership of the Moth with Paul, strapped me in. Just about everything in this airplane is original equipment, including the seat belt, a rather ingenious affair. It consists of four heavy leather straps with holes in them like a belt. Two belts come over your shoulders and two across your lap. Each belt is numbered.

You put the belts one over the other in the order numbered and then you push a spike through the holes linking them all together. A cotter pin type device holds the spike in place.

Before takeoff, Paul checked over the gossport to make sure my goggles were down.

"If a bug hits you in the eye at high speed, (90 miles an hour) you'll be incapacitated for awhile," he warned.

Paul taxied to the end of the runway at Trenton-Robbinsville Airport where the plane is based.

He ran up the engine and it purred like a contented kitten. Then off we went. In seconds we were airborne with the wind whistling past the cockpit.

Paul flew to a nearby area with long, broad wide open farm fields and he swooped down to within 50 feet of the ground and raced across the open land. It was something like watching those Cinerama scenes filmed from a helicopter. It was anything but the ordinary flying experience. Though the airplane was slow, soaring just a few feet above the ground made it seem like we were zooming along at high speed, and the wind blowing in your face didn't reduce that sensation.

Every once in awhile a long line of trees stretched out across the broad field we were flying over and seemed to approach at an uncommonly rapid rate. Paul pulled the Moth up, jumped over the trees and dropped down again on the other side.

And that is when I discovered why you dream the kind of dreams you dream, of helmet and goggles flying.

There were moments when I was sure we were returning from a successful World War I mission and were about to touch down at our home base where our cheering comrades would be waiting to congratulate us.

In 19 years of flying that was the most exhilarating experience I had known. People who have never experienced open cockpit, helmet and goggles flying, don't know anything about the real exhilaration of flight. What a pity.

When we glided in and touched down on the runway at Trenton-Robbinsville there were no cheering comrades. There was no one there to welcome us home.

I helped Paul push the Moth back into the hangar and then he told me about the two years and nine months he and Kurt spent restoring this aircraft that they bought from a fellow in New Hampshire. When they finished, it looked like it was ready for a museum, not for active duty.

Almost everything in the aircraft is original equipment. And absolutely everything in the aircraft is in gleaming, mint condition. Even the engine gleams. There is not a speck of dirt or grease on it. This past summer Paul flew the aircraft out to the Experimental Aircraft Association's annual fly-in at Oshkosh, Wis. It took him 22 hours to get there. He could have driven in less time.

Antiques and homebuilts and restored aircraft flew into Oshkosh by the hundreds from all over the country, Snoopy. There, many of these aircraft were entered into competition and judged by men who have seen them all. The aircraft that won the award for Category Champ for the World War II era was the beautifully restored Tiger Moth I had flown in.

11/25/73

Note: *That aircraft now hangs in the Air Force Museum at Wright-Patterson Field outside Dayton, Ohio*

THE LAST ONE STILL FLYING

The Savoia Marchetti S-56, the subject of the following column, was not only old, it was unique. It was the only airplane of its type still flying, although there is one more in existence. It's in a museum. The airplane is distinguished in another way. It was the first aircraft in the fleet of the New York City Police Department.

The man responsible for bringing this 1930 vintage aircraft back to life, "Buzz" Kaplan, is as unusual as the aircraft itself. He was an adventurer in the truest sense of the word. He flew to Greenland to assist the people of the Greenland Expedition in the recovery of a P-38 that went down on an ice cap during World War II. He went down 250 feet through a huge hole drilled in the ice to view a B-17 Flying Fortress, one of two that made emergency landings along with six P-38s.

He piloted one of four Caravans that flew to the Soviet Union in 1991 as part of a Friendship Flight when the Cold War was still going on and American general aviation airplanes were not generally welcome.

He bought and restored many rare antique aircraft. His 8,000 plus hours included flights above the Arctic Circle and into Africa. He was the only pilot since 1912 to land a seaplane, the 1930 Savoia Marchetti, on Lake Geneva, Switzerland.

In this instance the old airplane's pilot was as interesting as the airplane itself.

I f you're a Homo sapien, when you get old, no one wants to know you. But if you're an airplane, ah, that's a different matter. The older you get, the more they admire you. It's enough to make you wish you were an airplane.

Now you take the Savoia Marchetti S-56, an Italian designed, open cockpit, amphibious biplane. She celebrated her 60th birthday in January. That's pretty old for an airplane. But when she was scheduled to come to New York this past week to become part of the Italian Aerospace Show at the Intrepid Museum (aboard the carrier *Intrepid*, docked permanently in Manhattan), she was one of the items that reporters and photographers and TV cameramen were most anxious to see.

At one time there were 40 S-56s. Today, N194M is the only one in the world still flying. The only other example of the breed is in a museum in Rome and not in the best condition.

When R.W. "Buzz" Kaplan of Owatonna, Minn., discovered N194M it was a basket case. It was declared unrepairable. Even so, its owner in Washington State did not want to part with it. It took Kaplan two years to get him to change his mind.

If you saw pictures of what Kaplan bought, you would

understand why it was declared unrepairable. But Gary Underland, who had done a lot of work on other airplanes Kaplan owns, including the restoration of a Waco cabin biplane, wasn't about to accept the verdict that N194M couldn't be restored.

To rebuild it, however, he would need some drawings. What was left of her wasn't enough to go by. The original

R.W. "Buzz" Kaplan climbs out of the cockpit of his Savoia Marchetti S.56 Italian-designed amphibian that dates back to 1930. It was the first aircraft used by the New York City Police Department.

drawings were destroyed when the factory in Italy, where it had been designed, was bombed in World War II.

A company in Port Washington, N.Y., that built 40 S-56s under license, was long since gone.

Underland went to the Smithsonian's National Air and Space Museum in search of drawings. They had nothing.

He then went to the Eastern Region of the FAA at JFK Airport. That office would have had to approve any aircraft built in New York and would have to have drawings on file. They have tons of drawings in storage and finding any particular one is not a task they were anxious to undertake.

Invoking the Freedom of Information Act, however, Underland was able to get them to initiate the search. It took them two months to find the drawings he wanted.

"They found two boxes of S-56 drawings," Underland said. "They were in poor condition but the FAA copied them on microfilm for us and only charged $2 a copy."

Underland, with the help of carpenter Dana Ulen, spent 3 1/2 years rebuilding N194M. It is in mint condition today. It was shipped from Owatonna, Minn., and reassembled at Somerset Airport, (N.J.), to be landed on the Hudson River so it could be hoisted aboard the carrier *Intrepid*, now a museum, as part of the Italian Aerospace Exhibition. But that was not to be. Rough water in the Hudson prevented a landing and after traveling all the way from Minnesota for exhibition on the *Intrepid*, it never made it.

But it did get to fly over the Hudson. The S-56 was the first aircraft the N.Y. Police Department ever had. "Buzz" Kaplan flew her with a Newark Police helicopter escort. In its day, the New York police used it for harbor patrol.

Kaplan, who is older than the aircraft by six years, (he celebrated his 66th birthday on March 30), also appears to be in mint condition. A retired tool manufacturer, he learned to fly in 1946 after his discharge from the Army.

"I was in the infantry with Patton's Third Army," Kaplan said. "I looked up at the aircraft flying over us and said, 'Those guys are going to sleep in a warm bed tonight. I'm going to sleep in the mud.'

"I was discharged in April, 1946, got my pilot's license in May, and got married in June," he said.

Today, Kaplan owns a fleet of aircraft, including a turboprop Cessna Caravan on floats, an antique Waco cabin biplane on floats, a Cessna 185 and a J-3 Cub, both also on floats. Underland is rebuilding an antique Curtiss Robin for which they also have floats.

The S-56, that attracted a lot of attention earlier this week, has a normal cruise speed of 70 mph. It takes off at 40. The red line, (never exceed speed), is 100 mph. It has a range of 3 1/2 hours.

The aircraft has no brakes. It has a tail skid rather than a tail wheel, so it must be flown off a turf runway rather than a hard surface. It's powered by a 125-hp Kinner engine, with a compressed air starter. There are only about 25 such engines in existence today.

When Kaplan flew it out of Somerset Airport last weekend, he used the turf runway normally reserved for glider operations.

"Kaplan loves airplanes," Underland said. "I do, too. It's my hobby, my work, my life. He, (Kaplan), has enough money to make it work. I have enough savvy to make it work."

Together, Kaplan and Underland have turned out a real winner. N194M won the Antique Aircraft Association's Grand Champion Award and the Phoenix Diploma, awarded at the Paris Air Show in 1985. It was presented in New Delhi, India, at a meeting of the Federation Aeronautique International.

The aircraft was shipped to England in 1988 and it was flown in England, France, and Switzerland for a month.

So in spite of being 60, N194M still has a lot of get up and go. And wherever she goes, everybody loves her.

4/8/90

Note: *"Buzz" Kaplan died in June 2002 in an accident on takeoff in an antique JN-4 Jenny.*

THE PITCAIRN MAILWING

The days of the air mail planes and their pilots in the '20s and early '30s were among the most memorable eras in aviation history. Those air mail pilots were legendary. Charles Lindbergh was one of them. They flew biplanes with the limited instruments of the time through all kinds of weather, day and night. Many of them lost their lives. Perhaps the most outstanding of those aircraft was the Pitcairn Mailwing designed and built by Harold Pitcairn at Willow Grove Airport outside Philadelphia. Pitcairn not only produced what was probably the best mail plane ever built, but he pioneered the development of the autogyro which was the predecessor of the helicopter.

His son, Stephen, has done a marvelous job of preserving his legacy, along with some of the aircraft he developed.

What follows is the life story of a Mailwing that was the personal airplane of Harold Pitcairn which Steve acquired almost half a century after his father sold it.

One of the most colorful eras in the history of aviation in this country was the era of the mail plane. And one of the most distinguished of those great mail carrying planes of the '20s was the famed Pitcairn Mailwing.

There were about 140 of them built between the late '20s and early '30s. The last one rolled off the line in 1932. This is the story of one of those airplanes, NC 6708.

She was born on June 30, 1928. The price tag on her was $9,850. But she wasn't sold. Harold L.

Pitcairn Mailwing NC 6708

Pitcairn, developer and manufacturer of the airplane, chose her as his personal airplane.

In 1930, about the time of her second birthday, she went back to the factory outside Philadelphia for modification. The object was to increase her speed.

They changed her engine and upped her horsepower to 235, installing a new seven-cylinder Wright engine. NC 6708 was a PA-5 model, but by 1930 they were building PA-7s. They put PA-7 wings and tail surfaces on her. They changed her flat bottom to a rounded bottom.

There is no actual record, but it is assumed that these modifications increased her speed from 110 miles an hour to 120, and her top speed from 130 to 144.

She was sold in 1931. Her owner then became United Air Service Ltd. of California, a company owned by Paul Mantz, who achieved considerable fame in later years providing old airplanes for movies and also for his own stunt flying in movies. Since he was president of United Air Services, NC 6708 soon became a movie star. She was in several Warner Bros. movies.

By 1938, she had seen eight more owners and her price tag had dipped as low as $450. In 1941, Frank and Emil Stefanik bought her for $1,200 and brought her back home to Pitcairn Field in Willow Grove, Pa., where she was born.

With the onset of U.S. involvement, World War II civil flying on the east coast came to a halt. The Stefaniks disassembled her and put her into storage. There she remained for 28 years. She was then sold and moved to the 3M Airport in Bristol, Pa., just outside of Levittown.

On July 18, 1972, NC 6708 flew again for the first time in 31 years.

In 1973, she was sold once again, this time to the Owls Head Foundation Trust, that maintains an air museum in Rockland, Maine.

And here, once again, she met up with a famous personality. Ernest K. Gann, the author who had written the novel, *Blaze of Noon*, about flying the mail with Pitcairn Mailwings. He climbed into her cockpit and took her aloft.

Not long after that, the museum decided it wanted to concentrate on World War I and earlier period aircraft.

They contacted Stephen Pitcairn, son of the designer and manufacturer of the aircraft, and asked if he would like to buy NC 6708. Would he ever. That was the airplane that had been his father's. And that is how NC 6708 came back to the Pitcairn family after 49 years.

Today, NC 6708 is based at the Trenton-Robbinsville Airport in Robbinsville, in a new hangar that Steve Pitcairn completed earlier this year in which he also keeps a Waco CUC-7 cabin biplane, one of only two of that model still flying, a Culver Cadet, and a Luscombe. All of them shine with a mirror-like finish. There is also one of Harold Pitcairn's autogyros in the hangar. Steve flies them all.

All around NC 6708 are various models of the Pitcairn Sport and Mailwing aircraft that Steve Pitcairn's father built. It's like a museum, albeit a private one. Nowhere else in the country is there so much background on the Pitcairn mail planes as in this hangar.

Included in the collection is a picture of the first airplane Harold Pitcairn ever built, a three cockpit biplane.

Some of the early models pictured on the walls of the hangar were powered by the famed old OX-5 engine. There is a whole wall covered with blowups of photos of the Pitcairn autogyros manufactured from 1930 to 1940.

Steve Pitcairn flies NC 6708 about 30 hours a year now, but he lavishes much more time than that keeping her in tip top mint condition.

Gentry Smith, who helps Steve keep her in that condition, says of the Pitcairns, "I've been working on airplanes for 50 years. I've never seen another airplane that was as easy to work on. You can get at anything in that airplane with a minimum of trouble."

Steve Pitcairn figures that today, NC 6708 is worth somewhere around $50,000, a pretty good improvement from its low of $450.

12/30/79

THE SPARTAN EXECUTIVE

This column is kind of a twin of the preceding one. It's about an antique, the Spartan Executive, that found its way home after many years.

The Spartan was a sleek-looking aircraft with a huge rotary engine. It could carry five and cruise at about 200 mph, which would put it in the category of high performance single-engine aircraft of today.

It was, as the title implies, a truly executive aircraft. Less than three dozen of them were built, a fact that is an important part of this story.

The scene was enough to make you cry. George Mennen was 85 yesterday, and there was something very special about the occasion. After 17 years, he had a surprise reunion with *Mrs. Mennen.*

Mrs. Mennen was the name inscribed on a rare Spartan Executive aircraft that dates back to the days before World War II. The first one rolled out of the factory in 1935. With its low wing, big 450-hp radial engine and seating for five, the polished aluminum aircraft was 30 years ahead of its time. Its cruise speed was better than 200 mph. Only 34 were built. *Mrs. Mennen* was number 34, the last one off the line in 1940.

William G. Mennen IV with his grandfather, George Mennen, in front of the Spartan Executive which his grandfather had sold years ago and Will found at Oshkosh. He eventually bought it and brought it back to New Jersey and first showed it to his grandfather' on his 85th birthday.

It was originally owned by Texaco. The aircraft was very expensive. Most of them were owned by companies and a few by heads of states, including those of Mexico and Iraq. George Mennen bought his plane from the president of the Spartan Owners Association and named it after his mother.

He owned the airplane for 15 years and then donated it to the

Experimental Aircraft Association, (EAA), Museum in Oshkosh, Wis., when that facility opened in 1976.

Because of poor health, George has never been to Oshkosh to see his airplane on display.

At the time he owned the airplane, George Mennen was chairman of the board of the Mennen Co. of Morris Plains, one of the world's largest toiletries companies, with hundreds of millions in sales annually and 3,000 employees around the world, about half of them in the company's headquarters. He was also a part owner of Chatham Aviation, the fixed base operator at Morristown Airport where the airplane was based.

"Some of my fondest memories are of flying in that airplane with my grandfather," said George's grandson, William G. Mennen IV.

This past summer, Will, an attorney, was at the big EAA AirVenture 2002 show in Oshkosh and there he encountered a rare surprise. He saw the very airplane his grandfather used to take him flying in when he was a boy. There were six Spartans on exhibit at the show. "Less than 20 are still flying," Will said.

The airplane was now owned by Ben Runyan of Vancouver, Wash., a retired Delta captain who used to fly L-1011s across the Pacific.

"The plane was not for sale," Will said. But he had a very strong desire to own it and bring it back into the Mennen family. Mennen didn't give up because it wasn't for sale. "I exercised my keen powers of persuasion," he said. And eventually, he prevailed. Thus, via a chance encounter, Will became the owner of the airplane he had flown in with his grandfather many years ago.

Ben flew the airplane across the country with his wife, Sally, and last Sunday he landed at Somerset Airport where it will be based. Will who learned to fly at Somerset eight years ago and then earned a commercial license with instrument and multiengine ratings, also owns a Baron based at Somerset Airport.

Will did not tell his grandfather that he had purchased his old airplane. He wanted it to be a surprise. Yesterday was his grandfather's birthday and Will drove him to the airport. He pulled up to the hangar and opened the hangar door. It rose slowly and there was his grandfather's old airplane.

There is one more surprise to this story. The airplane Will bought did not have the green trim and the name "Mrs. Mennen" on it that was there when his grandfather flew it. The airplane was now polished aluminum with red trim. There was a reason for that.

When George donated the airplane to the EAA museum, they had a policy of exhibiting only the first aircraft ever built of a particular model. George's Spartan was not the first. It was the last. So it was not eligible to go into the museum. The first, as a matter of fact, no longer existed.

John Turgyan, a collector of antique aircraft, owned No. 2, which was based at Trenton-Robbinsville Airport, maybe ten minutes flying time from Somerset Airport. He agreed to trade his airplane for George's so the museum could have the earliest model of the aircraft in existence.

Turgyan's aircraft was then painted in Mennen's colors with "Mrs. Mennen" inscribed on the nose for exhibit in the museum and Mennen's aircraft was repainted with red trim.

So while it may have looked different, the airplane Will bought was the actual airplane his grandfather, George, had owned 32 years ago. It was an antique back then, although in appearance and performance it can still hold its own against aircraft built today.

Will thought it would be nice to take his grandfather for a ride in his old airplane, but he didn't think his frail, ailing grandfather could climb up into the cockpit. His grandfather surprised him. With a little help, he got up there and went for a ride to celebrate both his 85th birthday and the return of *Mrs. Mennen* to the family.

Some years ago, the noted aviation artist, Keith Ferris, painted a picture of *Mrs. Mennen* and he also built a small-scale model that is precise in every detail. George has a home in Chester, N.J., and another in Sarasota, Fla. The Ferris painting hangs in his Florida home so that even though the actual airplane has been some 3,000 miles away, and the one in his original colors was in Oshkosh, its image has never really been out of his sight.

But now, *Mrs. Mennen* is not only back home in New Jersey, but back in the family with Will flying it. And it's once again wearing its original Mennen colors.

10/14/01

Note: *George Mennen died on May 5, 2005.*

THE SWALLOW

The Swallow that dates back to the mid '20s, is the oldest airplane I ever flew in. It was an airplane used in air mail service and in the first commercial service. An open cockpit biplane, it lacked a few of the comforts we've come to expect in air travel.

The pilot with whom I flew in the Swallow was as distinctive as his airplane. He was an airline pilot, and a dedicated restorer of antique aircraft.

His exploits in the Swallow gained him considerable publicity and renown.

Capt. E. E. Hilbert makes his living sitting up front in a United Airlines DC-8. But flying is not just a job to Buck Hilbert. It's a love.

A lot of the flying he's done in the last 15 years he hasn't been paid for. Most of the flying has been done in airplanes as old as he is. These were airplanes with names like Ryan, Fleet, Porterfield, and Swallow.

He has owned about 16 airplanes in the last 15 years, each of which he rebuilt and restored with loving care.

Buck Hilbert flew into Newark International Airport yesterday in a restored Swallow biplane. It was this model aircraft that, 50 years ago, when Hilbert had barely learned to walk, made a flight

Captain E. E. "Buck" Hilbert talking to the reining Miss Colorado in 1976. His Swallow, built in the mid-20s, is behind them. It was the only one still flying when this photo was taken.

from Pasco, Wash., to Boise, Id., and then on to Elko, Nev., in what is recognized today as the beginning of scheduled airline service in the United States.

Last April 6, at 6:23 a.m., the same time that Leon Cuddleback took off a half century ago with six sacks containing 9,285 pieces of mail, Hilbert took off with the same load to retrace that original flight's route.

Everything was the same. Even the weather, which was cloudy and wet both times. When Hilbert landed at Boise,

Cuddleback, now 77, was there to greet him in the rain.

When Cuddleback made the original flight he was working for Varney Air Lines that merged with three other companies in 1931 to become United Airlines.

Buck's Swallow is the only one flying today and there's quite a story behind that.

About 11 years ago, Buck heard there was an old Swallow hanging in the rafters of a garage in Chicago. He tried to buy it, but the owner didn't want to sell. It was his dream to rebuild it himself, a dream he had nurtured since 1943 when he first put it up there.

Buck never gave up his hope of someday acquiring the aircraft and rebuilding it. After eight years, his patience was rewarded. The owner finally relented and Buck bought the aircraft with two partners, one of whom is Dario Toffenetti, the restaurateur. And, as it happened, he barely had time to restore it in time to reenact the historic flight of 50 years ago.

Buck, who is past president of the Antique and Classic Division of the Experimental Aircraft Association, and its current treasurer, is in the midst of a nationwide tour in the Swallow on behalf of United Airlines. This coming week, Tuesday through Friday, he'll be at the big Reading Air Show with it.

I met Buck in Denver last month at the Aviation/Space Writers News Conference, and I donned helmet and goggles to taste what flying was like 50 years ago.

Buck had hardly opened the throttle when we lifted from the runway at Arapahoe County Airport (now Centennial Airport). Once airborne, Buck gave me the signal to take the controls.

There were no instruments at all in the front cockpit. There was only a crude airspeed indicator hung out on the end of the top wing. What that told you was that when you hit 80 miles an hour you were getting just about all you could get out of the old bird.

If you put the wing down in a steep turn and put it on a point, it stayed there, steady as a rock. It was a bit noisier than my Arrow, there was a little more vibration and a lot of wind in the face, but a brand of flying every pilot should have the privilege of experiencing at least once.

The Swallow was designed in 1920 by Matty Laird who formed a company in Wichita, Kansas, to build it. After three years he sold the company to Lloyd Stearman and Walter Beech, and he went into designing racing aircraft.

Stearman and Beech later formed their own companies and produced their own aircraft.

In 1924, improvements were made to the Swallow and it became known as the New Swallow which earned a reputation as America's first commercial aircraft.

The 1927 model was priced at $2,485.

Buck Hilbert, as a DC-8 captain, is not unmindful of the debt we all owe the old-time aviation pioneers.

"I'm flying the Swallow," he says, "to try to gain recognition for the pioneers who built the air transport system we have today.

"Every time we step in a DC-10 or a 747, we're taking advantage of the foundation these people built," he says.

6/6/76

THE LITTLE YELLOW PIPER CUB

It is perhaps fitting that I end this chapter about old airplanes with what is probably the best known of all of them--the Piper Cub. This was the Model T of the airplane world. It was the first general aviation aircraft produced in great numbers. It introduced more people to the world of flying than any other aircraft of its time.

And when you speak of time, no aircraft, with the exception of the DC-3, has had as long an active lifetime as the J-3 Piper Cub. The DC-3 went into service in 1936 and the J-3 Cub came on the scene in 1937. The name actually became generic. Many people referred to any small aircraft as a Piper Cub.

The Cub entered the world as the Taylor Cub in the early '30s. The company went bankrupt and William T. Piper, a member of the Taylor Aircraft Board of Directors, was the only bidder for the company's assets. He bought them for $761.

In 1937, the company name was changed to the Piper Aircraft Corporation and the J-3 Cub was introduced the following year. It was always distinguished by its yellow color.

Summon the bugler. Let him blow taps. The Piper Cub is dead. The granddaddy of all general aviation aircraft, the worldwide symbol of the small airplane for more than half a century, has fallen victim to the insanity of the time we live in.

A Piper Cub landing on a platform atop a pickup truck at the Sussex (N.J.) Air Show.

Piper Aircraft will deliver the last 19 Cubs to Muncie Aviation in Muncie, Ind., the world's oldest Piper dealer, in June and July.

Thousands of pilots took their first flight lesson in the Piper Cub. Some of them wound up as captains of jumbo jets. Some became fighter pilots. At least one, and I'm sure there were many more, became aviation columnists.

But the Cub was not just a trainer, it had dozens of uses in war and peace. It was used for pipeline patrol, rescue work, and aerial photography. In World War II, it was used to direct artillery fire, for reconnaissance, as an air ambulance, and for transportation of personnel to remote areas. More than 6,000 were produced for the military during World War II.

Prior to the war they were used in the government's Civilian Pilot Training Program, where many military pilots got their start.

Piper produced more than 14,125 civilian J-3 Cubs, which with the 6,000 military versions added up to a total of more than 20,000 aircraft. Six thousand three-hundred and twenty were delivered in 1946. In contrast, the entire industry in the United States produced a total of 899 aircraft last year. Piper also built about 4,000 more advanced models of the J-3 Cub.

It was Piper Aircraft that announced the demise of the Cub, but it was the United States Congress that killed it.

The price of the Cub, like all general aviation aircraft, soared to levels that put them beyond the reach of those who constituted its market. A significant portion of those soaring costs didn't go to labor or for materials. They went for product liability, which is to say, it went to lawyers.

When they were introduced, the cost of a Cub was less than $2,000. Inflation boosted prices 10 to 20 times higher for many commodities over the past half century. The price of the Piper Cub rose to a level 40 times higher. The last of the breed to be delivered will bear price tags of $84,000. Although Muncie says it will sell them for $69,000.

Over the years the aircraft had earned a reputation as the most forgiving flying machine ever built, which is to say, the safest. A pilot could make all kinds of mistakes and not hurt himself or the aircraft.

If you are one of the thousands who flock to the Sussex (NJ) Air Show every year, you've seen a vivid demonstration of that. One of the show's favorite acts is a comedy routine in which a "farmer," unfamiliar with flying, gets into a Cub that proceeds to take off with him in it, with no pilot. He does everything you could possibly do wrong. It takes your breath away to watch him. But he does not hurt himself or the airplane. The things he does in the Cub you could probably not do in any other airplane.

Nevertheless, in a case in New Mexico involving a Cub accident, a jury decided the Cub is an unsafe aircraft and awarded the plaintiffs $2.5 million.

The aircraft involved had a camera mounted on the front seat. The pilot was flying from the back seat, which was standard procedure. A van drove out onto the runway to try to stop the Cub from taking off. In the collision that followed, the pilot injured his head when it struck the camera mount.

The lawyer for the plaintiffs convinced the jury that the Cub was unsafe because it had a tail wheel, (in contrast to the nose wheel on most of the airplanes built in the last couple of decades), and that configuration limits the pilot's visibility. Thousands of aircraft were built with tail wheels before the first general aviation aircraft was built with a nose wheel. That would make all aircraft built before the nose wheel, unsafe. You might as well declare all automobiles unsafe that were built before antilock brakes.

He also convinced the jury that Piper was derelict because the aircraft, built in 1970, did not have a shoulder harness, in spite of the fact that they were not required then.

Both the FAA, (Federal Aviation Administration), and the Department of Justice filed amicus (friend of the court), briefs pointing out that the aircraft was certified by the FAA which meant it had to pass rigid safety standards set by that agency. It costs millions to certify a new aircraft because of the multitude of tests to which it must be subjected before certification.

In spite of the fact that aircraft experts found that the Cub met all the safety standards and had been in service for 45 years, a jury of people who knew little or nothing about aircraft, judged the Cub to be unsafe. The aircraft involved was 13 years old at the time of the accident.

Since there is no statute of repose limiting the time of liability, Piper would have been liable even if the aircraft was 40 years old.

Awards like that $2.5 million are added to the cost of every airplane built after that. And that is not an isolated case, nor is it the most flagrant case on record. There are many that are far worse. In one example, a pilot admitted he ran out of gas and the manufacturer received a judgment against it of $25 million.

For a decade now, the general aviation aircraft industry and its associations in Washington have worked hard to get Congress to pass a reasonable product liability law. A half dozen times it has been voted down. There are simply too many lawyers in Congress. And the American Trial Lawyers Association has vast quantities of money and influence.

The industry has made heroic efforts to establish a statute of repose so that a manufacturer would not be forever liable for every aircraft it ever built. Their efforts have been unsuccessful.

Congress's steadfast refusal to pass any kind of liability reform has destroyed an industry in which the United States was once the world leader. Hundreds of thousands of skilled workers, many of whom spent the best part of their lives in the aircraft industry, are out of work. They cannot pass their skills and knowledge on to a younger generation. Skills that took years to develop are being lost. A valuable resource is slipping away.

Billions of dollars in overseas sales have been lost, contributing to our massive trade deficit.

Our children and our children's children will be paying to dig us out of the hole Congress has dug us into.

So weep not so much for the Piper Cub. Weep for those who destroyed it.

3/21/93

Note: *Since this column was written Congress passed the General Aviation Revitalization Act which limits aircraft manufacturers' liability to 18 years.*

CubCrafters of Yakima, Wash., is now building two aircraft based on the Piper Cub. One is called Top Cub. It is a beefed up version of the Super Cub. The other is a light-sport-aircraft version of the Cub. Both versions closely resemble the original Cub.

American Legend Aircraft Company of Sulphur Springs, Texas, manufactures a Legend Cub.

.

Chapter 14

Faster Than the Speed of Sound
(The Concorde)

Now that we've looked back at some of the pioneering great old airplanes that blazed the path to today's jet transports, it's time to look at where they have taken us. The greatest advance in the history of civil air transport was the SST (supersonic transport).

The only such aircraft to see commercial service was the British-French Concorde. It is ironic that after 27 years of operations, supersonic service has been wiped off the scene. The last Air France Concorde flight took place in May of 2003, the last British Concorde ceased service on November 24 of the same year. The aircraft that marked the greatest advances in commercial air travel are now museum pieces. They fell victim to economics. They were too costly to operate.

Nevertheless, I think those aircraft are worthy of a chapter of their own in this book. I will always be grateful that I had the opportunity to fly in them before the curtain was drawn.

PIONEER PILOTS OF THE SUPERSONIC AGE

Years before the Concorde was placed into passenger service, two pilots who had flown the airplane came to New York to talk with the aviation press about what it was like to fly a passenger aircraft that flew faster than the speed of sound.

Their audience hung on every word because they were forging new ground in aviation history flying supersonic transport aircraft. They were modern day pioneers.

The Russians had also produced a supersonic transport, but its career came to a horrible end when it crashed during a demonstration at the Paris Air Show before it ever went into service.

The United States had a competition between two major aircraft manufacturers, Boeing and Lockheed, to design and produce a supersonic transport. Lockheed won and a mockup had been built when Congress killed the project by cutting off funds because it was deemed too costly.

Senator Barry Goldwater, who was a pilot, said, at the time, that those congressmen who killed the project didn't know which end of the aircraft was supposed to go down the runway first.

What is it like to fly a supersonic transport?

Not many pilots in the world could tell you because there are not many supersonic transports flying. The Russians had one in the air and so did the British and the French in a joint venture. The one major power that never had one in production was the

The Air France Concorde in flight.

Courtesy of Air France

United States.

Two pilots who have flown such an aircraft, Jean Franchi of France and Peter Baker of England, were in New York recently to talk about their experiences with the next generation of aircraft and I thought pilots of slower and slightly smaller aircraft, as well as members of the general public would be interested in hearing their comments.

John Franchi, a Sud Aviation pilot, summed it up in two words, "It's easy. It was easy from the first day, from the first minute," said Franchi, a balding middle-aged fellow who is the father of four.

"Flying the Concorde is exactly the same as flying a subsonic jet," he said.

"In the traffic pattern, it's easier to handle than a subsonic jet," said Peter Baker. "There are no flaps or speed brakes to worry about."

Franchi and Baker are test pilots for Sud Aviation and British Aircraft Corporation, manufacturers of the Concorde. They might be inclined to be a bit prejudiced, so they had senior pilots from four airlines--Pan American, TWA, BOAC, and Air France--fly the aircraft and submit a report.

"If we submitted a report as favorable as they did," said Franchi, " nobody would believe us."

The four airline pilots concurred in the opinion that the aircraft was "pleasant and easy to fly," and "it imposed no excessive workload on the pilot, even in simulated failure conditions."

How about flying through the sound barrier?

"The sound barrier does not exist," said Franchi. "You don't feel anything when you go supersonic. Passengers will never know."

"Sound barrier," incidentally, is a term Franchi says he hates to use. Flight at supersonic speeds is quieter than current subsonic aircraft, according to the test pilots.

How about noise on the ground?

That is still a problem.

Noise on approach is slightly less than a 707 directly along the flight path. On takeoff, it's about the same as a 707. There is, however, more noise on the sides because the engines on the SST have no fan or bypass. This is a major problem which engineers are working on.

The Concorde, which is half the size of the proposed U.S. SST and 400 miles an hour slower, will cut flying times in half when it enters service, which is currently set for 1973. London to New York flight time will be reduced from 7 hours 35 minutes to 3 hours 20 minutes. A passenger will leave Europe at 2 p.m. and arrive in New York at noon. (The aircraft will whisk across the ocean faster than the sun.)

One thing the SST will accomplish, the aircraft's builders say, is to relieve peak congestion hours by spreading out arrival times, which are generally dictated by the time people wish to leave.

The SST is expected to have a significant effect on world trade. When any two places are brought within 12 hours traveling time of each other it provides a great stimulus to trade. This has been a fact since the days of the stage coach.

With the SST in service, everyplace in the world will be within 12 hours flying time of everywhere else.

The aircraft will operate at altitudes of 47,000 to 57,000 feet. Passengers in the SST will be the first to see the curvature of the earth.

It is interesting to note that France has supersonic corridors over the southern part of the country to avoid big cities. Concorde's builders assume supersonic flight will be banned over the continental U.S. It is of considerable importance, therefore, to note that the Concorde will burn only 5 percent more fuel flying at subsonic speeds.

So the French and the British, as well as the Russians, have a long jump on us in the SST business, which is somewhat surprising since most of the world's airlines rely almost entirely on American-built aircraft.

1/18/70

AN AIRPLANE LIKE NO OTHER

Captain Ken Larson was one of a handful of American pilots who flew the Concorde. That was because for a short time, Braniff Airlines operated the aircraft, under a complicated arrangement, from Dulles Airport outside Washington, to Dallas-Ft. Worth Airport. Larson wrote a book about that experience that contained a lot of interesting information. I used his book as a basis for a column.

In flight, it's a beautiful thing to behold. When it's coming in for a landing, it looks like a gooney bird.

No matter which configuration it's in, it will turn heads like a pretty girl in a bikini.

Up front, it has a needle nose that can droop like a Big Bird whose feelings have been hurt. In the rear, it has a little tail wheel. That's in addition to a big nose wheel.

It is a controversial flying machine and that is one fact that no one can deny. It is different.

The airplane in question, which you may have figured out by now, is the Concorde, the only supersonic transport in service today.

The aircraft is different in many respects, other than just appearance. It is the only transport aircraft that has no horizontal stabilizer. The wings have no trailing edge flaps, no leading edge flaps, no spoiler, speed brakes, slats, or trim tabs.

Three control surfaces on the trailing edge of each wing, called "elevons," do the work of both ailerons and elevators. All those other devices, common on subsonic transports, would cause too much drag on a supersonic aircraft.

The skin on the wings is not smooth but has gentle ripples throughout.

How did the world's first--and only--supersonic passenger aircraft become a reality? It was through the joint efforts, engineering genius, and steadfast determination of the British and French.

What is it like to fly the Concorde? There are not many Americans qualified to answer this question. Only a handful have had the privilege of flying that aircraft.

One of these is Ken Larson, who rose from a daydreaming Iowa farm boy, to a Concorde captain.

Larson has recorded his story, from farm, to B-17 bomber, to 747, to Concorde, in a new paperback titled, *To Fly the Concorde.*

He tells his story in the first person, so that when he goes through the checklist of the Concorde, you feel as if you're sitting there in the left seat along with him.

His is a story that has everything. There's a love interest. Her name is Sammy. Larson met her when they were both at Iowa State and he took her out on their first date when he had an upset stomach and was nauseous. He was afraid to cancel the date because she was a popular girl and he thought if he canceled the date, he might never get another chance.

She has been his wife since he returned from England after World War II. She is the mother of his three sons--all three are pilots--and this book is dedicated to her, "because I love her." There is a villain in the story as well as a love interest. A copilot who, on the flight across the Atlantic to take Concorde training, told Larson, a Braniff captain, "I will do whatever is necessary to get a captain's rating on the Concorde. I am not coming over here to be a copilot."

Later, when Larson was being briefed for the check ride with an FAA inspector, the copilot is quoted as saying to the inspector, "Bust his butt, Gene. Then I'll be a captain."

These are subplots that add a little seasoning to the story. The real hero, and the real fascination of the book, is the Concorde itself, an aircraft that cuts the size of the earth by more than half and overcomes tremendous obstacles to do it.

At Mach 2, twice the speed of sound, or about 1,350 miles per hour at altitude, the skin temperature of the aircraft rises about 300 degrees, so new metals were necessary to withstand those temperature changes. At cruising speeds of 50,000 to 60,000 feet, pressurization problems are created that don't exist at the lower altitudes of subsonic flight.

In Larson's words, and certainly they're not hard to believe, "the Concorde is the most sophisticated aircraft in the world today."

It is so sophisticated, as a matter of fact, that man can't even fly it. It was designed to be flown by black boxes. Those mysterious little electronic monsters, that, like computers, can do things man can't even dream of doing.

The Concorde has an AFCS, (automatic flight control system), that is as far advanced from the autopilot as the computer from the abacus.

The aircraft was designed to be flown by engaging the AFCS right after takeoff. This includes power settings and programming all changes by pushing buttons. "The pilot then," writes Larson, "will not touch any of the controls until the aircraft is on the ground after landing."

Lest you think that means the pilot does nothing, read the book.

There is a sad epilogue at the end of the book in memory of Braniff Airways, which went bankrupt after Captain Larson's manuscript was completed.

British Airways and Air France are the two major airlines in the world operating the Concorde today. For a time, however, Braniff Airways operated the Concorde, (subsonically), between Washington's Dulles Airport and the Dallas-Ft. Worth Airport, which took a bit of ingenious maneuvering.

There were some serious complications before this plan could be implemented. Regulations prohibit U.S. pilots from flying aircraft of foreign registry. Therefore, in order to be legal, Braniff had to "buy" the aircraft every time it arrived in Washington and sell it back every time it returned. They stuck US. registry numbers on the aircraft every time they bought the aircraft and tore them off when they sold them back.

In his introduction, Captain Larson says he wrote this book, "for the man in the street," but he admits, too, that parts of the book are quite technical. Even those parts that do deal with the technical aspects of the Concorde are quite readable and interesting and not likely to leave the average reader snowed under.

Captain Larson had a rare subject to deal with. He handled the assignment extremely well.

To Fly the Concorde is published in paperback by Tab Books.

1/23/83

IN THE JUMP SEAT OF THE CONCORDE

*During the 38 1/2 years that I wrote my column, I had a great
many memorable flights. The most memorable, however, was a flight
on the Concorde from New York to Paris, sitting in the jump seat
directly behind the captain.*

*In this column I tried to recreate that experience as faithfully
as possible. Now that the Concordes have ceased flying, that
experience is more memorable than ever.*

She's starting to age a little. But you would never know it.
When she passes by, all heads turn. And age hasn't slowed
her down. She still moves at more than twice the speed of
the new birds on the block, even though she's nine years older.

She's something special. There's still magic in the mention of
her name. Tell someone you're flying to Paris tomorrow and they'll
say. "Oh, isn't that nice."
Tell them you're flying on
the Concorde and their
ears perk up.

Captain Jacques Schwartz, left, and First Officer Gerard
Fourtier, in the cockpit of an Air France Concorde flying at
Mach 2 (twice the speed of sound) at 53,000 feet over the
Atlantic.

I perked up a bit when I
entered the aircraft. I felt
very wobbly, as if I had
imbibed a little too much.
They did serve champagne
in the lounge before
boarding, but a couple of
sips should not have left
me wobbly. The floor of
the aircraft seemed to be
moving under my feet.

I learned later that the floor is on rollers because of the high
degree of expansion resulting from the heat generated by supersonic
flight. A solid floor, I was told, would not provide for sufficient
expansion.

In the cockpit of Air France Flight 002, the Concorde that
departs Kennedy Airport for Paris at 1 p.m., everything seemed
quite routine. Captain Jacques Schwartz and First Officer Gerard
Fourtier, went through their checklists, along with the flight
engineer much as the student pilot in a Cessna 152 might go through
the checklist with his instructor.

Flight 002 pushed back from the gate at precisely 1 p.m. and taxied to Runway 31L. I am looking on from the jump seat directly behind Captain Schwartz.

We waited for a 747 landing on Runway 4R, and at 1:15 the tower cleared us for takeoff. The Concorde raced down the runway. It accelerated to 190 knots, (220 miles an hour), and rotated. It lifts off as easily as a two-place 152 trainer.

Shortly after takeoff, First Officer Fourtier, who was flying, made a steep left turn out over the water, a noise abatement procedure.

A couple of minutes later, the drooping needle-nose visor came up. Suddenly there's something in front of us that wasn't there a couple of minutes ago. Now we are looking through two windshields, the second one with a very gradual slope.

The nose droops on landings and takeoffs for better visibility. The maximum nose down speed is 270 knots because of the noise it makes at higher speeds.

Once we are established on our climb, which is automatic, Captain Schwartz turns around to chat.

He's been flying the Concorde for 10 years. He was an instructor for Braniff Airlines pilots when they flew the aircraft at subsonic speeds from Dulles Airport to Dallas-Ft. Worth.

Captain Schwartz learned to fly in the United States in the '40s.

"We were trained in the U.S. for the French Air Force," he said. "I learned in Orangeburg, N.C., and eventually flew the P-47 Thunderbird.

"I came to New York on Election Day, 1944. We were in a convoy and it took us 17 days. Now, I make the trip in 3 1/2 hours."

As we approached Mach 1, the speed of sound, Captain Schwartz called my attention to the fact that the afterburners were about to be turned on and he directed me to watch the fuel flow gauge. The speed of the fuel flow appears to double.

There is a slight feeling of getting a little extra shove as the afterburners are turned on, but as the Mach indicator passes through the speed of sound, there's no sensation at all. The afterburners are used only during takeoff and passing through the sound barrier.

"The engines look huge," Captain Schwartz explained, "but they are not as big as they look. The engine cannot take the air at supersonic speeds. It has to be slowed down. Half the nacelle is for slowing down the air so the engine can take it."

Air France made its first flight to New York with the Concorde on November 22, 1977, nearly two years after the aircraft first entered commercial service.

"It took us almost two years to get into New York because of the noise it was supposed to make," Captain Schwartz said.

"One time the Concorde couldn't land at Kennedy Airport because of the weather and it landed at Newark. A television reporter went around and asked people, 'Did you hear the Concorde when it landed at Newark Airport yesterday?' Nobody heard it."

Captain Schwartz is passionately devoted to the Concorde after 10 years in her cockpit.

"I flew the 747 for four years," he said. "It's like driving a big, heavy, American truck. Flying the Concorde is like driving a Formula 1 car. It handles like a fighter. It has the most accurate controls I have ever known."

We are now leveled off at 53,000 feet and flying at Mach 2, twice the speed of sound, approximately 1,150 miles an hour at this altitude and temperature.

Captain Schwartz says, "Touch the window frame." I do, and I withdraw my hand in a hurry. It's red hot. That is a graphic illustration of the fact that supersonic speed generates a lot of heat.

We are flying at the speed of a supersonic jet fighter. But there are 78 passengers back there, (capacity is 100), being wined and dined as if they were in one of the finer restaurants of Paris, not an airliner moving along at supersonic speed.

I leave the cockpit and go back into the passenger cabin to see how the other half is doing.

The seats of the Air France Concorde were recently redone in a rich red, which gives the impression of a plush restaurant. Actually, that's what it is, albeit rather mobile.

I had heard that the cabin is very narrow and, in fact, it is. Remember, this is a Formula 1 car, not a big, heavy truck. Certainly, it is not like the jumbo jets with 10 or 11 seats across and a couple of hundred people in one cabin.

The Concorde is divided into two cabins, 40 passengers in the front cabin, two seats on each side of the aisle, 60 in the rear cabin. The aisle is narrow, but the flight attendants seem to have no problem pushing the champagne carts up and down the cabin.

When I first took my seat in the rear cabin, I felt as if I was sitting rather low, but you soon got used to that. The seats are comfortable and certainly don't seem squeezed. By the time they're through wining and dining you, you're in Paris. There isn't time to show a movie.

You might expect a lot of celebrities on the Concorde. The fare to Paris is $2,248. (It was more than double that when the service was terminated.) Certainly, the aircraft does get more than its share of celebrities. Elie Wiesel, the noted author-lecturer, Nobel Peace Prize

Laureate, is aboard this aircraft. But the average passenger is a successful professional who is not among the ranks of celebrities. On this flight the passengers include a Boston criminal lawyer working on a drug case, a French professor who is doing research on rheumatology with several American research groups, a Hartford, Conn., investment analyst for a large pension fund, and a New York plastics manufacturer.

More than 59 percent of Air France's Concorde passengers have flown the aircraft before.

I did not return to New York on the Concorde. Space is much tighter on the westbound flight. It leaves Paris at 11 a.m. which means there is no need to wake up at an ungodly hour, and it arrives in New York at 8:45 a.m. There is a certain fascination about the prospect of arriving at your destination two hours and 15 minutes earlier than you departed. And it leaves the whole day for business.

As we disembarked in Paris, all agreed it's the only way to go if you can afford it. Said one passenger, shrugging, "Until they take passengers on the space shuttle, this will have to do."

6/23/85

Chapter 15

A Few of the Giants

I've talked about some of the great aircraft in aviation's history, now it's time to take a look at some of the great people. The history of aviation has more than its share of heroes--the Wright Brothers, Lindbergh, Amelia Earhart, Jimmy Doolittle, Eddie Rickenbacker, Paul Garber. And there are some whose names and contributions have been lost in the shadows of time.

There are many who deserve to be here and are not, simply because this is a compendium of stories based on my nearly four decades of weekly columns and I never had the occasion to write about them. There are others I've written about who might be included here if this were a book about aviation greats, but it's just one chapter in this broad view of aviation.

THE TWO MEN WHO STARTED IT ALL

It is only fitting that the first column in this chapter be devoted to the two men whose commitment, skill, diligence, and persistence lifted man from the status of earthbound creatures into flyers. There are two reasons for this. First, as the preface to this column is being written, it is more than a century since their accomplishment.

The second is that it is appropriate to start at the beginning and in the beginning there were Orville and Wilbur--the Wright Brothers. They started something with their 120-foot powered flight. Now, the moon is within reach.

Millions of people all over the world fly everyday now, thanks to Orville and Wilbur Wright.

Here is an account of their dramatic story based on a biography by Fred Howard.

There are some aviation stories that hold such fascination that they can be retold time and again and still generate fresh interest. The story of the Wright Brothers, who wrote the first chapter in the history of powered flight, is one of those.

Theirs is a story filled with intrigue, rejection, frustration, tragedy and triumph, all the ingredients of a rip-roaring good story.

The leading characters were unusual and fascinating men. Sons of a bishop in the Church of United Brethren in Christ, they had read and were influenced by the works of the renowned agnostic, Robert Ingersoll, that they found in their father's

Orville Wright making the first powered flight on December 17, 1903.

library. As a result, they never attended church, although they did observe the Sabbath and did not work or fly on Sunday.

Though they were only high school graduates, they had a masterful command of mathematics, which they employed in a very scientific fashion to unlock the secrets of flight.

They were extremely prolific correspondents and exhibited, particularly in Wilbur's case, an unusual literary bent in their use of the English language.

The brothers were what we might label today as "cool." They exhibited little emotion and no desire for the limelight.

Neither ever married and, as one of them explained, they had not the means to support a wife and a flying machine, too, an explanation heard frequently today from bachelor aircraft owners.

The latest work to chronicle this engrossing story is titled, simply enough, *Wilbur and Orville, A Biography of the Wright Brothers.*

Author Fred Howard, who was a member of the team that edited the papers of the Wright Brothers, spent nearly 15 years working on his book. The research is abundantly evident. There is a wealth of detail tracing every step, every struggle, every nuance in the drama of the brothers from Dayton.

Their great achievement, after painstaking study and experimentation, in the course of which they developed the first wind tunnel, was the realization that successful flight involved three axes and not just two. None of their competitors, who often claimed to have beaten or surpassed the work of Wilbur and Orville, ever realized this. The third axis is the one that permitted the aircraft to bank in a turn, which the Wright Brothers achieved through a system of wing warping.

This is what distinguished their work from that of their competitors, who sometimes achieved more recognition, though they had not achieved controlled flight.

The Wrights built their own engine in their bicycle shop, with considerable help from an employee, Charles Taylor, and they designed and fashioned their own propeller. They did it all with their own money.

Orville estimated the cost of their Wright Flyer at $1,000 in contrast to the $73,000 in grants spent by Samuel Langley, secretary of the Smithsonian Institution, whose aircraft took off from a houseboat on the Potomac River and plunged into the water.

The Wrights had to go to France to receive recognition and acclaim after the American military dismissed their efforts to sell them their flying machine.

But even after that, they suffered through long patent battles. This new biography, that is more detailed than any of its half-dozen predecessors, seems, through its use of letters and documents, to set the record straight.

Wilbur and Orville, was published by Alfred A. Knopf.

9/6/87

MY HERO

Jimmy Doolittle was my hero. He was a man who displayed tremendous courage on any number of occasions. He was a scholar, having earned a Ph.D. from MIT. He was an extraordinary pilot, a man who knew no fear, and a gentleman's gentleman.

I met him at a Wings Club banquet in New York where he sat on the dais with his wife, Joe, alongside him. My wife, Esta-Ann, asked if he would sign our program, which he graciously did.

On three occasions, I sent him copies of my "Wings Over Jersey" column. Twice, the column was about old friends of his. One was Addis Kocher, whose story appears in Chapter 12, and another time, it was a column about World War I ace Ray Brooks, who lived in the same building as Doolittle at an air base. (The story of one of Brook's unusual experiences is told in Chapter 4.) The third column was about a tribute to him in Boonton where he practiced for the first official blind flight on record. Doolittle's health did not permit him to travel from California to attend that ceremony, but his son, John, a retired Air Force Colonel, stood in for him and I chatted with him after the official proceedings.

In each case, I was surprised to receive a gracious note from Doolittle thanking me for sending those columns.

It is hard to put all his accomplishments between the covers of a book, but he did, with help from C.V. Glines, a prolific writer of aviation books whom I had met at numerous aviation events. The following column is based on his autobiography, "I Could Never Be So Lucky Again," that I recommend without reservation. For all the heroes aviation has produced, I do not believe any ever came close to matching Doolittle's accomplishments. His book is an inspiration.

The more you read about Jimmy Doolittle, the more you become convinced that here is one of the most accomplished men and aviators of our time.

His achievements are legend. He was one of the greatest of the pioneer pilots, a racer, record setter, and test pilot. He achieved our first victory in the Pacific in World War II by leading the raid on Tokyo early in the war. That achievement won him the Congressional Medal of Honor and promotion to the rank of brigadier general.

He is a three time member of the Caterpillar Club whose members all parachuted for their lives from disabled aircraft. His third was from the B-25 in which he lead the Tokyo Raid.

One of the most revealing stories of his indomitable spirit and courage, occurred in an incident in Chile in 1926. He went there to demonstrate the Curtiss P-1 Hawker in competition with a German aircraft, seeking sales to the Chilean Air Force.

A few weeks before the scheduled demonstration, at a party thrown by Chilean pilots, he did several handstands, duplicating some stunts they had seen Douglas Fairbanks do in the movies. The pilots cheered and applauded enthusiastically. Then they said they had seen Fairbanks do handstands on a window ledge. Doolittle climbed out on the ledge and duplicated that stunt. Then he decided to top it all by grabbing the edge of the window ledge and extending his body straight out, parallel to the ground one story below. The ledge gave way and he fell 15 feet, breaking both ankles, one in a number of places.

Jimmy Doolittle

They put a cast up to a point just below the knee on one leg and a cast that extended above the knee on the more seriously injured ankle and told him to stay off his feet for six weeks.

There was no way, Doolittle decided, that he was going to lay in the hospital while his competition was demonstrating its wares.

On his ninth day in the hospital, he had his mechanic Boyd Sherman, come in with a hacksaw and cut the longer cast to below the knee. Then he had him put clips on his flight boots so his feet wouldn't slip off the rudder pedals. The boots fit over his casts.

He had himself driven to the airport and hobbled on crutches to the plane. He was lifted into the cockpit and went up to practice aerobatics. The strain of the maneuvers he performed broke both casts.

He went back to the hospital and the doctors there would have nothing more to do with him. They wouldn't even let him back in the hospital. He got Sherman to take him to a prostheses maker who fashioned custom-made casts for Doolittle to wear while demonstrating the airplane.

The competing German pilot was in the air doing stunts to great applause when Doolittle took off. Doolittle performed some stunts and then got on the German pilot's tail. The German pilot couldn't shake him. No matter how he tried he couldn't get away from Doolittle and get on *his* tail. The German pilot was no match for Doolittle and broke off and landed. Doolittle looked down and saw the fabric on the German airplane torn on the top of one of the wings. So even though he couldn't walk, Doolittle won the competition that led to sales for the American manufacturer. That incident proved, early in his career, that virtually nothing could stop him.

During World War II, he commanded the 8th Air Force in the African campaign and later, in Europe, when it became the biggest Air Force unit in history, and still later when it transferred to the Pacific theater.

When it was suggested, shortly before the end of the war with Japan, that the 8th Air Force launch a mission so it could be said that they participated in the Pacific War, he refused on the grounds that the war was obviously about to end and he would not risk one man or one aircraft under those conditions.

In civilian life he headed NASA and the Air Force Association. He served on the board of directors of several major corporations, including Shell Oil and TRW. He served on many scientific commissions.

Doolittle earned a masters degree in aeronautical engineering from the Massachusetts Institute of Technology and then went on to earn a doctorate. His wife, Joe, to whom he was married for 71 years, helped him by typing his notes. She was a faithful and dedicated partner and earned distinction on her own for service to the nation during World War II.

It is not surprising that a number of books have been written about this unusual man. But until now, the story of his life has been told by others. Now, the story has been told by Doolittle himself, with the help of Carroll V. Glines, one of the nation's top aviation writers. C.V. was a guest at an Author's Reception at the prestigious Wings Club in New York several weeks ago, an event jointly sponsored by the club and the New York chapter of the Ninety-Nines, the international organization of women pilots.

"He never wanted to write an autobiography," C.V. told me at that event. "But when Joe died, he changed his mind. I had written a book about him and two books about the Tokyo Raid and he asked me if I would want to work with him on his autobiography. Would I ever!"

Doolittle could not have picked a better man to work with. This decision, like so many others in his distinguished career, was a superb one. C.V. is not only a fine writer, he knows the Air Force. He served as a pilot and was discharged with the rank of colonel. He currently writes for five aviation magazines. He has written more than a dozen and a half books. He was the perfect partner for the job.

There is great difference between books about Doolittle, (and most of them are excellent), and a book by him. This book, An Autobiography by General James H. "Jimmy" Doolittle with Carroll V. Glines, *I Could Never Be So Lucky Again*, provides deep insight into the man's character, philosophy and motivation--and into what made him tick.

For all his accomplishments, for all the awards he received, including the Congressional Medal of Honor for leading the Tokyo Raid, he comes across as a modest, down-to-earth, compassionate man. It's revealed in many of the letters to his wife, Joe, that he wrote during his service in World War II.

In one letter, written when he was in Okinawa, he says, "It's distressing to note that only two military services are constructive--the medics and the engineers. All the rest are destructive.

"I saw a little six-year-old with his hand blown off by a bomb fragment and a little sock over the stump. He was all alone, an orphan, leaning against a fence post. As I met his eye, I know that my glance showed guilt as well as pity. And that guilt is not only of us killers in the war, but it is on the American people at home, unless steps are taken now to see that we don't promptly have another war."

Many times he states that the best way to prevent war is to be well prepared. And he points out that we have usually not been well prepared because we demilitarize too quickly after each conflict in which we have been involved.

It is interesting to note also, that in spite of the compassion and guilt he displays, he was a great admirer of George S. Patton, one of the toughest field commanders we had in World War II. He refers to him constantly as "Georgie."

In the final paragraph of that letter to Joe, Doolittle writes, "Someday, I hope we can disband our military establishment and devote ourselves wholly to constructive pursuits, but until that time comes, let's do everything possible to train our children and so direct our nation as to give both the highest possible degree of security to the world in which they find themselves."

This book is remarkable on many levels. It provides a penetrating insight into the personality of one of the great men of this century. It contains excellent accounts of some of the most important air missions of the war. It provides interesting impressions of some of the other leaders of World War II.

It is also an account of an extraordinary relationship that spanned 71 years, his marriage to his school days' sweetheart who was always a close part of his life and a woman of distinction in her own right, whom he deeply revered.

Doolittle, now in his 90s, lives in California in an addition to the home of his son, John, and his wife, Priscilla.

His philosophy, as stated in the closing chapter of the book: "We should always pray for peace; to maintain it, we must remain so strong militarily that no nation will dare to attack us."

The book contains three appendixes, one describing the fate of each of the 16 crews on the Tokyo raid.

10/20/91

Note: *Jimmy Doolittle died on September 27, 1993, at the age of 96.*

THE INCREDIBLE BILL LEAR

There are those who will tell you that Bill Lear was a genius. And they would have no trouble finding many people to support their view. There are those who would tell you he was a wild man. They, too, could find plenty of supporters for their assessment of the man. There is a lot to support both views. The one thing no one can dispute is the fact that he was witty and he was funny, and he could accomplish some incredible things. He was not a man you could ignore.

He was, of course, the man who designed the very first business jet, the Learjet, that was, not surprisingly, named after him. He developed a host of other products, but it was the Learjet that launched his name into the limelight.

I remember being invited to a press event heralding the introduction of that aircraft. I told one of the sales representatives on the scene that I thought the cabin looked a bit tight. He shrugged, looked me in the eye, and said, "It's no tighter than a Cadillac." It sounded like a comment you would expect to hear from his boss. I wondered if he might have heard it from his boss.

Bill Lear was not a simple man. But that's what makes him a fascinating subject.

He was a genius. He was a tyrant. He was a philosopher.

He bent the rules. He broke the rules. He ignored the rules.

Bill Lear, right, with Charles C. Gates who bought Lear Jet Industries and became president of what was renamed Gates Lear Jet.

At one time he was indicted for white slavery and faced the possibility of going to prison. But he slipped out of that as easily as he slipped out of so many other tight spots in his life.

He had four wives, seven children, and dozens of mistresses.

He made millions and he lost millions. Between all that, he left a mark on the world of aviation that will not soon fade away--as he did in 1978, of leukemia.

Bill Lear is best remembered, of course, for his Learjet, the first jet specifically designed for corporate use. Two earlier business jet transport aircraft, the JetStar and

Sabreliner, were originally designed to carry military brass, not corporate brass. Lear was also responsible for the development of the Automatic Direction Finder, (ADF), the instrument landing system, and the automatic pilot.

He was a high school dropout, but he could take one look at a problem that had stymied top engineers for months and come up with an instant solution.

The complicated and fascinating life of Bill Lear is painstakingly dissected in a new book, *The Stormy Genius. The Life of Aviation's Maverick, Bill Lear,* by Richard Raske, the man who wrote, *The Killing of Karen Silkwood.*

One of Lear's earliest projects was the development of the car radio. He and his partner couldn't afford exhibit space at the radio manufacturers' show in Atlantic City, so they parked their Studebaker close to the boardwalk and dragged dealers over. They sold several dozen sets at $120 installed.

On the way home from Atlantic City, he and his partner dreamed up a name for the radio, Motorola--motor after the car and "ola" because popular brands of the day like Victrola and Radiola, ended in ola.

One time in 1934, when Lear was in deep financial trouble, he developed a multi-band tuner. RCA was interested in it. Lear was prepared to take as little as $2,500 for his idea because that would pay a lot of his bills.

He didn't know what to ask so he decided to let RCA president, E. T. Cunningham, make an offer. He walked away with a check for $50,000 and a commitment for $40,000 a year for five years.

When Amelia Earhart touched down at Newark Airport after the first nonstop flight from Mexico City, during which she set two speed records, she told a reporter that the Lear radio compass she carried worked perfectly and in her opinion would go a long way toward solving some of transport flying's most vexing problems.

On the 167th flight of Learjet No. 1, the aircraft crashed and burned. An FAA inspection pilot who was checking out the aircraft's single engine performance, made several successful runs, and then after one landing he took off without retracting the aircraft's wing spoilers. The aircraft wouldn't climb and he set it down in a cornfield with hardly a scratch. The FAA man and the Lear test pilot walked out unharmed. But a fuel line had broken and the aircraft caught fire and burned up.

The Reading Air Show in Reading, Pa., was in full progress and word spread that Lear and his jet were washed up. Lear's answer, "We just sold our first Learjet."

He needed the insurance money. A second Learjet that he had sold for cash, to his friend, Justin Dart, president of Rexall Drugs, was ready to go. They flew into the Reading Show for its first public appearance, and once again, Bill Lear had done the impossible.

His first ride in an airplane took place in 1917, when he was 19, after he had dropped out of high school six weeks after he entered. It was in a British de Havilland DH 4, the Jenny, an air mail aircraft known as the flaming coffin. The pilot made a hard landing and flipped the Jenny over on its back. Bill (he was known as Willy then) fell on his head but was unhurt. He still wanted to learn to fly.

In the summer of that same year, Willy was in Grant Park in Chicago when the Goodyear blimp landed. There was one seat open and Willy talked himself into a ride. But just before takeoff a newspaper photographer came along and Willy was bumped.

During the flight the blimp caught fire and it crashed. The captain and one mechanic parachuted to safety. But a second mechanic and the photographer were killed.

Bill did learn to fly and the number of aircraft he owned, including a Beech Staggerwing and a Bamboo Bomber, was almost as high as the number of mistresses he entertained.

I met Bill Lear just once, when he was guest speaker at a meeting of the Aviation/Space Writers Association in New York. He was hilarious. He was charming.

The story of his life, as told in this book, makes fascinating reading. It's published by Houghton Mifflin Company.

11/10/85

Note: *Bill Lear died on May 14, 1978 at the age of 75.*

A RUSSIAN IMMIGRANT NAMED IGOR

Igor Sikorsky was one of the great aviation pioneers. Though generally remembered for his development of the helicopter, he built fixed-wing aircraft as well, and was a pioneer in the development of the flying boat, a craft that forged the first transoceanic routes.

Sikorsky's love of aviation came from his mother, Zinaida, a physician. A woman physician was something extraordinarily rare in Russia in the late 19th century. When he was very young she taught him about Leonardo daVinci and his idea for a helicopter.

By the time he was 12, Sikorsky had built a rubber band model of a 'copter that actually flew. His father, Professor Ivan Sikorsky, one of Russia's outstanding physicians, imbued him with a sense of scientific curiosity.

The Wright Brothers were an inspiration to him, but his first love was the helicopter. He went to Paris to study aviation and engineering. He returned to his native Kiev to build a helicopter. Unfortunately, it didn't fly. So he turned his attention to fixed-wing aircraft. In 1914, he built and flew the first four-engine aircraft.

In 1917, he came to the United States with very little money and not much knowledge of English. The first few years here were rough, but then he formed a small company to build fixed-wing aircraft and he became a pioneer in designing and building flying boats. His first love, however, remained the helicopter, and in 1939, he built and successfully flew one.

The following column is an account of a talk about him given by his son, Sergei Sikorsky.

He talked about an 11-year-old boy who had a dream. It was a long time ago in a faraway city. It was in Kiev, Russia, in 1900. The boy dreamed of flying. In his dream he soared over coral beaches and green palm trees.

This was a rather strange dream. Everyone knew--even 11-year-old boys--that flying was reserved for the gods.

The speaker was addressing members of the Union-Morris N.J. Chapter of the Air Force Association. The young boy he spoke of was his father, Igor Sikorsky, one of aviation's great pioneers, particularly remembered for his work in the development of the helicopter.

"The idea of flight seemed so ridiculous," Sergei Sikorsky told his audience, "that when word of the Wright Brothers' first successful flight on Dec. 17, 1903, reached the *Paris Herald Tribune*, that highly respected journal pooh-poohed the story. They said it was a silly rumor.   Heavier-than-air   flying   machines   were   a   technical impossibility, they said."

But by 1906, even the French had achieved the impossible, he related.   A young Parisian art student became the first man to buy an airplane and then he won a 50,000 franc prize by becoming the first man to fly one kilometer.

The acclaim he received was so great--even the *Paris Herald Tribune* believed it--that the Wright Brothers rushed off to France. There, they forged new frontiers. In August, 1908, they achieved an altitude of 1,000 feet and remained aloft between 30 and 40 minutes.

The boy in Kiev, who dreamed about flying, was 18 years old now. He saw photos of the Wright Brothers and he dreamed of going to Paris. This dream was realized in a relatively short time.

Igor Sikorsky making the first helicopter flight wearing a fedora to protect him from the cold.

"He went to Paris and he saw grown men cry when they saw flight," Sergei Sikorsky said. "Something reserved for the gods became the province of man."

Igor returned to Kiev with some ideas of his own about flight.   "He built a helicopter in his backyard. It had one problem," Sergei related,   "It refused to fly." So Sikorsky turned to fixed-wing aircraft.   He was a bit more successful in this sphere. He built aircraft that actually flew and he constantly worked at improving them.

"In 1914, he built the world's first four-engine aircraft," Sergei told his listeners, "a machine that offered the luxury of an enclosed cabin."

And that wasn't all.   You could go places in it.   Igor Sikorsky flew it as far as 800 miles.

This aircraft was the forerunner of Russia's World War I Ilya Mourametz bombers that boasted machine guns up front and a tail gunner. They even put a 37 mm gun on it, but after one firing they decided not to try that again, Sergei related.

In 1917, Igor left Russia and came to the United States via France.   In the U.S. he built the 3NC flying boat that flew across the Atlantic.

"He started Sikorsky Aircraft in a chicken coop next to

Roosevelt Field on Long Island," Sergei said.

The first Sikorsky aircraft was sold to Roscoe Turner, one of the great heroes of the early days of flight. Later, Turner sold that aircraft to a young fellow named Howard Hughes.

After Lindbergh's solo flight across the Atlantic, Igor turned his talents to amphibians. The first one he built was referred to as "a collection of aviation spare parts flying in close formation," Sergei said.

Next came the first of the clipper ships. Igor was flying in one on the way to Florida. It had a paneled cabin. "It was the same cabin he saw in his dream in Kiev when he was 11 years old," Sergei related. "He looked out the window and there was the coral sand and the palm trees."

The career for which he is most remembered today, began in 1935 when Igor Sikorsky lifted off in a helicopter for the first time.

"One observer pointed out that while the machine lifted off vertically and could hover, and fly sideways and backwards, it never flew anywhere," Sergei said.

If his father could only see where they fly now.

12/10/78

FATHER OF THE AIR AND SPACE MUSEUM

Paul Garber was almost single-handedly responsible for the creation of the world's most popular museum, the Smithsonian National Air and Space Museum in Washington.

Garber served the Smithsonian Institution for more than 60 years. He chose the site of the museum's restoration facility in Suitland, Md., where many of the sparkling aircraft on display in the museum were restored to mint condition from pathetic-looking, timeworn relics.

He was responsible for the acquisition of a majority of the aircraft in the museum's unmatched collection, including two of the world's most historic aircraft, the Wright Flyer, that he got back from the British after many decades in a museum there, and Lindbergh's Spirit of St. Louis.

Garber was as dedicated a man as you will ever find. When he made up his mind he was going to get something done, it got done. He seemed, at times, to accomplish the impossible.

The Suitland facility, originally known as Silver Hill, was renamed the Paul E. Garber Preservation, Restoration and Storage Facility in 1980, when Garber was 80 and had been serving the Smithsonian Institution for 60 years.

Walter Boyne, the outstanding and prolific aviation writer and former director of the National Air and Space Museum, wrote a wonderful book, "The Aircraft Treasures of Silver Hill", that is a fascinating account of the marvelous Smithsonian aircraft collection and the skilled people who lovingly restored many of the rare aircraft in that collection. It was published in 1987, by Rawson Associates.

When Walter Boyne wanted to dedicate his book to Garber, a pilot who had served in both World Wars, Garber asked, "Why me? There are so many better known pilots."

That was the hallmark of the man, modest and humble to a fault, but he left a legacy that will long outlive all of us.

It was my privilege to have met Garber on a number of occasions and he was always very down-to-earth and friendly, but you could always feel yourself in the presence of a man of unusual accomplishments.

"What you are about to see occurred during the lifetime of myself."

And with that statement Paul Garber launched into a 2 1/2 hour dissertation, illustrated by slides, on the birth and early years of aviation. He used no notes. He didn't need them. He was on the scene from the time he saw the Wright Brothers fly as a boy.

He was a small man, barely five feet tall. But in the world of aviation, he was a towering giant. He was the father of the world's most popular museum, the National Air and Space Museum in the nation's capital.

Without him, the museum might never have come into being. And without him many of the museum's most treasured aircraft, including the *Wright Flyer* and *Spirit of St. Louis* would probably never be there.

A native of New Jersey, he was born in Atlantic City on August 31, 1899. In 1987, he returned to his home state to address a gathering of those who appreciate the colorful history of aviation in this country. His audience

Paul Garber

was assembled in the Sheraton Heights Hotel, (now the Hilton), in Hasbrouck Heights, just up the hill from Teterboro Airport.

Garber's appearance, under the sponsorship of Butler Aviation International of Montvale, was one of the major events in the yearlong celebration of the 15th anniversary of the Aviation Hall of Fame of New Jersey .

It is doubtful if any man has as much aviation history crammed into his memory as Paul Garber. Certainly, no man has done more to preserve that history.

To listen to him discourse on a subject to which he has been totally committed, since, as a boy, he watched the Wright Military Flyer put through its paces at Ft. Meyer, is an unforgettable experience. It was 1909, and he was ten years old.

Hearing Garber speak is like watching a one-man show. There is a quality about the man that would keep you riveted if he stood on his feet, and spoke for five hours. And he probably could.

At 87, he has a sparkle in his eye and a soft lilt in his voice. He has a sort of sly, mischievous look at times, like that of a boy who has just played a small practical joke on a friend.

You sense the satisfaction he gets every time he passes on a humorous incident from the vast collection of stories in his incredible memory.

He knew all the greats of aviation history, men and women most of us know only from aviation history books--the Wright Brothers, Glenn Curtiss, Charles Lindbergh, Wiley Post, Eddie Rickenbacker, Igor Sikorsky.

Many of the most prized aircraft in the National Air and Space Museum are there only because of the dogged persistence of Paul Garber in seeking them for the museum and in his friendship with the pioneers associated with those aircraft.

"I asked Glenn Curtiss for his airplane, and I got it," he told his audience at the Hall of Fame event. Curtiss, a rival and adversary of the Wright Brothers, built the first plane for the Navy.

"I asked Jimmy Doolittle for his racer. I got it," said Garber.

"I got the Pitcairn Mailwing from Eddie Rickenbacker. I asked him if he would give us an Eastern Airlines DC-3. He said, 'Yup.' " That airplane hangs in the museum today.

He found the Vin Fiz that made the first cross-country flight in 1911. It was in Pittsburgh, not exactly in mint condition. Garber rebuilt it and it's in the museum now. That historic event was duplicated last year on its 75th anniversary on a flight in a replica that took off from a street in Hoboken. (A story about the flight's reenactment is in Chapter 1).

Garber began his efforts to acquire the *Spirit of St. Louis* for the museum while Lindbergh was still winging his way across the Atlantic. The Smithsonian Institution didn't want anything to do with the project. They didn't think Lindbergh was going to make it.

But Garber has never been a quitter. When he made up his mind about something, he stayed with it until the end.

The happy ending to this story came when Lindbergh, after a tour of many thousands of miles following his history-making flight, flew his airplane to Bolling Field to turn it over to the Smithsonian. Paul Garber was at the field waiting to greet him.

It hung originally in the old castle-like Smithsonian building before the present Air and Space Museum was built.

A sensitive situation arose when Garber acquired the *Kitty Hawk Flyer* that resided in a British museum for 20 years. Orville sent it to England because he was furious over a claim that an aircraft flown by Samuel Langley was the first to fly.

After Orville's death in 1948, Garber got it back. Space for aircraft in the old building was very limited and Garber was asked where he was going to put it.

"I will put it in front of the *Spirit of St. Louis*," he said.

"Lindbergh won't like that," he was told.

"Let's call him up," he said. "I have his number."

Garber made the call and Lindbergh told him, "It will be a great honor to have it in the same hall."

Paul Garber, who is now historian emeritus of the National Air and Space Museum, came there in 1920 as a preparator, one who built models.

When he ended his active career with the museum, (although it never really ended until he died in his sleep on Sept. 23, 1992, at the age of 93), he was head curator of the Paul E. Garber Restoration, Preservation and Storage Facility of the Air and Space Museum in Suitland, Maryland, that now bears his name.

Garber first flew in 1915 in a glider. That made him a member of the Early Birds, a group of pilots who flew before 1916.

Last year--71 years later--he flew a glider at Kitty Hawk.

It's hardly possible to even suggest Paul Garber's contributions to aviation, both in the military and in civil aviation, in one brief column.

In May, Garber will return to New Jersey once again to be honored for his many contributions to aviation with his induction into the Aviation Hall of Fame of New Jersey.

No man could be more deserving.

3/1/87

THE AUTHOR OF THE BIBLE OF FLYING

There have been hundreds of books written over the years about the art of flying. But the book that most knowledgeable pilots consider the bible of the art, is one written 59 years ago. Many of the other books on the subject, a lot of them written long after this one, are long since out of print. But you can still find this book in virtually every pilots' shop in the country, as well as in most airports, many aviation museums and some book stores.

The book is titled, Stick and Rudder. Its author was Wolfgang Langewiesche. I met him quite by chance when I happened to land just ahead of him at an airport in Pennsylvania, that was part of a tourist attraction. He was flying with another distinguished aviation writer and publisher, Leighton Collins, whom I had met previously.

It provided a rare opportunity to chat with an author considered by many the ultimate authority on why an airplane does what it does in the air and what the pilot needs to know to fly safely and efficiently.

When this column was written, 28 years after the book was published, it was selling twice as many copies as it did when it first came out.

Shortly after I touched down on the turf runway at Penn's Cave Airport, the unusual tourist attraction in the Alleghenies of Pennsylvania, a Twin Comanche came gliding gently to earth.

Two men disembarked and I immediately recognized one of them. He was a fellow Jerseyan, Leighton Collins, editor and publisher of *Air Facts,* one of the oldest and most authoritative aviation publications in the country, published in Princeton.

Collins' companion was Wolfgang Langewiesche, frequent contributor to *Air Facts,* roving editor for *Reader's Digest,* and author of what most pilots consider the bible of the art of flying, *Stick and Rudder.*

On numerous occasions over the years, as a matter of fact, *Stick and Rudder* has come to the rescue of "Wings Over Jersey," my newspaper column, which was the source of these stories.

When readers questioned some fine point I might have discussed, I referred them to Langewiesche's book as the final authority.

So I was interested to learn more about the man I had leaned on more than once.

In the coffee shop at Penn's Cave, Langewiesche, who is as

interesting to talk to as he is to read, told me about some of the chapters in his aviation life.

His story opens in Chicago in 1933. That's where and when he learned to fly.

"They told me I could never get a commercial license because of my eyes," he said, "but they have since changed their minds."

Langewiesche was, at that time, working on a research fellowship at the University of Chicago. He had already earned a Masters in Economics at Columbia University's Graduate School, where he was accepted without an undergraduate degree.

Leighton Collins, left, publisher of Air Facts magazine and Wolfgang Langewiesche, author of Stick and Rudder, the definitive work on the technique of flying. They are pictured here after landing at Penn's Cave Airport in Centre Hall, Pa.

"You couldn't do that anymore," he commented.

"I think I was the only guy at the University of Chicago to fly. They thought I was nuts.

"But I spent so much time flying and so little time on my work at the university, that I switched to writing about airplanes. I was always interested in the airplane as a vehicle to see the United States."

In 1939, Langewiesche wrote a book titled, *I'll Take the High Road*, that he describes as being about "the glories of flying." It became a *Reader's Digest* book condensation.

Not long after he wrote that book, he began writing for *Air Facts*.

His first article was about a seaplane flight in a Taylorcraft from New York to Seattle. It was a ferry flight.

Langewiesche flew to the Wall Street Seaplane Base to begin his trip and he still recalls paying a fellow $5 to watch his plane overnight.

"I thought I was the first to make such a flight," he said, "but I found out a fellow in a Stinson did it before me."

Getting fuel was his major problem on that trip. There were almost no seaplane bases then and boat basins don't carry aviation fuel.

"Sometimes I had to use stove and lighter naphtha," Langewiesche said. "And sometimes I landed near bridges and hitchhiked to an airport and brought back gas in cans."

Other colorful chapters in the life of Wolfgang Langewiesche include stints as a test pilot for Chance Vought, flying Corsairs during World War II; working for Cessna, flying their Bamboo Bomber, and working for Kollsman Instruments after the war.

Even before all these chapters in his aviation life, Langewiesche was working on *Stick and Rudder*. He spent more than six years on that book.

How did he assemble all the facts to write a book that has remained the last word for 28 years?

"I read the technical books of the time," he says, "and I talked to people--people like Fred Welk, who designed the Ercoupe."

Langewiesche says the book sells about twice as many copies today (1972) as it sold when it first came out 28 years ago.

"We used to sell about 2,000 copies a year. Now we sell 4,000," he says.

Most airports keep the book in stock.

In all the 28 years since he wrote the book, Langewiesche says he has never changed a word, never added anything, never took anything out.

The only thing that has changed is the price. It used to be $3. Now it's $8.95. (Today's price, in 2007, is $24.95. It's still widely available and enjoys brisk sales.)

5/7/72

Note: *Langewiesche died on February 9, 2002 at the age of 94. Leighton Collins died on Jan. 16, 1995 at 92.*

A MAN FOR ALL SEASONS

Gill Robb Wilson wasn't your run of the mill pioneer. His credits could fill pages. He was a World War I combat pilot. He earned a bachelor of divinity degree and became a minister. Later, he earned a doctor of science degree.

He organized and became the first director of the New Jersey Department of Aviation. He was aviation editor of the New York Herald-Tribune. He created the Civil Air Patrol. He served as president and chairman of the board of directors of the Air Force Association. He formed the 119th National Guard Squadron at Newark Airport.

Wilson was first president of the Aerospace Education Foundation, president of the National Aeronautics Association, editor and publisher of Flying magazine. During his tenure in that position he wrote inspiring aviation poems in every issue. He was a riveting speaker. His autobiography was titled, "I Walked with Giants".

I had long conversations with him several times and always felt I was in the presence of a giant.

He would have been 100 years old yesterday.

He was born in East Brady, Pa., about 35 miles north of Pittsburgh on Sept. 18, 1893.

He died in California, where he lived his last years, on Sept. 8, 1966.

But much of his active life and a large measure of Gill Robb Wilson's major achievements took place in New Jersey. There is an airport named for him in Parkersburg, W. Va., where his parents lived and where he also resided for a time. There is a three-building flight line complex named for Gill Robb Wilson at Embry-Riddle Aeronautical University in Daytona, Fla.

His memory is preserved by a plaque in the Aviation Hall of Fame of New Jersey, commemorating his induction in 1980 into that reservoir of people who made aviation history in this state.

Wilson's aviation career began with the military. He flew with both the French and American Air Forces in World War I. On his return to the United States he followed in his father's footsteps and became a minister.

He received invitations from four churches to become their pastor. He accepted the post at Trenton's Fourth Presbyterian Church. He served in that post from 1920 to 1929 when he was stricken with cancer of the throat, the result of his having been gassed during World

War I.

He underwent surgery that cost him his voice and ended his preaching career.

He knew many of the top political figures of the day and they felt New Jersey should have a Department of Aviation. They were aware of his aviation background and came to him to organize a department. Wilson accepted and became the department's director. He had a secretary and no staff. He charged the state $7 an hour for the use of his airplane on state business-- enough to cover the cost of gas and oil. His friend, Colonel Norman Schwarzkopf, (superintendent of the State Police and father of Gen. Norman Schwarzkopf), gave him an office.

Gill Robb Wilson

Wilson set up the rules and regulations that would govern the department. New Jersey was one of the first states to have an aviation department. He served in that post from 1930 to 1941.

"We wrote a simple set of laws that set state standards for airworthiness for aircraft, airmen, and airports, in line with federal standards," he wrote in his autobiography, *I Walked With Giants*.

"We required no special state licenses, imposed no fees. Aviation gas would be tax-exempt.

"Realizing they were not to be bludgeoned by taxes or burdened by a multitude of regulations, the airlines, aviation industry, airport operators, and pilots cooperated readily with the department.

"It was my pride that the Depression did not put a single New Jersey airport out of business," he said.

Through painstaking efforts during this period, Wilson taught himself to talk again, speaking, as he put it "through the stomach."

When I interviewed him in 1963, he told me, "We sold the idea that New Jersey was a good place to locate. No income tax or sales tax. RCA located at Camden because of Camden Airport. Bendix came to Teterboro, creating hundreds of jobs. We kept a gas tax off airlines at Newark so they would come to New Jersey.

"At one time, 75 percent of all airmail carried in the United State went through Newark," Wilson said. "You know who was the best friend of Newark Airport in those days? Prudential Insurance. Air mail was important to Prudential and they did a lot to encourage the development of Newark Airport."

Wilson created the CAP (Civil Air Patrol) in New Jersey. He organized the 119th Observation Squadron of the Air National Guard at Newark Airport, which became the 119th Tactical Fighter Squadron. He was one of the founders of the AOPA (Aircraft Owners and Pilots Association).

He was a prolific poet. His subject matter was always flying. He captured the beauty of flying, the beauty of cloud formations, of the earth as seen from above. Many of those poems were published in a volume called, *The Airman's World*, long out of print.

For 12 years, Wilson was editor and publisher of *Flying* magazine and during that time one of his poems appeared each month on a full page with a beautiful photograph to go with it on the opposite page. He continued to contribute those poems even after he left the post of editor and publisher.

Wilson was friendly with many of the leading figures in politics and aviation in his day.

Among his many friends was a pilot named Hugh Fenwick. He was courting a girl named Millicent Hammond. Hugh wanted to impress her with his accomplishments and asked if he could borrow Wilson's Curtiss Robin. Wilson obliged. Millicent's reaction, as recorded in Wilson's autobiography was that, "flying was good for the liver, if nothing else."

Nevertheless, they eventually married and Gill Robb Wilson officiated at their wedding. The marriage lasted only six years during which they had a son and a daughter. Millicent Fenwick later distinguished herself as one of the most hardworking, dedicated members of the House of Representatives. (Coincidentally, my daughter, Amy Schapiro, wrote the first biography of Millicent Fenwick, *Millicent Fenwick: Her Way*.)

The Fenwicks raised full-blooded Guernsey cattle on their estate in Bernardsville. Wilson bought a heifer from them for his farm on Scotch Road near Trenton. He named the heifer, "Millicent," he wrote, "in honor of the lovely bride."

Wilson was one of the few people who defended Gen. Billy Mitchell for his strong advocacy of the future of air power that resulted in his court martial for defiance of superiors.

Like Mitchell, Wilson saw the future of aviation and was scoffed at.

Back in the early days of aviation, immediately following World War I, pioneering pilots all over the world were forging new frontiers of flying. Wilson, referring to their achievements wrote, "The few of us who had any long-range faith in the future of flight, warmed our hearts with each new achievement. The two pillars of my own faith were that in the sky we had found a universal highway and that the ingenuity of man was limited only by his capacity to dream."

He was a thoughtful man. He was down to earth. He was humble. And he wrote, while still in flight training:

> *So little time we walked the earth*
> *And peered into the sky,*
> *Deeming it rendezvous where judgment waits*
> *The souls of those who die:*
> *Do I then desecrate the past*
> *Or honor it the more,*
> *Seeking to climb the laddered atmosphere,*
> *To knock on heaven's door?*

His autobiography was titled, *I Walk With Giants.* Though he would never consider himself such, he was one of them.

9/19/93

Note: *Gill Robb Wilson died in 1966 at the age of 73.*

THE UNKNOWN HERO

In the preface to this chapter I wrote that there were heroes no one ever heard of. The following column was about one of these.

It is about a man who made the first flight from the United States to Norway in 1935. That flight made him a true pioneer. But that was not what made him a hero, except in his native Norway. There, he was honored by the king and wildly acclaimed by the populous.

In the United States, his achievement received almost no notice in the press. Unfortunately, the day before he arrived in Norway, one of early aviation's most revered pilots, Wiley Post, was killed in a crash in Alaska, along with the beloved American humorist, Will Rogers. It was a tremendous shock to the nation and the newspapers were filled with stories about the tragedy. There was no room for news of the achievement of Thor Solberg.

The act that made him a hero in the United States five years later, was related to his flight across the Atlantic that had remained virtually unknown and unheralded. However, that act never received much notice, although it was a vitally important element among the events of World War II, as the following story relates, and it may have changed the course of history.

He was the kind of man who could set an impossible goal for himself and then, in the face of untold obstacles, fulfill that goal.

His name was Thor Solberg and his dream was to become the first man to fly from the United States to his native Norway.

That goal became a reality 50 years ago this coming August.

"It was a great day in his life" said his son, Thor, Jr. "But he had the misfortune of landing in Norway on the day after a major air tragedy. Wiley Post and Will Rogers were killed in a crash in Alaska so he didn't get much space in the papers here."

Last Wednesday, however, the Aviation Hall of Fame of New Jersey paid tribute to that achievement by inducting Solberg into their ranks along with other New Jersey aviation pioneers and other New Jerseyans who left their mark on aviation history.

The successful flight was not the first attempt to realize his dream. He had tried to do it in 1932 in a sturdy Bellanca Airbus, one of the first aircraft to have retractable landing gear.

The flight ended in the Bay of Fundy in Nova Scotia. As he was flying, Solberg was suddenly enveloped in fog. The air turned frigid and the engine quit. The carburetor had iced up and the aircraft was not equipped with carburetor heat.

Fortunately for him, Solberg was a proficient instrument pilot and he had studied his charts well and had a pretty good idea of where he was even though he couldn't see anything.

He had been flying over mountains, but he thought he was now near the Atlantic coastline. He was right. He splashed down in the water and a fisherman told him he was in the Bay of Fundy, which is where he thought he should be.

The fisherman towed him to shore and the aircraft was beached with relatively little damage.

The next morning, when Solberg went out to inspect the airplane, it was completely stripped. The instruments were gone, the fabric, even the wire, the prop and engine parts were taken.

The trip had been financed by friends and Solberg was now deep

Thor Solberg Sr.

Courtesy of Pat Reilly

in debt to them. For another man, that might have been the end of the dream. But not for Solberg. He repaid his debts with the proceeds from a thriving picture frame business in Brooklyn and he began to plan another attempt.

In 1933, he found a Loening Amphibian Air Yacht built in 1929 and proceeded to overhaul it. He installed larger gas tanks and enclosed the cockpit.

Solberg named his aircraft the *Leif Erickson* and set out on July 18, 1935, with radio operator Paul Oscayan, to retrace the route of his famed countryman, but in the opposite direction. He reached Norway on August 16, after many stops and weather delays. But few people in the United States were aware of it because it was overshadowed by the Post-Rogers tragedy.

While he was wildly acclaimed in Norway and honored by the king, it wasn't until after the invasion of his homeland almost four years later, on April 9, 1940, that his history-making flight received any kind of recognition in the United Sates.

Solberg believed that the Nazi advance into Norway was a stepping stone to an attack on the United States. He remembered sites in Iceland and Greenland that he saw on his historic flight, from which he thought the Nazis could strike major cities in the

United States, perhaps Boston or New York.

He expressed his views in a letter to President Roosevelt and he was invited to the White House where he discussed his ideas with the President in some detail.

President Roosevelt sent the Coast Guard to investigate and sure enough, they found the Nazis hard at work establishing a base right where Solberg had indicated they might. The Nazis were captured and interned, ending what might have been a national disaster for the United States. A U.S. base was built on the site.

That event has never received much publicity and is still little known.

Solberg became an airport owner like thousands of others. In 1940, he began acquiring property in New Jersey on which to build an airport. That airport, in Readington, which bears his name and is operated by his son and two daughters, was opened in 1941. The first hangar was built with steel from the Florida Pavilion at the 1939 New York World's Fair.

After a few months the airport was closed because no civilian fields were allowed to operate near the Atlantic coast after the U.S. entered World War II. Solberg went to Massachusetts where he trained some 5,000 pilots for the Civilian Pilot Training Program.

After the war, he became a distributor for the SeaBee, an amphibious aircraft, and then the distributor for Cessna aircraft sales in Norway. For many years, Cessnas were crated at Solberg Airport for shipment to Norway.

"He probably had a more dramatic effect on aviation in Norway than he did here," said his son, a flight engineer with United Airlines. (He later became a captain.) "He brought general aviation and amphibians to Scandinavia. He operated a flying school in Norway and started a scheduled service there using seaplanes. He spent half his time in Norway and half here."

Young Thor and his two sisters have scrapbooks filled with clippings about their father's exploits. A majority of them are from Norwegian newspapers, largely because the Post-Rogers tragedy diverted U.S. attention from his pioneering flight.

Today, Solberg's name is probably better known than his exploits. The airport at Readington still bears his name and there is a VOR (a radio navigation aid), on the field known as Solberg omni, which is a departure fix used by airliners flying out of Newark, as well as other airports. An inlet in the Arctic has also been named for him.

"He felt the airplane was going to change the nature of transportation," said his son. "He was one of those inspired people who had aviation in his blood."

5/26/85

Note: *Thor Solberg, Sr. died in 1967.*

Chapter 16

The Movers and Shakers

In the early days of aviation virtually every pilot was a hero. The biggest hero of all, of course, was Charles Lindbergh, with Amelia Earhart a close second.

But strangely, as the years progressed and aviation grew from a novelty to a vital part of every day life, the bloom fell off the rose. Regulations and restrictions on general aviation mushroomed, slowly eroding the freedom to fly. Extremely vocal anti-airport and anti-noise groups, often making highly exaggerated claims in emotional outbursts, exercised influence far beyond their numbers. Many of them moved into neighborhoods near airports and immediately begin to attack operations at those facilities, whether they serve airlines or general aviation.

Aviation, which has shrunken the world, adding tremendously to the quality of life on this planet, became an enemy of the people in areas surrounding airports. Never mind that it provides vital services to virtually every family. It brings perishable, out-of-season fruits and vegetables not previously available to tables all over the United States, including those of the protesters. It gets mail to your door in record time from all over the country and the world. It delivers lifesaving human organs that could not reach hospitals in time by any other means of transportation. It has given the nation's businesses, large and small, a new tool with which to expand their areas of operations and sales, which expands the nation's economy and creates jobs. It delivers important packages overnight. In spite of these contributions to our quality of life, (and there are many more), aviation suddenly had to fight for its right to exist. All because some people who are sensitive to aircraft noise chose to live near an airport and protested loudly enough to attract the attention of their legislators.

A small group of dedicated men and women picked up the cudgels and with great energy, dedication, and knowledge, assumed the leadership to stop the erosion of this enormous gift which the Wright Brothers gave the world more than a 100 years ago.

These men include Phil Boyer, president of the 413,000 member Aircraft Owners and Pilots Association (AOPA); Paul Poberezny, founder and first president of the Experimental Aircraft Association (EAA); Jack Olcott, who recently retired from his post as president of the National Business Aviation Association (NBAA); James Coyne, former congressman and current president of the National Air Transportation Association (NATA); and Ed Stimpson, founder and former president of the General Aviation Manufacturer's Association (GAMA), and U.S. Ambassador to the International Civil Aviation Association (ICAO)[4]

They are the leaders of today's general aviation community. They are general aviation's future. Their stories follow.

---

[4] Ed Stimpson retired from his post as ambassador to ICAO in December, 2004

THE PIED PIPER OF GENERAL AVIATION

Phil Boyer is the leader of the largest pilots' organization in the world, the Aircraft Owners and Pilots Association (AOPA). More than four hundred thousand pilots look to him to represent their interests. And he is always there.

He is everywhere. He testifies before Congress. He meets frequently with top people in the FAA, and the TSA (Transportation Security Administration), and other regulatory bodies. He flies a jet and he conducts pilot meetings in all 50 states. There is constant communication between him and his members via the organization's magazine, AOPA Pilot, that has the largest circulation of any general aviation publication in the world and in which he has a monthly column. He reaches pilots via AOPA's online newsletter. He has boundless energy and enthusiasm for the mission he performs. He leads a team of AOPA professionals who work together under his leadership as a highly coordinated team.

One of the hallmarks of his constant effort to remain close to his membership and to keep them up to date on what is going on, is his Pilot Town Meetings that he conducts at locations around the country. It sometimes seems as if he has the capacity to be at more than one place at a time. A Cessna Citation he flies, helps him create that impression.

The following is an account of one of his Pilot Town Meetings. Though this meeting took place several years ago, it focuses on the wide variety of problems aviation has faced and Boyer has dealt with head-on.

Phil Boyer, president of the Aircraft Owners and Pilots Association (AOPA) visited New Jersey recently to conduct one of his Pilot Town meetings at the Glenpointe Marriott in Teaneck. A capacity audience of 300, almost all pilots, filled the ballroom for his presentation.

It was a shame there weren't 3,000 non-pilots there. By the end of the session Boyer would have had every one of them dashing to their nearest airport to sign up for flying lessons.

He has a rare ability to create excitement and his talk, interspersed with slides and videos, made two hours seem like 30 minutes and sent his audience home feeling enthused about the fact that they were part of the wonderful world of flying.

He spoke about the need to get more people to find out about that world. AOPA has had numerous special programs aimed at accomplishing that. There is also a Pilot Instructors Program to bring new people into the fold, with special incentives to instructors.

AOPA photo

Phil Boyer

And if all this isn't enough, AOPA will give away a new Cessna 182 later this year. Any new member of AOPA is eligible to win the aircraft as well as any current member who renews his or her membership. (This column was written ten years ago and Cessna still gives away an airplane every year. Each year it is a different make of aircraft.)

The aircraft, coming from a new factory in Independence, Kans., will be the first piston aircraft produced by Cessna in ten years. Once the world's largest producers of general aviation aircraft, Cessna ceased production in 1988 when outrageous and unreasonable liability awards made it impossible for the industry to profitably build small general aviation aircraft.

Russ Meyer, president of Cessna, pledged to resume production if Congress would pass the General Aviation Revitalization Act, designed to bring liability laws back to reasonable levels the industry could live with. Congress passed the act and Meyer lived up to his promise.

The first new piston-powered Cessnas will roll off the line later this year. Meyer has announced the company's intention to build 2,000 aircraft the first year.

Boyer pointed out that Piper Aircraft, also hard hit by product liability laws, has emerged from bankruptcy, greatly expanded its work force, and is producing increasing numbers of new aircraft.

The old product liability laws that virtually wiped out the nation's substantial general aviation manufacturing industry, had a domino effect. All phases of general aviation activity dropped precipitously. Student starts, which were once at a level of 140,000 a year, dropped to 60,000. The objective of the AOPA's efforts is to bring the student pilot population back up to 100,000 by the year 2,000. (In mid-2003, the figure was up to 67,036 in spite of 9/11, one of the worst streaks of winter weather in years, and one of the wettest springs on record.)

While he was in the area, Boyer also met with members of the New Jersey General Aviation Study Commission and he discussed the student pilot situation with them as well.

AOPA, Boyer told them, conducted a survey of people who were into such activities as golf and boating. Those surveyed were over 25. (The average age of student pilots today is 38.) "Eleven percent told us they would be very interested in learning to fly," Boyer said.

The survey also revealed some of the reasons that people who were interested didn't go ahead and learn to fly.

"There were many misconceptions," said Boyer. "Many of the people we talked with thought it cost $200 an hour to rent an airplane." The cost (in 1996) is actually well below half of that--with an instructor.

Another common misperception was that it took two years to get a license. It depends on how often the student flies, but the average student these days gets a license in a little more than 50 hours and many students do it within a year. Some students do it in two or three months.

The reasons given for wanting to fly were interesting. The top reason people gave was that they could get to where they wanted to go in less than half the time. The second reason given was, "It's something I can do with my family."

Other factors that encourage people to fly are the romance of flight, and the fun and utility of it. The romance of aviation flourished in the pioneering days of aviation when the world was excited by aviators establishing one new record after another in the days when flying was a novelty and not yet a means of public transportation. That sense of romance, associated with breaking the bonds that tie us to the earth, has really never faded.

The thought of handling the controls of an airplane is a dream that thousands share, but only a small percentage of the population realizes. The ability to go places that might not normally be accessible is intriguing. AOPA programs are designed to capitalize on those facts.

In the number of publicly-owned airports, New Jersey ranks number 41. That figure is in the process of changing with a pair of airports on the way to public ownership.

Boyer left little doubt in the minds of those who heard him last week that general aviation is experiencing a vital rebirth. But he said that to make the most of it, a coalition of aviation organizations, aircraft manufacturers, avionics manufacturers, and others is needed. Such an organization has been established by AOPA and the General Aviation Manufacturers Association with 36 founding members.

In the five years since he took over the reins at AOPA, Boyer has been in the forefront in representing the interests of general aviation on the legislative front. Among the accomplishments in which he was a leading figure were the defeat of the FAA's efforts to change medical standards for pilots and make them more restrictive, with absolutely no statistics or facts to indicate a need for such action.

Another major achievement was taking the aviation trust fund off the general budget. The money consisted of funds collected from aviation, but its use for aviation needs, including safety improvements, was severely restricted because as long as it remained in the general budget--and it was a sum well up in the billions--it was not all used for aviation purposes. And the amount held back was used to make the federal deficit look smaller.

Boyer has exhibited such initiative and has proven so effective in his efforts that there is no question but that he has played a significant role in the current resurgence of general aviation.

Perhaps the greatest example of his effectiveness has been in his leading the organization to an all time high in membership during a period when general aviation was in a steep decline.

When he was chosen the new president of AOPA five years ago, the organization had about 300,000 members. (In 2007, the figure was 412,000 plus). It will come as no surprise if he does the same thing with student starts, the future of general aviation.

Today's students are the people who will buy the new general aviation aircraft that will be rolling off the lines in increasing numbers. Future airline pilots are the students now learning to fly at local airports.

With Phil Boyer as president of AOPA, those of us in the wonderful world of aviation are in good hands.

5/5/96

THE FATHER OF THE EAA

A half century ago, on Jan. 26, 1953, a World War II pilot who had an interest in homebuilt aircraft, assembled a group of some 30 like-minded people to discuss the formation of a club in which they could share their knowledge and experience with others.

The pilot, whose name is Paul Poberezny, had built his own homebuilt in his father's garage in 1952. He went on to fly P-51s and has flown something like 170 other types of aircraft, and has logged more than 30,000 hours of flying time.

That meeting was the beginning of what eventually evolved into the EAA (Experimental Aircraft Association) which today has 170,000 members around the country.

The organization is probably best known for the show it stages in Oshkosh, Wis., every summer. For years it was known simply as Oshkosh. Today, it bears the name AirVenture. In terms of attendance, it is the biggest air show in the world, attracting about 800,000 attendees.

Paul Poberezny, who never envisioned the little group of homebuilt enthusiasts would grow into a nationwide organization, served as its president until 1989 when his son Tom, an accomplished aerobatic pilot, stepped into his father's shoes.

In addition to running the world's biggest air show, (in attendance), it presents the largest display of antique aircraft, classics, homebuilts, and warbirds in the world. The show also offers dozens of seminars and workshops where show attendees can learn the skills necessary to build an aircraft.

Perhaps the greatest service EAA has done for general aviation, is to introduce millions of non-flying people to the world of aviation at their annual air show, in an exciting atmosphere where they can get a firsthand picture of what general aviation is all about and have a good time in the process.

One other thing the EAA does for its members is to publish several excellent magazines.

There are thousands of pilots in the country who have built their own aircraft, most of them with an incredible degree of old-fashioned skill and precision. Thousands more dream of building their own aircraft. Perhaps Poberezny's greatest personal accomplishment has been in helping so many of those dreams come true.

The following column was based on a talk by Poberezny in 1986 when general aviation was, perhaps, at its lowest ebb.

Pilots have a rather strong need for reassurance these days. To anyone who knows what's going on in the industry, the future of general aviation seems like it was yesterday and not tomorrow. Cessna Aircraft, the General Motors of the industry, discontinued production of all piston-powered aircraft a couple of weeks ago, laying off 900 workers in the process to add to the thousands the industry has already laid off. In its announcement, Cessna said production will not be resumed before October 1987, at the earliest.

Paul Poberezny

Prior to this announcement, production of two-place trainers had already been discontinued by all of the major manufacturers.

To pilots who have a love of flying and for those for whom general aviation aircraft are an important business tool, it is not a very pretty picture.

But several hundred pilots who flew in to Pennridge Airport in Perkasie, Pa., a week ago Saturday, left feeling just a mite better about things, perhaps, than they did when they flew in. The occasion was the third annual Pennridge Super Saturday Fly-In and FAA Safety Seminar. And the reason for the little ray of sunshine was a fellow named Poberezny.

Paul Poberezny, founder and president of the Experimental Aircraft Association (EAA), the most dedicated group of aviation enthusiasts in the world, was guest speaker at the event that featured films, seminar sessions, and a lot of hangar talk.

A World War II Air Corp veteran, a 30,000-hour pilot, and a man who has designed and built 16 aircraft himself, Poberezny has been an inspiration to thousands of people in aviation for nearly four decades.

Recognizing the fact that general aviation is "at a low point on the totem pole," he pointed out that if there are very few airplanes being produced, there are still large numbers of aircraft under construction in basements and garages.

So general aviation, admittedly not what it should be, is still very much with us. And that was certainly indicated by the large number of aircraft that flew into the Super Saturday event, including many beautiful homebuilts and marvelously restored antiques.

But if general aviation is still very much with us, so too, Poberezny admitted, are the problems.

"Many of our neighbors who don't fly, think pilots are alcoholics," he said. That struck a responsive chord with me immediately. Only the night before, a friend indicated he held such a view.

In 32 years of flying, I don't recall ever encountering a pilot who had been drinking. I know of only a very few instances where alcohol was a factor in an accident. Most accidents result from pilots flying into bad weather and exceeding their capabilities.

But my friend remembered an accident which happened years ago in which alcohol was a factor and it made a lasting impression. There have been hundreds of thousands of safe flights in New Jersey since then, but he only remembers that one unfortunate flight.

Poberezny said he asked the assistant medical examiner at the FAA about this problem and was told that accidents in which alcohol was a factor have really dropped.

"I asked him, 'Why don't you put out a release?' " Poberezny said. He told me, "If we did, people would think we're not really concerned."

That is one of general aviation's biggest problems. There is a tendency among those who don't fly to emphasize the negative and completely ignore the positive. Last year was the safest year in general aviation history, but nobody not involved in aviation remembers that.

Product liability costs are another major factor depressing the industry. The manufacturers simply cannot afford to produce aircraft at a price within reason because of unreasonable and outrageous product liability awards.

"A few years ago," Poberezny said, "when Sen. Bob Kasten of Wisconsin, proposed liability legislation, the Trial Lawyers Association raised a half million dollars to defeat him.

"People think money comes only from insurance companies," he said, referring to the many multimillion dollar judgments brought in by juries. "How many people are qualified to make a $10 million business decision?" he asked.

"Progress is being hindered because people are afraid to put their assets on the line to market all sorts of products."

And that, the last time we looked, was supposed to be what our free enterprise system was all about.

Poberezny pointed out how liability is affecting the big EAA show that attracts hundreds of thousands to Oshkosh each year. "Last year insurance for the show was $151,250. This year, Lloyds of London, the only company that will quote on it, is asking $347,000. In addition, it costs $20,000 to $25,000 to insure the camper area plus air show insurance and insurance for the warbirds. The total bill will be $600,000 to $700,000.

"People think we make a lot of money at Oshkosh," he told his audience. (The event attracts about 14,000 aircraft and hundreds of thousands of people every summer.) "Last year we cleared $105,000 on food concessions. But the toilets cost $143,000. We'd have been better off if we didn't eat."

But the very fact that Oshkosh continues to attract huge throngs every year and the fact that it is a family event, is evidence that general aviation is a potent and vital force. That leaves hope that we will yet see better days for general aviation. And that is the feeling most pilots carried home with them from Pennridge.

6/22/86

A PIONEER IN BUSINESS AVIATION

Over the years I wrote dozens of columns on various aspects of business aviation. The very first business aviation column I wrote ran on September 1, 1963. That was a little more than a year before the first Learjet was delivered.

My first business aviation column was about John W. "Jack" Olcott, who was director of flight training for Linden Flight Service, a company that had a unique executive flight training program. Some three decades after that column ran, Olcott became president of the prestigious National Business Aircraft Association (NBAA), a position he held for more than ten years until his resignation in 2003.

Linden Flight Service was one of the business aviation pioneers. They were among the first companies to manage business aircraft, which meant providing crews, maintenance, scheduling etc. Among their customers were Pfizer, Purolator, Hess Oil, and Paul Tishman, a major builder.

Bob Meyers, who headed Linden Flight Service, signed a long term lease for Linden Airport in the early '50s. Olcott credits him with being one of the pioneers in the aircraft management business.

Olcott, himself, was a key figure in one important part of the company's business aviation initiatives. He ran the flight training program designed specifically for executives and eventually became vice president of the company.

Youngstown Airways in Ohio, was the father of the aircraft management business, Olcott told me, and was its biggest operator, managing 21 aircraft.

Today, Olcott heads his own consulting firm, General Aero Company, based at Morristown Municipal Airport in New Jersey.

Olcott is widely known as one of the most knowledgeable spokesmen for business aviation and one of its leading advocates. But few know the story of his beginnings in business aviation described in the following column written more than 40 years ago.

It's getting so that many business executives whose corporate activities are spread over several states would no more think of being without a corporate aircraft than they would think of being without an automobile. And the more executives who come to realize the value of an airplane in the operation of their business, the more executives want to learn to fly.

As a consequence Linden Flight Service at Linden Airport has inaugurated a unique new flight training program tailored exclusively for the busy executive.

"We have a professional man's flying school," says John Olcott, director of flight training for Linden Flight Service, who conceived the idea for the executive flight training program. "We offer a single price package program leading to a private license.

"The FAA requires a minimum of 35 hours for a private license," says Olcott. "But statistics show the national average is 63 hours. We have a single price no matter how many hours it takes, and it's a guaranteed course. We will refund an executive's money if, in our opinion, we determine he won't make a safe, efficient pilot.

"We give all training in new Beechcraft Musketeers. When the executive finishes the course he can go right on flying a Musketeer. He doesn't have to go through any transition training from a smaller, lighter training plane. (The Musketeer is a four-place aircraft.)

"And there are no extras," Olcott added. "The single price includes ground school, books--everything needed to complete the course." And when he says tailored to the busy executive's needs, he means it.

Jack Olcott

"One executive," said Olcott, "wanted a lesson at 6:30 a.m. He got it. We schedule flights at the executive's convenience.

"Our program is designed for the busy professional man who, when he starts a program wants to finish it, and wants personal attention."

Linden Flight Service initiates this new service with plenty of experience under its belt in catering to the needs of corporate flying. The company runs a charter and air taxi service, it leases aircraft to corporations, and it manages corporate aircraft.

"Under the management plan," says Olcott, "we supply the crew, maintenance, and storage for a company-owned plane. We are actually the company's aviation department. They use our experience and have no headaches. We send out an itemized account monthly of how the airplane was used and the cost." Linden Flight Service operates all kinds of aircraft under this plan, including

Twin Beeches, a DC-3, and a Convair.

"One drug company came to us a few years ago," says Olcott, "and said they were wasting too much of their executives' time driving from one point to another. They would often spend a whole day on the road and then be too exhausted to tackle problems with the energy needed. We studied the company's transportation problem to determine how best its needs could be met, through ownership, rental, lease, air charter, or our management program.

"The drug company now owns two twin-engine planes that we manage, and the program has solved their transportation problem to their complete satisfaction."

9/1/63

JIM COYNE TELLS IT LIKE IT IS

Jim Coyne, president of the National Air Transportation Association (NATA), seems to personify Teddy Roosevelt's counsel to "speak softly and carry a big stick."

When he speaks publicly, though he may advance strong arguments in regard to a specific issue in a very convincing manner, he is rather soft spoken. But when he is advocating legislation or calling for a change in regulations, he is forceful and dynamic. He speaks with a strong voice.

Coyne served in Congress in 1980 for one term following which he became Special Assistant to President Ronald Reagan and Director of the Office of Private Sector Initiatives.

He has held many other executive positions including President of the American Consulting Engineers Council, founder and President of the American Tort Reform Association, and President of Americans to Limit Congressional Terms. He has served as a director of several private and public firms.

Coyne holds a bachelor's degree from Yale and an MBA from Harvard. He has taught at the Wharton School of Business at the University of Pennsylvania.

He flies a Beechcraft Baron and a King Air.

NATA represents some 2,000 FBOs, charter operators, and small aircraft commuter operators.

Coyne, as president of NATA, is a vital voice representing the interests of small aviation businesses, (generally less than 500 employees) that are the foundation of general aviation activities.

"If we want to see the future of New Jersey, we have to ask, 'What kind of transportation system are we going to have?' "

Those were the words of Jim Coyne, President of the National Air Transportation Association (NATA) in Washington, D.C., and former congressman from Bucks County, Pa., addressing the recent annual meeting of the Mid-Atlantic Aviation Coalition, a New Jersey group.

Coyne once lived in Washington's Crossing (N.J.) and he took his first flight lessons when he was a resident of New Jersey. He used to fly out of Collins Field, a private strip that was located between the Turnpike and Route 295. It's been gone for years now.

"How many airports we used to know are not there anymore?" he asked rhetorically.

Speaking in a calm and thoughtful manner, Coyne pulled no punches. He talked about the serious decline in the number of airports, resulting in large measure from relatively small, extremely vocal local groups, and the effect that it is having on the national transportation system.

Jim Coyne

"We are at the dawn of the second century of aviation," he pointed out. "Which way will we go? It was the automobile in the 20th century, the railroad in the 19th century. It will be aviation in this century."

But aviation does not have as smooth a road to traverse as the earlier forms of transportation that contributed so significantly to the economic growth of the nation.

"We've allowed aviation to be separated into the airplane and the airport," Coyne said. "Somehow, they think we can do without airports and still have aviation. They never separated the automobile and the highway or the railroad and the railroad tracks.

"Local politicians are deciding whether their airports can exist. Why don't they decide whether they're going to let railroads in their town or not? Suppose they decided to shut down the New Jersey Turnpike at night because of the noise of trucks? They devote their efforts to trying to break down a transportation system we've built up over a century," Coyne continued. "The real threat is at the local level.

"We asked the railroads, how do you deal with the local communities? They said, 'We show them the Constitution.' The federal government has the right to regulate interstate commerce.

"When I mentioned the situation to one of the justices of the Supreme Court, I was asked, 'Have you ever heard of the commerce clause of the Constitution?' " That clause relegates control over transportation to the federal government. Coyne pointed out that if you rely on commercial aviation transportation, "it will take significantly longer today to get to your destination than it did 25 years ago. This is the result of the hub-and-spoke airline system, (which usually requires changing planes), the much larger number of people who fly today, the long lines at airline counters, the long trip from the parking lots or rental car stations, and more," he said.

"Small jet engines are now here," he pointed out. "Think of the potential of an airplane weighing 2,500 pounds, (the average weight of a four-place, single-engine piston aircraft), that can fly at 450 knots. It will be the fastest form of personal transportation the world has ever known." The price of the Eclipse, a light jet, will be about a third that of the least expensive business jet available today.

He referred to the widely acclaimed new book by James Fallows, *Free Flight: From Airline Hell to a New Age of Travel*. The book, which was excerpted in the June issue of *Atlantic Monthly*, refers to two aircraft that will make a difference in personal travel, the Cirrus, a four-place piston aircraft that comes equipped with a parachute for the airplane, and the Eclipse, which has the potential to revolutionize personal jet travel. The Cirrus is approved by the Federal Aviation Administration and many are already flying.

"Fallows has pointed out an era of unbridled potential for aviation," Coyne said.

"The benefactors of aviation are all over the country. Polls show that 75 percent of the people support airports or have no objection to them."

NATA created a list of the 100 most needed airports in the country. Six out of the hundred are in New Jersey. Those six are Bader Field in Atlantic City,[5] Greenwood Lake, Morristown Municipal, Solberg, South Jersey Regional, and Teterboro. "There are 1,500 airports right now on the most endangered list," Coyne said.

"We went across the country," he said, "to visit airports which we think are going to be critical to aviation over the next century."

7/29/01

---

[5] Bader Field closed in September 2006. Greenwood Lake Airport has been purchased by the state. Solberg is the center of a heated debate over its future between the airport owners and Readington Township, its host community. The Port Authority which owns and operates Teterboro Airport has called for a reduction in traffic at that facility. The area's congressman, Steve Rothman, has demanded a cut of 25 percent in traffic. Morristown Airport which is owned by the town, is relatively stable.

A MAN OF DISTINCTION

Edward W. "Ed" Stimpson has been an imposing figure on the general aviation scene for more than three decades. He was the U.S. Ambassador to ICAO, the International Civil Aviation Organization in Montreal, from October of 1999 to December 2004, when he retired.

Stimpson is best known as president of the General Aviation Manufacturers Association (GAMA), a position he held for 25 years. During that time he interfaced with leading members of Congress and officials of the Department of Transportation, the FAA, and other high level organizations and individuals. He testified frequently before Congressional committees. He was a member of many key aviation committees and advisory panels, including both NASA and FAA groups. He is a past chairman of the board of Embry-Riddle Aeronautical University and is currently a member of the board.

Prior to joining GAMA, Stimpson served as assistant administrator of the FAA under three administrators. During his years with the FAA he was honored with the U.S. DOT's Meritorious Achievement Award and two FAA awards, The Meritorious Service Award and the Decoration for Exceptional Service.

He left GAMA in 1990 to serve for two years as senior vice president of the Morrison Knudsen Corporation, following which he returned to GAMA.

At the time he received his appointment to ICAO which he served at the will of the President, he was chairman of the Be-A-Pilot, GA Team 2000, a nationwide program to increase the number of student pilots.

He has probably received more major awards than anyone else in general aviation. These include: The Aero Club Trophy for Aviation Excellence, the Brewer Trophy, the Aviation Week & Space Technology Magazine's Laurel of Aviation. He was named Man of the Year by Flying and Business & Commercial Aviation.

In 1998, he was awarded the prestigious Wright Brothers Memorial Trophy by the National Aeronautics Association.

He graduated from Harvard Cum Laude in 1956 and received an MPA (Master of Public Administration) from the University of Washington in 1959. Stimpson is a private pilot.

Although the column that follows was written nearly a quarter of a century ago, it points out facts about the growth of business aviation that seemed amazing and almost unbelievable at the time, but have proven valid as the years passed.

T here are now more general aviation jets in this country than there are airliners in the domestic airline fleet.

The bearer of this news is Edward W. Stimpson, president of the General Aviation Manufacturers Association.

Ed Stimpson

The business jet fleet now numbers 2,600 and the domestic airline fleet 2,300, Stimpson said at a luncheon meeting of the prestigious Wings Club in New York.

"By the end of the next decade, an estimated 6,000 general aviation jets and 7,300 general aviation turboprops will fly a total of 7.2 million hours annually, which will nearly equal the 8.2 million hours for the forecast fleet of 3,100 air carrier airplanes," Stimpson said.

What Stimpson was trying to impress on his audience was the growing importance of general aviation in the nation's transportation system.

(Figures through the end of 2006 report a total of 7,626 jets and turboprops in the U.S. airline fleet and 10,687 jets and turboprops in the business aviation fleet.)

"The major reason for the growth in general aviation is business flying," said Stimpson.

"And the reason for that growth," he pointed out, "is the discontinuance of airline service to smaller communities.

"Now, with the Airline Deregulation Act, the airline cutback of service to smaller communities on less profitable routes is accelerating.

"In the past three years," Stimpson pointed out, "1,000 plants a year have been located outside major metropolitan areas. Many of these areas either are not served at all or are served inadequately by the airlines, leaving general aviation as the only means of access by air.

"One thing this illustrates most dramatically is the urgent need for airports to cater to the growing general aviation fleet serving business and industry.

"In spite of this urgent need, almost $3 billion in the Airport/Airways Trust Fund, collected expressly to modernize the airport/airway system, remains uncommitted, Stimpson declared.
"The funds available for reliever airport development should be at least five times the current amount that is authorized," he said.

"The legislative proposals now before Congress recognize the need for reliever airports. Our concern is that they do not go far enough. The time is past due for a major program. Industry studies show there is an immediate need for more than $250 million.

"Relief will only come by making better use of what we have and by retaining every square foot of existing real estate. There are more technical concepts that will increase airport capacity, such as automatic metering and spacing of aircraft on approaches, reduction, or at least detection of wake vortices, improved runway turnoffs and taxiways, and more navigation aids.

"What we need," Stimpson told his audience, "is the increased use of underutilized non-strategic military fields, the preservation of privately-owned airports that are succumbing to other real estate demands, and the development of all metropolitan area airports into attractive reliever airports by providing them with instrument landing systems, lighting and weather reporting."

Stimpson pointed out the tremendous need in the New York Metropolitan Area for additional general aviation airport capacity. He specifically pointed out some encouraging steps taken here in New Jersey.

"A promotional campaign by Teterboro encourages business aviation to come to that airport. The campaign reads, 'At Teterboro the business airplane, not the airliner, is the big duck, so air traffic delays are less, ramp delays are shorter, and you can come and go with a minimum of inconvenience.'"

The removal of the landing fee and quota at Newark is encouraging.

"The first objective should be to keep airports open that are now in existence. We cannot afford to lose any airports. Several years ago, Caldwell Airport was threatened with closing. The airport was saved and now it is an important reliever."

12/16/79

Chapter 17

Women in Aviation

There are women today who are captains of jumbo jets, women who fly the nation's hottest jet fighters off the decks of aircraft carriers. There are women astronauts. But getting there was a long, tough struggle.

Going back to the early days of aviation, women who wanted to learn to fly had a tough time finding somebody to teach them. Flying was perceived as something for daring, dashing, macho men. It was not a thing for ladies. In spite of that, some women did learn to fly in the very early days.

Bessie Coleman's story is one of the most remarkable examples of prejudice in the early days of flight. She had not one, but two strikes against her. Not only was she a woman, she was black. No flight school in the United States would accept her. She learned French, saved money and went to France where they did not have the racial barriers the U.S. did at that time, and she got her license in 1921. She returned to the United States and became a popular air show performer.

As late as World War II, women pilots were treated like second class citizens. Women who flew in the WASPS, (Women's Air Force Service Pilots), flew every aircraft in the inventory from fighters through bombers. They received absolutely no benefits. When one was killed, (38 WASPS died in the service of their country), the government would not even cover her burial costs. Her fellow women pilots had to collect money for her burial.

It wasn't until 1977, more than three decades after the end of the war, that they were recognized as veterans and received the same education and medical benefits as other veterans.

In spite of that, women have attained a remarkable record of achievement, even flying into space. The columns in this chapter tell only a very small part of the story of women's achievements. There are numerous books that tell much more. But this chapter will give you a taste of the struggles women faced--and overcame.

THE NINETY-NINES

The greatest symbol of women in aviation is the Ninety-Nines, the international organization of women pilots founded in 1929 in a hangar at Curtiss Field in Valley Stream, Long Island, N.Y. At the time of its founding there were 117 licensed women pilots in the United States and 99 of them were charter members, which explains where the name comes from.

One of the women at that meeting was Amelia Earhart and she was elected first president of the organization. It was international from the beginning. One of the original 99 women was from Germany and another from Australia. Today there are 35 nations throughout the world that have Ninety-Nines chapters.

The Ninety-Nines is one of the most active aviation groups in existence. They are involved in aviation education and safety. They grant scholarships. They help organizations that operate mercy flights. They are energetic and willing to undertake almost any task that will serve the best interests of general aviation.

Today there are a total of about 6,000 members. They own and manage the Amelia Earhart birthplace museum in Atchison, Kansas, and the Forest of Friendship there.

They have their own headquarters building at Will Rogers Airport in Oklahoma City. On the second floor of the building they have a small Women in Aviation Museum, an aviation library and a resource center on women in aviation.

The following column was written on the occasion of the organization's 60th anniversary convention held in New York City. On that occasion I interviewed three of the Ninety-Nines charter members, one of whom, Fay Gillis Wells, a long time friend, died Dec. 2, 2002 at the age of 94.

George Bernard Shaw once said, "Youth is wasted on the young." He could never have gotten away with that if he had attended the 60th Anniversary Convention of the Ninety-Nines at the Marriott Marquis Hotel in Manhattan. The Ninety-Nines, of course, is the international organization of women pilots.

On the occasion of that anniversary they honored their charter members, women who attended their first meeting at Curtiss Field in Valley Stream, L.I., on Nov. 2, 1929.

Here were women who had the courage and daring to learn to fly more than 60 years ago in primitive, open cockpit aircraft with the wind blowing in their faces. And 60 years later, though most are no longer flying, they are still active, dedicated, and as stimulating as they surely must have been when they were true aviation pioneers.

I talked with three of the charter members who were among the 400 Ninety-Nines gathered here from all over the world. Some members flew in from Australia for the occasion.

Fay Gillis Wells, now a resident of Alexandria, Va., was one of the original signers of the letter that went out to all 117 licensed women pilots in the country, proposing they join together to form an organization. There were 99 women at the meeting at Curtiss Field in Valley Stream, when the organization was formed. The figure has since grown to 6,000.

Fay soloed on Sept. 1, 1929, in a Curtiss Fledgling at Valley Stream. At the time, Curtiss test pilots were putting a souped up Fledgling with a 225-hp engine in place of its standard 165-hp engine, through all kinds of aerobatic maneuvers to see how much it could take. "They were trying to tear it apart," Fay said.

The day after she soloed it was her instructor's turn to fly the experimental aircraft. He invited Fay to come along and promised her some aerobatic instruction.

Fay Gillis Wells, left, one of the founding members of the Ninety-Nines, with Alice Hammond, president from 1951 to 1953 at the group's 60th anniversary convention in New York City in 1989.

They took off, and her instructor, John L. H. (Sonny) Trump, put the aircraft through some violent maneuvers.

"The tail started vibrating," Fay recalled, "and the vibrations shook the engine off its mount." They were upside down when the wing buckled and they both fell out. They pulled the ripcords on their chutes and both wound up hanging from the same tree.

It took an hour for firemen to get there and get Fay down. Then they rushed her to the airport and put her in another airplane. "They didn't want to lose a customer," she said. "They were getting $600 for ten hours of dual and ten hours of solo time."

That parachute jump made Fay the first woman member of the Caterpillar Club, an organization of pilots who have had to jump for their lives. "Jimmy Doolittle became a member of the club for the second time on that same day. He jumped from an aircraft at the Cleveland Air Races," Fay said.

Fate took good care of Fay on one other occasion. She was a friend of Wiley Post's and he invited her to join him on a flight to the Orient. She declined the invitation in favor of a honeymoon in Africa. Humorist Will Rogers took her place. Both men were killed in a crash in Alaska on August 15, 1935.

Fay's many accomplishments include service as a correspondent in Russia. She was a founding member of the Overseas Press Club. Later she was a White House correspondent and one of three women chosen to accompany President Nixon on his historic trip to China in 1972 and then to the Soviet Union.

Fay was a founding member of the International Forest of Friendship in Atchison, Ks., birthplace of Amelia Earhart. If she had a hash mark on her sleeve for every honor she's received, they'd have to make her sleeve longer. She typifies the caliber and spirit of the Ninety-Nines.

Another of the charter members I spoke with was Ila Fay Loetsche, now 85, the first woman in Iowa to receive a pilot's license.

A former resident of Somerville, (N.J.), where she lived for more than 10 years in the '50s and '60s. She now lives on Padre Island off the Gulf Coast of Texas. She has received nationwide recognition for her efforts over the past 25 years to save the Atlantic Ridley sea turtles from extinction.

In a conversation at the convention, she recalled receiving phone calls from Amelia Earhart encouraging her to participate in the formation of the organization that became the Ninety-Nines.

Mary Jensen of Weathersfield, Conn., another charter member, told me about how she had wanted a job on a newspaper. The editor of the *Hartford Courant* told her, "If you become the first woman to fly in Connecticut, you've got a job."

She really wanted that job, but she had competition from another female student pilot. Mary soloed first, however, and got the job. She served as aviation editor for three years.

Mary holds a sport pilot's license from the Federation Aeronautique International, signed by Orville Wright who was then national chairman of the official French record keeping organization. She crossed the Atlantic in the *Hindenburg* in 1936, and spent many years in the public relations business before she retired.

One of the early Ninety-Nines, though not a charter member, was Alice Hammond of Millville (N.J.) who served as the group's president from 1951 to 1953. Alice got her license in 1931 and joined the group the following year. She has logged more than 6,500 hours.

Judging by the energy and enthusiasm these women have today, it's hard to imagine what they must have been like 60 years ago. Maybe flying keeps you young. Certainly, their enthusiasm for flying has kept their spirits youthful.

The closing banquet was emceed by Roland Smith, WOR-TV (N.Y.) anchor man and a pilot, who told the Ninety-Nines, "I had one instructor from my first lesson to my last and she was a Ninety-Nine."

It's not easy to convey the tremendous spirit of unity among these women, but Doris Renninger Brell, who was the first woman helicopter pilot in New York and manager of the prestigious Wings Club in New York for nine years, probably came as close as anyone could when she offered the invocation. She asked everyone to join hands with the person sitting next to them as she told them, "We celebrate this evening, the life and accomplishments of all who fly."

You could not be in the presence of these women, some relatively new to the world of aviation, some who were there in the early days, but all young in spirit, without being awed by them. You could sense the quiet feeling of pride in the contributions they've made to aviation, particularly in education and safety.

If there was a pilot's license in your pocket, you had to leave with a special feeling of pride in being a pilot that you never felt before.

7/16/89

THE POWDER PUFF DERBY

The event that probably drew more attention to women in aviation than any other in its time, was the Powder Puff Derby. It was an all women transcontinental air race. Its clever name was probably responsible for helping it attract the amount of attention it did. Witty humorist Will Rogers came up with that name for the event.

The Powder Puff Derby is gone now. The last race ended in Tampa, Florida, in 1977, after 30 years.

The event was to have ended the year before because of lack of financial support but the Smithsonian Institution's National Air and Space Museum suggested that the 30th anniversary of the first race be commemorated with one last race following the route of the first contest from Palm Springs, Calif., to Tampa, Fla. That race had all of two starters registered, one of which didn't get off the ground.

For years, Kay Brick, a former WASP, ran the event from a little office on the second floor of an old hangar at Teterboro Airport that was piled high with papers. It was an enormous task, but it did not phase Kay. Very little did.

The race was a great event and its termination marked the sad end of a great tradition.

The Powder Puff Derby was replaced by the Air Race Classic, sponsored by the Ninety-Nines, an event that is still held annually.

As already stated, the race got its share of publicity as the column that follows illustrates.

It was a race that WCBS-TV, the network's New York outlet, used as a feature. The copilot was a WCBS-TV news gal, Joan Murray, who learned to fly with TV cameras focused on her for showing to millions of TV viewers.

The pilot, Merle Chalow, was the attractive young daughter of Rudy Chalow, who owned a turf field called Rudy's in Vineland, N.J. He was known as one of the best aircraft engine experts in the east.

I bumped into Merle many years later at the Flying W Ranch in New Jersey. She was as pretty as ever and had her attractive teenaged daughter with her. She was not only striking, but she wore a stylish outfit that stopped traffic.

By then she was flying the family Learjet that she and her husband owned and flew from their own private strip.

What do two girls talk about when they're on a coast-to-coast flight competing in the Powder Puff Derby?

The greatest authority on this question is a fellow

named Bob Wiemer. He listened in on every word spoken during the 14-hour flight of TAR (Transcontinental Air Race) Entry 92, an Aero Commander 200.

Wiemer is producer of WCBS-TV's "Eye on New York." About a year ago, he did a two-part program about "The Light Plane Boom." In the program, WCBS-TV news gal Joan Murray was shown learning to fly under the careful tutelage of Bill Whitesell, head honcho at the Flying W Ranch in Lumberton, N.J., and a former Eastern Air Lines pilot.

This year, Bob climbed into Whitesell's camera-equipped B-25 and chased two pretty girls across the country. He had a tape recorder going all the time they were in the air. After the race, Bob took the

Merle Chalow, left, and CBS-TV news gal, Joan Murray, ready to take off in the Powder Puff Derby.

tape home and sat and listened to the girl talk--all 14 hours worth.

Next Sunday, via CBS-TV's "Eye on New York," you can do a little girl watching and a bit of "eavesdropping" of your own.

In another two-parter, "A Powder Puff for Joan," Wiemer will give the viewer an insight into the actual flight of TAR No. 92, an unofficial entry in this year's Powder Puff Derby, from Seattle, Wash., to Clearwater, Fla.

Merle Chalow who piloted Aero Commander 899RS, is a chemistry major at Bucknell University. Her copilot was WCBS-TV's Joan Murrray whose flight lessons were a little different from normal. They were televised for several million viewers.

So what did they talk about? "At one point," Bob Wiemer revealed, "Joan asked Merle, 'Would you hand me my purse?' And then they both started laughing as Joan started putting on lipstick when they were several thousand feet in the air where there was nobody to see them."

On the show you'll also hear them talking to control towers, you'll hear them go through their check lists. You'll hear them wonder if anyone is ahead of them. As in all races where various models of airplanes are entered, each aircraft is assigned a handicap speed and they fly against the handicap not against the other aircraft.

The girls actually had a companion flying with them--a little wooden one-toothed gremlin. "We thought anything that ugly would bring us luck," they said.

Flying along in the chase plane were Wiemer, Whitesell, sound man Dave Scott, cameraman Bernie Dresner, and an observer from the Powder Puff Derby to see that the B-25 didn't give any navigational aid to the WCBS-TV entry.

Part one of "A Powder Puff for Joan," will be devoted to the preparations for the race. Part two, to be aired the following Sunday, will show them in the actual race.

9/18/66

SOME GREAT STORIES ABOUT THE POWDER PUFF DERBY

Kay Brick, the former WASP, mentioned earlier, knew more about the Power Puff Derby than anyone else because for years she was the heart and soul of the event. Kay had tremendous energy and she poured it into everything she did.

She had some wonderful stories about the event that she recounted at a meeting of one of the oldest aviation groups in New Jersey.

Back in 1947, a little two place Ercoupe with Carolyn West as pilot and Bea Medes as copilot, took off from Palm Springs, Calif., in an all-women air race to Tampa, Fla. They didn't beat anybody, but they won the race. They were the only entry.

After the two intrepid women pilots arrived in Tampa, they learned that the only other plane entered had never gotten off the ground.

And that was the somewhat inauspicious beginning of what is now the famed Powder Puff Derby.

They tell a lot of stories about the 29 races that have been run since then, and nobody knows more of those stories than Kay Brick, who served for 17 years as a member of the Derby's board of directors and for the past six years as chairman of that board.

Kay Brick in the office at Teterboro Airport from which she ran the Powder Puff Derby.

A few weeks ago, the Mid-Atlantic Pilots Association had Kay as its guest speaker, and some of the stories she told were well worth repeating. So here goes.

There was the time, for example, when the sponsor of a woman pilot from Greenville, Miss., came up with an absolutely sensational idea for solving the wardrobe problem.

Now this fellow knew all about the problem. He knew that the women all flew with the air vents closed to eliminate drag.

And he knew that an airplane can get pretty hot in July with the air vents closed.

He also knew that a gal could carry a big wardrobe and keep changing, but a big wardrobe adds weight and that is not what you want when you're racing. She could wash her dress at the one or two overnight stops they'd be making, (The women only fly during daylight hours.) But then she might be wearing a wet dress the next day.

So this ingenious gentleman dreamed up the idea of paper dresses. Wear 'em and throw 'em away. They weigh next to nothing so there's no weight problem.

A gal from Greenville was game. She climbed into the airplane wearing her paper dress and flew with great skill and precision to Rock Springs, Wyo. She alighted from her airplane with nymph-like grace and began walking to the terminal, whereupon the good citizens of Rock Springs blinked and gaped and blushed. The back of the young lady's dress, it seems, was still pasted to the seat of her airplane.

Then there is the story of the Lady and the Tiger. The women often find ingenious ways of drawing attention to the products or services of their sponsors. Last year, one gal went so far as to wear a tiger suit while she flew.

Now it happens that the race committee usually arranges to have young Civil Air Patrol Cadets rush up to the airplanes when the ladies land, to help them alight and to help them unload such things as the little bags into which they throw their banana peels and sandwich wrappings.

Last year, when the race terminated at Chattanooga, an enthusiastic young cadet dashed up at great speed to the tiger lady's airplane, opened the door and came bounding away at twice his original speed.

The Associated Press, in a story carried by newspapers across the country, reported that the red-faced cadet reported back that the lady in the airplane had told him. "Wait. Let me get my clothes on."

What the lady had actually said was, "Wait. Let me get my head on." She was wearing her tiger suit, but the head was in the back seat.

And then there was the entry sponsored by Calaveras County, Calif., the county that gained wide fame from Mark Twain's account of their celebrated jumping frogs.

On the outside of her airplane, Carol Kennedy had a painting of a frog lying contentedly on its back, arms behind his head, legs crossed, with his fat white belly pointing toward the sky. Inside the airplane, Carol and her copilot carried two Calaveras County frogs in a basket with cool water and the kind of water lilies that make frogs happy.

At night they took them to their hotel room and put them in a bathtub filled with cool water because if frogs are not kept cool and comfortable, they will die.

On one occasion the frogs escaped from their especially prepared cool basket into the lobby of the hotel. This added greatly to the reputation of Calaveras County, but did little to enhance the image of the hotel.

This was in 1964, the year the race terminated in Atlantic City. The women thought it would be a nice gesture if, at the banquet in honor of the participants, they presented the frogs to a city official.

Frogs are kind of wet and clammy and women are usually thoughtful and considerate. So they knitted turtleneck frog sweaters for the ceremony, because they thought the city official would appreciate the gift more that way.

They were wrong. "He couldn't have wanted anything less in this world," Kay explained.

The frogs were reported to have been turned loose in a swamp area near Atlantic City. So it is entirely possible that there is a colony of Calaveras County jumping frogs in southern New Jersey, courtesy of the Powder Puff Derby. But nobody can really be certain because nobody ever knew if one of the frogs was a boy frog and the other a girl.

11/13/66

AN UNUSUAL REUNION OF WOMEN WARTIME
PILOTS

The role U.S. women pilots played in World War II has, over the years, received some degree of exposure. But the story of Russian women pilots in that war is much less known. Unlike their American counterparts, they actually flew combat missions.

In 1990, a group of former WASPs had the unusual opportunity to go to Russia to meet with some of their counterparts. I spoke to a couple of the women who made that trip.

Nine years prior to this, a British television reporter named Bruce Myles, wrote a book about the sacrifices of the Russian women combat pilots, many of them teenagers. It is a relatively rare, although fascinating account, of a little known phase of women's role in World War II.

War is a man's business. But somebody forgot to tell that to Alice-Jean Starr, Faith Richards, and Anne Shields.

World War II WASPS Faith Richards, left, and Alice-Jean Starr, hold hard cover and paperback editions of "Night Witches," a book which tells the story of Soviet women combat pilots in World War II.

Between them, the three New Jersey women flew such World War II combat aircraft as the P-47 Thunderbolt, the P-51 Mustang, and the B-24 Liberator bomber.

They were members of the WASPs (Women Airforce Service Pilots). They flew these aircraft on ferry flights, mostly to training bases or to locations from which they were shipped overseas, like Newark. They also served as test pilots for aircraft coming out of maintenance.

WASPs were not permitted to fly in combat or to fly overseas.

Thousands of miles away, Galina, Ludmila, and Natalya , were flying combat aircraft, too. They were flying the PE-2 twin-engine light bomber that carried a crew of three, and the single-seat Yak-1 fighter. Some also flew the PO-2 wooden biplane trainers later pressed into service as night bombers. The aircraft they flew had the red star of Russia painted on their sides.

The Russian women, a majority of them still in their teens, flew those aircraft in combat. They fought in some of the fiercest air battles on the Eastern Front and some of them saw service in a night bombing regiment that earned the women pilots the title, "Night Witches."

Last month, Alice-Jean, Faith, and Anne, flew to Russia as part of a group of 49 former WASPs, to meet their Soviet counterparts.

Although they had never met before and nearly a half century had passed, it was an emotional reunion. When they arrived in Moscow late in the evening, a group of former Night Witches, bearing flowers, greeted them with hugs and kisses.

The trip was arranged and planned by People-to-People, a Spokane, Wash., organization that sets up trips for groups that share interests with people abroad.

The women attended dinners and visited aviation museums and war memorials. They were like a mutual admiration society. *Pravda*, the Soviet newspaper, carried stories and pictures of the two groups. Some of the Russian women said it was the first time since the war that anything had been done to honor them.

During their conversations, Faith mentioned that she has a helicopter license. One of the Russian women, also a helicopter pilot, invited her to dinner in her apartment. It turned out she not only had dinner, but her hostesses had arranged for her to spend the night with her family. The two women helicopter pilots were joined by an interpreter and they talked into the wee hours of the morning. They had much to talk about.

Both the American and Russian women were familiar with Bruce Myles' 1981 book, *Night Witches*, which tells the moving story of the Russian women combat pilots. It is a stark and poignant account of the awful personal tragedies spawned by World War II. Reading the story of the young girl combat pilots is an unusually emotional experience.

Most were just kids in their teens. A few were married and left young children with grandparents. Their husbands were already at war.

A majority of the girls were tiny. Many sat on pillows when they flew. Some had to have blocks put on the rudder pedals so they could reach them. But they could match skills with any male pilot, and sometimes they had to fight to prove it.

Many were very attractive and they caught the starry eyes of the male pilots. There were many love affairs between male and female pilots separated by constantly shifting assignments. Many of the affairs ended with the death of one or both pilots.

The women had their share of kills and they suffered their share of losses. The loss of any of them weighed heavily on her comrades because close bonds grew between them, but the survivors climbed back in their cockpits to avenge the deaths of their friends.

The Night Witches were sometimes caught in the crisscrossing beams of German searchlights reaching up into the sky like fingers trying to pluck them down to earth and to their deaths.

Although the American WASPs did not see combat, 38 were killed and 32 injured in accidents.

"We flew with no insurance," recalled Faith Richards. "We were civilians, even though we flew military aircraft, so we couldn't get military insurance. And because we were flying military aircraft, we couldn't get civilian insurance. The families of the 38 girls killed in the line of duty had to pay for their funerals, usually with help from her comrades.

"In 1979, the WASPs were granted veterans rights. Now, I can go to a veterans' hospital and when I die, my daughter can get a flag," Richards said.

The WASPs wore military uniforms which they had to buy.

"One day when I was coming into the air base at Romulus, Mich., where I was stationed, an MP stopped me," Starr said. "I was wearing my uniform with the U.S. insignia on the collar. The MP told me I wasn't entitled to wear it and made me take it off."

Both Alice-Jean Starr, who lives in River Vale, and Faith Richards of East Orange, feel women should be allowed in combat. Alice-Jean thinks all young people (that includes women, of course) should serve in the military for two years. Anne Shields of Haddonfield, who also made the trip to Moscow, Leningrad, and Kiev, was unable to join her friends for this interview.

All three are active members of the Ninety-Nines, the international women pilots organization. The most lasting impression of their trip to Russia was the strong feelings expressed by the Night Witches they met. "All we want is never to see war again. We want peace."

A proclamation stating those sentiments was signed by all the women from both sides to be submitted to Presidents Bush and Gorbachev.

6/24/90

WOMEN IN AVIATION INTERNATIONAL

Although the Ninety-Nines, which dates back to 1929, is the oldest and best known women pilots organization, another relatively new group has made extraordinary strides in representing the interests of women, especially those who seek careers in aviation. The organization, Women in Aviation International, had its beginning in 1990. Its major mission was to aid women seeking career opportunities in aviation.

A nonprofit organization, it wasn't formally established until 1994. Its membership today, of more than 15,000, includes corporate pilots, airline pilots, astronauts, maintenance technicians, air traffic controllers, aviation business owners, educators, journalists, flight attendants, high school and college students, air show performers, and airport managers, among others.

The organization now awards as much as $1 million a year in scholarships, in all areas of aviation careers. These grants are sponsored by 25 organizations and companies.

WAI holds an annual conference that has attracted increasing numbers of attendees each year. It has grown in importance as a resource for women in aviation, and its scholarship grants have expanded tremendously.

The following column was an account of the WAI's annual conference in Memphis in 2000.

Maybe you think flying an airliner is a man's job. Talk to Jackie Basinger's seven-year-old son and you'll find out how wrong you are. Jackie is a first officer for Atlantic Coast Airlines, a commuter line that operates as United Express. She has three children, the oldest of whom is a seven-year-old son. One day a couple of years ago she asked her young son if he'd like to be a pilot. His response: "Gee, mom, that's a girl's job." Do you need more proof than that?

Well, there was more proof two weeks ago when Women in Aviation International held its 11th annual conference in Memphis. The first year the conference was held it drew 150 attendees, including spouses and children. This year there were 2,000, not all of them members of the organization, though membership now totals 4,300.

Two New Jersey members who attended were Lynn O'Donnell of Denville, who flies a 747-400 for United Airlines, and Linda Sollars of Kinnelon, a pilot with Atlantic Coast Airlines. They were both quite impressed with the progress women have made in aviation. Twenty-five years ago the airlines wouldn't talk to women about flying jobs. A woman in the cockpit was unthinkable.

At this year's conference, 18 of the more than 100 exhibitors were airlines. They were there to recruit women. It is not all that unusual today, for airlines or commuters to have all-women cockpit crews.

The conference's general session featured an address by Eileen Collins, the first woman space shuttle commander. She commanded the flight of the Columbia last July that deployed a telescope to study exploding stars, quasars, and black holes. It was her third space mission.

Among the many other notable women at the conference were Jerrie Cobb, one of the world's most decorated women pilots, and Patty Wagstaff, aerobatic champion and air show star. There were many WASPs and women who have participated in the Air Race Classic.

The conference is an inspiration to women who have found or are aspiring to find, careers in aviation. Four years ago, when Linda Sollars attended her first conference, she was working on Wall Street and doing very well. The conference inspired her to seek a career in aviation eventually resulting in her becoming a commercial pilot.

The event provides dozens of seminars offering an opportunity to meet other women in aviation, to learn from their experiences and to establish meaningful friendships.

One of the highlights of the conference is the closing awards banquet at which the scholarships are presented. When the program was initiated in 1997, $11,000 in scholarships were awarded. This year, 46 scholarships worth $461,570 were handed out.

Linda won scholarships in both 1998 and 1999. In 1998, she won the $6,000 Cessna Citation Maintenance Scholarship, sponsored by Flight Safety International. In 1999, she won a Boeing 737-200 type rating from United Airlines worth $10,000.

There were 1,300 people at this year's awards banquet. "The accomplishments of the women in the room at that banquet just blew me away," said Lynn O'Donnell, who, as a 747 pilot, has not done badly herself.

Lest you get the wrong impression, Women in Aviation International, founded by Peggy Baty, who has been a leader in aviation education, is not an organization for women pilots alone. Its membership roster includes mechanics, controllers, aeronautical engineers, women in aviation sales and in manufacturing, astronauts, flight attendants--and even some men. Nobody could have dreamed of this 25 years ago.

3/26/00

AMELIA EARHART WAS MUCH MORE THAN A PIONEER PILOT

I think it is fitting to close this chapter on Women in Aviation with a pioneer woman pilot who was the symbol of women's accomplishments in the golden days of flight and whose name is still the most highly revered of all women pilots, Amelia Earhart.

There are many books about her, but the column I have chosen is based on a book written by her sister.

I think it is an honest and accurate account of the woman who achieved such fame before her untimely disappearance on an around-the-world flight that was to be her last adventure.

One of the most magical names in aviation is Amelia Earhart.

There are two reasons for this. One is the extraordinary courage displayed by this aviation pioneer, in her solo flight across the Atlantic in 1932, the first flight from Hawaii to the mainland in 1935, and a record-setting flight from Mexico City to Newark just a few months later.

A second reason her name holds such magic is the mystery surrounding her disappearance on an around-the-world flight in 1937. A mystery is always intriguing.

The Amelia Earhart biography, "Amelia, My Courageous Sister," written by Muriel Earhart Morrisey (with Carol Osborne).

Martin Balk photo

There is no shortage of books about Amelia Earhart. Most of them deal with her disappearance, research on the subject, and theories. Few of them tell very much about the woman who inspired so many headlines in her short lifetime.

There is a new book that does just that. And it was written by a woman eminently qualified to write on that subject, her sister, Muriel Earhart Morrisey, in collaboration with aviation historian, Carol L. Osborne.

Even if they ignored all the achievements that won her worldwide fame and admiration, there's still the story of a fascinating, many-faceted woman. She had been a teacher, a nurse, a magazine writer, and a social worker. She even wrote some poetry.

She was a champion of the underdog. She loved animals and tried to intervene when she observed cases of cruelty to animals. She advocated social reforms long before such programs gained any kind of acceptance.

Amelia and her sister Muriel--they called each other "Meelie" and "Pidge"--were tomboys during their childhood days in Kansas.

They lived through good times and bad during their early years and Muriel reveals incidents that provide an intimate insight into the character of the woman the world knew only in headlines.

She was a woman who actually didn't like being in the headlines and would much rather fight for the principles in which she believed than take credit for accomplishments that she felt were more deserved by others.

When she became the first woman to cross the Atlantic by air (as a passenger), for example, she captured most of the attention, although she felt rather strongly that she didn't deserve it, since she was only a passenger and she felt the credit should go to the pilots.

Perhaps her modesty and compassion came from a somewhat unstable home life. Her mother's parents were opposed to their daughter marrying Edwin Earhart. He was a lawyer, but they felt his earnings were too meager. (Their maternal grandfather was a well-known judge.)

They lived through lean years, but as youngsters that didn't seem to affect them very much. And then their father's fortunes turned when he was hired by a railroad company as a claims lawyer and finances improved considerably.

But just when things were looking up, their father fell victim to the bottle.

One of the most moving incidents described in this book took place during that period.

Both girls were looking forward eagerly to attending a church party to which two boys whom they knew through church activities, had encouraged them to come.

Their father had promised to take them to the party, as was the custom. The boys would escort them home. And their father had promised to dance once with each of them. Sometimes, it seems, the boys were a little slow to ask the girls to dance.

"He was a beautiful waltzer," Muriel writes.

They were assured by their father that he would come home in plenty of time to have dinner, bathe, and dress by 8 o'clock.

Dinner and hot water were ready and waiting at 6 o'clock. By 7 o'clock the food was dried up, the bath water was getting cold. Amelia and Muriel were still at the window watching for him.

Seven thirty came and went, then 8 o'clock. He showed up at 9 o'clock. They never got to the party.

Later in the evening they heard the voices of the boys who would have escorted them home, as they passed the house.

Several years later, their parents were divorced.

Amelia was a very sensitive and compassionate woman. While she was visiting her sister, who was attending college in Toronto, she saw many wounded soldiers. She was attending school in Pennsylvania at the time and immediately left school and took a Red Cross course in first aid and became a volunteer at a military hospital.

After the war, Amelia enrolled as a pre-med student at Columbia University and Muriel went to Smith College.

Amelia did well, but in 1921 she began to take flying lessons that set her on a course she followed the rest of her life. She never returned to Columbia after the first year.

One insight into Amelia's character is reflected in a poem she wrote during an emotional period when she rejected a proposal of marriage. She called the poem, "Courage". It began with these lines:

Courage is the price which life exacts for granting peace
The soul that knows it not, knows no release
From little things
Knows not the livid loneliness of fear
Nor mountain heights where bitter joy can hear
The sounds of the wings

The book is filled with family photographs, photos of newspaper clippings, documents, and personal letters.

The final chapters are devoted to a detailed documentation of all that is known about the flight on which Amelia Earhart was lost.

Her sister discounts most of the theories. She believes they ran out of gas when they couldn't find tiny Howland Island and went down in the ocean.

It is doubtful we will ever know for sure just how that flight ended. But you will certainly know a lot more about the woman who became an American hero by the time you finish this volume.

Amelia, My Courageous Sister was published by Osborne Publishing Incorporated in Santa Clara, Calif. and distributed by the Aviation Book Company in Glendale, Calif.

4/3/88

Chapter 18

Blacks in Aviation

One of the more dramatic stories of World War II was one which, for a long time, was swept under the rug.

When the Japanese attacked Pearl Harbor thousands of young men left their jobs, their schools, their families, to enlist in the service of their country. That was no secret.

But there were hundreds of worthy young Americans eager to serve their country who were turned away. These were men who wished to become combat pilots. They were turned down not because they were unqualified, but because top Air Force brass concluded, without giving them an opportunity to take tests to indicate their capabilities, that they were not capable of becoming pilots. Why? Because their skin was dark.

Eventually a flight training school for black pilots was established at the Tuskegee Institute, a black college in Alabama, and some 900 black pilots were trained there. They became known as the Tuskegee Airmen and formed their own fighter group, the 332nd, that established an incredible record. Flying as fighter escorts for bombers there were very few aircraft lost.

Nevertheless, the indignities suffered by these men were almost beyond belief. But these men carried on in spite of it.

It wasn't until years after the war, after many of these former combat pilots speaking all over the country, mostly to local groups, that they drew attention to their plight. A television film was made telling their story. It was a powerful piece and it was aired numerous times. Several books were written about the Tuskegee Airmen.

I spoke to many of them and I wrote a number of columns about them. I am including several of those columns in this chapter because I think their stories are incredible and deserve to be told again and again, and again.

THE ULTIMATE INDIGNITY

In retrospect it is hard to imagine the indignities heaped on American servicemen in the uniform of their country. Perhaps none could be more humiliating than the occasion when black Americans, often in officers' uniforms, were put off trains so their seats could be given to German prisoners of war.

"**I** cried when I saw it," the aging veteran said.

Ed Jenkins of Montclair was talking about the HBO film that aired several weeks ago recounting the experiences of the Tuskegee Airmen, the black pilots of World War II, who had to fight for the right to fight for their country.

Jenkins was one of those men.

George Wanamaker who lives within walking distance of Jenkins, is another. His reaction to the film that revived memories of experiences more than half a century ago, were similar.

"My daughter was sitting next to me when I watched it," said Wanamaker. "Tears welled up in my eyes."

Tuskegee Airmen Ed Jenkins, left, and George Wanamaker, hold a copy of "Lonely Eagles," a book about the black fighter pilots of World War II.

"I had been through some of the same things shown in the film," said Jenkins. "One of my friends was killed in an accident. I saw the crash. I didn't know who it was at the time. I had to gather up his things and send them home. He was from my hometown, Montclair."

There was a scene in the film where black inductees were put off a train to make room for German prisoners of war. Both men recalled similar incidents happening to them. "I was scheduled to go overseas," said Jenkins, "and I got a pass to go home to see my mother in Nutley before being shipped out. I was in an air conditioned car. At Florence, S.C., I was ordered to get off. 'You're not supposed to ride in this car,' I was told. 'This car is for white people.'

"I looked back at the people in the car. They were all German prisoners. I was in my officer's uniform, wearing my lieutenant's bars and wings.

"I was put on a Jim Crow car, the first behind the engine. All the smoke and cinders blew in that car. It was very dirty and dingy. By the time we got to Charleston I was covered with soot."

Wanamaker recalled an occasion when he was put off a train.

The two New Jersey men first met at Tuskegee. "I was having trouble with my formation flying," said Wanamaker. "My instructor asked if I knew Mr. Jenkins. I said, 'No.' He said, 'Ask him to give you some pointers.' "

Wanamaker contacted him and they set up a date to fly. "I flew with him," said Jenkins, "and he did okay."

Jenkins who had two years of pharmacy training at Howard University before he enlisted in the Air Force to become a pilot, got his chance to earn Air Force wings by an unusual twist of circumstances. Initially, he was rejected for pilot training.

"A doctor who examined me when I went to Whitehall Street in New York to enlist said there was something wrong with my heart. He said I could go to Tuskegee, but I couldn't fly.

"I worked in administration and I was sent to several schools for administrative training. Then I was sent to Baton Rouge, La. I met a doctor from Texas there who was white and we became quite friendly. I had two years of pharmacy training and we talked medicine.

"I told him my goal was to fly. He said, 'Come to my office. Let me look you over. He examined me and said, 'I don't find anything wrong with your heart.' He got me on orders separating me from my job on the base. Shortly after that I was sent to Keesler Field in Mississippi for tests and after I passed them I was sent to Tuskegee.

"The outfit I had been with in Baton Rouge went overseas and was wiped out."

George Wanamaker worked at the Picatinny Arsenal as an explosive operator. His job was to fill shells with explosives. He earned $6 a day.

"I saw a story in the newspaper that said Negroes were being accepted for the Army Air Corps. I went to Newark and volunteered. I was given a physical and a written test I had already passed. I was worried. What if I didn't pass it this time?" He passed.

Wanamaker was sent to Tuskegee where he became a PAC, or Pre-Aviation Cadet until he got into a class.

Both men took primary training in a Stearman and then advanced into a T-6.

Jenkins had learned to fly at Westfield Airport before he enlisted. But he never told the Air Force.

"I had soloed an Aeronca C-3 after an hour of instruction," he said. "I had 40 hours and got a license. Then I flew with Ed Gorski at Teterboro." Gorski, who had been Amelia Earhart's mechanic, and his wife, Julia, ran Teterboro Airport before World War II.

Both Jenkins and Wanamaker recalled an instructor at Tuskegee named Gabe Hawkins who was very tough on trainees. They referred to him as "The Hawk." He was the major in command. Cadets had good reason to be a little unsettled when they were scheduled for a check ride with him. Passing such a check would put a fledgling flyer on Cloud Nine.

One of the dictums he instilled in his men was, "If you lose an engine on takeoff, don't turn back. Go straight ahead."

As it happened, The Hawk lost his engine one day on takeoff in a T-6 and he turned back. What happened was exactly what he said would happen: He stalled and crashed. Jenkins witnessed the crash.

They pulled him out of the wreckage and got him to a hospital. He needed blood. The Hawk was white. Most of the people on the base were black. They gave him a black man's blood. His wife found out and divorced him.

Jenkins flew P-40s and P-47s. Wanamaker flew P-47s and B-25s. Both were ready to go overseas when the war ended.

But their battle to receive equal consideration, based on their experience and qualifications, didn't end. It continued when they sought employment after their discharge.

"I saw an ad in the paper for oil burner trainees," said Wanamaker. "It said they preferred pilots. Apparently they thought pilots were pretty smart and had mechanical aptitudes. I applied and was told they were looking for people who had pilot training.

"I took out my credentials and the man I showed them to was flabbergasted. He never knew there were black pilots. He said, 'The boss is not in.' They called me the next day and said there were no openings for oil burner mechanics but they could give me a job as a truck driver. "I had two children. I needed a job. I drove a truck for two months. Then I was accepted as a chanceman (probationary policeman) with the Montclair Police Department. I was with the department for 41 1/2 years and retired as a captain."

After the war, Jenkins joined the Air Force Reserve, then flying out of Newark. In 16 years with the Reserve he flew P-51s, C-46s, C-45s, T-28s, and the T-33 and F-80 jets.

Jenkins had seen an ad that said, "Be a pilot and your future will be assured."

"I was training pilots in the Reserve at the time. I went to the airlines. They wouldn't hire me. But they hired all my students."

Jenkins finished his pharmacy studies while he was in the

Reserve. He became a registered pharmacist and had a 34-year career with Roche Pharmaceuticals as a biochemical engineer with a specialty in genetic engineering.

9/17/95

Note: *Ed Jenkins died in June 1998. George Wanamaker died in September. 2006.*

OVERCOMING PREJUDICE

Dr. Roscoe Brown was a Tuskegee combat pilot who flew 68 missions and was the first member of the 15th Air Force to shoot down a German jet. After the war he earned a doctorate in educational research from New York University and he became president of the Bronx Community College.

As part of the Black History Month activities, the New Jersey Aviation Hall of Fame and Museum had Dr. Brown as its special guest speaker. The following piece was based on his talk.

He reminded one of the highly acclaimed Italian film, "Life is Beautiful," that finds hope, even humor, in the midst of the Holocaust, one of the darkest events in human history.

Dr. Roscoe Brown, speaking at the New Jersey Aviation Hall of Fame and Museum at Teterboro Airport for a Black History Month program, found something positive in every road block thrown in the path of African-Americans who wanted to fly for their country in World War II.

Dr. Roscoe Brown

As he recounted incident after incident of prejudice, he shrugged off each one with a declaration, of "that's all right."

He won his wings at Tuskegee and joined the 332nd Fighter Group in which he became commander of the 100th Fighter Squadron. He was made a captain and was awarded a Distinguished Flying Cross and the Air Medal with eight Oak Leaf Clusters.

To illustrate the degree of unconscionable prejudice to which blacks were subjected, Brown told the story of Benjamin O. Davis, Jr., who became commander of the Tuskegee Airmen Fighter Group. When Davis was admitted to West Point in 1932, no student would talk to him. That never changed during his entire four years at the Academy.

Davis lived with that and went on to graduate 38th in a class of 330. He became a member of the first class at Tuskegee Institute that numbered a total of five. He became the first African-American lieutenant general.

Even though they were overseas, fighting for their country, the

Tuskegee Airmen continued to encounter and endure prejudice in many forms.

"One time, " Brown related, "a B-24 bomber was forced to land at our base. We invited the crew to stay with us, but two or three men refused to sleep with us. They decided to sleep in the plane.

"The weather was bad and the temperature dropped to ten degrees. There was no heat in the plane," Brown said. "At two o'clock in the morning there was a knock on the door."

The spirit that helped the Tuskegee Airmen gain flying status prevailed when they were in combat. On one of the missions Brown's squadron was assigned to attack Athens Airport. They didn't come in low enough to hit the aircraft lined up on the tarmac. Wires kept them too high. They returned the next day, flew under the wires at an altitude of 50 feet and destroyed the airport.

On a mission over Berlin escorting bombers, Brown in his P-51 was the last plane in the last group. He spotted three Me 262 jets. He peeled off to the rear, flew under the bombers, came up on one of the Me 262s and opened fire. The plane burst into flames. He and his gun camera saw the pilot bail out as his plane went down. Brown was the first member of the 15th Air Force to shoot down a German jet.

The Tuskegee Airmen flew P-51s with red tails. Bomber crews, many of whom didn't know there were black pilots in those planes, were always happy to see them because it was well known that the "Red Tails" had a sterling record of protecting the bombers they were escorting. Brown flew 68 combat missions. "I was shot at over every capital in Europe," he said, "except London and Paris."

Brown holds a doctorate in educational research from New York University. For 16 years he was president of Bronx Community College. He later served as a professor at NYU and is now a graduate professor at the City University of New York.

2/21/99

HE LEFT A PERMANENT RECORD

Roy LaGrone was a most unusual man. He was a Tuskegee Airman who flew 50 combat missions out of Italy in a P-51. He was also a talented artist.   Before returning to the United States, his commanding officer, Gen. Noel F. Parrish, told him, "You're going to document this." He was referring to the achievements of the Tuskegee Airmen.

After the war LaGrone joined the Air Force Art Program and he did 21 paintings of Tuskegee Airmen for them. One of his paintings depicted the five men in the first Tuskegee class, including Benjamin O. Davis, Jr., who became commander of the famed 332nd Fighter Group and later became the first black lieutenant general.

Most of LaGrone's paintings were portraits of Tuskegee Airmen, usually with the airplane they flew painted beneath the portrait.

LaGrone was a friendly, matter-of-fact kind of guy in spite of his outstanding record of achievements and his special talents. I met and spoke with him a number of times, usually at exhibits that featured his works. He always reflected great enthusiasm for what he did.

For many years he was art director and graphic coordinator for the Robert Wood Johnson Medical School in New Brunswick, N.J.

Roy LaGrone was inducted into the Aviation Hall of Fame of New Jersey in 2001.

There were four inductees that year including Jack Olcott, who had been president of the National Business Aircraft Association for more than ten years. (His story is in Chapter 15.) I wrote profiles of all four inductees, leading off with Roy LaGrone.

The following is the brief profile of LaGrone.

He was studying for a career as an artist when the Japanese attack on Pearl Harbor put a slight detour in his path. But it didn't keep him from reaching his goal. It just added another dimension to his career, a dimension that contributed to the distinction he eventually achieved.

That distinction will bring special recognition to the late Roy LaGrone, an acclaimed aviation artist and Tuskegee Airman who will be inducted into the Hall of Fame of New Jersey in May.

LaGrone was studying art at the Tuskegee Institute in Alabama on Dec. 7, 1941, "a date which will live in infamy." While he was still in school he joined the Civilian Pilot Training Corps and earned his

Roy LaGrone

private pilot's license.

When the Tuskegee Airmen program was established to train African-Americans to fly, he left school, joined the Air Corps and eventually got into the flight training program and became one of the black pilots to graduate in that program.

He flew more than 50 combat missions in a P-51 Mustang, escorting B-17 bombers on missions over Germany. After the war he attended Pratt Institute in New York and went on to study at Florence University in Italy, before launching a highly successful art career. The crowning achievement of that career was a series of 21 paintings executed under the auspices of the U.S. Air Force Art Program, illustrating in oils some of the history of the Tuskegee Airmen of World War II.

2/25/01

ANOTHER VIEW OF LaGRONE

A few years before Roy LaGrone's induction into the Aviation
Hall of Fame of New Jersey, aviation writers, Ann and Charlie Cooper,
wrote a book about him that includes color prints of a couple of dozen of
his paintings.
These are excerpts from a column about that book.

After more than five decades, with many of the leading characters gone, the spotlight is being focused on the story of the black fighter pilots of World War II, the Tuskegee Airmen.

It is a true story, but it has the elements of a novel, strong characters who face obstacles which seem to be insurmountable, persistent struggles, bitter disappointments, but a final chapter in which they prevail.

The story is told in beautiful style by Ann and Charlie Cooper. It deals with a subject that is variously controversial, inspirational, and in the end, rewarding. The reader shares the rewards with the men who earned them.

Titled, *Tuskegee Heroes, Featuring the Aviation Art of Roy LaGrone,* the book is double barreled on two counts. One, it not only tells the story of the black fighter pilots of World War II, but in an opening chapter it tells of the pioneering black pilots who paved the way for future black pilots.

Second, it combines the best qualities of a well-written account of a memorable chapter in the nation's aviation history with the eye-appealing qualities of a coffee table book. It is printed on slick stock, it contains dozens of photographs and 24 plates of paintings and sketches by the late Tuskegee Airman Roy LaGrone, who died in September, 1993.

LaGrone was active in the Air Force Art Program, and he recorded the story of the Tuskegee Airmen on canvas. His paintings are, for the most part, portraits of distinguished members of that group, usually combined with a background scene from their wartime career.

The portrait of Wendell O. Pruitt for example, contains a scene depicting the sinking of a German destroyer by Pruitt and Gwynne O. Pierson, a feat achieved without bombs or torpedoes. They hit ammunition with their 50 caliber machine guns and the ship exploded and sank.

Each portrait is accompanied by a text describing the background and accounts of missions on which they distinguished themselves.

Keith Ferris, one of the nation's leading aviation artists, who had been a good friend of LaGrone, has written a short, "Introduction to the artist" that appears in the front of the book and details his many accomplishments as an artist.

Chapter One of the book details the travails of many early black pilots, including Bessie Coleman, the first black person in the world to become a pilot.

Yet in spite of all the obstacles thrown in their path the Tuskegee Airmen established a remarkable record that is recounted in great detail in this book.

Tuskegee Airmen, Featuring the Art of Roy LaGrone was published by Motorbooks International of Osceola, Wis.

2/23/97

PEACETIME PREJUDICE

The Tuskegee Airmen stories that preceded this column dealt with wartime prejudice. But prejudice did not end with the war. African-Americans faced countless obstacles in the pursuit of their career dreams long after the war to liberate Europe and bring peace back to the Pacific.

Like the story of the Tuskegee Airmen, it has a positive ending because black pilots persisted in their efforts to attain equal treatment and eventually their tenacity opened up doors that had been closed to them.

Today, there are black pilots, both male and female, in the cockpits of the nation's airliners.

The struggle African-Americans had to endure to find their way into the cockpits of those airliners was very much like that which the Tuskegee Airmen suffered. They were not given a chance to prove their capabilities. They were rejected by the airlines solely on the basis of the color of their skin.

In order to dramatize the struggle African-Americans had to endure to achieve their place in airline cockpits, I talked to a black airline pilot who lived through the rejections and frustrations.

His story details the long path laced with obstacles he had to clear in order to make his dream come true.

In the '50s if an application for an airline pilot job had the word black or Jewish on it, there was no chance that individual would be hired, Perry Jones was telling me.

Perry Jones is an airline captain. Perry Jones is black. He knows a little bit about the problems blacks had getting into the flight deck. He learned the hard way.

Jones, who lives in Montclair, is a graduate of Montclair High School, class of 1954. As a member of the track team he held the state record for 800 meters and the county record in 400 meters.

He went on to earn degrees in aeronautical and mechanical engineering from the University of Pittsburgh. Since he had been in the ROTC, he was called up within months of going to work for Lockheed Aircraft. He wanted to fly, but the road to flight school was a bumpy one.

He was sent to preflight training. It seemed he was on his way. He was one of 10 blacks in the class of 240. Before flight training commenced the Air Force said they needed navigators. Of the 10 blacks in the class, all but one were sent to navigators school. Jones went to navigator school.

His first break came when he helped a general's wife prepare for a Christmas party. He met the general who asked him what he wanted to do.

The general told him he had to put in two years as a navigator, but then he would recommend him for the air training command.

In 1962, he went through primary and basic flight training at Big Spring, Texas, in a class made up mostly of Air Force Academy graduates. When he finished, SAC (the Strategic Air Command) needed pilots, so he wound up flying KC 135 tankers. But he wanted to be a fighter pilot.

Perry Jones

Eventually, after flying tankers in Vietnam, he went through F-4 Phantom training in California and he went back to Vietnam where he flew 126 missions out of Da Nang Air Base.

When he was discharged in November 1965, Pan Am was hiring. "On Dec. 6, 1965, I went to work for Pan Am," Jones said. "I flew the 707, which is the same as the KC 135."

Later, he few the L-1011 and the 747. He's flown to every corner of the world. He is currently an Airbus A310 captain.

Many black pilots have had a much harder time breaking into the airline business than Jones. But considerable progress has been made since Jones was hired. There are now 482 black airline pilots in the country out of a total of 50,000, about one percent. There are five black female pilots. Three fly for United, one for UPS, and one was just hired by Delta.

Black pilots still face problems. Many airlines have been laying off pilots recently, and because blacks weren't hired years ago, most of them have low seniority and are the first to be laid off.

The Organization of Black Airline Pilots represents the interests of these pilots and tries to help young minorities realize their potential in aviation and achieve that potential. President of the organization is Perry Jones.

The organization was founded in 1976 by Ben Thomas, an Eastern Air Lines pilot.

Today, the organization has 380 members. The vice president is Larry Parker of Somerset (N.J.).

Parker went to school in Kansas City and worked in the post office at the airport after school.

"One day I was walking through the terminal," he relates. "It must have been in 1968 or '69, and I ran into a black pilot who was flying for TWA. I stopped and talked to him and said I didn't know they had any black pilots."

That pilot encouraged Parker and kept in touch with him and his parents.

Larry Parker

"I got a job as a lineman," Parker said. "I washed airplanes and did all kinds of jobs. I worked for some flight lessons and I paid for some.

"I went to Penn Valley College in Kansas City where they had an aviation program. Then I worked as a TWA flight attendant for five years. My goal was to be a pilot. TWA people encouraged me to fly for a commuter airline.

"I was flying charter out of Republic Airport on Long Island while I was working on my instructor's rating when I was hired by Altair, a commuter line." In time, Parker became a captain on an F-28 jet.

Then he got a job with People Express where he became a 727 captain. When United Parcel started its own flight department, it went to the Organization of Black Airline Pilots looking for minority pilots. Parker was hired.

His first job was in personnel interviewing prospective pilots. Then he went into flight operations and became a check airman on the 727. Now he is in management as a 747 captain training 747 pilots.

The Organization of Black Airline Pilots has numerous programs to help minority youth achieve the goals Jones and Parker have.

Members go to high schools--predominantly black schools--to talk about opportunities in aviation and ways to take advantage of them.

There are black high schools in Louisville and Houston that have flying in their curriculums and A&P (aircraft and power plant) mechanics courses, Parker related. The Martin High School in Queens is an aviation school that offers A&P courses, and some of its students get flight time at Republic Airport on Long Island. Perry Jones is active in the work at that school.

The Organization of Black Airline Pilots holds an annual week-long convention, always at some hub city. Airlines help sponsor the convention. One day each year is dedicated to local youths. One hundred students--mostly minorities--are taken to lunch where they hear a guest speaker.

Perhaps the outstanding program of the organization is its participation in the summer flying program at Tuskegee, Ala., that was started by the Negro Airmen International, a group made up mostly of general aviation pilots.

At Tuskegee where the black fighter pilots of World War II were trained, they hold a two-week session for 30 to 40 students each summer. It includes both flight and ground school instruction. The cost for each student is about $1,000, including room and board. The Organization of Black Airline Pilots sponsors about a dozen students.

Last year, 17 of the 30 students soloed.

"A female was the top student last year," Jones said. "She's from an inner city school in Detroit. She graduates from high school this year and she's going to the Naval Academy at Annapolis.

"One of the students we sponsored," said Jones, "was Ernesto Perez of Newark. He was a West Side High School student. He's now in Seton Hall University.

"He's the kind of boy you would like your daughter to marry. He is every person's dream," says Jones.

3/10/91

A PIONEERING BLACK AVIATOR

He went where no black man had gone before. And he did it more than once .

He was a medical doctor, but he became enamored with flying. This was in the early '30s, before the advent of the DC-3 and the real establishment of aviation as a viable means of transportation.

If you mention the name Dr. Albert Forsyth, it will not ring a bell with many people, even with many aviation historians. But Dr. Forsyth created aviation history.

In 1933, if you told anyone you were contemplating a flight across the country in a single-engine airplane, they would probably look at you as if you were crazy. If you were black and made the same statement, they would know you were crazy.

But they would be wrong.

Dr. Albert Forsyth

It was a time when a black man couldn't learn to fly because nobody would teach him. But a fellow named Ernie Buehl didn't consider the color of his skin when a young physician named Albert Forsyth said he wanted to learn to fly.

"Most professional men played golf," said Dr. Forsyth, now 88 and a resident of Newark. "But I had an interest in flying. I learned to fly at Somerton (Pa.) Airport with Ernie Buehl. I was one of the first to get a transport license."

Dr. Forsyth became enamored with flying after he flew from the island of Jamaica, where he grew up (he was born in Nassau) to the United States in a Pan American Flying Boat in 1912. "There was no airport in Jamaica then," he recalls.

He came to the United States to go to college. "I went to the Booker T. Washington School at Tuskegee for two years, but they had no pre-med school so I went to the University of Illinois and then the University of Toledo where I graduated."

He received his M.D. and Master of Surgery degrees from McGill University in Montreal.

After he learned to fly, Dr. Forsyth, who had established a

practice with another physician in Atlantic City, bought a Fairchild 24 that he based at Bader Field.

In the back of his mind was the thought of making a series of flights to prove what black people could do. "I developed a plan for three different flights. The first would be from Atlantic City to the West Coast and back. The second would be an international flight from Atlantic City to Montreal. I knew I could get a large gathering to meet me at Montreal because of my McGill connections. The third flight would be from Atlantic City to Nassau, where I was born, and on through the Caribbean and West Indies.

"I had met another black pilot, C. Alfred "Chief" Anderson of Bryn Mawr, Pa., known as "the Father of Black Aviation," when he was on a visit to Atlantic City. He was a real flying enthusiast and a natural and I invited him to go with me."

Anderson agreed and, in 1944, the two men made the coast-to-coast round trip together in Forsyth's Fairchild dubbed, *The Pride of Atlantic City.*

On the trip to California they ran into hail storms, gusty winds, and a lot of rain. "But we flew a strict schedule," Dr. Forsyth said. "We had problems getting over the Rocky Mountains because we didn't have all that much power. Over the Mojave Desert the engine overheated and we couldn't climb. We landed in the desert.

"When we landed in Glendale, Calif., Rochester, from the Jack Benny program was there to greet us. We got a lot of press coverage. And when we came home, 15,000 people came to a parade in Newark for us.

After that trip Dr. Forsyth thought he should have a new airplane to make the next two flights, so he and Anderson flew to Robinson, Mo., outside St. Louis where the Fairchild was traded for a new 90-hp Lambert Monocoupe.

There they met Charles Lindbergh who was at the factory to pick up a 200-hp version of the same airplane.

"He talked to us for an hour. He gave us a lot of advice about our flight."

They flew the airplane to Tuskegee, landed it on a farm and then taxied it up to the grave of Booker T. Washington, where the aircraft was named for the man who founded the Tuskegee Institute.

"In 1934, when we were planning the flight to the Bahamas and the Caribbean, I wrote to President Roosevelt. His secretary wrote back that the President was glad we were going to make the flight because it was in keeping with the Good Neighbor Policy.

"We couldn't afford all the things we needed," said Dr. Forsyth. "We had no radio, no navigation instruments, no turn and bank indicator. Only a compass.

"When we flew from Miami to Nassau, we received a cablegram that said, 'Fly to the lighthouse and make a right turn onto a dirt road.' They wanted to know when we were going to arrive. The editor of the newspaper there arranged with the authorities to let us land. They had to cut telephone and electric wires so we could get in. We were the first to set a land plane down in Nassau.

"People had little faith in black flyers," Forsyth said. "Before we left Miami, the airport manager called me over. He almost had tears in his eyes. He said, 'We're going to leave the lights on at Miami Airport so if you can't find Nassau, you can come back.' " They found Nassau.

From there they flew to Cuba. "President Batista invited us to visit him and he treated us royally." Dr. Forsyth recalled.

They next landed on government grounds in Jamaica. There were thousands waiting for them including Pan Am officials. Pan Am serviced their plane everywhere they went.

One Pan Am official said, "Dr. Forsyth, that was the finest landing I ever saw anywhere."

They went on to Haiti, the Dominican Republic, Puerto Rico, St. Thomas, Grenada, and Trinidad. On one leg of the flight they flew 600 miles over water.

After that flight, Dr. Forsyth sold his airplane and concentrated all his efforts on his medical practice. He maintained a practice in Atlantic City from 1930 to 1951 and then in Newark until 1978.

Anderson, who is now near 80, is still chief instructor at Tuskegee, a position he has held for 50 years. Among his more notable pupils was the late Chappie James, the combat pilot who became one of the Air Force's top generals.

"He's still teaching flying," said Dr. Forsyth, "and we still talk to each other once in awhile."

6/2/85

Note: *Dr. Forsyth died on May 6, 1986 at 88. C. Albert "Chief" Anderson died on April 13, 1996 at 89. He took Eleanor Roosevelt for a 40 minute ride at Tuskegee in 1941, which led to the establishment of the military training center for black pilots where the Tuskegee Airmen were trained.*

Chapter 19

Learning to Fly

Each spring for 25 years, I wrote a series of three columns about learning to fly. I usually interviewed five students for each column.

My object was to find out why they wanted to learn to fly in the first place and what their reactions were after they got at least as far as their first solo. I wanted to pass their thoughts along to others who might be thinking about taking flying lessons, as well as to the general public, many of whom I thought might want to learn to fly if they knew a little more about it.

A majority of the flight students I talked to told me that learning to fly was something they wanted to do all their lives. But, for various reasons they hesitated, sometimes for years.

There are many reasons for that. For one thing, people are hesitant because they have so little knowledge of what flying is all about. It's an entirely unfamiliar world. For another they have misconceptions about the length of time it usually takes to get a license and what the cost would be.

In many cases, people are afraid to come out to an airport to ask questions because they think they will sound stupid.

In an attempt to overcome these fears and misconceptions I began the annual Learn to Fly series.

I always ran it the first three Sundays after Easter because spring is a time of rebirth. It's a time to get out and try something new after a long winter of cabin fever.

A student had to have soloed to be eligible for inclusion in the column. By that time the student has a pretty good idea of what learning to fly is all about and their experiences can prove helpful to would-be students.

I tried to find students for the series who represented a cross section of the population: a senior citizen, a teenager, a professional, a blue collar worker, a housewife, a secretary, a minority. My goal was to have someone in the series with whom almost any reader could closely identify, as well as to indicate that people from all walks of life and backgrounds learn to fly.

In the series I tried to answer the most frequently asked questions about learning to fly, questions about costs, the time it will take, medical requirements, and both the flight and written exam requirements. The students also talked about the rewards of flying, the beauty of flight, the self confidence it builds, the sense of achievement it provides.

The three-part series I have selected for this book ran in 1997. Its subjects include a senior citizen, a computer science engineer, an account manager, a secretary, a businessman, a schoolteacher, a priest, a toxicologist, a student, a ceramic tile specialist, a mechanical designer, and two flight students who learned to fly after overcoming serious health problems. Every year I wonder "What can any student tell me that I haven't heard before?" And every year it's a new experience. The people I interview are always interesting and invariably I hear comments that put learning to fly in a new perspective for me.

FROM 16 TO 50, THEY PURSUE THE SAME GOAL

The first column in this three part annual series features a senior citizen, a teenager 50 years his junior, a French woman who is a computer science engineer, an account engineer, and a secretary.

The column answers a lot of the most frequently asked questions such as how much does it cost, how long does it take, and what is it that gets people started after many years of thinking about it.

It also provides a sense of the broad spectrum of people who are flight students.

—

F rank Toolan is 66. But you wouldn't call him old at 66. It would seem incongruous. There's nothing old about him. Although he is a grandfather eight times over.

Behind his broad smile lies an unbridled bundle of energy, enthusiasm, and initiative. He uses all those qualities to good advantage as a flight student.

Toolan's interest in flying goes way back.

"I built and flew balsa wood models as a kid," he recalls.

What finally got him up in the air after all those years? His wife, Pat.

Knowing he always wanted to fly, she asked him one day, "Why don't you?" He had no ready answer, but Pat did.

For Christmas, she gave him a gift certificate for an introductory flight lesson.

He has now logged 60 hours as a student at Somerset (N.J.) Airport. He's soloed and passed his FAA written exam. He still has to complete the cross country requirements.

But a pilot's license is no longer something he always wanted. It's something he almost has. "People my age feel that our capabilities are not limited," he says. "There's a place in the sky for people my age. Flying opens new horizons."

Pat had a sense of those new horizons when she encouraged Frank to learn to fly.

"She sees flying as a way to visit our children (they have four) and grandchildren (eight) and bringing the family closer together," says Frank. Their children live in North Carolina, Pennsylvania, and Massachusetts.

Toolan who holds a Ph. D. in education from Rutgers University, spent 31 years in personnel with AT&T, then had his own career counseling and placement business.

He now teaches fifth and sixth grade English and social

studies at Shoreless Lake School, a New Brunswick Catholic School.

* * *

Jordan Meek of Lawrenceville is a half century younger than Frank Toolan, but he too, is a flight student.

Jordan, a sophomore at Lawrence High School, had his interest in flying piqued by a simulator flight program on his computer.

"My mom knew I wanted to fly and when somebody she knew started to take flying lessons she thought it would be a good time for me to start," he says. "I was 14."

Turns out it was a good decision. When he reached his 16th birthday on Feb. 13, he soloed at Princeton Airport where he is a student at the Raritan Valley Flight School. You have to be 16 to solo and 17 to get a license.

What does a 16-year-old feel like when he takes an airplane up all by himself for the first time?

"My heart was pounding," says Jordan, "but it was pretty routine."

Jordan, who swims the 100-meter backstroke and 200-meter freestyle on the Lawrence High varsity swimming team, the Central Valley division champs, would like to make flying his career and he's off to a flying start.

***

A lot of people who would like to learn to fly hesitate because of their fear of the cost. They ought to talk to Karine Mule, a student at Million Air Flight School at Teterboro Airport. Mule is overwhelmed at how cheap it is. "It costs half as much here as it does in France," she says with a burst of glee.

A native of France, Mule took some lessons there before coming to the United States. The cost of getting a license here generally runs between $4,500 and $5,000. Dual instruction averages about $70 an hour, solo flight about $50. (These are 1997 prices,) Prices vary, largely due to the type of aircraft used, two-place or four-place, and today gas prices are a factor.

It takes most students a little more than a year to get a license, so the cost is spread out over that period.

Another difference in this country compared to France is the attitude toward women in the cockpit.

"I wanted to become a commercial pilot," said, Mule, "but there's more discrimination against women pilots in France than in the United States. (A switch from the early days.)

"I took the army tests for flight training. I did better than a lot of the men. But I was not accepted. I was told the quota for women was filled. Many of the men accepted did not do as well as I did."

Mule's introductory flight at Million Air was a gift from her husband for their first anniversary. She has now completed almost all the requirements for her private license.

She works as a computer science engineer, "but the idea of a career as a commercial pilot is still in my head," she says.

***

What inspires people to learn to fly? A surprising number of people have hidden in their subconscious, a latent desire to do so. There are many factors that bring that desire to life.

One of the most common is a gift certificate for an introductory flight. A close second is the experience of flying with someone else.

For Jerome Rifino of Dunellen, an account manager for Digital Equipment, the latter was the route to the pilot's seat. His father, a World War II fighter pilot, is still an active general aviation pilot. Young Rifino had flown with him in his Piper Cherokee many times.

One day last spring, after a flight with his father, he said, "This is the time to do it." The next day he took his first flight lesson at Solberg Airport.

To start with, it was a new experience because his father's Cherokee is a low wing airplane, and his first flight lesson was in a Cessna, which is a high wing airplane. He had never flown in a Cessna before. But after only ten hours, he soloed. That's far less time than most students require, but he had learned a lot from his dad.

"It was very exciting," he said. "The first solo landing was the best I ever made. My father was at the airport to watch me."

***

It was a flight with a friend's husband that brought Jennifer Codding of South Amboy, a secretary for a construction firm, to the pilot's seat.

"We took off from Old Bridge Airport," she said, "and we flew up the Hudson River past Manhattan and then back down and along the New Jersey shore."

That flight convinced her she'd like to learn to fly.

Last August she took her first lesson at O'Brien Aviation's Flight School at Old Bridge Airport.

"My first flight lesson was very exciting. I thought it would be a long time before I did anything. But the first time I sat in the airplane I taxied, and once we were in the air I did turns and climbs and descents. Flying was much more exciting when I was doing things myself."

Codding flies on weekends. Every Monday morning when she gets to work, everybody in the office wants to know what she did this week.

Her husband doesn't fly, "but he thinks it's real neat that I'm learning," she says.

4/6/97

HEALTH PROBLEM DIDN'T HOLD THEM DOWN

The first interview in this second column in the 1997 Learn to Fly series is about a man who's 30-year-old dream of flying was seemingly grounded when he was struck by a heart attack.

If you have heart problems, you can't get an FAA medical and without that you can't get a license, and if you already have one and you lose your medical, which needs to be renewed regularly, your license is invalid.

Albert Harmon is proof, however, that if you have a health problem, you shouldn't surrender too quickly. He underwent procedures that restored his health and he went on to pursue his longtime dream.

He is not alone. Another student in this column is a woman whose health problem was overcome by flying. It's another example of the fact that what may appear to be insurmountable obstacles can be overcome.

It's a good lesson even without the aviation overtones that were pertinent in these cases.

Y ou can't keep a good man down.

Albert Harmon of Montclair is proof of that. Two-and-a-half years ago he had a heart attack and his dream of flying that goes back more than 30 years, to his days as a student at George Washington University in the Nation's capital, went up in smoke.

At the time of his heart attack he had an angioplasty and artereotomy. The thought that he would never be able to realize his decades old dream was tough on him psychologically.

A year ago, he went for a stress test. "The cardiologist, who was a pilot, told me I was in great shape. He said I could pass the Federal Aviation Administration's medical."

The FAA medical examiner could not issue him a medical certificate on the spot as is normally the case when the exam indicates everything is okay. Because of the heart attack all of his records had to be sent to the FAA's medical center in Oklahoma City for review.

A few weeks went by before his medical certificate arrived. "It was one of the happiest days of my life," he said. Because of his heart attack, Harmon must take a thallium stress test every year in order to keep his medical valid.

Last June, Harmon enrolled in the MacDan Aviation Flight School at Essex County Airport. It was the culmination of a dream that started when he tried to enlist in the Marine Aviation Cadet Program in the 1960s. He was turned down because his vision didn't meet Marine standards.

That is history. Private pilot medical standards are not as stringent as those of the military. He has now soloed and is working on the required cross country flights.

Harmon is an independent member of the New York Stock Exchange. He trades on the floor for companies that don't have a seat on the exchange. It's a chaotic, stressful job. Flying is the perfect antidote. He describes it as "a serene experience."

***

Pat Holden of Carteret is another flight student who had a health problem, one that seemed impossible to cure--until flying cured it.

She lost her father in 1944. It was sudden and unexpected. "It left me in a tail spin," she says.

Pat suffered from depression that was affecting her life and that of her two children.

"I went to a counselor," she relates. "The counselor said, 'What do you want to do with your life?' I told her, I'd like to fly. She said, 'Well, do something about it.' I did."

She went out to Alexandria Field in Pittstown and started taking lessons. "The minute we took off on the first flight I felt a feeling of total exhilaration and freedom," she said.

Pat had worked for Eastern Air Lines reservations for 16 years. Then she worked for a travel agent and following that she taught travel courses in a business school.

In 1988, she went to work for the City of Carteret (N.J.). She serves as Community and Economic Development Director, helping senior citizens who have problems they can't handle and she writes grants for housing and rehabilitation.

She soloed last July. "When I looked at the empty seat next to me I said, 'Okay dad, you're right here with me.' When I got down I couldn't get the smile off my face. Flying brought me back to being me."

Her children, Katie, 17, and Ty, 15, both outstanding students and athletes, are thrilled about their mom's flying. "It's great to have mom back," is the way they put it.

***

Warren Saunders of Westwood had a different reason for learning to fly. Warren is a partner in a business that provides sales and service for computer controlled laboratory instruments that determine the chemical components of substances. His work entails long hours on the road. The business is expanding throughout the East Coast which will mean even more travel.

He is married and has one child. "I don't like the overnights," he says. "I wanted to be home with my wife and 5-year-old son.

"My office is near Teterboro Airport. I pass it every day. One day I said, 'Why don't I pull in and ask questions?' I did. I went to Air Fleet Training Systems and asked a lot of questions. And then the instructor asked me a question. 'When do you want to start?' I said, 'Tomorrow.' That was last October."

He soloed in November. "That's something no pilot ever forgets," he says.   "There's a great feeling of accomplishment in knowing you can do it. It's a confidence builder."

It won't be long now before he has his license and then he's looking forward to buying a plane so that he can expand the range of his business and still be home with his family most nights.

***

Bud Thomas of New Egypt, an electronics technician for the Justice Department, caught the flying bug on a business trip to the Caribbean. He was in Puerto Rico and had to make a trip to St. Thomas and St. Croix. He took a small plane.

"The view of the islands and the water was beautiful and that got me interested in learning to fly," he says.

"My wife gave me a gift certificate for an introductory flight as a birthday present. That convinced me I wanted to do it.

"I started flying with O'Brien Aviation at Lakewood Airport last spring. I didn't know what to expect, but I handled the controls on my first lesson

"There's a lot more to it than you would think. Landings are the hardest thing to learn, but on Jan. 29, my instructor got out of the airplane and she said, 'Go.' I made three solo takeoffs and landings."

Thomas would like to fly to Canada and the Caribbean with his family when he gets his license. He has two daughters, 2 and 6. His 6-year-old told him she would like to fly with him. The 2-year-old hasn't discussed it with him yet.

***

Joyce Watson, a schoolteacher in Yardley, Pa., says, "I knew 20 years ago when I went for a flight with a relative, that learning to fly was something I wanted to do."

She finally did it last year when she soloed on May 31, her 46th birthday.   She is a student at Ronson Aviation, at Trenton Mercer Airport.

"I started in the summer of 1995," Watson said. "My daughter was a teenager and more independent. The time was right."

Watson nourished her interest in aviation and space in 1995 when she went to the Teachers Space Camp in Huntsville, Ala., where she went through space simulation.

"The emphasis," she said, "was on how to bring that back to the classroom."

She did that by organizing a Young Astronauts Club which meets once a week during the lunch recess.

She was invited to Washington, D.C., last summer to take a three credit course given by the University of Alabama at Huntsville. The class visited with congressmen on the aviation subcommittee, then went to the National Air and Space Museum, the Naval Academy in Annapolis, Md., and the Goddard Space Center in Greenbelt, Md.

Her pupils, gifted students in grades one through five, are fascinated by her accounts of these experiences, but they're most excited by the fact that their teacher is learning to fly and has soloed. "I let them know I'm still learning," she says.

Watson's 15-year-old daughter has been a big booster. She sat in the back seat during one of her mom's lessons. "Sometimes I get discouraged, and she encourages me," she said.

And she continues to encourage her students' interest in aviation.

4/13/97

PICTURE A PRIEST TUMBLING AROUND IN THE SKY

A priest, a 71-year-old retiree, a teenager, a toxicologist, and a ceramic tile specialist, a pretty diverse group, are the subjects of the final article in this Learn to Fly series.

Flying is such a lofty experience that it's difficult to describe. Every student you talk to sums it up in his own personal way. "From a small plane you can really see the beauty of the earth," said Father Don.

"It's an uplifting experience," said Gabriella Adam-Rodwell.

"Flying is a great feeling. There's nothing like it," said Michael Maskileyson.

"Once you become introduced to it, it becomes a way of life," is the way John Anaeiros summed up his feeling about flying.

"I don't need a destination. I just like to fly," said Dave Freiberger.

The column that follows tells a little more about this diverse group of flight students.

Father Don Sheehan

Father Don Sheehan, pastor of St. Mary's Roman Catholic Church in Dumont, has a smile that projects warmth, compassion, gentleness. So when he talks about doing loops and rolls in an old Stearman biplane, it makes your eyebrows rise.

But that's only the beginning.

Those loops and rolls go back two years. He's come a long way since then.

It started when Father Don's friend Jim Culligan, a retired Eastern Air Lines pilot, invited him for a ride in a Stearman biplane and then tumbled it around the sky a little bit. "I thoroughly enjoyed it," said Father Don.

Flying was not something altogether new to him. "Twenty-five years ago, I used to go for rides at Teterboro Airport." he said. "I loved it. I wanted to learn to fly. What finally made it happen was my relationship with Jim. I had a lot of confidence in him and he gave me my first few lessons.

"I can remember reading, *God Is My Co-Pilot,* and *Into the Wind* when I was a kid. I was intrigued about what makes a plane fly."

Father Don is now a student at Lincoln Park Aviation Flight School at Lincoln Park Airport. He soloed last July. When his instructor got out of the airplane and told him to do three takeoffs and landings, he recalls, asking himself, "Why am I doing this?" His answer: "Because I want to. Flying is an experience," he says. "There's a sense of accomplishment.

"I'm doing this for the sheer joy of it. It's so different from the ordinary experience. I love the exhilarating feeling of looking down on the world below. From a small plane you really can see the beauty of the earth, especially around here with the lakes and hills.

"I like the challenge and the rewards of flying. I'd like to encourage kids to have an interest in aviation."

Of his own flying he says, "It's a gift from heaven and Jim Culligan."

***

Gabriella Adam-Rodwell of Hillsborough, a toxicologist at Colgate-Palmolive's Technical Center in Piscataway, is not one to take a back seat in anything she does. Her husband, also a toxicologist, has been a pilot since 1981 and she's done a lot of flying with him.

"One day," she relates, "I said, 'It's my turn now.' "

Her husband told one of the instructors at Central Jersey Regional Airport in Manville that she was thinking of learning to fly.

"The instructor lit up with enthusiasm," says Gabriella. "I asked her, 'If I don't have what it takes, will you tell me?' 'You better believe I'll tell you,' she said."

You don't have to talk to Gabriella very long to know that she has what it takes. And you come to understand what she means when she says she doesn't take a back seat.

Born in Romania, she earned a Ph.D. there before she came to this country. But people made her feel that her degree didn't count because she got it in a socialist country.

So she went to the Medical College of Ohio and earned another Ph.D., this one in medical sciences.

Gabriella soloed in November, an event she describes as, "an uplifting experience."

"I could do other things with my money," she says, "but I wouldn't have the same satisfaction. It's worth it."

***

Like Gabriella, Michael Maskileyson of Wayne, came to the United States from a socialist country. He was born in Riga, Latvia, formerly a part of the Soviet Union. Michael, who is 17 and a senior at Wayne Hills High School, came here when he was 10. His interest in aviation came from looking up at the sky.

"I watched big jets flying over and I thought, 'I'd like to fly one of them,' " he says.

That thought brought him to the Caldwell Flight Academy at Essex County Airport.

His father, a software analyst, does a lot of flying in commuter planes. When Michael went for his introductory flight, his dad rode in the back seat of the Cessna 172. It was Michael's first flight in a single-engine airplane.

"It was a weird feeling the first time," he says, "but I liked it. My father loved it. He said this was much better than the commuters.

"Flying is a great feeling," said Michael. "There's nothing like it. I think a lot of people don't understand that. But that's because they have a lot of misimpressions about flying."

Michael will be studying computer sciences at Fairleigh Dickinson University in Madison (N.J.) in the fall. He would like to get into police work eventually.

He's given up the idea of flying one of those big jets because it takes too long. But he hasn't lost his enthusiasm for flying. That's soaring as high as ever.

***

John 'Shake" Aneiros, a ceramic tile specialist, who has his own construction business, remembers walking to the airport when he was a kid to watch the airplanes. But when he was a teenager, he was into motorcycles instead of airplanes.

Last spring he sold his motorcycle to buy tools for his business. But it left a big void in his life.

"I needed another activity," he says. "So I walked into TR Pegasus Flight School at Greenwood Lake Airport. I asked questions. I got answers.

"I came back a few days later to take my first flight lesson. It was the most heart-rushing, adrenalin-pumping experience I ever had. And I rode a motorcycle since I was 13. I knew I wanted to fly."

"Shake," who got his nickname when he was an amateur boxer at Lou Costello's Gym in Paterson, (his record was 15 and 7), hung around the hangar where Tom Steeves and Ron Gertsen, owners of TR Pegasus, rebuilt aircraft, largely of World War II vintage.

"One day they were spray-painting," he says, "and they showed me how to do it. The next thing I knew I was coming in after work and on weekends spray-painting."

He sums up flying like this: "Once you become introduced to it, it becomes a way of life."

***

Dave Freiberger, 71, of Stillwater, got into flying as a result of a new type of license introduced by the FAA a couple of years ago, the recreational pilot's license. It's easier to get than a private pilot's license, but it has a number of restrictions.

Cross country flights are not required, radio navigation instruction is not required, nor are night landings.

As a result the recreational pilot is restricted from night flight, from landing at towered airports, and from flying more than 50 miles from the point of departure, a restriction that can be extended with special permission and which may be amended.

Also the recreational pilot cannot carry more than one passenger and cannot fly any aircraft with more than 180 horsepower.

For some people, however, that's perfect. Dave Freiberger is one of those people.

Freiberger retired after 20 years as a mechanical designer at the Picatinny Arsenal, where he still works 20 hours a week. He doesn't want to fly at night and he doesn't need to fly to far away places.

"I don't need a destination," he says. "I just like to fly."

He's taken training in Piper Cubs and Aeronca Champs (tail wheel airplanes) at the Andover Flight Academy at Aeroflex-Andover Airport. That gives him an advantage over most pilots who learned to fly in aircraft with nose wheels and have never flown a tail wheel aircraft.

Actually, a tail wheel aircraft takes a little more skill to land and the pilot who has never flown one has to take training to get checked out. Freiberger flies several times a week for the sheer joy of flying.

He likes to recall the day he first soloed. "My instructor said, 'Hey, you feel like doing it yourself?' I said, 'I thought you'd never ask.' "

And he'll tell you, he is very glad he was asked.

4/20/97

Chapter 20

Business Aviation

Businesses have spread their wings over the past couple of decades. Years ago, most major companies were confined to a single location. Today, many of those companies have plants all over the country and, in many cases, all over the world. Top executives need to be on site at these widely spread facilities to oversee and monitor their activities on a regular basis. There is no way they can do this except by business aircraft. Aircraft have, therefore, become one of the most important tools a company can have.

Airlines were once widely used by corporate executives, but they no longer serve their needs. Executives' time is money and airline travel today wastes a lot of time. It is necessary to get to the airport hours in advance. The executive can't travel at the time that's convenient to him or her but at the time the schedule dictates. The hub and spoke system frequently makes direct point-to-point flights impossible. A stop is often required and can even involve a time-wasting layover or a change of planes.

Using business aircraft the executive can leave when he or she wishes. He or she can fly directly to their destination. No stops. No changing planes. Often it is possible to visit more than one facility in a single day and be home that same night where using airline schedules might make it impossible to return the same day even with a single destination.

This has given birth to a multibillion dollar business aviation industry that employs hundreds of thousands of people. The industry includes aircraft manufacturers, charter operators, fractional ownership organizations, fixed base operators, who cater to business aircraft, maintenance facilities, avionics facilities, in-flight catering services, and the need for hangar facilities.

Virtually all of the Fortune 500 companies use business aircraft. The National Business Aviation Association, which, as of this writing, represents 7,348 companies that use corporate aircraft, is one of the largest aviation organizations in the country. One of its major functions is promoting safety among its members. There have been years in which business aviation safety records have exceeded that of the airlines.

The stories in this chapter indicate the importance of business aviation to the nation's economic welfare.

HOW A $1,000 AIRPLANE LED THE WAY
FROM $500 IN SALES TO $700 MILLION

I've written many columns about business aviation over the years. I am, however, indebted to Hank Rowan, president of Inductotherm Industries, for the best business aviation story I've ever run into.

It is the story of how a company grew from an initial $500 order to a $700 million worldwide business. Rowan attributes the phenomenal growth of his company in large measure to his use of airplanes.

He started with a used, two-place Ercoupe and through a process of constant upgrading, he wound up flying a Learjet 31. (He was a World War II B-29 pilot.)

I know of no story that proves the value of business aircraft as convincingly as that of Hank Rowan's. This, incidentally, was not a "Wings Over Jersey" column. Twice a year I put out a comprehensive business aviation section for the Star-Ledger. One was in the paper's annual year-end "Outlook" section and a "Top 100" section each September. The aviation section of Outlook filled as many as four pages. This story ran in an Outlook section.

Henry "Hank" Rowan built his first furnace in his garage. His wife helped him assemble it and he was paid $500 for it. This fiscal year Rowan's business will gross somewhere between $600 and $700 million.

Henry "Hank" Rowan, president of Inductotherm, in front of his Learjet 31A at the airport on the grounds of company headquarters in Rancocas, N.J.

To what does he attribute this phenomenal success? In large measure, he will tell you, the growth of his company was the result of his use of an industrial tool called the airplane. He can provide endless illustrations of how aircraft helped his business grow into the world leader it is today.

Rowan is president of Inductotherm Industries, a worldwide group of companies which manufacture electric induction furnaces used principally to melt metals.

Just outside his sprawling headquarters plant in Rancocas, N.J., about 15 miles south of Trenton, there is a 3,850-foot paved runway where many of the company's fleet of a dozen aircraft are based, including the newest addition, a 500-mph Learjet 31 that Rowan flies himself.

Rowan, who had flown the B-29 in the service just before the end of World War II, wanted to test the value of business aircraft when he founded his company. Inductotherm was only a couple of years old when he bought his first aircraft, a used, 90-mph Ercoupe for which he paid $1,000. "I bought it myself because I didn't think the company could afford it," he said.

The first trip Rowan made in that aerial flivver was to the Crucible Steel facility in Syracuse, N.Y. He flew home with a $10,000 order for two 3,000-pound vacuum metal furnaces.

After that experience, he reasoned that if he had an airplane that could move a little faster, he could probably land more business. So after eight months he traded the Ercoupe in for a used Bellanca, a much more expensive aircraft ($6,000) that had a greater range and was considerably faster.

Soon after he acquired it he learned that Corning Glass in Corning, N.Y., had an interest in a special furnace to melt glass in a research lab. Corning was four hours away by car but only one hour by plane.

He called them. "They told me not to come. The issue was closed. I can be there in an hour, I told them. Give me an hour of your time. They said, 'It won't do you any good,' " he related in the large, comfortably furnished sitting area of his office in the Rancocas facility.

After much insistence on his part, they reluctantly agreed to see him. Rowan met with executives there and flew home with the order which was worth $30,000.

Chalk up one more sale to an airplane.

In 1962, Inductotherm added its first flying salesman to the staff. "We hired a salesman who was a pilot and bought him a Twin Comanche. He covered Wisconsin, Illinois, and Indiana, an area he could never have covered without an airplane."

By that time, Rowan himself was flying a twin engine airplane.

Rowan is so convinced of the value of aircraft in building sales that he offered to pay for flying lessons for any of his salesmen who wanted to learn to fly so they could expand the territories they covered and serve their customers better. He offered to buy an airplane for them after they got their license. A half dozen salesmen took him up on that offer and he says the increase in their sales has more than paid for the cost of their flying lessons and an airplane.

The increased sales also meant increased employment, Rowan pointed out. "We employ 900 people in New Jersey. We have plants in Camden and Cherry Hill as well as here in Rancocas. We also have three plants in Detroit and six plants in England, one in Belgium, one in Germany, and one in Italy. We even keep an airplane in Europe

"In 1972, the company hired its first professional pilot. Now, in addition to Rowan, a professional pilot flies the Learjet and professional pilots also fly the piston and turboprop aircraft in the fleet.

The company flies potential customers to the Inductotherm plant to see the operation and to the sites of companies which have installations where they can talk to users of the company's furnaces.

"There is a big advantage to getting the customer to our plant to see our equipment being manufactured, and to learn about our company's culture," says Rowan.

A walk through the spacious plant is an impressive experience. It is as spotless as a medical laboratory, and the employees look immaculate and professional.

"If we were to ask a top executive to visit our headquarters plant, as well as a couple of our customers in distant cities, it would usually involve a three-day trip. You're not going to get a company president to give up three days," Rowan says. "If we send the Learjet to pick him up, we can make the same visits and still get him back home the same day. And he doesn't have to keep looking at his watch worrying about catching the 6:30 flight. He just walks outside the door, boards the aircraft, and is home in an hour or two. With the Lear, we can get the president of the company here and not one of his subordinates."

Rowan recalls that this service was especially successful in one recent transaction. "We picked up a Mexican executive in Texas with the Learjet. He ran the largest foundry in Mexico and we flew him to foundries in Texas and Pittsburgh and finally to our plant here in New Jersey.

"He didn't initially think of us as a likely supplier because he already had several furnaces built by a competitor in Europe," he says.

However, after the trip, the executive placed an order for a 12.5-metric-ton furnace that cost $3 million.

"Many executives think of aircraft as being an expensive

luxury," says Rowan. This businessman, however, has a different philosophy.

"The airplane is a salesman's tool, that can double his coverage and his value to the company. It actually saves money.

"There are savings in airline tickets, overnight stays, car rentals or taxis. And you need less salesmen. When you fly yourself you can almost always land at an airport closer to your customer's plant. And they are always anxious to come out to the airport to pick you up and see your aircraft. It starts things off on a very positive note," he says.

"Aviation has been a key factor in the development and growth of our company," Rowan declared. "Without aviation we wouldn't be the company we are. Our aircraft and our landing strip give us a huge advantage over our competition."

1/29/95

THE BUSINESS AN AIRPLANE HELPED CREATE

It is not a well publicized fact, but there are literally thousands of businesses across the country that were started from scratch and grew into multimillion dollar enterprises that their owners will tell you couldn't have happened without the use of an airplane. The previous story was an outstanding example.

These companies create employment for thousands of people. They pay millions in taxes every year. In many cases they are a boon to local economies. Together, they make an impressive contribution to the national economy.

One fact that should be pointed out is that this couldn't happen without a national network of airports. Airplanes are as useless without airports as automobiles without highways. Yet we are losing local airports on a regular basis as a result of a handful of highly vocal people who choose to live near airports and then complain about the fact that they live near an airport. Often they grossly exaggerate the impact the airports have on their communities that didn't exist when the airports were built. People moved into those communities of their own free will and they are free to leave if they consider conditions intolerable.

Elected officials often take up their cause because they are so persistent and vocal that they create the impression that these people represent great blocks of votes. However, that may not always be the case. They lose sight of the economic benefits these airports bring to their communities. They overlook the fact that in addition to their economic impact, airports have been used in a wide variety of emergencies from flood relief, fire fighting, hurricane rescue operations, traffic reporting, emergency medical services, and as weapons in the constant fight against crime.

I have written many columns about companies whose growth has been attributed by their owners to the use of aircraft. Such stories don't usually get much play in the press so it is understandable that members of the general public and their elected officials are generally unaware of the tremendous contribution general aviation makes to our lives every day of the week. Here is one more example of how an aircraft helped build a business.

"My business wouldn't be where it is today if it weren't for my airplanes," said Stan Rosania of Stockton. Where is his business today? It's at $28 million plus and growing. He started the business from scratch in 1967 with a partner whom he bought out three years later.

Rosania had been a plumbing and heating contractor. The business he heads today is Structural Foam Plastics of North Branch, an injection molder of plastics.

When the business started Rosania had no knowledge of plastics. His partner did. Rosania learned the business and made the most of it.

"I have 12 competitors in the country today," Rosania said. "We're number two.

"A supplier introduced me to flying when he took me to visit a customer in Groton, Conn., in his Cessna Skylane. It took an hour and a half each way. I said, 'This is for me.'

"I started taking lessons at Solberg Airport in 1975. I wanted the availability of an aircraft when I wanted it. So before I had my license I bought a new Cessna 182.

"While I was working on my license, the supplier who introduced me to flying flew me on business trips in my airplane. I learned what an asset an airplane can be.

"I kept my 182 for a year, but then I wanted more capability so I bought a twin Cessna 337. It was faster and could carry more. Also, I did a lot of night flying and I preferred a second engine."

Rosania's business grew, and as it did, so did his airplanes. He's owned eight airplanes, each a step up from the one before. Today, he owns a pressurized Cessna 421, a piston twin and a Citation II Cessna jet based at Solberg.

Each is designed to perform a different mission and frequently both are out at the same time. "I can respond to customers more rapidly by personal visits," said Rosania. "I fly to Mississippi in the Citation, a comfortable range for it, although we have flown to the West Coast several times when we had several people to see out there."

Rosania also visits his other plants in Liberty Center, Ohio, and West Chicago, Ill., and a new one is in the works in Winchester, Ky.

His main plant in Branchburg employs 180 people, more than twice as many as the other two plants combined.

Specifically, how do his airplanes help his business?

"We had a call from IBM in Charlotte, N.C., at 10 o'clock one morning," he recalls. "They wanted to know if we could be there by 3 p.m. to give a quotation that had to be completed that day.

"By 2 p.m. we were in the IBM offices. They wanted front pieces for an ATM machine. It was a brand new project and they had to get it off the ground as soon as possible.

"We got a $300,000 order and there were sizable follow-ups.

We became a preferred vendor because we could respond so rapidly.

"A similar situation arose with the GE Aircraft Engine Group. We designed an in-house material handling pallet to carry heavy engine parts within the plant.

"In that case we had received a call from GE in Cincinnati asking if we could attend a meeting in Detroit that same day to give our input on a new project. Our ability to respond that day gave us an edge over our competitors.

"We were the only vendor able to make the meeting that day. It resulted in a $1.4 million order with follow-ups."

Rosania recounted other examples of how his airplanes have helped his company grow.

There are many other companies that have similar stories to tell.

But constant pressure from anti-airport groups in New Jersey is forcing many of those companies to look elsewhere when they need new facilities. And some have moved out of New Jersey, taking jobs and tax revenues with them.

Every time a company finds a more friendly atmosphere elsewhere for its aviation operations, word gets back here and other companies begin the search.

These companies are run by responsible people who have made a real contribution to the welfare of New Jersey. Many of the airport opponents could hardly be called responsible. Time and again many anti-airport charges have been proven highly exaggerated or groundless.

3/27/94

Chapter 21

Lighting the Fire

Aviation has probably created more career opportunities than any other industry. When people think about aviation jobs, they usually think of only one thing--pilots. Actually, there are hundreds of aviation jobs outside the cockpit, many of them very rewarding and challenging. Aviation needs maintenance technicians, avionics technicians, engineers, designers, dispatchers, meteorologists, airport managers, and a hundred other specialties.

Young people who need to think about their future are generally unaware of all that aviation offers.

There are many people and many organizations dedicated to arousing interest--lighting the fires--in the hearts and minds of young people. The Experimental Aircraft Association had a program to have its members give a million free airplane rides to youngsters by Dec. 17, 2003, the centennial of the Wright Brothers first heavier-than-air powered flight. They achieved that goal about a month before the actual centennial and their Young Eagles program continues to give airplane rides to youngsters. The EAA also has a summer encampment program for teenagers at its Oshkosh home base.

The "Be A Pilot" organization has an active program to attract new students. Working with flight schools they offer special introductory flight coupons that are publicized on cable TV and in print media.

The Civil Air Patrol has a very successful cadet program. And they have a program that offers top cadets the opportunity to solo an aircraft during a one-week summer encampment held at an airport. The Boy Scouts have an aviation division, as well as an aviation badge. Local airports conduct tours for youngsters to bring them up close to general aviation aircraft and explain to them what flying is all about. Many grade school teachers incorporate aviation into their curriculums.

The Ninety-Nines offer aviation scholarships and at least one local chapter we know of holds Annual Student Pilot Forums at which instructors and other knowledgeable people in aviation present information on learning to fly and answer questions for prospective flight students. There are many programs designed to bring the benefits of aviation to the attention of youngsters and to get them involved. The Ninety-Nines and the Women in Aviation offer a wide variety of scholarships. The EAA has its Young Eagles initiative, and the NBAA has its AvKids program. It was announced at AirVenture 2006 that the latter two had merged. AOPA offers educational material for youngsters through its website www.aopa/path

In many cases aviation has been used as a tool for improving student grades. It has also been used to give inner city youths a goal that has lifted them above the bleak and depressing surroundings they find themselves in through no fault of their own. It has been used to help mentally challenged youngsters.

Aviation has grown phenomenally in its first hundred years and there is every reason to believe the pace will accelerate in the next hundred years.

AVIATION MADE HER STUDENTS WANT TO LEARN

Many teachers have discovered that if they incorporate aviation into their curriculums, they can arouse a higher degree of interest in learning many subjects. They have used it, for example, in teaching math. Let's say they give their pupils a problem that states: An airplane flies 150 miles an hour. How far will it travel in two hours and 15 minutes? It has been found many times over that if the problem is stated in aviation terms, the results will be far better than if it was stated in general terms.

Probably no one ever put that knowledge to better use than Margaret Kiernan. And she did it working under difficult conditions. Her students were disadvantaged and mentally challenged. She had a teaching career that spanned three decades and she left her mark. Her dedication and devotion to getting the best they were capable of out of her students, made her stand out among her compatriots. Probably none of her students ever found employment in aviation, but her teaching methods made a difference in their lives and were so innovative they deserve special notice.

They called her the "Grand Lady of Aviation Education" in the state of New Jersey. She spent 34 years in the Newark school system before her retirement last year at 71. For much of that time she developed innovative ways to use aviation to motivate her students, many of them emotionally handicapped.

Example: She obtained a multi-band radio and tuned in the Newark Airport Tower in class.

"I had them write down what they heard," said teacher Margaret Kiernan, "including numbers. That taught them concentration. It increased their attention span. And they picked up phrases like, 'maintain altitude.' "

For the last seven years of her career, Margaret Kiernan taught in the Floyd Patterson High School, a special school for the classified handicapped, which includes socially maladjusted students and

Margaret Kiernan with a paper airplane made by one of her challenged students.

perceptually impaired, that is, those with learning disabilities. This can be a tough assignment. But not for Margaret Kiernan. She always found ways to make it exciting, for herself as well as her students.

Her success in reaching them was graphically illustrated recently when she paid a visit to the school from which she had retired last year. One student after another, spying her seated in a classroom, lit up with excitement and rushed in to embrace and kiss her.

Though she's no longer on the staff, evidence of her work is prominently displayed in the school's front lobby. Hanging from the ceiling are a couple of dozen very simple, elastic-powered balsa wood and tissue Delta Dart flying models made by her students.

"When they make them you can tell if they can follow instructions. You can tell about their manual dexterity. You can even learn if they have a vision problem. If they hold their work very close to their eyes, you know they have a problem.

"You're always looking for new things," said Mrs. Kiernan. "When I got state funding, I began taking them on field trips."

Her students visited the control tower at Newark Airport, Butler Aviation, the general aviation facility at the airport, the Dobbs House airline food preparation facility, Lockheed Electronics in Plainfield, Bendix Aerospace at Teterboro and Weston Instruments in Newark. Some of her students even visited the National Air and Space Museum in Washington, flying down in the morning and back in the afternoon.

Even her vacations were tied in with her work. She used vacation trips to visit the United Airlines maintenance base in San Francisco and the American Airlines Training Center in Dallas, where she saw a flight simulator demonstrated.

On one vacation she visited the Johnson Space Center in Houston. She returned to her alma mater, Purdue University, many times to speak with the people in the aviation department and to visit the aviation archives. She came away with materials to use in the classroom--slides, film strips, photographs, pamphlets, maps, charts.

"You have to go out and get it," she says. "It's not going to come to you."

Her own introduction to aviation came when she was a student at Purdue in her home town of Lafayette, Ind.

Purdue has always had an outstanding aviation program and today it has its own airport.

In 1935, when Mrs. Kiernan was a student, Amelia Earhart visited the campus and addressed the students and faculty.

"I'll always remember her standing there in a navy blue, satin gown. She was very much interested in careers for women and she lectured on that subject at Purdue.

"The Lockheed Electra in which she was attempting an around-the-world flight when she was lost in 1937, was outfitted at Purdue," Mrs. Kiernan said.

"She came to the campus once a month in 1937 as a career counselor," she said.

From 1943 to 1947, Mrs. Kiernan served as a public relations officer in the Navy. During that time she had the opportunity to fly several times in everything from a two-place aircraft to a large military transport.

"My first commercial flight was from Newark to Indianapolis to go home for Christmas in 1938 in a TWA DC-3. I was working as a personnel director at Sears in Philadelphia. My coworkers, knowing I was going to fly home, made a parachute out of a cot-sized sheet and tied it to a basket in which they put a bottle of Mother Sills Seasick Pills.

"Coming back I was on a sleeper. That was an experience. It arrived at 4 a.m. but you didn't have to get up until 7. You were strapped in your berth and you could look out the window and see clouds. How much closer can you get to heaven?

"I was in the upper berth. The man in the lower berth was completely bald. When I climbed out of my berth in the morning, I put my foot right on his bald head.

"I've told my students about these experiences," says Mrs. Kiernan. "You have to make your presentations human."

When she decided to take a friend's advice and go into education, Mrs. Kiernan lacked only one course from getting a permanent teaching license. She took the course at Seton Hall University and insisted on doing practice teaching, part of it in special education. She later earned a master's degree in special education from Columbia.

She has always been active in a host of aviation organizations. For 14 years she was chairwoman of the Aerospace Intermodal Transportation Curriculum Committee for the Newark District.

Among the other organizations in which she has been active is the New Jersey Aviation Education Advisory Council. At a recent meeting of that organization, the Federal Aviation Administration recognized the work and accomplishment of Margaret Kiernan in the form of a bound Certificate of Appreciation.

It addressed her as "The Grand Lady of Aviation' in the state of New Jersey.

12/14/86

COURTESY OF THE CIVIL AIR PATROL

The Civil Air Patrol (CAP) is most often thought of as a search and rescue organization. It is that, but it is much more. It flies human organs for transplants. It also flies missions in emergency situations and participates in disaster relief. And it does conduct search and rescue missions for downed aircraft, lost hikers, and others. Over the years it has saved many thousands of lives. Its operations are conducted solely by volunteers.

A phase of its work that is less well known is its cadet program. In addition to the senior members who are, for the most part, pilots, it has a large and active cadet program. Under this program youngsters are given aviation orientation and ground school classes. They frequently have the opportunity to fly with senior members.

One of the most exciting phases of the CAP's cadet program is a summer encampment program in which select cadets over 16 who have excelled are given the opportunity to solo an airplane.

The CAP was founded in 1941 by the late Gill Robb Wilson, author, lecturer, editor, poet, pilot, minister, and New Jersey's first state aviation director. It was founded to fly volunteer coastal patrols at a time when German U-boats lurked off the east coast sinking many American ships carrying war supplies. Most of the missions were flown out of Atlantic City.

When the war ended the CAP assumed a new role in peacetime that has been equally effective.

In war or peace, its work has always been carried out by volunteers.

Over the years, hundreds of youngsters have been given the opportunity to solo an airplane courtesy of the CAP. Many of these youngsters would never have dreamed of such a thing before they became a CAP cadet. But even then, they had to be the cream of the crop to qualify.

Many of them have gone on to become private pilots after the CAP "lit the fire." And some of them have gone on to become airline pilots, while others have gone to the Air Force Academy and have had rewarding careers as Air Force pilots.

Here is a column which describes the excitement of that program.

S he was soaking wet but what really told the story was not the water dripping off her, but the huge grin spread across her face. When she cut the engine and stepped out of the Cessna 172 at the Lakehurst Naval Aviation Engineering Center, she was greeted by a hosing from one of her fellow students. And for an encore, a couple of other guys in her group dumped a large garbage can full of water over her. All this was by way of welcoming her into the world of solo pilots. What a welcome!

Less than a week ago, Kathryn Fricks, 16, of Toms River, had never handled the controls of an aircraft. Now, she had just completed three solo takeoffs and landings.

Kathryn was one of seven Civil Air Patrol cadets who soloed during the 13th New Jersey solo encampment. (An eighth cadet in the group was prevented from soloing by bad weather on the last day.)

These seven brought to 151 the number of cadets who have soloed since the program began in New Jersey, according to Dick Donica, commander of the one-week encampment.

"In the 13 encampments, only eight cadets haven't soloed," said Donica, who has been with the program since its inception.

That's a rather remarkable record. But these are remarkable youngsters. They are the cream of the crop of 600 CAP cadets in the state.

Take Fricks, for example. A student at Toms River High School, her goal is to be an astronautical engineer. Toward that goal, she would like to study at the Massachusetts Institute of Technology, generally considered the nation's premiere university for the study of mathematics and engineering.

Naturally, only top students are accepted. One of the criteria universities look at closely is the SAT (Student Aptitude Test) scores of applicants. A score of 1,200 out of a top score of 1,600, is generally enough to get a student into one of the better colleges. Kathryn scored 1,500.

Guiding the students through the one-week encampment that includes 20 hours of ground school in addition to the flight time, were six instructors, one of whom, Alex Baldi, was once a cadet in this program himself. All of the instructors are volunteers who take time off from their jobs and donate their services.

The Navy makes barracks available to the cadets at no cost. Cadets pay $90 for the week's encampment that covers food, log books, supplies, and incidentals.

Four aircraft are used, a Cessna 150, a 152, and two 172s. Three of them are owned by the New Jersey Wing of the CAP. One was borrowed from New York.

In most cases, the CAP receives funds from their states. Until last year, all funds for the New Jersey Wing were raised by the cadets themselves. Last year, the state contributed $7,500 for radios and for aircraft expenses

The cadets in the 13th solo encampment, in addition to Kathryn Fricks, were:

- Liesl Breikner, 17, of Toms River, a student at Monsignor Donovan High. Liesl would like to become an MD or a veterinarian. She would also like to get into the Air Force Reserve.
- Peter Carraba, 17, of Manalapan, a graduate of Marlboro High, is going on to the Norwich Military College of Vermont and eventually hopes to become a military pilot.
- Pat O'Brien, 16, of Freehold, is a student at Freehold Borough High. He hopes to get into a military academy or ROTC program. His goal is to fly the F-14 Tomcat in the Navy.
- Joe Martinez, 16, of Wanaque, a student at Lakeland Regional High. He hopes to go to medical school and then get into the Air Force.
- Peter Reed, 17, of Ewing, is a graduate of Nassau Christian School in Princeton. He's taken courses at Mercer County Community College and is entering Parks Air College to study aerospace maintenance engineering.
- Joe Schultz, 17, of Howell, is a student at Freehold Township High. He's hoping to get into the Air Force pilot training program.

The volunteer instructors, in addition to Donica, were Janice Blackburn, like Donica, an Eastern Airlines pilot; Fritz Range, a corporate jet pilot; Bill Reda, a computer science and math teacher at Passaic County Tech., Tom Flieger, an aerospace education teacher at Middletown North High, and Alex Baldi, who has flown for commuter airlines.

8/30/87

GIVING INNER CITY KIDS A CHANCE

Sometimes opportunity knocks and sometimes you have to go out and find it. For inner city kids it doesn't knock very often and if any of them look for it, they discover it's not easy to find.

It did knock, however, for a bunch of inner city kids in Newark when a black minister saw a situation he didn't like and decided to do something about it. What he saw was kids hanging around corners instead of going to school. What he did was to organize an aviation group for them that not only taught them about aviation but taught discipline and helped them with their school work, resulting in much better grades. He had to be pretty persuasive to get these kids off the streets. And he's a very strict disciplinarian.

The youngsters in this group are as disciplined as West Point cadets. When addressed in class by the Rev. Russell White they respond with a loud, sharp, "Yes, sir."

He taught them to do silent close order drills in which they execute a wide variety of marching maneuvers with no audible commands. They memorize the routines that they execute with the highest degree of precision. Rev. White obtained discarded Air Force uniforms that they wear when performing. They frequently perform at public events. They practiced for many hours on one of the streets in the inner city.

Rev. White believed parents should be involved. As a result he conducted classes for parents to keep them up on his programs and to explain their responsibilities.

Some of his cadets have become airline pilots. At least one became a 747 captain. A number of them got into the Air Force Academy and became Air Force officers. It changed the course of their lives for every youngster who participated in that program.

He was a halfback on the Bloomfield High School football team in 1945-46-47. His coach was Bill Foley, one of the finest high school coaches in the history of the sport in New Jersey.

"Russell," he said to his halfback one day, "The world doesn't owe you a thing. If you need something, go out there and earn it. If you need help, somebody out there will help you."

Rev. Russell White of the Bethel Baptist Church in Orange, never forgot those words. The inspiration they provided has lived with him all his life, and the philosophy they expressed has provided the basis for one of the most successful inner city youth programs in the state.

It started in 1977 when Rev. White, who was employed in internal security at East Orange High, found boys hanging around, cutting classes.

Rev. Russell White at the airport briefing some of his Young Eagles students.

He was a student pilot and he took some of those boys out to Morristown Airport with him one day. There they met Fred and Nancy Huykman, who operate the Certified Pilot Center Flight School, and Jerome Lee, an instructor on their staff.

They helped Rev. White form the Eagle Flight Explorer Post 290, a unit of the Boy Scouts of America which offers youngsters ground school and flight training.

The City of East Orange gave the group a grant of $3,200 through its Community Development program. They have received annual grants ever since. This year's grant which the group just received, was $5,000.

These funds, along with other contributions, help provide flight training up through solo for members of the group. If they can, the youngsters also contribute something on their own.

The group today has 37 members, including nine girls.

Since the group was formed, 40 of its members have soloed.

Many have gone on to the nation's top aeronautical schools, such as Embry-Riddle Aeronautical University, the Florida Institute of Technology and the Hawthorne School of Aviation.

Three have gone to the Air Force Academy and a fourth has been accepted.

A number have gone on to become professional pilots. One former member of the group became a pilot with Prinair, an airline operating in the Caribbean. Another is now a captain with Transair, also operating in the islands.

One former member is a pilot with Combs Airways in Denver, and one is a jet mechanic in the Marine Corps.

That's a pretty impressive record, but Rev. White hopes to do better. And he's making progress toward that end.

The Eagle Flight Explorer Post owns its own aircraft, a Cessna 150 based at Hanover Airport. (That airport closed and the airplane was moved to Morristown Airport.)

The airplane was donated by a Rochester, N.Y., businessman who met the group on a trip into Morristown Airport. It's in good shape and the group is using it for training, but it could use a paint job. Don Redpath, manager of maintenance for Falcon Jet at Teterboro Airport has agreed to provide the paint.

The operator of Hanover Airport is providing the post with tie-down space. In return, the group is cutting grass at the field.

One of the instructors at Hanover, Walt Castle, has agreed to donate some time to give flight training.

The post owns a second aircraft, a Piper Tri-Pacer, but this one is not in flyable conditions yet. It was donated by a Silver Springs, Md., man after he saw an item in the EAA (Experimental Aircraft Association) magazine, *Sport Flying*, saying the group was looking for an aircraft.

The fuselage is in Rev. White's backyard. The wings are in a third floor factory loft donated by Manufacturers Village of East Orange.

Ground school is provided for the youths at Rev. White's church every Thursday evening by Victor Alesio, a member of EAA Chapter 730 of Teterboro.

FAA physical exams are provided at no charge for all members when they become 16 by Dr. Eugene Simms of East Orange.

Members of the post have made many field trips to control towers, flight service stations, air shows, and military bases. They were the guests of Dr. Robert H. Max, principal of Clifford Scott High School in East Orange, who serves as wing commander for a transport group at McGuire Air Force Base.

But the most exciting trip they made was to the EAA convention and air show in Oshkosh, Wis., the biggest general aviation event in the world. Last year, 33 members made the trip. This year, 25 are signed up. They rent a bus and camp out at the convention. The group pitches in and does volunteer work at the eight-day show. They are currently soliciting funds to buy a bus of their own. (They did raise enough to buy their own bus.)

At Oshkosh, the group met Paul Poberezny, founder of the EAA, and his son, Tom, executive vice president and one of the nation's top aerobatic pilots.

"They have been very helpful to us," says Rev. White. "If there are any angels, they hang around airports."

Of the members of his post, he says, "If they're willing to try, there are at least 10 people standing in the wings ready to help."

They've had ample evidence of that.

And it's pretty much what coach Foley told White 35 years ago.

6/27/82

THE AIRPORT AS A CLASSROOM

Local airports are seldom thought of as education centers, even though virtually every local airport has a flight school. Many airline pilots began their aviation training at these airports. And many became Air Force pilots.

But there is another phase of aviation education that local airports are involved in that is even more unnoticed. Thousands of youngsters visit airports every year to gain an introduction to aviation. These include school children, Boy Scouts and Girl Scouts, church groups, even preschoolers.

The airport owner or operator or an instructor conducts tours showing the visitors airplanes and airport facilities. They explain airplane controls, take them into the maintenance shop, explain the things pilots need to learn including navigation, weather, and Federal Aviation Regulations.

In some cases, airports have gone a step beyond this. They've invited airline pilots to participate and discuss their careers and experiences and instructors conduct ground school sessions for the youngsters.

Here is an account of a well-organized tour for middle school students.

One of the services local airports offer their communities that you seldom hear about involves their contribution to education. I'm not talking about the flight training offered at these airports. I'm talking about the thousands of tours offered every year at local airports all over the country to students ranging from preschoolers to college seniors.

In a world in which air travel plays such a preeminent role in our transportation system and in commerce, the average person has little awareness of what aviation is all about.

An airline captain speaks to middle school students in a hangar at Somerset (N.J.) Airport.

Most people have never been to a local general aviation airport except, perhaps, on rare occasions to attend an air show or special event where the airport and its every day functions are not paramount.

How are small airplanes used? How far can they fly? What keeps them in the air? What's involved in learning to fly? How expensive is it?

Ask these questions of the average adult and in most cases you would not be able to get answers. Ask the 40 students from the sixth and eighth grades of the Warren (N.J.) Middle School who visited Somerset Airport in Bedminster a couple of weeks ago. They'll tell you.

They got an education from a group of dedicated people who were happy to share their aviation knowledge.

The students were welcomed in a big hangar that still had some airplanes in it, by Mary Sullivan, a pilot and volunteer for a variety of aviation activities, and Ellen Parker, co-owner of the airport with her brother, Dan Walker.

Sullivan explained runway orientation, which is how runways are laid out according to the compass. The main runway at Somerset, 30-12, is headed 300 degrees in one direction and 120 degrees in the other.

She explained the difference between controlled airports (airports with control towers) and uncontrolled airports (small airports without towers).

The vast majority of airports in the United States are uncontrolled, which means they don't have towers. Only bigger, busier airports have control towers. This is not to say that smaller airports have no control. Every airport has a radio frequency on which pilots receive airport advisories, such as, which is the active runway. Pilots use that frequency to report their position when they are in the pattern for landing so other pilots know where they are. This system works very well for smaller airports.

Ellen Parker told the students how her father, George Walker, built the airport.

"There was nothing around here then," she said. "The main runway was laid out by Gill Robb Wilson after a study of the prevailing winds."

Esta-Ann Elliott, who fixes dinner for me every night, told some of the highlights of New Jersey's vast aviation history. The first flight in the new world (in a balloon) ended in South Jersey. In more modern times, Kathryn Sullivan, a native of Paterson, was the first woman to walk in space. Two of aviation's best known aviators,

Charles Lindbergh and Amelia Earhart, flew in and out of New Jersey airports many times and for a time, Lindbergh lived in New Jersey. Earhart's mechanic, Ed Gorski, once ran an operation at Teterboro Airport and then owned and operated Lincoln Park Airport for many years with the help of his wife, Julia.

After their welcome and briefing in the hangar, the students were divided into four groups. One went into a classroom for a ground school lesson from Angus Kydd, one of the airport's instructors. Another group went into the maintenance hangar to hear Lee Weber, an FAA licensed mechanic, discuss aircraft and engine maintenance.

A third group stayed in the hangar to listen to Captain Mark Benton of Continental Airlines talk about his job, and the fourth group went outside where retired TWA captain, Jim Carley, showed them a new Cessna aircraft and one of the Pipers used for flight training, and explained how the controls work.

The groups were rotated so each student had a chance to attend all four sessions.

Kydd explained what keeps a plane in the air. The answer lies in Bernoulli's Theory that the faster a liquid or gas (air in this case) moves, the lower the pressure. This theory is applied to flight by making the top of the wing curved and the bottom flat. Air moving over the top has further to go to get to the back of the wing than air moving along the bottom of the wing and therefore has to move faster (lowering the pressure) than the air moving across the bottom, where the pressure is higher. Lower pressure on top of the wing and higher pressure on the bottom generates the lift necessary to sustain flight.

Kydd also told the students about the four forces that act on an aircraft in flight, lift (created by the shape of the wing), drag (the resistance created by the aircraft structure), weight (sometimes referred to as gravity, the force that causes an object to fall to earth), and thrust (the force that propels the aircraft).

In a prop plane, the propeller screws its way through the air the way a wood screw twists its way into a board. Jets are propelled by compressed air ejected under pressure from the rear of the engine, pushing the aircraft through the air. These forces create the speed necessary to sustain flight.

Captain Benton told the students something most airline passengers don't know. Pilots never eat the same food as passengers. And the pilot and copilot may not eat the same food. "If I eat a turkey sandwich, the first officer has to eat something else," Benton said. "And pilots never eat at the same time." All this is a safety measure to protect passengers in the unlikely event of contaminated food.

Benton also emphasized that opportunities abound for women

in aviation today. Ten percent of Continental's 10,000 pilots are women, he told the students.

"A woman pilot gave me my last check ride," he said.

Benton owns a Pitts Special aerobatic biplane that he flies at air shows and in aerobatic competitions. He pulled it out of his hangar and taxied it over to the big hangar so the students would have a chance to see a plane that was a little bit different.

Like Benton, aviation technician Lee Weber emphasized the opportunities in aviation for women.

"My FAA's mechanic's license is signed by a woman." he told the students. He explained also that all aircraft must undergo an annual inspection in order to remain in flying status.

Weber explained that all aircraft have dual ignitions. There are two spark plugs in each cylinder. If one should fail, the engine will continue to run on the other.

Captain Corley gave students a chance to get up close to an airplane and see the controls and instruments. He also gave them a briefing on the cost of aircraft and the cost of operation.

Their tour of the airport was an important part of their education about the world they live in. Aviation is, and will continue to be, an important part of that world.

6/18/2000

Chapter 22

A Few of My Favorite Stories

I have always felt fortunate to have run across so many memorable stories over the years. By now you've read a good number of them. But there are certain ones which, for one reason or another, are special favorites of mine.

Most of these columns, as it happens, didn't lend themselves to the way this book is organized. They just didn't fit into any particular chapter. So I decided to give them a chapter of their own. To me, they were just too good to leave out.

I hope that by the time you finish this chapter you will agree.

AN UNFORGETTABLE FLIGHT

If you met Florence Johnson, it's a sure thing you wouldn't soon forget her. Though she was a nonagenarian when I had the delightful experience of interviewing her, she had more spirit and wit than a lot of people I've interviewed over the years. She recounted events that took place three quarters of a century ago as if they happened yesterday. One of the events she related was her first airplane ride. That took place in 1911. It was in a single seat aircraft. She was not a pilot. She was a passenger.

This is her incredible story.

I f Florence Johnson lives to be a 100, she won't forget her first airplane ride. Mrs. Johnson is 98 now and that first airplane ride took place 75 years ago in March 1911.

Florence Johnson with one of her scrapbooks of newspaper stories about her husband's flights in 1911.

Alert, perky, and witty, Mrs. Johnson told me about the circumstances leading to that flight during a visit in her cozy room at the Haddonfield Home in Camden County, (N.J.) where she has resided for the past 10 years. She was living in the Finger Lakes town of Bath, N.Y., where she was born, when she became one of the first women in the world to fly.

"Some of my friends came to my house and asked if I wouldn't join them to go see the 'bird man' fly," she said. "I put on my hat and coat because it was very cold, and went with them.

"The bird man was flying off the ice on Lake Salubria. He came over and asked me if I wanted to fly across the ice. There was only one seat in the airplane. He lifted me up and put me on the wing.

"We went across the lake a few times and the next thing I knew we were flying and he said, 'Hold on.' I held on to the wing strut.

"I wasn't exactly scared because it happened before I realized it and it was exciting."

The pilot's name was Walter Johnson and he said he wanted to see if he could get off with 50 extra pounds. " I weighed more than 50," Mrs. Johnson said.

"I didn't say anything about it when I got home. But my father went uptown to the post office. There was no mail, but everybody went to the post office. When he got there everyone was talking about my flight."

"What did he have to say when she got home?" Mrs. Johnson was asked.

"Plenty," she replied.

"And later you married the pilot?" she was asked.

She pointed her finger at herself and said, quite emphatically, "He married *me*."

A newspaper clipping dated March 6, 1911, describes the flight of Florence Strafford (her maiden name) that it said took place last Friday afternoon and attained a height of 25 feet. Under the headline, "Bath Woman Passenger on Airplane Trip," the story concluded, "Miss Strafford is the recipient of many congratulations, upon her exhibition of nerve and daring."

That clipping is one of dozens of newspaper stories she has, most of them from 1911 and 1912, about the exploits of the bird man, whom she married about a year later.

Describing his courtship of her, Mrs. Johnson said, "He'd fly all day and come and see me in the evening. He'd put his head on my lap and go sound asleep.

"Everybody thought I was crazy to marry a man who flew because they thought he would be killed," she said. Johnson died in 1961 after they had been married 49 years. They had three children.

The airplane Johnson was flying was a Thomas "headless" biplane with a Kirhan engine. It was made by two English brothers, W.L. and Oliver Thomas, who came to the United States and settled in the remote rural community of Bath.

"I don't know how they came to a place like this," Mrs. Johnson said.

The newspaper stories about Johnson described him as the son of a Rochester physician. He played football in high school and was a high jumper at Syracuse University.

One story in Mrs. Johnson's thick scrapbook carried the headline, "See Football Game From Exclusively Reserved Seat." It describes Johnson flying over a football game that was suspended for a few minutes while the players "stood and watched the young man, who two years before had circled their ends with amazing swiftness, perform much faster, daring circles in the air."

"He taught himself to fly," said Mrs. Johnson, "and during World War I, he taught flying for the military.

"After the war, he was sent to Russia to teach the Russians to fly flying boats. (A newspaper clipping reported that he took 100 Curtiss seaplane bombers across the Arctic Circle and delivered them to Russia in 1915.)

"He had trouble getting out of Russia," said Mrs. Johnson, "because his flying boat broke. He got out by flying across the Scandinavian countries to England. He wrote to me, but I never got any of the letters."

There were dozens of stories in her scrapbook about early records Johnson set, headlines like "Sixteen Miles Covered in Fourteen Minutes at Height of 500 to 1,500 Feet." and a story about a flight of 3 hours and 51 minutes with a passenger on the wing.

"But there was no money in it," said Mrs. Johnson, "so he had to get out of it."

Johnson became a banker. He worked for the Camden (N.J.) Trust Company for many years, during which time they lived in Collingswood, and he became head of the bank's estate organization division.

In a newspaper story dated August 18, 1939, at which time he held that post, he was quoted as saying, "In my opinion, the next war will be decided in favor of the nations which have air supremacy."

It was less than a month later that World War II started with the Nazi dive bomber attack on Poland, and it was allied air power that eventually won the war.

6/8/86

THE CHICKEN COOP GANG

There are a lot of airplanes flying around these days that didn't come out of factories. They came out of garages and basements and living rooms. The numbers of homebuilt aircraft have been increasing steadily while production figures for factory built airplanes have been sliding.

Home builders, most of whom belong to the EAA (Experimental Aircraft Association), are a very tight group. They lend help and advice to each other all the time. Many are superbly skilled craftsmen and they share their skills and know-how with their fellow homebuilders.

Some builders spend eight or ten years turning out an airplane. But when they finish, their products reflect the long years of loving care that went into them. You can see hundreds of these aircraft at the EAA show in Oshkosh every summer.

I've talked to homebuilders who took over their living rooms and converted them into airplane factories for a period of years. Somehow, they talked their wives into tolerating that. In many cases, I've discovered wives actually became part of the project.

What made this particular column stand out above all the others I've written about such projects, is the unusual location in which these aircraft builders carried out their work. Until I wrote this story I thought a living room was an unusual place to build an airplane.

They call themselves the Chicken Coop Gang.

It's an appropriate name when you consider they replaced 18,000 chickens. There are 15 regulars in the gang. They are all flyers. There are those who will tell you that 15 flying birds are worth more than 18,000 non-flying birds any Friday of the month.

I had been invited to Ernie McOdrum's chicken coop on several occasions, but I was not too hasty about accepting the invitation. I have been invited to all kind of places...but a chicken coop? The idea of visiting this place did not exactly whet my appetite, not even when they told me they were building airplanes there.

There are more general aviation piston airplanes being built in this country today in basements, bedrooms and garages than in factories. However, as far as I've been able to determine, chicken coop production is not high.

I finally ran out of resistance and I made my way to the chicken coop.

Some chicken coop! I had envisioned a small building where the roof sagged in the middle and admitted more rain than it kept out. But here was a huge concrete block building with cement floors.

The building is 220 by 50 feet. It's two stories high. When you walk in you are immediately greeted by several aircraft fuselage frames in advanced stages of construction. And stretched out on the far side of the room is a newly recovered wing with skin as smooth as a baby's elbow.

Members of the Chicken Coop Gang recovering a wing. Left to right, Al Douglas, Bill Leavens, Bob Kroll, Konrad Kundy, and Ernie McOdrum

It's Friday night because that's the night the gang assembles to do their thing. And they are busy doing it. A couple of guys are cutting strips of tape for the wing with shearing scissors. Several more are doping the wing fabric. A couple of others are ironing the fabric on the wing to shrink it.

These are craftsmen of the old school. You sense immediately the pride they take in their work. Their standard is perfection.

These are specialists in this "chicken coop" in every skill necessary to take metal, wood, or composite materials and fashion them into beautiful flying machines.

Among them are men who excel in welding, metal work, wood work, fabric, electrical systems, and engines. They pitch in and help one another. They work together like a finely tuned team. You need five guys for a job, you've got five guys. You know every one of them loves doing what he's doing.

They are members of EAA (Experimental Aircraft Association) Antique and Classic Chapter 7 that meets in Flanders. They range in age from 20 to 74. The junior member is Matt Kiener, a videographer. That, if you are wondering, as I did, is a guy who videotapes weddings, bar mitzvahs, 50th anniversaries, and other memorable occasions.

At 74, Bill Tuckler qualifies as the senior member. He owns a machine shop. Ernie McOdrum, who falls somewhere inbetween, owns this chicken coop somewhere in the wilds of Lebanon (N.J.). His calling is general contractor.

Ernie bought the three acres that provide a home for the coop and the 105-year-old house he lives in, 15 years ago. How did the coop become a hangout for this unlikely gang?

"It just happened," said Ernie. "Bill Tuckler needed a place to assemble a Sky Bolt wing. I told him I had room for the wing."

Somehow, word about the coop leaked out. There are now seven airplanes either being built from scratch or undergoing complete rebuilding in the coop.

Members of the Chicken Coop Gang are building an Emeraud, an all-wood aircraft of French design, two Pietenpols (one of them is Ernie's), an aircraft designed in the '20s that is still very popular with homebuilders, and a Sky Bolt. They are rebuilding two Taylorcrafts and an Aeronca Champ.

This is Ernie's second Pietenpol. He built one in the early '70s in a shop on his property when he was a resident of Warren Township.

He rebuilt two airplanes in the coop, a Taylorcraft and a Cessna 170. It took him two years to rebuild the Cessna and when he finished it, he flew the aircraft to the EAA's Sun'n Fun Fly-In in Florida.

"A guy saw it there and fell in love with it," said Ernie. "He kept calling me about buying the airplane. I didn't want to part with it. But he kept raising the offer. I finally sold it to him.

"He's a retired chemical engineer. Last April, he flew it to Sun 'n Fun and from there he flew it to every one of the contiguous 48 states. He returned home in mid-July. He sent me postcards from all over the country."

Ernie still takes pride in showing pictures of the airplane. Pride is one thing there is no shortage of here in the coop. Let Bill Tuckler explain his work on the Sky Bolt and you know you're listening to a perfectionist and a guy who takes tremendous pride in his work. It's a quality he shares with the other members of the gang.

You also sense the feeling of camaraderie among these men in the sharing of what, for all of them, is a labor of love.

The coop has come a long way from the day when it was home to 18,000 chickens. Ernie is pretty sure that figure is no exaggeration. There was plenty of evidence.

"When we moved in here it took us two years to clean out the manure. It was layered. A layer of manure, a layer of straw, a layer of manure, a layer of straw. It was halfway up to the ceiling."

It would have taken an active and vivid imagination to envision then what Ernie and the gang turned this place into.

May the chickens forgive them.

9/22/91

TO DREAM THE IMPOSSIBLE DREAM

This is a story I can never forget because it is an example of a guy who had what many people might consider an impossible dream, but he was willing to make enormous sacrifices to pay the price to achieve his goal.

He was a truck driver and he wanted to be a professional pilot.

Ed Ordway talked about how he had to drop out of college after two years because he couldn't handle the cost. He became a truck driver. His boss, who was a pilot, introduced him to flying and Ordway started taking flying lessons. It took six years until he got his license.

He drove a tractor-trailer to Washington every night while he was working on getting all his ratings. After he had all his ratings, which consumed a lot of time and a lot of money, he discovered it was not easy to find a job as a pilot. But he kept focused on his goal. His determination to achieve that goal never wavered. He is an outstanding example to anyone who ever had a career dream, whatever it might have been, of what can be accomplished by hard work and determination.

E d Ordway has been a driver all of his working career. But there have been some big changes in his career since he started driving in 1958. In those days he was driving an 18-wheel tractor-trailer. Today, he "drives" one of the most sophisticated corporate jets.

It was his boss back in 1958 who was responsible for the dramatic change in the type of driving he does.

"Paul

Ed Ordway, left, in the captain's seat of a Grumman GV simulator. In the right seat is Paul Rietschel, who flew with Ed for 10 years.

Courtesy of Ed Ordway

Mische, president of Suburban Transfer Service, (a Carlstadt, N.J., service) was my boss and he got me interested in flying, even though he was an inactive pilot himself at the time," said Ordway.

"He took me out to North American Flying Service, a seaplane base on the Hackensack River in Little Ferry, where he learned to fly. I thought I would try it.

"I started flying as a hobby, but I did it in drips and drabs and didn't get my license until 1965.

"In 1966, I decided I wanted to make flying my profession."

Ordway had studied mechanical engineering at Penn State for two years before he had to drop out for financial reasons. He started driving a truck.

While he was driving the 18-wheeler he got his commercial pilot's license and he took his instrument ground school.

"I drove to Washington every night," he says, "leaving at midnight and returning the next morning." That's about nine hours of driving, plus the time for them to unload his cargo.

"As soon as I got back from my trip I would go out to the airport and fly for a couple of hours. Then I went home and went to bed.

"I woke up at 6 p.m. and had breakfast. Then," he says, "I went to ground school from 7:30 p.m. to 10:30 p.m."

After ground school, Ordway headed straight for his truck for the run to Washington. He did that for 11 months. At the end of that time his ratings included multiengine and seaplane.

Then came the tough job-- finding somebody to hire him as a pilot.

"I started knocking on doors," said Ordway.

"A good friend of mine was Iggy Kaufman, a Bergen County police officer, at one of the Teterboro terminals. He asked every transient pilot, 'Do you need a good kid as a co-pilot?'

"After six months, one chief pilot said, 'Have him write to the home office.' I did.

"Six months later I got a call from the chief pilot. He said he wanted to talk to me at Morristown Airport.

"After the interview he said, 'You're on the payroll starting tomorrow.'

"So at last I had a job flying--at half the salary I got driving a truck. "I flew a King Air and Twin Beech and qualified as a captain on the King Air.

"Then I was approached by a company operating a turboprop Mitsubishi MU-2 and a Jet Commander. I took that job and my salary jumped to what it had been as a truck driver," said Ordway.

A year later he had an opportunity to join the aviation

A year later he had an opportunity to join the aviation department of National Distillers which operates a Grumman Gulfstream I and two Gulfstream IIs out of Teterboro Airport.

For the past five years he's been flying one of the finest corporate jets in the world for a top ranked corporation.

"I'm doing what I want to do," says Ordway. "I love to fly. I'd rather fly than do anything else in the world.

"Some pilots get blasé. Not me. Every single takeoff and landing sparks something," he says.

When he's not flying the Gulfstream, which is based on the east side of Teterboro Airport, you can find him on the west side of the field helping out his old boss.

No, he doesn't drive a truck. His old boss, Paul Mische, is now president of Suburban Aviation, a Fixed Base Operator, and he still runs Suburban Transfer, the trucking company.

Ordway spends his free time as an aircraft salesman for Mische.

He's not about to forget his old boss--or that trip to the seaplane base on the Hackensack River that changed his life.

1/11/76

Note: *Ed Ordway was the 15th pilot in the world to be type rated in the Gulfstream I, II, III, IV and V.*

THE MASTER OF ALL FLYING MACHINES

People who have done something nobody else has done are not easy to find. But I found one. His name is Jack McNamara. He earned an instructor's rating in every type of flying vehicle that the FAA licenses. In addition to that he has every ground instructor's rating they issue.

Accomplishing that was no mean feat. It took him 25 years, a lot of ingenuity, and a bunch of money.

Nine-year-old Jack McNamara was riding his pony, Dolly Grey, when he met a very friendly fellow working on the lawn in front of his house about two miles down the road from the McNamara family farm in Morris Plains. They got into a conversation over the man's hedge and before very long the conversation turned to aviation.

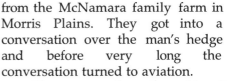

The man on the other side of the hedge was Tom Buck. Anyone who knew Buck would know that any conversation with him would soon turn to flying. Buck, who lost a leg in an aircraft accident and continued to fly with a wooden leg, had a mad love affair with aviation that he wanted, with a passion, to communicate to the rest of the world. I wrote about him more than 20 years ago when he was flying out of the now defunct Somerset Hills Airport. (Two of his sons, Kern and Rinker flew to California and back when they were 17 and 15 respectively in a Piper Cub that they rebuilt. See Chapter 3.)

Jack McNamara, who holds every ground instructor and flight instructor rating the FAA issues. Pictured in front of his home.

In his zeal to communicate the thrill and uplifting spirit of flying, he invited the young pony rider for an airplane ride. Dolly Grey was soon tied up at Buck's house, and they were off to the airport.

"We did loops and rolls and I loved it," McNamara recalled the other day, chatting on the porch of the pre-revolutionary house on his 130-acre farm in Far Hills. "When I got home, I told my parents about it. They called Tom Buck and read him the riot act for taking me up without their permission."

That was in 1950.

Today, Jack McNamara is a pilot--a rather unusual one--and he firmly believes he doesn't take second place to anyone so far as his love of aviation is concerned.

There is another aspect of flying in which he takes second place to no one. So far as anyone, including the FAA, knows, he is the only pilot who holds every rating issued. This includes single and multiengine land and seaplane ratings, a jet type certificate in a Cessna Citation, glider pilot (approved for both tow and winch launches), helicopter, gyro plane, hot air and gas balloons, and a lighter-than-air ratings. There are five ATPs (Air Transport Pilot) ratings, that are kind of the Ph.D.s of flight ratings. He holds all five.

There are seven flight instructor ratings--airplane, instrument, multi-engine, helicopter, helicopter instrument, gyroplane, and glider--and he holds all of them. In addition, he has given instruction in a blimp. There is no blimp instructor's rating. Anyone who holds a commercial lighter-than-air rating has the privileges of an instructor. He also holds advanced ground instructor and instrument ground instructor ratings.

You may have the impression by now that McNamara is in the aviation business. Negative. He's an attorney.

Not surprisingly, he specializes in aviation law. He represents pilots, airports, flight schools. He has even represented some airlines.

It is McNamara's theory that the more he knows about aviation, the better he'll be able to represent his clients and the more ratings he gets, the more he'll know.

That is the reason he put forth the extraordinary time, effort, and investment to acquire all these ratings. It is a feat of monumental proportions.

The toughest rating to get was the lighter-than-air (blimps and dirigible) rating. There are no schools that provide this rating. When Goodyear needs a blimp pilot, they hire and train one.

McNamara overcame that stumbling block by going to England. Although there are no schools there either, Per Lindstrand, the first man to cross the Atlantic in a hot air balloon, along with Sir Richard Branson, has a company that manufactures balloons and blimps and McNamara worked out an arrangement with him to get the 50 hours needed for his lighter-than-air commercial rating.

The last rating McNamara got was for the gas balloon. All those balloons you see at the balloon festivals are of the hot air variety. There are not many gas balloons around so it is not easy to find a place to get that rating. Since he already had a commercial hot air balloon rating, all he needed was two, two-hour flights. He flew from Quakertown to Perkasie, Pa., and then from Perkasie to Rosemont, N.J. Having done that, he had every rating in the books.

His pursuit of all these ratings started at Somerset (N.J.) Airport in 1960, when he was 19. He and a boyhood friend took enough money--$135--out of their bank accounts for ten hours of flight time, enough to get themselves soloed. Then he went back to school--Georgetown University--and that ended his flying for awhile.

He got his license in 1965 in a Helio Courier, a STOL (short takeoff and landing) aircraft, that is larger and more powerful than a trainer, owned by a friend of his. He had a TWA pilot teach his two children to fly and Jack made a third. They learned on a landing strip on his friend's farm.

During his last year at Fordham Law School, McNamara owned a piece of a Piper Comanche with several partners, none of whom were pilots. He flew passengers from LaGuardia Airport to East Hampton, L.I.

After he got his law degree, one of his clients had a helicopter charter operation that had a great deal of paperwork associated with it, so he made McNamara president in charge of the paperwork. That gave McNamara the opportunity to learn something about the aviation business from the operator's point of view. In addition to understanding his clients' problems first hand, McNamara was interested in discovering exactly what high standards are in the world of aviation. He discovered that at the University of North Dakota where he got a couple of his ratings.

"I'm convinced," he says, "that the University of North Dakota is teaching to the highest standards." The growth of the university's aviation program would seem to indicate that they are, indeed doing something right.

"Ten years ago they had two instructors and one leased aircraft. Today they have 100 aircraft including seaplanes and two jets," McNamara says. "And they have 20 simulators including full motion simulators similar to what the airlines use."

McNamara owns a twin-engine Piper Apache that was based at Solberg Airport. (Currently it's based at Somerset Airport.) He holds a world speed record that he established three years ago in a flight from Grand Fork, N.D., where the University of North Dakota is located, to

Morristown Airport.

But that record pales in comparison with his record number of ratings. It took him 25 years from the time he got his first rating until the last one, the gas balloon rating that he got in June. Anyone who wants to tackle that record has their work cut out for them.

8/26/90

Note: *Jack McNamara was inducted into the Aviation Hall of Fame of New Jersey in 2007.*

YOU GOTTA BELIEVE

You've never met anybody like John Joseph. That's because he's a one-of-a-kind.

After you talk to him for a little while you get the impression that he's a man who could walk through a stone wall if he made up his mind that he really wanted to get to the other side.

Everybody knows, for example, that you can't build a landing strip on top of a mountain. John Joseph didn't believe that. So he built it. He had to do some creative landscaping in order to accomplish that feat. He happens to be in the blasting business and that helped some. He blew off the top of the mountain and flattened it. He now has his own, paved landing strip right in front of his home.

If John Joseph had believed his doctors, there wouldn't be a landing strip where that mountain top once stood because John Joseph wouldn't be here. He was diagnosed with cancer of both kidneys. The doctors said his days were numbered. He didn't buy that either. Now, several decades later, he's perfectly healthy. He has no cancer.

There's a lot more about John Joseph that's unusual. Read on.

Every time I think I've seen it all, I find out how wrong I can be.

Some weeks ago, Dave MacMillan, a trustee of the Aviation Hall of Fame and Museum of New Jersey, freelance flight instructor, and licensed mechanic who holds an IA (inspection authorization) mechanic's rating told me that in spite of all the years I've been writing about aviation, I hadn't seen anything yet. Last weekend he proved it.

John Joseph standing next to his aerobatic Christen Eagle wearing his father's full headdress.

I met MacMillan at Lincoln Park Airport and he flew me in a Cessna 172 up over the hills of West Milford, where he circled over a brand new, 2,100 by 40 foot paved landing strip stretched across the top of a mountain that had been flattened.

News of any new landing strip in New Jersey borders on the unbelievable, but what was even more unbelievable in this case, is that it is not a public use airport. It is a private strip on private property.

All of the private landing strips in New Jersey are turf. There is one paved corporate strip (Inductotherm Corp.) that is not a public facility. This is the first and only paved, purely private, strip in the state. At an elevation of 940 feet, it is also the highest landing strip in the state. John Joseph calls it "Hilltop."

On high ground overlooking the runway is a brand new house with a deck overlooking the runway. And alongside the runway there is a large hangar.

It would take an extremely imaginative person to envision a landing strip on top of a mountain and to conceive the idea of leveling the top of that mountain to accomplish this.

But there's more. John Joseph, who did it, might qualify in almost anybody's book as one of the most unusual characters they ever met.

One of the first things you learn on meeting him is that he is a Native American. "My father," he told me, "was in a tribe that was part of the Algonquin Nation. He was an Adirondack hunting and fishing guide and he was an expert carpenter."

He showed me a large photograph of his father who looked quite distinguished in a full Indian headdress. That headdress is one of John Joseph's proudest possessions.

His mother came from Riga, Latvia. Her father was president of The Bank of Riga, one of the largest banks in the country. He held a very distinguished position.

When the Soviets took over Latvia after the Revolution, four soldiers came to their house to take their 15-year-old son (the brother of John Joseph's mother) off to service. Their mother said she did not want them to take her son away. She embraced him and said, "He's too young and too little to go into the army."

One soldier said, "All right. Step outside."

The whole family stepped outside and one of the soldiers shot the boy in the head and told his mother. "Now he won't have to go into service."

The family fled Latvia and came to the United States via Switzerland and France, arriving here penniless.

His mother worked as a governess and met his father when they were both working for the very wealthy Schultz Cigar family.

John Joseph told me these stories in the comfort of his new home overlooking his runway. He heads one of the state's largest blasting companies, a company that bears his name.

He is, of course, a pilot. He flies a Cessna 210 and, when he can find the time, he likes to do aerobatics in a beautiful, prize-winning Christen Eagle biplane.

Joseph, who takes extreme pride in maintaining the highest standards in everything he does, holds a commercial license with single engine, land, sea, and glider ratings. He was five when he announced he was going to be a pilot.

"Some Waco UPF7s on floats came in to Long Lake, N.Y., where I was born and grew up," he said. "They took people for rides and my father let the other four children in the family go, but he said I was too young to appreciate it, so I couldn't go. I told him when I grow up I'm going to fly."

Joseph's first flight came four years later, in 1939, when he was nine. He went for a ride in a Stinson out of Floyd Bennett Field in Brooklyn.

He was 16 when he soloed an Aeronca on floats at Long Lake after four hours of instruction. He's logged about 3,000 hours since.

The idea for his new airport was born in 1979. That's when he bought 57 acres of rocky, mountainous land in West Milford. At the time, he thought about putting a landing strip on the property, although probably no one else could have envisioned such a thing on that rough tract of land.

He was spurred into action two years ago when the land was reassessed. "The taxes went up considerably," he said. He and his wife, Doris, who celebrated their 40th wedding anniversary last Monday, decided that if the town decided the land was worth much more, then they ought to use it.

And now, two years later, they are using their land like no other couple in the state. If they want to fly to Seattle or to the Bahamas, two places they have flown to, all they have to do is walk downstairs, get in their airplane, and go.

Joseph, who is tall and lean, wears a perpetual smile and peppers his conversation with good humor that gives no hint of the adversities he overcame before coming to his present state.

At 11, he was constantly beaten up by schoolmates, because he was a half-breed, half Native American, half Caucasian. He never said anything to his father until one day when he took a particularly bad beating and his injuries were quite visible when he came home. His father was incensed and told him the next time he was attacked he should beat his assailants within an inch of their lives. He did, and they never bothered him again.

Of the six children in the family, he was one of only two who didn't go to college. Of the four who did, three were valedictorians and one a salutatorian.

John Joseph has lived through some trying times. His father became seriously ill and was hospitalized for a long time. John Joseph took over and supported the family. His father was not expected to survive, but eventually his problem was diagnosed as gall stones. He underwent surgery and after a long period, he recovered.

Years later, John Joseph had some serious health problems of his own. In 1983, he learned that he had cancer in both kidneys. "I went on a microbiotic diet," he says, "seaweed, brown rice, grain, and fresh vegetables. No dairy. No sugar. In nine months, my kidneys were clean." He's in good health today.

"I enjoy life," he says "My philosophy is: today is the best day of my life and tomorrow is going to be even better."

12/2/90

GUYS, IT PAYS TO LISTEN TO YOUR SPOUSE

This is a story about a notable career that blossomed because of a man's love of flying and a wife who understood that. But it's not just a story about flying. It's a story about a family. It's the kind of story any writer would like to write. That's probably why it's one of my favorites.

I knew the subject of the column from the earliest days of a career that he pursued to the very top. That made writing this story all the more rewarding.

Sometimes guys, it pays to listen to your spouse.

Jim Peters listened. It was one of the smartest things he ever did.

It was 1963. Jim and his wife, MaryLela were newly married. He was a new trainee at the National Community Bank and he was attending Fairleigh Dickinson University, nights and weekends.

Jim had soloed an airplane at Teterboro Airport when he was 16 and a student at Rutherford High. But he didn't get his license. The funds to accomplish that just weren't there.

Jim Peters

MaryLela knew he still longed to fly, but supporting a household and paying tuition made that impossible.

One day, MaryLela said to him, "Someday you're really going to need a license and you love flying so much, Why don't you get it?" She was working as a secretary for a building products company.

"She paid for me to get my license," said Jim. "She was paid every other week and she handed me her check."

MaryLela never dreamed how right she was when she said someday he was going to need a license and she agreed to finance it.

Last November, Jim was named president of the National Community Bank, an institution with 105 branches and assets of $4 billion. His pilot's license had more than a little to do with his reaching that pinnacle. Actually, it had everything to do with it.

At the time he got his license at Totowa-Wayne Airport (now defunct) in 1963, he went to work for Bert Rose, chief lending officer for the bank. Bert, though now retired, is still a member of the board of directors and he comes in three days a week as a consultant.

"Bert taught me how to analyze credits and how to make loans," said Jim.

There was an idea in the back of Jim's mind at the time. He thought the bank should establish an aircraft financing department.

"I knew the flying business," he said, "but I had to learn the lending business. When I did, I proposed the idea to Bert Rose. He was a very conservative man, but he let me go ahead and do it, and he was very supportive.

"We started slowly, but in the first year, 1964, we financed a million dollars worth of airplanes, all singles or light twins."

Jim flew a rented Cessna 172 to New York, Pennsylvania, and around New Jersey to drum up business.

The March 13, 1966, "Wings Over Jersey" column was about a young banker, 26-years old, who was not sitting behind a desk waiting for people to come in and ask for loans, but was flying around in a Cessna 172 bringing in business. His name, of course, was Jim Peters.

The bank later bought him a Cessna 182. The aircraft was equipped with two Mark 12 navigation/communications radios, a Bendix ADF, a three light marker beacon, and a transponder.

The airplane cost $18,500 new. (By contrast, in March 2004, Cessna began selling 182s with a multifunction glass panel. The price of the aircraft was more than $300,000. Advance sales are being recorded at a good rate.)

"Flying gave me a lot of visibility," said Jim. "I was the most visible guy in the bank, not only to customers, but to the board of directors, because what I was doing was unusual. I might have gotten lost in the crowd, but I didn't."

Today, with the United States having lost its world leadership in the light plane industry largely because of our liability laws, and with Cessna no longer producing light planes and Piper Aircraft in bankruptcy, the aviation financing business is not what it was. Nevertheless, the National Community Bank has $25 million in aircraft loans outstanding, a tiny fraction of its business, but quite significant in terms of today's aviation market.

Jim had the most original idea we've heard yet about how to deal with the aircraft liability problem. "Cigarette companies print a surgeon general's warning on each pack which says, 'Smoking could be injurious to your health,'" he points out. "People die every day from cancer attributed to smoking, but nobody ever wins a suit against the cigarette companies.

"Maybe they should put a little plaque on airplanes similar to the surgeon general's warning. It could say, 'There are inherent risks in aviation. Maximum liability $200,000.' What's wrong with that?"

In the years since we wrote about the 26-year-old banker 26 years ago, he's come a long way.

After six years of night school and weekend classes, he earned a master's degree in business administration.

Since I talked to him for the 1966 column, his family has grown. His oldest son, Jim, loves flying as much as his dad, and he now flies charter for MacDan Aviation out of Teterboro Airport.

His oldest child, Abby, made him a grandfather for the first time last July. Son Jon is a student at Ramapo Valley College, and youngest son, Will, is a student at Pompton Lakes High School. He wants to start taking flying lessons at 15 1/2 so he can solo at 16.

There have been some changes in the Peters household since I last wrote about Jim, but it's probably a safe bet that one thing hasn't changed. When MaryLela speaks, Jim listens.

1/12/92

Chapter 23

A Touch of Nostalgia

There are not too many people around today who inhabited this planet when the Wright Brothers lifted from the earth's surface in a powered aircraft at Kitty Hawk, N.C., on Dec. 17, 1903. But there is no shortage of those who love to recall the old days when flying was a true adventure, when airplanes were flimsy, open cockpit biplanes, with engines that were not always as reliable aa they might be, and people who flew wore a helmet and goggles--and a parachute.

I've covered a lot of aviation history and recounted stories on all aspects of the world of flying, so I thought maybe before I wind it all up and put "the end" on the last page, I might indulge in a bit of nostalgia, part of the aviation story I've tried to tell.

THE KID AT THE AIRPORT FENCE

Where better to start talking about nostalgia than right in your own backyard. As a matter of fact, I felt a twinge of nostalgia when I reread this column that was written three decades ago. The personal events took place more than twenty years before that.

Times have changed and something has been lost along the way. Rereading this column helped me rediscover the fascination of a day gone by. Many years may have passed, but the fascination has not.

I saw an ad in an aviation magazine recently that touched a sensitive nerve.

"Whatever happened to the kid at the airport fence?" it asked.

I remember when I was that kid. I rode my bicycle from Bloomfield to Newark Airport (about seven miles) Saturday after Saturday to watch the airplanes (DC-3s) come in over the fence by the road and settle down onto the runway.

There was nothing more exciting than to watch those airplanes land and to dream of flying in one of them some day.

The dream of actually flying an airplane seemed so far-fetched that it was a kind of secret dream.

But just to watch them coming in, hour after hour--to see them and listen to the sound of the engines--made for many a memorable Saturday.

At smaller airports, fields like Pine Brook, which I remember, and which eventually succumbed to Route 46, kids lined the fence every Saturday and Sunday and stared in awe at the wondrous flying machines. And sometimes they could get their fathers to agree to go up for an airplane ride with them. That was how I had my first airplane ride--in an open cockpit biplane. It was a New Standard biplane with two cockpits. The pilot sat in the rear cockpit and there was a large forward cockpit with four seats. My father and I, and my younger brother, Herb, were in that front cockpit. I was about nine, my brother seven.

It was an incredible experience to lift off the turf runway with the wind blowing in your face, climb into the sky and look down at the countryside and the tiny houses and automobiles. And it was all over so fast. But the memory never faded.

There was a fascination, whether you were a kid or an adult, in just standing there at the fence watching other people climb into that cockpit and have one of the ground crew people buckle them in. There were kids who sat and watched that scene every weekend. Those kids were never bored.

Today, you seldom see kids at the airport fence like you used to, but you do hear about kids who are bored.

Maybe airports have grown so big and so impersonal since the grass roots, open-cockpit days, that there's no room or no time for the boy at the fence anymore.

Or maybe in this age of walking on the moon, airplanes no longer hold the fascination for today's youngsters that they did for youngsters years ago. That's sad.

Many of the kids at the fence 30 or 40 years ago are pilots today. Airplanes have lost none of their fascination for them.

There are some efforts to do something about this situation. Mostly they are based on the theory that if the youngsters won't seek out aviation, then aviation must seek out the youngsters.

Increasing numbers of aviation courses are being offered in the public schools and there are groups like the Explorer Scouts that have formed some aviation posts.

Their efforts are commendable, but so tiny.

Youngsters should still be fascinated by flight, by its potential and its future.

I know many pilots in their 40s and 50s who dream of flying their own plane to Rio de Janeiro at carnival time or even across the Atlantic like Marion Hart, the grand old lady of aviation, who at 81 recently completed a solo flight across the Atlantic Ocean, a feat she's accomplished numerous times. She's lived a lot of years, but she's really not old. She's young in spirit and that's what counts.

It's wonderful for older folks to have dreams of flights to faraway places full of adventure and excitement.

But it's the youngsters who should be the real dreamers. And if we lose them, we lose everything.

12/30/73

TURNING THE CLOCK BACK

If you wonder how much nostalgia there is about the old days of aviation, you have only to visit the Old Rhinebeck Aerodrome in Rhinebeck, N.Y. From May through October they put on shows featuring World War I and pre-World War I aircraft. You can actually see some of the earliest airplanes fly, airplanes dating back to the Wright Brothers' days.

Rhinebeck has been in operation for decades using a short turf strip with a dog leg. There are large crowds every weekend--and the majority of them are not pilots. They are just people fascinated by old flying machines, and you will always find a large number of youngsters at the shows. Rhinebeck is a perfect destination for families.

Visiting Rhinebeck is a trip back in time.

I f they didn't have an announcer up on a high platform describing the action over a 1975 vintage public address system, you might very well think it was 1918 and you were at a little Aerodrome in wartime (World War I) France.

As it is, you might feel you're on a movie set. More weekends than not there is a camera crew filming a short, a commercial, or a television bit.

The German DR-1 triplane of World War I in flight at Old Rhinebeck Aerodrome.

The action every Saturday and Sunday from mid-May to the end of October, consists of a reproduction of all the elements--sight, sound, and smell--of the infant breed flying machines. On Saturdays, they fly pre-World War I aircraft and on Sundays, they re-create the atmosphere of World War I and those daring young men in their flying machines.

This takes place at Old Rhinebeck Aerodrome north of Rhinebeck, N.Y., across the Hudson River from Kingston.

It's been a number of years since my last visit to this re-creation of aviation history and there have been many changes.

There is a greatly expanded museum, filled with a wide variety of antique aircraft, engines, and photos, going back before World War I. There is also a large gift shop now with everything from coloring books and pennants for the kids, to antique aircraft model kits.

Adjacent to the runway are long rows of benches sufficient to hold thousands of spectators on Saturdays and Sundays when the flying shows are held. Those benches are usually all filled.

Sunday is the really big show. That's the World War I show that starts at 2:30. But you should get there a lot earlier to see all the marvelous exhibits on the field and in the museum spread out over several hangars that seem as old as the planes.

In the Sunday show you not only get to see all the World I airplanes fly, but they stage a whole drama with a villain, a good guy, and a pretty heroine, plus a supporting cast, all appropriately costumed in the sartorial splendor of the time.

The villain is the evil, strutting Black Baron who tries to conquer the sweet and innocent Trudy Truelove. Happily, Sir Percy Goodfellow comes to the rescue. In the course of the afternoon you also see World War I era automobiles, trucks, ambulances, and even a vintage tank.

On Saturdays, there is a different treat. They fly flimsy pre-World War I aircraft. On the Saturday I was there they flew a replica of the warped wing Hanriot, originally built in 1910. It doesn't get up very high or go very far, but when you see it fly it's as if you're watching aviation history in action.

Another oldie they flew was the 1916 F.E. 8. This was a pusher-type fighter plane. The engine was put in the back because the aircraft was built before they figured out how to synchronize machine guns and propellers. This aircraft actually flew around the pattern.

In the Sunday show realistically simulated war scenes help lend an air of authenticity to the production. The old birds come swooping down to drop "bombs" on the evil Black Baron, right in front of the audience. And they drop them with remarkable accuracy, usually coming breathtakingly close.

The bombs explode with a bang and a puff of black smoke, filling the air with noise and the smell of gunpowder, that blends with the smell of castor oil from the old engines.

For the climax, they stage a dog fight between the bad Black Baron in a German Fokker Triplane and the virtuous Sir Percy Goodfellow in a French Sopwith Pup.

It's a great show for the whole family. The kids especially

love it.   But you also see a sprinkling of senior citizens who might remember way back when.

To get there I flew up past Greenwood Lake to the west of our course, then past the west side of the West Point restricted area (though it is usually inactive this time of year), then up the Hudson past Stewart Airport at Newburgh, past Poughkeepsie, and on into Sky Park, across the river just north of Kingston. It's a five minute station wagon ride to Old Rhinebeck.

It's an experience that calls for repeat visits.

10/12/75

A SENTIMENTAL JOURNEY

Seventy years after it first made its way into the sky and into the hearts and memories of so many pilots, a lot of people still think of any small airplane as a Piper Cub. Thousands of pilots were trained in little yellow Cubs.

There are still hundreds of them flying and the pilots who own them harbor great pride in that ownership.

The J-3 Piper Cub was the first mass produced trainer. There have been thousands of pilots--some of them who eventually worked their way up into jet airliner cockpits--who took their first lessons in the Piper Cub.

Back in 1986, a Piper Cub fly-in was established in Lock Haven, Pa., where these airplanes were built. They called it "Sentimental Journey to Cub Haven."

In 1987, I flew to Lock Haven, Pa., to attend the second Sentimental Journey to Cub Haven. It was a kind of personal nostalgia trip for me since, like so many others, I took my first flight lessons in a Piper Cub.

But unexpectedly, it turned out to be a sentimental experience for another reason as well. A fellow with a white mustache read my name tag and identified himself as the kid I had taken for rides when I owned a Stinson Station Wagon based at Morristown (N.J.) Airport back in the late '50s. He had his pilot's license now and he worked as an air traffic controller.

Although all this took place 16 years ago, the memory is still fresh.

This a story of a "Sentimental Journey." It turned out to be more sentimental--or maybe nostalgic--than I anticipated.

The journey took me to Lock Haven, Pa., former home of the Piper Aircraft Co., for the second annual "Sentimental Journey to Cub Haven," an event to which Piper owners from all over the country were invited to fly their aircraft. This year (1987) marked the 50th anniversary of Piper Aircraft and the Piper Cub.

My flight from Somerset Airport took me over the Poconos and Alleghenies, over Hazelton and Milton, Pa., to Lock Haven, 148 miles away. I made the trip on the second day of an eight-day event to the birthplace of thousands of Piper Cubs, the most famous of the "little" airplanes and the most revered aircraft among old-time pilots. Thousands of them learned to fly in the Cub. Some 10,000 were built before World War II and the military bought close to 7,000 for war service.   Thousands more were built after the war. (Cub Crafters, a Yakima, Wash., company, is now building a beefed up version of the Super Cub called the Top Cub priced at more than $150,000.   They also build a Light Sport version.   American Legend Aircraft Company of Sulphur Springs, Texas, also builds a Legend Cub.)

The first "Sentimental Journey" was staged last year as a test run for this year's 50th anniversary event. It was organized by a group of aviation enthusiasts including some key people who are not pilots, in conjunction with the City of Lock Haven and Clinton County.

When I flew in a week ago Saturday, there were a couple of dozen Cubs on the field from all over the country, in spite of the fact that flying conditions were not the best. It was excessively hot and humid and there was the accompanying haze and fog that cut visibility.

Some of those Cubs had come from as far away as California, Washington State, and Arizona.   There were Cubs from Kansas, Wisconsin, and Illinois.

It was a bit nostalgic for me looking at them lined up wingtip-to-wingtip in lines as straight as a line of West Point cadets.

I took my first flight lessons in a Cub at Westfield (N.J.) Airport in the late '40s and couldn't recall having flown in one since then. (I got my license in a Piper Super Cub.)

When William Schaeffer of Manhattan, Kansas, asked if I'd like to go for a ride in his J-3 modified to a later model PA-11, with tandem wheels on each gear (four main wheels) for rough field landings, I leaped at the opportunity.

When you fly in a Cub you know why it is so revered by old-time pilots.   It's not fast, it's not plush, but it makes you feel you were born to fly.

We took off from the grass strip alongside the 3,350-foot paved runway, and flew over Lock Haven, framed on one side by a mountain ridge and on the other by the Susquehanna River. The upper and lower halves of the door on the right were open, and the window on the left was open. That created a feeling of grass roots flying you don't get when you're closed in.   Short as it was, the flight was a kind of Sentimental Journey back to days long since past.

But it wasn't until after that flight that I encountered another bit of nostalgia that took me back more than 20 years to another period and another airport.

A white-haired fellow looking at my name plate said, "Jack Elliott."

"That's right," I responded

"You used to own a Stinson," he said.

"That's right."

"At Morristown Airport," he said.

"That's right."

"You took me up in it when I was 15," he said. "I polished it for you. I was the airport bum. You got me a ride in the American Airlines Ford Trimotor when it visited New Jersey. I soloed when I was 16. You did a column about me."

I remembered that boy. His name was Del Coller. He is now an air traffic controller and he lives in Pennsylvania.

Del Coller

I met a lot of other people from New Jersey I know, but no others I hadn't seen in well over 20 years.

I also met a lot of the Cub pilots who flew in for this event. They are a cross section of America. Some of them like Daro Myles of Camp Lake, Wis., acquired Cubs that had seen better days and with tender loving care, brought them back to life.

Myles bought his personal Cub 12 years ago as a basket case. He paid $900 and spent two years restoring it to flying condition. A Cub in good condition will bring somewhere between $8,000 and $10,000 today.

(Note: Not anymore. You'd be lucky if you could find one at three times that price today.)

Dick Stone of Marlboro, Mass., has owned his Cub for 22 years. He restored it last year, finishing the day before he flew it to Lock Haven where he won second prize in the judging.

George Bruce, who flew his Cub in a flight of two from Kansas with William Schaeffer, is a captain in the Kansas Highway Patrol. Schaeffer is a warrant officer in the army and flies the military version of the King Air 200.

Aside from the old airplanes, there were exhibits in one of the hangars, dozens of forums, films, tours of places of special interest in the area, cookouts, and even a "Sentimental Journey" parade in town.

There was a Piper Museum housed in a giant trailer. Among the exhibits were ads for the early Cubs. In one aviation magazine dated May 1940, an ad proclaimed, "Down payment as low as $333".

Prices in the ad ranged from $985 for a 40-hp model to $1,948 for a 65-hp model.

The whole city seems to be enthusiastically involved in the Sentimental Journey. The hospitality is genuine and unrestrained. I was having a hamburger and milk shake when local residents, the Johnsons, introduced themselves. Mrs. Johnson offered to take me on a tour of the city and invited me to stay over at their house. "We have a big house," she said.

Unfortunately, I had to return that night.

The big Piper factory here is now closed. There are only memories of better days when 2,700 workers were employed there. All Piper facilities are now in Vero Beach, Florida.

But Bill Piper and his Piper Cub have left their mark on Lock Haven.

Piper has built more than 128,000 airplanes. The majority of them first saw the blue skies here in Lock Haven

There will likely be a lot more Sentimental Journeys here. They are already at work on next year's.

7/19/87

MEMORIES OF LONG AGO

If I didn't know how much nostalgia was associated with flying, readers of my "Wings Over Jersey" column certainly reminded me. Stories about personal memories of the old days were the subject of many letters.

One that referred to Hadley Field, the eastern terminus of the transcontinental airmail service in the '20s, inspired the column that follows. Historic old Hadley is now a shopping mall.

Hadley was not exactly a pristine airfield. It had turf runways. And there were places where there was no turf. At one point where runways intersected there was a good sized depression. After a heavy rain it became Lake Hadley. But if it didn't have paved runways and if the hangar looked like something out of a movie about the old days, Hadley had something more important. It was an integral part of aviation history.

Bell Labs based aircraft there that were used to test the first aircraft radio communications. World War I ace Ray Brooks was Bell's chief pilot. He liked to tell the story about how he flew over his house in Summit and called his wife on the phone from the airplane they were testing. She answered and said, "I can't hear you. Some damned fool is flying an airplane over the house."

The airport closed in 1968 and it is still mourned by many pilots.

They came back home, back to the place where the hangar once stood that protected their aircraft from the elements. That was a half century ago.

Now they sat in a Holiday Inn and ate prime ribs while down the hall a new generation bounced up and down to the ear shattering rhythms of a combo that could drown out the sound of those old engines that were heard here so long ago.

World War I ace Ray Brooks, now in his 80s, was here. He flew from the airfield that once occupied this spot in South Plainfield, testing aviation communications equipment for Bell Labs from 1926 to 1939.

Here at this spot in South Plainfield was where Hadley Field stood and this is where Ray Brooks flew the Fairchild FC2W, the Fairchild 71A, and the Ford Trimotor. Bell Labs developed communications systems for aircraft here, until the government, in its wisdom, forced Bell Labs out of the business in 1939.

Matt Selesky, another World War I ace, was here. He was a

pilot for the original owner of the field, Ken Unger, a Canadian World War I ace, who now lives in Pompano, Fla.

Parker Runyan was here. Runyan put up a lot of the money that went into experimental aircraft at Hadley Airport. He boasts a license signed by Orville Wright.

And Ed Lawler was here. When he first came to the airport that was here, Ed was a boy of 11 or 12. He used to wash airplanes and run errands and sometimes some of the pilots would give him a quarter. Ed served in the Navy during World War II and flew every amphibian in the Navy inventory. After the war he became a Pan American pilot and flew jets across the oceans. He's a businessman today and flies his own twin-engine Cessna all over the Western Hemisphere, often to South America.

There was even a Hadley here, John R. Hadley, who grew up on the farm that became Hadley Field when his uncle, who lived in the Midwest, leased it to the Post Office Department for an airmail terminus.

Airmail flights had originated at Heller Field in North Newark in what is now part of Branch Brook Park, famed for its cherry blossoms that rival those in Washington. The runway at Heller Field was too short, which led to many accidents, and the operation was shifted to Hadley Field in December of 1924, where it remained until the airmail was shifted back to Newark in 1930, this time to Newark Airport that was a much more suitable facility.

But in those years, during the '20s, when Hadley was a cradle of airmail operations, three of the nation's top airlines had their beginnings there as airmail carriers.

Pitcairn Airways eventually evolved into Eastern Air Lines, Colonial Air Transport became American Airlines, and National Air Transport became United Airlines, all after many mergers.

Ten years ago I wrote about my last flight into Hadley just a few days before the historic Field was closed.

All that remains of Hadley Field today is a granite monument in front of the Holiday Inn adjacent to the Middlesex Mall. It looks like a grave stone. As a matter of fact, that's exactly what it is.

And most of those mentioned in this story who attended the Hadley reunion are gone now to the aviation heaven where Hadley Field rests.

11/12/78

Chapter 24

A Few Delicious Leftovers

I' m convinced Yogi Berra was right. It ain't over 'til it's over.

After I finally finished the last chapter of this tome, I came across a folder of columns I had intended to include, but for which I had never found a home in any particular chapter. Most of them could probably have fit into the chapter on My Favorites, because as it turns out, they were columns that I particularly liked.

I cogitated on it for awhile, and then I thought, gee, these are leftovers, but they prove how good leftovers can be.

And then my brain began thinking in something of a Yogi Berra vein. What if we served the leftovers for dessert?

And so kind reader, here is your dessert.

A FLIGHT TO NOWHERE

There must be a thousand celebrations planned in this 100th anniversary year of the Wright Brothers' first flight at Kill Devil Hills, N.C., on Dec. 17, 1903.

The main one of course, is the one at First Flight Airport in Kitty Hawk, N.C., on Dec. 17, 2003. As this is written, that occasion is still a few months off, but I doubt I will be there. Part of the reason is related to my flight from New Jersey to that same site twenty years earlier on the occasion of the 80th anniversary of the history-making flight.

When you read the story of that adventure you may conclude that it was an exercise in frustration. Sometimes you don't know whether to laugh or cry. It's better to laugh. So this was written with my tongue firmly tucked in my cheek.

Dear Orville and Wilbur:
          Nobody said it was going to be easy.
          A week ago yesterday, they paid tribute to you on the 80th anniversary of your historic achievement at Kill Devil Hills, North Carolina.

There is a 3,000-foot paved strip now on the sands where your first flight took place. Appropriately enough, they have named the strip First Flight. That is where the celebration was held. Unfortunately, you couldn't be there. Neither could I, but for a different reason.

I was looking forward to it with great enthusiasm. It was to be a family trip, the first one in a long while. The kids were filled with anticipation. For some reason or other they seem to have an enormous interest in flying.

All week long we all watched the weather reports, hoping that Saturday would be a good VFR (visual flight rules) day.

On Friday, the outlook was excellent. I called the sponsor of the event (who shall remain nameless) to double check on arrangements.

The field would be closed from noon to 2 p.m., he told me, for a demonstration by a replica of the Wright Flyer. He confirmed that there was no fuel available on the field.

Saturday, the 17th, was a rare day in December. Clear. Excellent visibility. Very little wind. Predicted high temperature for the Kill Devil Hills area was 52 degrees.

OCEANFRONT ROOM, $6 A NIGHT

My first overnight stop in Mexico was an eye-opener. I had no idea what to expect, but when I registered at a hotel in Mazatlan, I have to admit it was not what I expected. I enjoyed my brief stay there and the next morning flew on to a more interesting destination--Puerto Vallarta.

It was a primitive village when I was there, but it had a great deal of charm. It's a popular resort area today.

Few people had ever heard of Puerto Vallarta until Elizabeth Taylor and Richard Burton were there for the filming of Tennessee William's "Night of the Iguana". Burton was in the film. Elizabeth Taylor was not (Ava Gardner played the female lead), but Burton and Taylor were the hottest gossip column item at that time.

It wasn't exactly the kind of place you would expect to find a movie queen and one of the most distinguished actors of his time. It was beautiful, but primitive. I met interesting people there and my visit was one of the most enjoyable interludes of my trip.

Outside the terminal at Mazatlan, I found a friendly looking cab driver and I opened my Diner's Club Directory and showed it to him asking for recommendations. His English is on a par with my Spanish. So I pointed to the first listing. He looked at it and said, "Yes." I pointed to the second listing and he said, "Yes." And so on for every hotel on the list. It was obvious that he thought every hotel on the Diner's Club list was a good one. But I had to pick one.

There must be many solutions to a situation like this. Mine was to pick the tallest waterfront hotel. In this respect, the Freemont Hotel towered above all others.

"Do you want a room in front for $6 or a room in back for $4?", the man at the hotel counter asked. On my first night in Mexico, I decided to splurge.

The room was rather spartan. It had a nice balcony overlooking the Pacific with two comfortable beach chairs. The room was comfortably furnished, but not exactly plush. It had wall-to-wall concrete, the floor, the walls, the ceiling were all concrete. It looked like it wasn't finished yet. The waterfront hotels in Mazatlan are not in the Miami Beach or Acapulco league, but then, neither are the rates. (I'm sure that's changed by now, but I haven't been back.)

This being a famous fishing port I decided on seafood for dinner, which was no mistake. I dined at a pleasant looking place called La Copa de Leche on the waterfront just a short walk from the Freemont.

The red snapper was as good as you'll find anywhere. And they served two good sized fish.

In the morning, after an American-style breakfast of hot cakes and bacon at a restaurant not far from the hotel on the street that ran along the waterfront, I proceeded out to the airport for the relatively short flight to Puerto Vallarta.

As I untied 197 Charlie I spied another fellow nearby pre-flighting a shiny Beechcraft Bonanza with "Nut Tree" painted on the side.

Nut Tree restaurant in California with its adjacent airport and miniature railway from the strip to the restaurant, is as famous out west as New Jersey's Flying W is in the east.

I walked over to say hello and met Edwin I. Power, Jr., one of the partners at Nut Tree that is located near San Francisco.

He introduced me to his wife, Sophie, who turned out to be a Jersey girl. She graduated from Clifton High in 1940. In the yearbook she's McPhee Unesco.

Two fellows pre-flighting a Citabria, were also from California, and they said they were headed for Puerto Vallarta also. They took off just behind me and after I had made one circle over the city shooting pictures they were on my right side heading down the coast.

The Citabria slowly pulled away from 197C and after 75 miles I lost sight of it. When I landed at Puerto Vallarta, a town that still has no highway, but does have jet service, the Citabria was not there.

A small boy was at the paved parking area that had no tie downs. He found a chock and placed it under one wheel, then he gathered stones to place on both sides of the other wheels. All efforts to get him to smile for a picture were unsuccessful, which was unusual since the Mexicans are generally a very happy people.

After I closed my flight plan and came back for my bags, the two fellows in the Citabria taxied in. They had circled the town to look down at the hotel they were staying at that has its own private beach.

Puerto Vallarta turned out to be my favorite stop of the trip. It's small, it's rather primitive, with dusty cobblestone streets. It's quiet, and it's beautiful.

The town is built on the side of a hill and some of the streets are just steps. I was walking up one such street shortly after I got settled in Hotel Aero when I spotted a sign saying "Chez Elena."

My friend Peter Callers of the Mexican Tourist Council in New York had suggested I look up Elena when I stopped at Puerto Vallarta.

He described her as "a garrulous character who had been there a long time and knows more about the place than anyone."

The description turned out to be bristling with accuracy and we were not in the least surprised. An ample woman of half Mexican, half American ancestry and background, she described herself in exactly the same terms Callers had.

"Puerto Vallarta will never become another Acapulco the way some people think," Elena said, "because we only have a hundred small beaches. We don't have one big beach and that's what you need to have an Acapulco." (She turned out to be wrong about that. Puerto Vallarta is a major resort today).

I returned a few hours later for dinner on the beautiful open patio high up the hill. When one of her guests asked for a dry martini, Elena said, "Would you like to make your own?" Pretty soon everybody was at the bar mixing their own.

During meal service, Elena chased her waiters and kitchen help like an angry mother hen clucking away at errant chicks. She had been away in Guadalajara for several days "and everything went to pot," she grumbled. The meal was delicious and piping hot, even though a bit slow in arriving.

"The secret of running a good restaurant," Elena said, "is first, atmosphere, then good food, then good service. Cleanliness is indispensable," she added, "and I would also have to add, the food should be hot."

I dined here with Ken and Maggie Howe, Americans now living in Mexico who made enamels that they sell at the one-day-a-week Bazaar Sabado in Mexico City.

When I said I planned to leave the next day for either Manzanillo or Zihuatenajo, Ken thought I was crazy because he thought I would be leaving paradise to head for something less.

He told me I would be foolish to leave without taking the all-day boat ride across the bay to Yelapa where I would discover what he described as "instant Tahiti."

So I stayed. I took the boat ride that followed the coast for 22 miles past such points of interest as the house where "Night of the Iguana" was filmed with Ava Gardner and Richard Burton. "The house," said our guide, Benjamin Medina Duenas, "is 262 years old. But the movie company renovated it."

At Yelapa there was a lovely beach and a hotel with thatched-roof cottages that was exactly what Ken Howe had described: "instant Tahiti."

I hiked up a trail in Yelapa, a village of 175 people all belonging to three families descended from the Aztecs. They raise coffee in the hills and dry the beans in the village. Two hundred and fifty thousand pounds of coffee are shipped from the village every year.

There is no electricity. There are no roads, only trails. But the people are well dressed. The shirts on the lines look like they might have come from Bamberger's department store. They look good and they are the whitest white you ever saw.

Climbing up a rocky trail from the village you come to an 84-foot waterfall, also called Yelapa. The word means "meeting place" and this is where the Aztecs met with the tribe from across the bay.

The next day I left Puerto Vallarta with considerable reluctance. But Acapulco was waiting for me.

3/26/67

ACAPULCO, HERE I COME

Acapulco was one of the top watering places for the Hollywood set. When you took the boat ride around the bay they pointed out the homes of the rich and famous in the hills looking down on the picture postcard scene below. The fancy homes were on the other side of the bay from the hotels.

Here, under the warm, bright, winter sun is where the jet set congregated. I hardly expected to rub shoulders with these people, but following up on a lead from an airline public relations friend in New York, I wound up in their midst and found out something about how the other half lives.

When I got ready to take off from Puerto Vallarta bound for Acapulco, one of my major stops on my flight to Mexico, I had to wait for a Comet to land. (The Comet, built by the British, was the first passenger jet to go into service.) Whoever would come to Puerto Vallarta would come by plane or by boat because there is no road to the town. They've got 35 more miles to go and they will be connected to the rest of the world by road.

On this leg of the trip I would be following the coast, cutting a corner here and there where a point of land jutted way out. My first stop was at Manzanillo where the chart indicated I would find a 3,764-foot gravel strip. My Jeppesen Airport Directory chart was dated May 25, 1965. This was almost two years later and the strip had been paved since then. The field is several miles from town and is surrounded by flat, open land. When you taxi up to the little gas shack you feel like you've landed a long way from anywhere. But when I opened the door I was pleasantly surprised to be greeted by a fellow who said, "Hi there." Everywhere I had landed previously I couldn't understand them and they couldn't understand me.

The welcome came from a fellow whose business card reads: R.E. (Robert) Hallsey, Piloto, Aviador. Piloto Hallsey, I learned, has lived in Manzanillo for 13 years and for the last four he has been running the airport--a non salaried job.

Before retiring to Manzanillo he ran an air charter service out of San Francisco.

Hallsey admired the paint job on Stinson 197C and asked how much it cost. When I told him, he thought awhile and then said, "I'll do a job like that for less than half of that--$240. And we use the best paint. Somebody can fly down here and have a free vacation with the money they'll save. We just finished painting that Bonanza. We'll paint a twin for $450."

I asked him how come I couldn't pick up the Manzanillo radio beacon and he told me there was a good reason. Although it's on the charts, there is no beacon in Manzanillo. I asked him about the radio at Mazatlan that I couldn't pick up either. He told me, "Yes, they do have one, but they sometimes turn it off unless an airliner is coming in."

Hallsey went over my ON chart and pointed out all the airports shown that aren't really there and marked a great many that are there but aren't on the chart. Many of them were private strips on huge ranches. I was anxious to get to Acapulco before dark since it's illegal to fly VFR after dark in Mexico. But he kept telling me things I didn't want to know and I couldn't stop him. I just kept getting more concerned about getting off.

When I was finally able to get him to let me go, I thanked him and off I went for Zihuatenajo, some 210 miles further down the coast. The strip at Zihuatenajo lies between two ridges. The only way to get in is to fly around the back of one of the ridges on the downwind leg. But the ridge was high enough to obliterate the view of the runway. You flew downwind until you came to an opening in the ridge which put you on a 45-degree angle to the runway to get on final toward the ocean. You glide in over a cemetery that had graves close to the end of the runway.

Although Zihuatenajo is a tiny town, the runway here is a long, wide blacktop and they were working to make it even bigger. As a matter of fact, there was heavy equipment in the middle of the strip that never budged as I made my approach. Fortunately, there was plenty of room to land short of the equipment.

I was gassed up promptly here (with gas coming from drums, as it did at Manzanillo). While four little boys briskly wiped down the airplane I paid my landing fee, gave the little boys some change, and I was out of Zihuatenajo within half an hour. There were two planes on the field, incidentally, one of Mexican registry, and one American. I did not have to file a flight plan here or at Manzanillo since I filed from Puerto Vallarta to Acapulco with two stops.

Just over an hour later I flew over the bay at Acapulco, as lovely a sight as you could ever hope to see.

Driving into town in a cab, I stopped at one beachfront hotel after the other along the main avenue, inquiring as to the availability of a room. Everywhere, the response was the same--nothing. I asked him to stop at hotels that were not on the beach. No rooms in any of them either. I finally asked the cab driver to take me to an address given me by a friend back home. The address took us to a small

Spanish-style building with a courtyard in the center and ten rooms opening off the courtyard. It was not on the beach. It was in town. It was unlisted, unadvertised, unheralded, and not exactly in the tourist area--but they had one room available. I lucked out. Someone had left unexpectedly earlier that day. I learned the hard way that it is definitely not a good idea to go to Acapulco at the height of the season without a reservation.

Back in New York, my friend Lillian Sessions, who sings the praises of flying to Mexico — and points south — via Braniff International Airlines, suggested that when I got to Acapulco I give her friend Sloan Simpson a buzz. This is the same Sloan Simpson who was the top model in New York before she married Mayor Bill O'Dwyer and became the first lady of New York City. Later O'Dwyer became the American Ambassador to Mexico which made her the ambassador's wife.

When I phoned, she said, "I'm having a few people over tonight. Why don't you stop over?" I arrived early and found Miss Simpson looking chic enough in silk slacks to still be a top model.

Her home has a long, covered patio from which all rooms in the house open. There is a lovely garden running the full length of the patio. By the time her "few friends" stopped arriving there were several dozen people on the patio and in the garden.

The fashions worn by the women were creations you would hardly expect to see outside the pages of *Vogue*. And there were some gorgeous women poured into those fashions.

One of the loveliest, a strikingly beautiful blonde, turned out to be a model from Iceland who has done numerous TV commercials and has had a number of small parts in movies.

Another strikingly dressed girl turned out to be from a family that owns one of the largest chains of movie theaters in the U.S. We met a woman designer who said she gave Sloan her first job as a model.

And then we met Buck Rogers--and that's for real--a fellow who used to be the manager of the upscale Pierre Marques Hotel in Acapulco and who now has plans to build a 500-room hotel with a golf course. It would be the first golf course in Acapulco.

And among the attractive young ladies present was his daughter, who, when she's not enjoying the social life in Acapulco, makes her home in Princeton, N.J.

So, on our first night in Acapulco, thanks to Lillian Sessions, and Sloan Simpson, we discovered the jet set. It was one of the highlights of this visit to Acapulco.

4/2/67

OBSTACLES ABOUND ON FLIGHT TO MEXICO CITY

Mexico City is a beautiful metropolis, but getting there in a single-engine aircraft can have its problems.

The city, which sits in a bowl at an altitude of more than 7,000 feet, is ringed by mountains that reach up to more than 12,000 feet.

The mountains that surround the city do not permit the pollution, which is high, to blow away. It is confined to the bowl. This creates restricted visibility to aircraft flying in.

I surmounted these obstacles without great difficulty and felt, after sampling all that the city had to offer, that it was worth whatever challenge might have been encountered in getting there.

I had many warnings about flying into Mexico City. The smog and haze are very bad, I was told. And the blowing sand is worse. Get there early because it's at its worse in the afternoon, I was advised.

I left Acapulco at 8:30 in the morning. The weather report at Acapulco said there was four miles visibility at Mexico City in smoke and haze. And if I was to believe what I was told, it would get worse. Weather information is good at Acapulco and Mexico City. At most other places in Mexico, forget it. However in the winter in Mexico--except on the Gulf Coast--weather is near perfect all the time.

There was heavy ground fog in the valleys as I climbed out, heading for 12,000 feet because the pass into Mexico City on the highway is 10,000 feet high, with peaks as high as 12,917 feet on one side and 12,096 feet on the other. If your altimeter reads 11,000 feet, you're 1000 feet over the highway.

When I arrived at Mexico City (field elevation 7,340 feet), visibility at the airport was about 4 miles in smoke and haze. The weatherman was right. The runway boundary lights were on.

The big three--Cessna, Piper, and Beech--all have facilities here and you can take your choice for parking and service. I thought *Charlie* might feel more at home among the high-wing Cessnas (*Charlie* is a high wing airplane), so that's where I headed.

The Cessna facility looked much neater and cleaner than most operations you would find back home. The long hangar, open at one side, was crowded with many twins, including 411s and 310s.

A lineboy met me, clipboard in hand to record my needs. His English was, as I had encountered previously, somewhat akin to my Spanish--virtually nil.

But when a Mexican lineboy can't understand you, he sticks with it until somehow or other he figures out what you want. Between the two of us, the form on his clipboard was filled out without too much trouble.

The commandant's office, where my flight plan had to be closed, is on the other side of the field and the only way to get there is by cab.

The wait for the cab was considerable, but then, the cab driver waited for me at the terminal and watched my bags and cameras while I finished my business with the commandant's office which took only a few minutes. And then I took off for the city. Of the major cities of the world that I've visited--including Paris, London, Rome, Zurich, Brussels, Honolulu, and Tel Aviv, Mexico City ranks right up there.

Its boulevards, particularly the broad, landscaped Paseo de La Reforma, are among the most beautiful in the world. Likewise, the monuments and fountains. There are strikingly beautiful buildings. You'll find fine hotels and magnificent restaurants.

But the one thing that counts even more than all this is the people. They are friendly. They are helpful. You never get the feeling that they've got you spotted as a tourist and they're going to "take" you, that you get in many other countries.

Wherever you travel in Mexico City you will find an abundance of art works. There are brilliant murals in the lobbies of hotels. One of the most colorful graces the outside of a movie theater.

On Sundays in Mexico City there is a park that becomes a Garden of Art. There, artists from all over the country display their works in an open air gallery. You can find works here of every style and technique. A great deal of it is of high quality. We don't recall any exhibit in which we saw so many works we would like to own. And happily, prices are in most cases, unbelievably reasonable.

On Saturdays there is the Bazaar Sabado, an old, Spanish style building where all kinds of arts and crafts works are on sale. Here, as in the Garden of Art, which, incidentally, has different artists every week because many come from far away and come only periodically, you will find many unusual things. It's a good place to pick up gifts and souvenirs that are a bit out of the ordinary.

Mexico City's Palace of Fine Arts contains many world-famous paintings. And in the auditorium here, every Sunday, you can see the colorful Ballet Folklorico de Mexico.

The new Museum of Anthropology houses one of the world's finest collections of archeological objects tracing the history of man in a building that is as noteworthy for its architecture as it is for its exhibits.

Mexicans are extremely proud of their country and its capital. One wealthy Mexican I met summed it up best. "It is so important that we have the Olympics here in 1968," he said with great conviction. "It doesn't matter," he said, "if we win the 100 yard dash or the discus throw. What is important is that the whole world will see that we are first in art and culture."

If the Mexicans love art, so too, do they love music. And in Mexico City there are many places where you can find it. One of the best known is the Plaza Garibaldi where Mariachis play in the street. There are usually eight to ten musicians in a group--guitars, violins, trumpets. They play with great gusto, if not always great intonation, and frequently two or three groups are playing at once, stirring up a cacophony that attacks your ears with a vengeance.

They will serenade you for a contribution of ten pesos (80 cents) per selection. When this grows to be too much for your ears, you can retire to one of the surrounding bars such as Guadalajara de Noches, where your ears will be subjected to but one group at a time and the quality of the music is much higher than what you encounter on the street.

Many of the hotels and night clubs have groups for the more refined ear.

One more thing that should not be overlooked when you are talking about Mexico is the bullfight. We will discuss that subject in the next column.

4/9/67

THROWING THE BULL--MEXICAN STYLE

Bullfighting is a passion of the Mexicans the way baseball, football, basketball, and hockey are to Americans in the United States.

The largest bullring in the world is in Mexico City, but the passion for bullfighting extends far beyond that ring. In one instance I encountered an unusual bullfight on the beach at Acapulco.

In another ring I became the matador--with unfortunate consequences.

And finally, I went for the big time in an effort to discover what it was about this activity (I hesitate to call it a sport) that fired such passion in Ernest Hemingway and continues to excite spectators as if every bullfight was the seventh game of the World Series.

Ferdinand the Bull would not have liked it in Mexico. Mexicans do not take lightly to shy, peace-loving bulls. In Mexico City they like brave bulls.

The life expectancy of a brave bull, once such bravery is put on public display, is about 20 minutes. The Ferdinands live longer.

I attended four bullfights in Mexico before returning to the side of the Rio Grande where the bulls and the tap water are safe. The first of these was at the bullring in Acapulco. Here, I learned that there are better things to watch in Acapulco than bulls. The second was at Paradise Beach in Acapulco. The third at Texcoco, some 35 miles outside of Mexico City. Here, for a small fee, you can enjoy the thrill, etc. etc., of fighting your own bull. And the fourth was at Plaza de Toro in Mexico City, the world's largest bullring.

At Paradise Beach in Acapulco I was hardly prepared for a bullfight. I was just sitting around in the open air restaurant on the beach drinking watered down pineapple juice while innocently watching the girls in the bikinis do the hully gully or whatever it is they call it nowadays.

All at once the music stopped and the girls all took their bikinis back to their coconut cocktails.

When the dance floor was bare, the band struck up what was unmistakably bullfight music. And hark! The black-bearded fellow who only moments before was the maitre'd, was suddenly a matador in a brocaded red jacket with a bullfighter's hat and a red cape.

He strutted proudly into the arena, bowing and doffing his hat to the assembled aficionados who welcomed him with enthusiastic approval. He was tailed by an entourage of flunkies bearing white table cloths over their arms.

Enter the bull. This bull bears a strong resemblance to my waiter. But he is much braver than any waiter. He carries a pair of horns and lowers his head and makes pass after pass at the matador's red cape. He is magnificent. But the people cheer the matador.

Enter the picador--a little boy riding on the shoulders of a "horse," holding a broom. He sticks the bull with his broom and one of the flunkies spills a soup plate full of ketchup on the bull's back. It is not a sight for weak stomachs.

Now it is time to place the banderillos. The matador rears up on his toes, runs swiftly at the bull, and places the banderillos (two straws) in the bull's back. The crowd cheers wildly. They are strongly anti-bull.

The matador makes some good passes and the crowd (even the girls in the bikinis) is beside itself with excitement, shouting "Ole, Ole!"

Then the matador struts around the dance floor (er, arena), pointing thumbs down and the audience is in a terrible frenzy. The bull is doomed.

The kill is swift. The approval is unrestrained. The matador waves his prize up high. Is it the ears? No. The tail? No. Let us just say if the bull were still alive, he would be a Ferdinand.

My next encounter with the bull was a very personal one. This took place at the beautiful new Plaza de Toro la Morena in Texcoco. Here, for a modest fee, you can meet the bull face-to-face. The fee for this privilege is $20, but it can be divided among four would-be matadors.

In the dressing room, the boys put the chaps on you. (You look more like a cowboy than a bullfighter.) They put a big Mexican hat on your head. They drape a cape over your arm and they point you toward the ring.

The doors swing open. The bullfight music blares from the loudspeakers, and you march into the ring to the place marked "Authorities" where you bow low. Then comes the bull. He is small and he looks harmless enough. The professional bullfighter who is in the ring with you makes some passes and you can see the bull knows exactly what to do and it is all very simple.

Enter Matador Elliott from behind the barrier. The bull has a kind of "I don't believe it" look in his eye. Matador Elliott waves the cape (Bulls cannot distinguish color--they are all color blind--only motion.) That red cape jazz is for the spectators, not the bull.

The nice little bull comes running across the ring. He misses the cape completely. He hits the matador. Matador Elliott is on the ground rolling around in the sand, looking up at the bull.

Eventually, when he regains his feet, Matador Elliott feels like he has been riding a horse for a week or so. He stumbles bravely behind the barrier.

Soon the professional bullfighter comes over and says, "Now would you like to try the muleta?" That is the red cape with a stick in it. Matador Elliott is very honest. He says, "No."

The professional bullfighter goes out and plays with the bull. They both seem to be having a good time. Then the pro comes over and says to Matador Elliott, "Now would you like to try the muleta?"

What do you say after you've said, "No?" Matador Elliott takes the muleta. He has great difficulty walking out to the ring. The bull is over there. Matador Elliott is over here. A great distance separates the two adversaries.

A voice from the crowd shouts, "Go closer!" In his best flamenco style, Matador Elliott triple steps closer. More advice. The voice from the stands shouts, "Wave the cape." Matador Elliott waves the cape. A fatal mistake. The bull sees it.

The bull puts his head down and comes at the cape full speed. Brave Matador Elliott does not run. This is the biggest mistake of all. Matador Elliot goes flying--without benefit of airplane. When he comes down, it is not on his feet.

Very slowly, very painfully, very stiff-leggedly, Matador Elliott retires from the ring--forever.

Let it never be said that Matador Elliott is a bull thrower.

The next day was Sunday and I dragged my aching posterior to the huge bullring in Mexico City. I was accompanied by Rene Ruiz and Luis Garrido from the office of the Mexican Tourist Council. The council had obtained permission for me to shoot movies of the bullfights from the corridor between the bullring and the stands...but not without many warnings that the bull sometimes jumps over the fence and into the corridor. While I photographed the action, Luis Garrido, an expert on bullfighting, described the action on my reel-to-reel tape recorder. He explained the passes made by the Spanish bullfighter Diego Puerto, and he described each of the stages of the bullfight, following the initial "feeling out" of the bull with the cape.

First comes the picador on a padded, blindfolded horse. As the bull attacks the horse, the picador "punishes" the bull by driving a steel-pointed pole into the bull's back. This stimulates the bull to fight and it weakens certain muscles in the shoulder, causing the bull to lower his head so that the bullfighter can make the kill.

The next step is the placing of three sets of banderillos, brightly-colored sticks with steel-pointed tips, in the bull's back.

Following this, the matador will make passes until he has the bull under control and is ready to make the kill. The kill, when perfectly executed, is accomplished by driving the sword up to the hilt and into the heart of the bull.

In the bullring, as in some other places, it takes two to tango. Diego Puerto was brave and skillful, but the bull did not always provide him with the best opportunity to demonstrate his skill. But then, Puerto gets $15,000 for an afternoon of work. The bull has less incentive.

Before the fifth fight (there are six on the program), Luis Garrido chided me about the fifth bull. It is usually the one that jumps over the fence.

Enter the fifth bull. The toreador waves the cape. The bull runs like crazy--the other way. A toreador on the other side of the ring waves the cape. The bull turns and runs away. He's not dumb.

Garrido turns to me. "It is a coward bull," he says. "We never see a coward bull. The coward bull is the one that jumps over the fence."

Luis was right. The bull jumped over the fence. And not on the opposite side of the ring either. He hurtled the fence just a few feet from the barrier where the retired bullfighter, Matador Elliott, sought shelter. He fortunately turned the other way and attacked the next shelter, splintering the corner and ripping the trousers of one of the men who sought shelter there. I decided then, not only to retire from the ring, but from the shelter as well.

The next day I did my flying in 197 Charlie from Mexico City to Tampico to refuel, and head for Matamoras where I checked out of Mexico. Then I hopped just across the Rio Grande to Brownsville, Tex., where I checked back in to the United States.

On the following day I flew from Brownsville to New Orleans. From New Orleans I flew to Danville, Va., where I had spent the first night of this trip.

The following day, the exact same winds that were blowing the day I left (which held my ground speed to 54.5 miles an hour), were still blowing--this time in my favor.

On the final leg of the flight I made an average ground speed of 140 miles an hour. It had been a wonderful trip, but the runway at Princeton Airport was a beautiful sight. One of the most beautiful of the entire trip.

4/16/67

Chapter 26

Mexican Encore

If it was an adventure the first time, it was no less so on my second flight to Mexico. This time, however, there were two differences; I had a newer aircraft with better equipment, and I had good company, my wife, Esta-Ann.

On this trip we visited Guadalajara, where neither of us had been before, Puerto Vallarta, where both of us had been previously (but not together), and Zihuatenajo where I had stopped on my first flight but where Esta-Ann had never been.

I didn't suffer a fractured tail wheel on this flight because the Arrow we were flying on this trip doesn't have a tail wheel. And this time I didn't fight any bulls. I had been fully convinced that once was enough.

It was a memorable flight nonetheless.

THE FIRST TWO DAYS WERE DIFFERENT THIS TIME

Our first stop in Mexico on my second trip south of the border was Guadalajara, the country's second largest city which I had not visited on my first flight.

This was a new adventure and a pleasant one, in spite of the glitches that you can usually count on if you're making a long trip and are flying into another country.

This time, in spite of headwinds, we made New Orleans, our first overnight stop, in one day instead of two. We arrived a bit later than we planned, but we spent our first night in the wild and wooly Fun City near the mouth of the Mississippi.

The second night of this trip we had a delicious dinner in Mexico.

At 7:23 on Saturday morning, March 1, some 17 minutes before the sun poked its head above the horizon, we lifted off the runway at Somerset (N.J.) Airport in Cherokee Arrow N4858J bound for another country and another seacoast.

Piper Arrow N4858J in flight.

Tony Link Photo

Ahead of us lay 2,800 miles of geography--cities and open country, marshes, swamps and towering mountains. And at the end of the line the tiny fishing village of Zihuatenajo on the Pacific Coast.

It was our hope to get to New Orleans the first day. We planned to have dinner at Brennan's and then take a Saturday night stroll down famed, carnival-like Bourbon Street.

The weather briefing we had received from New Jersey Weather Service at Morristown Airport had told us we could expect clear weather and excellent visibility all the way, but with high winds, mostly on our nose, and with turbulence. The forecast turned out to be quite accurate.

We planned to follow a flight plan prepared for us by AOPA (Aircraft Owners and Pilots Association). This lists each omni station along the route, magnetic headings, point-to-point distances, total distances and airways to follow. All of which saves hours of flight planning time and makes it simple to file flight plans. (Today's avionics equipment does all this for you.)

The flight plan form also provides a space for estimated time to each station, actual time and ground speed. Taking care of all of this bookkeeping was Esta-Ann's task on the flight.

Although we had hoped to make New Orleans (1,156 miles) with one stop, the headwinds canceled that idea and we wound up following the AOPA flight plan that had scheduled two stops, one at Greensboro, N.C., and another at LaGrange, Ga., just south of Atlanta.

Because the headwinds were stronger at higher altitudes, we spent the first day's flight at low altitudes, mostly at 2,500 feet. The higher altitude flying would come later in Mexico.

We arrived in the New Orleans area several hours later than anticipated and just in time to encounter an evening thundershower. As we ran into it, 35 miles east of New Orleans, approach control picked us up on radar and advised us of heavy cells in our path, but said there was no rain at our destination, Moisant International Airport.

While they watched us we veered off course enough to go through the fringe of the shower, still picking up some pretty heavy rain.

It was 7:30 when we touched down, many hours later than planned because of the headwinds all the way, but we still had dinner at Brennan's and enjoyed our Saturday night stroll down Bourbon Street that is now closed to vehicular traffic and consequently more carnival-like than ever. The street was swarming with people soaking up the noises of the jazz houses, the strip joints, and the hawkers in front of both.

Our fuel bill to New Orleans was $66.50. We checked the airline coach fare and found it would have cost us $104 each.

At 9:38 on Sunday morning we were off for Laredo, Texas, on the Mexican border.

Again, the weather report was generally favorable with improving conditions reported along our route. We planned to make one stop at Corpus Christi, per our AOPA flight plan. But the en route weather reports indicated that the low ceilings forecasted at our scheduled stopping point were not lifting as early as predicted.

So we landed at Palacios, Texas, instead, refueled and filed a flight plan for a route a few miles further north where the weather was better.

We arrived at Laredo at 3:40 p.m., checked into a motel near the airport and headed for the International Bridge to walk into

Mexico.

It costs five cents to walk across the bridge over the Rio Grande River (which is very narrow and unimpressive here) from the U.S. into Mexico. Coming back it cost a penny.

Nuevo Laredo, on the other side of the bridge, was much more impressive than I had remembered it when I stopped here in 1967 on my flight in Stinson 197C.

The honky-tonk look I remembered was largely gone. There were a couple of very fine shops and even the tourist souvenir shops were rather nice. But don't try to get Mexican currency in change. All the tourist shops in Nuevo Laredo, Mexico, have only American money.

Several people in Laredo, on the other side of the border, had recommended a relatively new restaurant called the Winery in their sister city to the south.

Downstairs there was an intimate cocktail lounge with Mexican music. The restaurant was on the second floor. To reach it you walked a wide curved staircase with tropical plants on both sides.

The heavy, dark Spanish decor was attractive and the menu, a combination of both Mexican and American dishes, was impressive.

Esta-Ann found one Italian dish, Fetuccini Alfredo, on the menu. She may be the only woman who ever flew to Mexico for Italian food, but that's what she ordered.

She raved about it, so I tried some and found it to be as good as any Fetuccini Alfredo I ever ate anywhere--including Italy. We didn't worry about cholesterol in those days.

The check was brought to the table in the yellowing pages of a book that was more than 125 years old. That surely takes your mind off the size of the bill, which in this case wasn't really necessary since the whole tab came to $15.40, including wine.

That night we got to bed early to be ready for the mountains of Mexico, en route to Guadalajara the next day.

3/23/75

OVER THE MOUNTAINS TO GUADALAJARA

There is always something intriguing about visiting a city for the first time. Every city has a personality of its own, reflected in its people, its buildings, its main thoroughfares, its hotels, its restaurants, its museums.

Neither Esta-Ann nor I had ever been to Guadalajara, Mexico's second largest city, so we were both looking forward to it. And getting there in our Piper Arrow was not quite the routine way to get there. So when we took off from Laredo, Texas, for Guadalajara, we had a lot to look forward to. Here is an account of that leg of our trip.

We filed our flight plan from Laredo, Tex., to Monterrey, Mexico, 130 miles to the south, and took off at 9 in the morning.

The weather report for Monterrey was clear, but it was overcast at Laredo. After take off we climbed to 1,200 feet. That was as high as we could get and still stay under the overcast, and we flew across the Rio Grande into Mexico.

A half hour later we were down to 800 feet, and with mountains more than 4,000 feet high just this side of Monterrey, we decided it would be a good idea to turn around and come back.

Guadalajara's main square with the city's beautiful cathedral in the background.

One hour later it was clear at Laredo and we took off again. After just over an hour's flight time we were on the ground at Monterrey.

A young fellow in a bright orange jacket, pushing a hand truck for baggage, came out to meet us.

Since we were heading for Guadalajara after going through all the port of entry formalities, we didn't need to unload.

The young man in the orange jacket was our escort through all the entry procedures.

First, he took us to a neat, new-looking office where we had to close our flight plan and pay our landing fee. In Mexico flight plans are mandatory and you must close them in person.

At every airport where we stopped there was a man at a typewriter who very quickly filled out a landing fee form ($1.60 a landing) and gave us a form to fill out to close our flight plan. In every case these men spoke English.

"!!Viva Mexico!! Have wife. Must travel " is the inscription on the tail of a Cessna with Mexican registry which Esta-Ann found parked at the airport in Guadalajara.

In the same office we bought a RAMSA card for $6.25. This entitles a pilot to unlimited use of communications and weather facilities. Otherwise you must pay a separate fee at each stop. It's a small fee, but if you're going to make more than two or three stops, it pays to buy the card.

Only once were we asked if we had the card, and a couple of times when we filed flight plans we were given weather at our destination without being asked for it.

After we paid our landing fee and closed our flight plan the boy in the orange jacket took us to customs where our tourist cards were stamped.

Then he took us to still another office, immigration, where an attractive young lady typed out our general declaration form indicating ownership of the aircraft, number of passengers, etc.

He then escorted us back to the original office to file our flight plan for Guadalajara.

Our only problem came when we asked the line crew to fill our tank with 100 octane gas. "No 100 octane," the line boy said, "manana" --tomorrow. This seemed unbelievable at an international airport. Line crews, incidentally, generally spoke no English.

After a bit of haggling, and with the help of the English speaking man in the office, we finally got 100 octane and took off for Guadalajara, 435 miles to the south.

On this leg of our trip we did not follow the AOPA (Aircraft Owners and Pilots Association) flight plan route. That route was 250 miles longer than the direct route.

At first we couldn't understand it, but after a little study of the charts it became clear. The direct route was a jet airway that means flight levels above 20,000 feet. There was no low level airway.

The obvious reason for this is the fact that directly to the south of Monterrey there is a broad band of mountains more than 12,000 feet high. AOPA would not route a single-engine aircraft over a jet route and the only alternative was the long way round--if you were going to follow airways.

But we discovered still another alternative. By flying west from Monterrey for about 50 miles, you can fly through a pass (off airways) and then turn south and pick up the Salinas omni more than 200 miles away.

The fixed base operator at Laredo had assured us that this was the best route because once we flew through the pass we would be flying over a level plateau 7,000 feet high to the outskirts of Guadalajara.

We flew the route at 10,500 feet and had no difficulty. We did carry two tanks of oxygen, but even at 11,500 feet we felt no need for them.

At Guadalajara, elevation 5,012 feet, a young man helped us park the airplane and tie it down and then picked us and our luggage up in a van and drove us to the general aviation terminal.

We had first gassed up and charged it on a Master Charge card. Every airport we stopped at pumped gas from a truck or a pump (no oil drums this trip) and everywhere they accepted Master Charge, which was not the case on the first trip.

Every tower controller spoke clear English. That wasn't always the case on our first trip either.

We found personnel at Mexican airports to be universally helpful, polite and efficient.

Guadalajara is a busy, bustling metropolis. Avenida Juarez, the main shopping street, is crowded with people and vehicular traffic and at night brightly colored electrical signs gave it a glowing atmosphere.

It is not a Mexico City, but it does have some lovely sections and some beautiful boulevards, monuments, parks, arcades, pretty squares, a magnificent cathedral and good restaurants.

It was an interesting experience to visit a major city that is not on every tourist's itinerary.

Our next scheduled stop was Puerto Vallarta.

3/30/75

CRISIS IN THE COCKPIT

The most memorable thing about our flight from Guadalajara to Puerto Vallarta was the fact that immediately after we took off I knew something was wrong, but I didn't know what. It was one of those occurrences that hits you unexpectedly, and in this case it was something I will never forget.

When we got to Puerto Vallarta, after solving the problem, we met a lot of fellow Jerseyans, an experience that creates the feeling that you're never far from home.

O n the morning we planned to fly from Guadalajara to Puerto Vallarta, a thick layer of haze and smoke hung over the city. From our hotel window you could barely see a couple of blocks.

As the morning wore on, the haze lifted only slightly. But since the weather report was good, we headed for the airport. As we got out of town the fog evaporated. The airport was clear.

We took off at 11:19 under a blazing sun on the 128-mile flight to the Pacific Coast resort.

After takeoff, the climb out was unusually sluggish. The airport elevation was 5,012 feet which would account for the poor performance to some extent. And it was quite hot, which would also affect the rate of climb.

It took us more than ten minutes to reach 7,000 feet--a climb of only 2,000 feet. Even under the existing conditions it shouldn't have taken more than four or five minutes. Something was definitely wrong. But I could not figure out what it was.

I circled in the vicinity of the airport and checked all the instruments. Everything was in the green. The engine sounded normal. Then I leaned over to check the gear lever. I don't know why. It was clearly visible without bending over. It was in the up position where it belonged. As I leaned over I cast a shadow on the three gear lights. All three green lights were on indicating the gear was still down despite the gear lever being in the up position.

With the extremely bright midday sun shining on the lights, they were not visible.

The gear hanging down would create considerable drag and combined with the altitude and temperature, the climb performance would be sluggish.

Why was the gear down when we had pulled the gear lever up to raise it? The Cherokee Arrow has a system that automatically lowers the gear when the power or speed are reduced as would be the case in a landing approach. This is a safety feature to prevent a gear-up landing if the pilot should be forgetful.

On takeoff the same system prevents gear retraction until the aircraft reaches a speed of approximately 85 miles an hour. I had lowered the nose numerous times in the course of our climb to bring the speed up to 100 miles an hour, but the gear had not come up. At higher altitudes, the speed at which the gear will come up increases.

When I discovered what the problem was, I pressed the emergency gear up lever that cuts off the automatic system and the gear retracted immediately. And at once the plane behaved differently.

Aurora Puga, right, shows Esta-Ann Elliott where her architect husband is planning a community of luxury homes on a mountainside where "Night of the Iguana" was filmed.

We climbed to 10,500 feet and in less than an hour we came over the mountains and the Pacific Ocean hove into view along with the Puerto Vallarta airstrip stretching toward it.

Our stay at this resort was at the Posada Vallarta, the largest, the best known, and probably the most luxurious hotel in the city made famous by Elizabeth Taylor and Richard Burton during the filming of Tennessee Williams' "Night of the Iguana." (A great many luxury hotels have been built since our visit.)

One of the first things we wondered was whether there were any other Jerseyans at the Posada Vallarta. We had our answer soon enough.

On our first turn around the grounds I spotted a fellow on the beach reading the *Wall Street Journal*. I hadn't seen a newspaper and hadn't heard any bad news in nearly a week.

Turned out the fellow had picked up the newspaper on the plane from St. Louis that morning.

I said that we were from New Jersey and a couple in the group said, "We're from Princeton." They were Ruth and Marty Wolfson.

I mentioned that there were no *Wall Street Journals* on our flight in the Arrow from Somerset Airport. As soon as I said Somerset, they said, "Oh, we know Dick Nierenberg who runs Kupper Airport in Manville." That's only a few miles from Somerset Airport.

We mentioned the *Star-Ledger* and they said, "Oh, we know Al Stein of the *Star-Ledger's* ad department."

Before 24 hours had passed we had met the George Wains of North Bergen, the Taubert Steins of Ridgewood, and the Julian Falks of Paramus.

The following day we met William Phillips of Fort Lee, who was in Mexico selling a water-saving device called Aqua Miser that saves two gallons on every flush of a toilet.

We stopped in to chat with Elena, proprietor of Chez Elena, whom I had met on my first flight to Mexico. Her establishment up on the hill overlooking the bay, was still an "in" place not generally frequented by first time tourists.

Elena, was in Guadalajara for a few days but we visited with her husband, Joe Reneghan, an easy going, fascinating fellow who was a transplanted Bostonian, whom I had not met before.

Chez Elena had not lost any of its charm and the food was still very good.

The next morning we were off for Zihuatenajo, a beautiful, little-known resort, on a lovely bay about 120 miles north of Acapulco.

4/6/75

GREAT DINING--ON A MEXICAN BEACH

Mexico had a well established, "Don't eat the food or drink the water" reputation, so it is understandable that when it was suggested that we order dinner on the beach at Zihuatenajo we were reluctant. But fellow Jerseyans we met, who had been here for several days before we arrived, recommended it highly.

You wouldn't exactly expect gourmet food in Zihuatenajo, a primitive village where most of the streets are dirt. But we had a very pleasant surprise. Our friends were right.

Dining under a thatched roof on the beach was not only delicious, it was exotic.

Zihuatenajo is a small fishing village on a picturesque bay, some 120 miles north of Acapulco. This was the next port of call on our Mexican flight after Puerto Vallarata. Although both towns are on the coast, we did not follow the bulging coastline but took the AOPA (Aircraft Owners and Pilots Association) flight plan route direct to Manzanillo (also on the coast) that carried us about 40 miles inland, over mountains that stretched to more than 8,000 feet. And from Manzanillo our course was directly to Zihuatenajo flying about 20 miles inland and always in sight of the coast. The 345 mile flight took us two-and-a-half hours.

Looking down at Zihuatenajo from the air, the scene below looked like a fairy tale setting. The bay is surrounded by mountains with small buildings nestled between the foothills and the sea. There is not a high-rise building in sight.

Any pilot who has not landed at Zihuatenajo before, or at least talked to a pilot who has, is in for a real experience. This is the airport where there is a tall ridge right alongside the runway that points toward the water. As you look down from the air your impression is that they would have to move the mountain so you could land.

They have no tower so you couldn't even call to ask them to move the mountain.

Before we left Puerto Vallarta we met a pilot from California who perked up when he heard us say we were going to Zihuatenajo.

"Do you know how to get in there?" he asked.

We told him we had stopped there once before en route to Acapulco.

"I couldn't figure it out," he said, "so I came in over the water and landed downwind."

The solution, we found out in our flight eight years earlier, is simple. When you fly the downwind leg, you fly on the far side of the ridge. The runway is blocked from sight until you come around the end of the ridge and turn onto what could loosely be called a base leg. It was actually at about a 45-degree angle to the runway.

As you fly between the mountains, the runway comes into view.

Zihuatenajo is still relatively unknown to tourists. It is peaceful, uncrowded, unspoiled, and completely relaxing.

The biggest hotel in town, the Posada Caracol, where we stayed, has 52 rooms. Only two other hotels are listed in the AAA guide to Mexico. They have 33 and 45 rooms. All are rated good. There are no luxury hotels that are usually rated excellent or very good and have excellent to very good rates.

However, we found the Posada Caracol with our two-story-high room and the big ceiling fan from another era, quite comfortable and the food, served family style, was plentiful and good. Everybody sat at long tables in a friendly and festive atmosphere.

Just after Esta-Ann and I checked into our room, I strolled out onto the wide veranda just outside our room with a view of the bay and a beach about a hundred feet below us.

Three steps below the veranda there was a lovely pool with a very attractive young lady splashing about adding tremendously to the charm of the setting.

We asked her about beaches.

"Don't go to the one down there," she advised. "There's a much better beach not far from here called La Ropa. And there's another good beach called Los Gatos. You have to walk to town and then take a boat across the bay to get there."

She gave us some more helpful information and then said, "I'm going back to La Ropa. My husband is there. If you want to go now, I can show you the way."

On the way, we learned that our guide was Pat Eisel of Franklin Lakes, N.J., former model and before that a schoolteacher in Union City and then Summit. Her husband, Russ, is a plant service supervisor for the telephone company.

At La Ropa, Russ and a circle of friends were lounging in chairs strategically placed under thatched umbrellas on the beach where they were enjoying the cool breezes and cold beer.

After awhile they decided it was time to dine. Food is prepared and served right on the beach. There are tables in the shade of thatched roofs.

Ordinarily we wouldn't have eaten there on a bet, but with the recommendation of our knowledgeable friends we joined the crowd.

They presented us with a menu and I ordered red snapper. In a few minutes a little girl appeared holding a freshly caught fish (by the eyes) for our inspection.

It turned out to be fabulously good (they cook it over a hard wood fire and season it with a healthy amount of garlic). It was so good that the next day at Los Gatos we ordered the same thing at Arnold's ("English spoken, a little"), a primitive place on a dirt path. The snapper here turned out to be equally good.

Carlos, center, holds a red snapper, which he recommends to Russ, left, and Pat Eitel, for their dinner on the beach.

The village of Zihuatenajo is primitive. The streets are dirt or cobblestone. The shops, too, are rather primitive, but well stocked with souvenirs and attractive, good quality shirts and blouses.

Shopkeepers generally will not bargain. If you want to buy, fine, if not, that's okay, too. We saw them let lots of people walk out. That was quite unlike Acapulco or other cities in Mexico. Because it was so relaxed and without pressure, Zihuatenajo, was our favorite spot on this trip, even though the accommodations were rather spartan.

But it won't stay that way for long. It is scheduled to be built up into the next big resort area. The village was served by Twin Otters (19 passenger commuters) from Mexico City when we were there.

A week after we left a new airport opened that will be served by jets carrying a hundred passengers.

I'm afraid if we wait five more years to come back, everything will be changed. Instead of $33 a day for two with meals, there will be fancy 300-room high-rise hotels at $75 a day without meals.

Then we will just have to look for another Zihuatenajo.

4/13/75

FRUSTRATIONS ON THE HOMEWARD FLIGHT

When it's time to go home you're usually in a bigger hurry than
you were when you went away. It's all over and now you're anxious to
get home. So when the unexpected moves in to throw roadblocks in your
path, it's particularly frustrating.

The flight back from Mexico to Somerset Airport had a few
problems we could have done without--notably two days in
Galveston, Texas, waiting for tornados to blow themselves out.

If we had been living in the late '40s, it might have been more
exciting. In those years Galveston (an island) was a booming sin city
with gambling, loose girls and all that usually goes with it.

But they blew the whistle in the early '50s and today it is a
very proper seaside summer resort that simply dies in the off season. It
is virtually abandoned and looks sad and shopworn.

Before we were grounded in Galveston we had traveled 1,200
miles on our return trip and had spent a most enjoyable two days in San
Antonio.

It had been our hope when we took off from Zihuatenajo at 8:15
a.m., to get to San Antonio before nightfall. But we had our doubts. We
had to make a stop to check out of Mexico and another to go through
customs on reentering the United States. The trip from Zihuatenajo to
San Antonio was nearly a thousand miles and we would lose one hour
when we came across the border.

We made a fuel stop at Guadalajara and took off without the
little gear problem experienced on the way down.

Monterrey, where we planned to check out of Mexico, was 440
miles to the north. We made this leg in 2 hours and 57 minutes which
put us down at 1:51 p.m.--reasonably early.

The paperwork was finished quickly, but when we were being
refueled we noticed a broken aerial wire.

We had trepidation about finding someone who could fix it, but
in a few minutes a Mexican mechanic was at work. He had it repaired
in a short time and there was no bill. He was most appreciative of a
tip.

The hour we were to lose between Monterrey and Laredo, Texas,
was a problem.

If you arrive at a Port of Entry airport before 5 p.m., there is no
customs charge. After that you pay up to a maximum of $25, depending
on how many aircraft use the service during the time period before the

next regular work shift.

We took off from Monterrey at 3:07. Since it's about an hour's flight that would be no problem--except for the loss of an hour.

About ten minutes before the hour we called the Laredo Flight Service Station to advise them that we would arrive shortly and that we would require customs.

A young lady came right back and said, "You better step on it. The customs man goes at 5. After that we have to call another inspector to come out to the airport."

We arrived at 5:10 and were instructed not to leave the airplane until the customs man got there. Since he had been called before we landed, he was there in less than five minutes after our arrival. (If your bladder is bursting, you have to sit there and let it burst.) You can't get out of the aircraft until the customs man arrives. At times that can be more than half an hour.

Customs only took a few minutes. The bill comes in the mail.

We climbed back in the airplane and took off for San Antonio, 150 miles north. As we approached the city we ran into some light rain and haze. But approach control was most helpful, as they were throughout the trip.

There was a twin-engine Piper Aztec about a half mile to our left.

They instructed us to follow him into runway 12 Right. So we just played follow the leader.

We spent two days in San Antonio and enjoyed every moment.

During our stay, we visited the Alamo, right in the heart of the city, where Davy Crockett died with 181 other gallant defenders.

We went up the 500-foot tower built for the 1968 Hemisphere that still has a revolving restaurant on top. We walked through La Villita (little village) a quaint group of mid-18th Century dwellings reconstructed during the depression of the '30s to create work for youth and now occupied by arts and crafts dealers and a small museum.

Our favorite place in San Antonio was the Paseo del Rio, the river walk along the San Antonio River. It looks more like a stream than a river but it's clean and filled with tiny, brightly colored tropical fish.

Both sides of the narrow river have lovely paved walkways. As you stroll along the edge of the water that is below street level, you pass umbrella tables, shops, nightclubs where you can hear good Dixieland jazz or romantic Spanish guitar.

You walk under beautiful arched bridges. You see rented paddle boats that the venturesome ride like a bicycle.

There are excellent restaurants. One night we ate in the Fig

Tree on the banks of the river in a house that was once a private home in La Villita.

It was this kind of place: Wine was served in silver goblets. There was a gold knife rest at each place setting so you wouldn't have to put a dirty knife on the tablecloth. After serving the house salad they brought a long stemmed glass dish of fruit-flavored shaved ice--to clear the palate of the garlic before the main course. All entries were $11.

When we left San Antonio, our destination was Atlanta. That's when we wound up in Galveston, 50 miles south of Houston. We had tried to make it into Houston, but the weather was down. It was no dice. We were lucky to be able to get to Galveston, following a highway, under a low ceiling.

The next two days were very long ones. Most everything was closed, including most of the hotels, motels, and restaurants. We were lucky to find a nondescript motel that was open. The weather remained poor and there was no place to go and nothing to do. But what a great feeling after two days of total boredom to take off for Atlanta.

After one night in Atlanta, visiting family, it was destination Somerset.

The last entry in Esta-Ann's log read, "4:08 p.m." and in capital letters under it. "HOME."

We had traveled more than 6,000 miles during our two-week trip in 43 hours of flying time (Average speed, 141 miles an hour).

It was a great trip. But at the end, that four letter word that closed the log in capital letters, looked beautiful.

4/20/75

Chapter 27

Swan Song

All good things come to an end. My "Wings Over Jersey" column had been a good thing for me. It was a labor of love and I hope that was evident in the stories the column produced. I think readers considered it a good thing as well. Over the years, the number of people who told me, "That's the first thing I turn to every Sunday morning," numbered in the hundreds. More than five years after the last column appeared (as of this writing) I still encounter people regularly who tell me they miss the column.

However, after 38 1/2 years, it came to an end on December 30, 2001, the last Sunday of the year. The column that follows is that last column. It is brief and to the point and I think it made a fitting ending for its long run and I think it makes an appropriate fini for this book.

Writing the column was a rewarding experience and I hope that you have found reading this book a rewarding experience as well.

I t's been a long flight. We took off on June 9, 1963. I wasn't quite sure where I was going. Certainly, I never anticipated breaking any records. But after more than 38 years, I have set an endurance record. No other newspaper aviation column ever survived for so long.

It has been a marvelous journey, exciting and personally fulfilling. It has taken me to great air shows all over the world, Paris, France; Farnborough, England; Abbotsford, British Columbia; Oshkosh, Wis.; Lakeland, Fl.; Reno, Nev.; and Sussex, N.J.

I've had the privilege of meeting many outstanding aviators, including Jimmy Doolittle, Jimmy Stewart, Bob Hoover, Leo Loudenslager, Fay Gillis Wells, Diane Hakala, Sean Tucker, Patty Wagstaff, Malcolm Forbes, and many VIPs who were pilots, Sen. Barry Goldwater, Arthur Godfrey, Johnny Carson, Hugh Downs, and Mitch Miller, among them.

The most intriguing stories of the past 38 years have been those about people not in the spotlight or the front page, but ordinary people--secretaries, schoolteachers, clerks, truck drivers, sales people, computer programmers, doctors, lawyers--who found in flying something that enhanced and enriched their lives.

I've written about many people who found rich and rewarding careers in aviation. Doug Schwartz, aviation director for a company near the top of the Fortune 500 list that bases its aircraft at Morristown

Airport, summed up the feeling those people have better than I ever could. "The best thing about aviation," he said to me during a recent interview, "is that when you go to work you are surrounded by people who are living their dream."

Over the years I've had the privilege of flying in a wide variety of memorable aircraft, from the antique 1929 Swallow and the old Ford Trimotor to the supersonic Concorde.

I took off on this Journey in Journalism with the notion that general aviation had a colorful and exciting story to tell that wasn't being told and my intention was to try to tell it. I have done my best to do that.

There have been columns about incredible flying achievements and I have concluded this book by recounting two personal experiences about memorable flights from New Jersey to Mexico.

The column has won a half dozen national awards and scores of local awards and there is a sense of pride in that.

And now it's time to come back to earth, to shut down the engine, to push our wings into the hangar and shut the door.

I do that with thanks and appreciation to the hundreds of people who helped me stay aloft for so long and with best wishes to them for many more years of happy landings.

And I dip my wings to the many readers who wrote over the years to tell me they enjoyed reading "Wings Over Jersey." I especially treasure the letters I've had from people who said they were not pilots but enjoyed reading about flying, because they were the people I wanted to introduce to the wonders, the beauty, and the utility of personal and business flying.

Another source of gratification was the receipt of letters from all over the country that came from people who told me they read "Wings Over Jersey" every week because a friend, a relative, or a former neighbor, mailed it to them after they moved to other parts of the country.

I have had my share of happy landings over the years along with a few bumpy ones. I would wish for all my good friends and loyal readers that they would have as many happy landings in the future as I have had in the past.

12/30/01

The End

INDEX